PORTRAYING THE LADY

PORTRAYING THE LADY

Technologies of Gender

in the Short Stories of Henry James

Donatella Izzo

University of Nebraska Press   *Lincoln and London*

Acknowledgments for the use of previously published work
appear on page vii.
Manufactured in the United States of America
♾
Library of Congress Cataloging-in-Publication Data
Izzo, Donatella.
Portraying the lady: technologies of gender in the
short stories of Henry James / Donatella Izzo.
p. cm.
Includes bibliographical references (p.   ) and index.
ISBN 0-8032-2503-2 (cloth: alk. paper)
1. James, Henry, 1843–1916—Characters—Women.
2. Feminist fiction—History and criticism.   3. Repression
(Psychology) in literature.   4. Sex role in literature.
5. Women in literature.   I. Title.
PS2127.W6198   2001   813'.4—dc21   2001027348

"N"

CONTENTS

ACKNOWLEDGMENTS

Over the eleven years spent writing this book I have incurred several debts that I gratefully wish to acknowledge. Cristina Bacchilega, Paola Cabibbo, Mario Corona, Anna De Biasio, Annalisa Goldoni, Giorgio Mariani, John Rieder, and Luisa Villa read drafts or parts of the manuscript and offered comments, suggestions, criticism, consent, and dissent in the course of desultory talks or endless conversations, over lunches or dinners, prior to classes or afternoon naps, through e-mail messages or telephone calls that extended well into the night. Most importantly, they created the constant network of friendship, interest, discussion, and humorous support without which the enterprise of writing a book becomes a truly unrewarding and solipsistic task. Susan Gunter and Pierre Walker read the complete manuscript and offered the resources of their scholarship and insight: I feel lucky to have been able to benefit from their attention. To Paola Ludovici MacQuarrie I owe much gratitude for her invaluable assistance in preparing the final version of the manuscript: her unique combination of intellectual acuteness and friendly enthusiasm, as well as her competence and professionalism, helped this project more than I can say. Sonia Di Loreto, Carlo Martinez, and Stefano Tani generously responded to my recurrent cries for help in tracing out-of-the-way items in the huge James bibliography, providing speedy customized book supplies at various crucial stages of the work (the latter occasionally adding refreshing sarcasm). Ladette Randolph has been as promptly responsive, universally competent, and unfailingly supportive an editor as any author may dream.

Earlier and shorter versions of the first three chapters appeared respectively in *RSA Journal* 5 (1994), *Igitur* 7:2 (1995), and *Merope* 1:1 (1989). I am grateful to these journals for permission to reprint.

For lifelong friendship, relentless scrutiny, and endless laughter, this book is dedicated to Cristina and to Paola—two ladies whom no portrait can frame.

PORTRAYING THE LADY

Introduction
The Manifold Arts of Re-vision

To revise is to see, or to look over, again—which means in the case of a written thing neither more nor less than to re-read it . . . The "old" matter is there, re-accepted, re-tasted, exquisitely re-assimilated and re-enjoyed . . . ; yet for due testimony, for re-assertion of value, perforating as by some strange and fine, some latent and gathered force, a myriad more adequate channels. It is over the fact of such a phenomenon and its so possibly rich little history that I am moved just fondly to linger—and for the reason I glanced at above, that to do so is in a manner to retrace the whole growth of one's "taste," as our fathers used to say: a blessed comprehensive name for many of the things deepest in us.

—Henry James, Preface to *The Golden Bowl*

Portraying the Lady, a re-visioning of the title of *The Portrait of a Lady*, appears to me as the most expedient, though perhaps obvious, way to point to the object of this book. By expanding and distancing the terms of the well-known title, my own title draws attention to both of them separately, thus defamiliarizing the apparent naturalness of their combination and the untroubled appositional placing of the woman. What becomes visible, by changing the noun to a verb, is the problematic nature of the act that conjoins the portrait and the lady, that is, representation.

Representation is a complex notion, as semiotics, the critique of ideology, and cultural studies have pointed out: it bears on art, as re-production of reality according to aesthetic and rhetorical codes, and on all processes of signification that as such produce not only meanings but also codes of intelligibility and positions from which the meanings may be perceived and consumed—ideology, in a word, in which cultural processes interface with social practices, power structures, and modes of production on the one hand, and with individual subjectivity on the other. In the field of sexual difference, this translates as *gender*: both a product and a process of representation, as Teresa de Lauretis has argued in the essay to which my subtitle refers. A theoretical abstraction, but one that men and women live out in the numberless social and cultural practices that endlessly reproduce it ("technologies" in Foucault's sense), gender is to my mind the ideal theoretical tool to bring out the implications of Henry James's treatment of women in his short stories. As my readings will show, these are not just stories *about* women. In them, the problematic notion of representation becomes itself central to the textual project, and gender is investigated both theoretically, as an ideological framework that dictates the construction of woman as subject in history and discourse, and mimetically, in its concrete operation through the minute actualities of the experience of bourgeois women in the Victorian age. Although specifically narrative in nature, means, and resources, James's investigation results in a conceptual outlook comparable to the achievements of present-day feminist theory and gender studies.

By defining the object of my study in these terms, I have already delimited implicitly my theoretical framework and methodological orientation. Before attempting to define them more explicitly and precisely, though, it seems necessary to position my work in relation to its more immediate contexts, such as the directions of the recent James revival, and the many critical studies produced on James's approach to the "woman question" and the ideological paradigms of his time. Through a critical appraisal of these two contexts I hope to outline my own terms of reference, the problems that my work sets out to address, and the problems that my work itself poses. Considering the story of this book, this preliminary positioning is all the more necessary. This book is not the result of a "strong" hypothesis. Rather, it started coming together, more than ten years ago, when works of feminist theory and the short fiction of James that I was reading at the same time and in the same place, albeit with different purposes in mind, became a sort of "parallel text." That coincidence produced interactions and synergies, which I have attempted to reproduce in my approach to the texts. This book found its own interpretive hypothesis and its own unity along the way, as it were. What follows is then, at least in part, a reconstruction "from the end"—an involuntary act of mimesis of the problematic Jamesian authorship—an attempt at understanding and outlining the intellectual necessity of apparently casual and unrelated writing events, and ultimately an effort to justify the need, not at all taken for granted, of yet another book on Henry James.

The many Henry Jameses who populate contemporary culture are altogether different from the relatively monolithic Master we used to know before the 1970s.[1] The multiple Henry Jameses are no longer singularly expert in narrative form and technique; they have different roles and expertise. The philosopher: follower of Nietzsche (Donadio), of pragmatism (Hocks, Posnock), of Wittgenstein (Hagberg), of phenomenology (Armstrong, Williams).[2] The ideologue of the bourgeoisie (Jameson); the author who reproduced its power structures in his texts (Seltzer); the critic of the public domain (Salmon); the expert in the publishing industry and mass communication (Jacobson, Margolis, Anesko); the polyglot lover of popular fiction (Veeder, Tintner, Walker); the social critic and forerunner of the Frankfurt School (Posnock, Rowe) who questions, with equivocal results, the status of women and ethnic minorities in society (Habegger, Posnock, Blair); the distinguished representative of the "homosexual panic," or else of a marginal male subjectivity, perhaps triumphantly *camp* and potentially subversive of the prevailing phallic cultural model (Kosofsky Sedgwick, Person, Savoy, Silverman, Moon, Stevens).[3]

There is something odd, almost uncanny (in the Freudian sense of the familiarity of the repressed), in these critical developments, which, in the space of a generation, have transformed the "writers' writer," the artist in the ivory tower, into a social critic whose commentaries range from women's rights to multiethnic society, from the Jewish question to financial capitalism. On one hand, it is a historically and theoretically necessary development, a reflection of the way cultural paradigms have been transformed by the "culture of dissensus." On the other hand, this transformation is so radical and conspicuous that it raises a number of perplexing questions.

To examine the meaning of this Jamesian revival, I would like to look briefly at the latest and, in my view, most explicit product of the new Jamesian scholarship, *The Other Henry James*, by John Carlos Rowe, published in 1998 in the important and innovative series of the "new Americanists" from Duke University Press. Rowe, an influential Americanist and experienced critic of James, published *Henry Adams and Henry James: The Emergence of a Modern Consciousness* in 1976 and *The Theoretical Dimensions of Henry James* in 1984.[4] The latter study constitutes the foundation for a theoretically grounded reading of James in which texts and theories engage each other and test their own premises, thus mutually exposing their limitations and strategic repressions.

In many respects, *The Other Henry James* extends Rowe's 1984 approach to new theoretical interests that now include gender studies, critical theory, and ethnic and class differences. The book, though, sets forth a different kind of critical approach, where the critical performance loses or hides any deconstructive self-consciousness of its own historical and ideological limitations and therefore presents the "other" Henry James as a full-fledged figure, not so much "other," mobile, and subversive in its contingency, but rather *alternative.* When Rowe describes "the transformation of the pompous figure of James as master of the novel . . . into the vulnerable, sexually anxious, and lonely writer struggling with the new modern art and new age" (ix), he claims this new figure as more relevant to, and with more currency for our times, than the old master of style, thus appearing to be substituting post hoc one critical assessment for another without questioning the terms of the contemporary construction or altering the terms of the old one. For example, Rowe's rescuing of the noncanonical short stories is justified by a thematic concern for what they tell us on "James's historically specific attitudes toward women, gays and lesbians" (xii–xiii), a concern that is kept separate from the aesthetic one ("in strictly aesthetic terms they are certainly minor writings in James's career" [xiii]): the oppositional status of the two terms is neither questioned nor discussed. Likewise, in his concluding chapter Rowe offers an impassioned apology for James's continued relevance to the humanistic syllabus resulting from the new theoretical approaches, in which he systematically construes a concept of the author's "transformation" in binary terms: "from an ivory-tower aesthete into an important subject and object of critical theory" (191), from the secluded artist to the human being in conflict and *engagé*, from the limited bourgeois writer to the precursor of postmodern consciousness.[5] This transformation is also the precondition for a new "readability": the reading centered on "technical issues of little interest to all but creative writers or professional scholars" is replaced by a reading focused on "general themes and fictional aims" (197) more in line with our contemporary interests.

At this point, I should acknowledge that, leaving aside Rowe's concern for the syllabus, dictated by circumstances specific to universities in the United States, I am in perfect agreement with the general drift of his argument or, better, with his evaluation of the Jamesian revival and the theoretical approaches on which it is based. My book is a further attempt in that direction, whose fruitfulness is evident in Rowe's outstanding readings of Jamesian texts. On the other hand, exactly because *The Other Henry James* is a mature essay that sums up a coalesced critical revision, it appears to me as the place where some of the problems posed by the present Jamesian revival stand out more clearly. The recurring rhetoric of *transformation* runs the risk of substituting for the elitist Master of Form another image, opposed to but as critically reified as the preceding one and perhaps as unwilling to question its own premises.

According to Rowe's definition, as "important subject and object of critical theory" James would seem to play simultaneously two different and complementary roles: as object, he is again marketable in academic syllabi within the new theoretical framework that would have otherwise eclipsed him, and as subject of critical theory, he is reinstated at the top of the literary charts, albeit according to premises far removed from those of the preceding critical generation. It is hardly worth noting that any text, literary or otherwise, may constitute the *object* of critical theory. Therefore, Rowe's claims, together, have strategic rather than heuristic value. The Jamesian revival dismisses James as formalist and aesthete, canonizes him anew on ideological and ethical premises, and ends up acclaiming him again as the Master: the King is dead, long live the King.

Such a development may be interpreted, of course, from two opposing points of view. From the vantage point of an ontology of literature, it would seem to indicate the intrinsic qualitative superiority of James's work, which, because of its flexibility, comprehensiveness, richness, and linguistic texture, is easily amenable to the critical paradigms and questioning of every generation. It is the "masterful adaptability" that Rowe celebrates in the very first page of his book (where a parallel is established between the recent flurry of screen adaptations from James's works and those from Shakespeare, the Immortal Author par excellence). From a purely materialistic vantage point, this development could be interpreted, with Bourdieu, as a salvage move on the part of academic critics who are unwilling to risk their "cultural capital" and are ready to play it out by changing the rules, even when this move may involve reaffirming the authority of the modernist canon while adopting the theoretical stance that was supposed to undermine it, and invoking the preterhistorical authority of the Author as a justification for its own demise.[6] It is important to underscore that the Jamesian revival has very little to teach us, for example, on race or class relations *from a theoretical point of view*—a transcodification that has undoubtedly more solid theoretical and political foundations in relation to gender. Rather, it is a development "internal" to Jamesian scholarship, dictated by its premises and needs, that is, by the necessity to produce new readings and new approaches to reading, assuming Henry James simply *as a starting point.*[7]

A similar ambiguity between the revisionary and the recuperative mode is certainly at the root of my book as well: I too assume Henry James as a starting point—the "authority" from which my work originates and the field of expertise that gives it authority. As a critic, I was raised in the 1970s at the school of the Master of Narrative Form and of structuralist analysis, and therefore I have my own investment (one that is more psychological and existential than intellectual and academic) to protect by preserving the image of Henry James and retooling it, as it were. Indeed, in this regard my project can be considered *doubly* recuperative. Not only do I appropriate the image of James as social critic, by providing yet another contextualization within feminist theory, gender studies, and critique of ideology—which are the three privileged domains of the new Jamesian scholarship; but I do so through the same "textual" and "formal" approach that produced the first canonization of Henry James and his almost painless recanonization by deconstructionism. My premise is that James as critic of ideology is neither theoretically nor critically incompatible with James as sophisticated artist of narrative techniques. The two are absolutely interdependent and need to be put into focus using each other as a lens, even at the price of a certain theoretical "eclecticism," so that each may question the other and both their public. I will now clarify my approach by engaging the existing critical studies on Henry James and his relationship to women.

As several critics have already noted, the opinions on the aesthetic and personal relationship between Henry James and the woman question are curiously polarized. On one hand, the proliferation of scholarship on this topic attests to its centrality; on the other, the divergence of interpretations would seem to indicate its essential ambivalence and instability, or else the great divergence in critical methodology employed to tackle it, or perhaps both. Therefore, I will first outline briefly the main interpretations that Jamesian scholarship offers on this topic, bringing into focus their theoretical premises and procedures.

With the sole exception of the 1978 study by Edward Wagenknecht, marked by an extremely traditional approach to characters as content and theme, the early critical production of the 1970s on James and women was not a product of feminist criticism or strictly Jamesian scholarship; rather it was the result of more generalized inquiries.[8] Lisa Appignanesi's *Femininity and the Creative Imagination* includes James in a triad of writers, with

Proust and Musil, whose writing and psychic organization is dominated by the "feminine," in a general psychoanalytic sense, as the principle that foregrounds inner life, fluidity, the personal sphere over the external and collective sphere, and the rigidity of ritual and dogma.[9] *The Faces of Eve,* by Judith Fryer, and *The New England Girl,* by Paul John Eakin, both published in 1976, are thematic studies of the archetypal or historical dimensions of female characters in American literature.[10] *A Rhetoric of Literary Character,* by Mary Doyle Springer, attempts a rhetorical classification of characters following Wayne Booth's approach, in which James's female characters are chosen on the basis of either memorable characterization or variety of roles (that is, on the basis of an ontological and formal notion of character) and not on the basis of gender.[11] Indeed, in discussing *Washington Square,* Springer underscores the specificity of the status of women portrayed in the novel and the role of "implicit social critic" (87) assumed by James, but she is almost apologetic about it and feels she has to invoke a wealth of textual evidence to support the necessity of her reading.

The appearance of Judith Fetterley's influential book *The Resisting Reader* (1978), along with *Communities of Women,* by Nina Auerbach, was the point of departure of feminist readings of James centered specifically around his way to present women's oppression in patriarchal societies.[12] In both books, the reappraisal of Henry James from a feminist point of view is based on the rediscovery of a relatively noncanonical work (at least to the extent of its not being included in the New York Edition) like *The Bostonians.* According to Auerbach, the novel describes in sympathetic and prophetic terms the historical necessity of women's emancipation, whereas according to Fetterley, the novel is the most honest and extreme representation of women's oppression in the literature of the nineteenth century. Thus, notwithstanding James's "fatalism," which sees such oppression as inevitable and "natural" because it is based on the inherent balance of power inscribed in men's and women's sexuality, "there is revolution latent in James's novel, and, while he would be the last to endorse it, being far more interested in articulating and romanticizing the tragic elements in women's powerlessness, *The Bostonians* provides the material for that analysis of American social reality which is the beginning of change" (xvii).

Fetterley's analysis presents almost all the elements that will be renegotiated, under different guises, by the critics to follow. First is the thematic-ideological approach to the novel, based on a comprehensive reading of the economic, historical, and sexual contexts inscribed in the characters and in the plot. Next is the dichotomy between James as authorial presence (and/or as the biographical James, suspicious and fatalistic in respect to women's liberation) and his power of representation, which, in the general sense used by Marx and Lukács for Balzac, makes him an "objective" ally of feminism: the novel, therefore, has consciousness-raising value in regard to women's oppression and conveys a latent "revolutionary message" (152) for a radical feminism where woman-centered relationships would lead to liberation.

Most scholars of the 1980s adopt the same themes and critical stance, within an explicit feminist framework. Both Virginia C. Fowler and Joyce W. Warren (1984) examine the question of women in James by intersecting a psychological reading of the female protagonists with the statements of the author and the contemporary cultural contexts.[13] Both scholars underscore the suffering and sacrifices of James's female protagonists but end up absolving the author of the male chauvinism present in the literature of his time because of his ability to relate to women as "persons." In another 1984 book, Carren Kaston takes the issue of renunciation in James's novels as a point of departure to examine the ambivalent textual connotations of this topic: James's keen awareness of the dynamics of submission and control (both authorial and social) gives rise to a search for narrative relationships that are exempt from those dynamics and from the renunciation that they entail. In his search for a "shared fictionalizing, or the mutual creation of experience," writes Kaston, James is close to feminism, since "[s]uch collaboration . . . is the essence of feminism." The analysis and critique of his stereotypical submission plots, therefore, should not ignore "the interrogation to which James subjected the assumptions behind the stereotypes."[14] In her 1987 book, Mary Suzanne Schriber maintains explicitly that James-the-artist was capable of transcending the limitations of the patriarchal ideology to which both he and his culture subscribed. "Provoked rather than subdued by the ideology of gender, the imagination of James . . . provided aesthetic solutions to questions raised by the culture's horizon of expectations for women," thus distancing "his conscious perception of social reality and his imaginative capability."[15] Schriber's assessment represents the culmination of the romantic-modernist notion of the artist—a notion shared, perhaps less explicitly, by other scholars. The idea of James's intellectual commitment and artistic control is also proposed in studies that take different methodological approaches, as is the case with the important 1984 book by Elizabeth Allen. Her semiological investigation focuses on women as signs of male "signified," reduced in the cultural domain to a representational function that negates them as persons: James's novels, no matter what the ideology of the author was, betray his awareness of the signifying process that constitutes characters *qua* women and, therefore, explore "the conflict of the woman as sign and as self."[16]

The rhetoric of "artistic control" declines with the rise of poststructuralism in Jamesian scholarship. What does not change is the image of an oeuvre in which there is unprecedented space for the emergence and display of the feminine, no matter how it is formulated, and more often than not formulated as psychic, philosophical, or linguistic positioning or principle. Lynda S. Boren in her *Eurydice Reclaimed* (1989) outlines this emergence in Lacanian terms.[17] Peggy McCormack describes James as "both feminist and feminine in his writing," because of his "extraordinary sympathy" for women's position in an economy based on economic-sexual exchange, and because of his use of an open, fluid, and antilogocentric *écriture féminine*.[18] Priscilla L. Walton, in her *The Disruption of the Feminine in Henry James* (1992), follows French poststructuralism and its definition of the feminine as absence, alterity, instability, and linguistic openness, which destabilize the phallogocentric closure of the referential/realistic text; she claims the "feminine" in James as that internal factor, often associated with but not confined to the female characters, which undermines the referential stability sought by realist texts and generates the plurality of language.[19]

My excursus, of course, has covered only some of the works that stand out for their critical comprehensiveness and influence, leaving aside, out of necessity, the exuberant production of articles on a single novel or short story. Let me now offer a few preliminary comments. Apart from general considerations on James's reappraisal within a feminist framework and the many original readings this approach has produced by revisiting noncanonical texts or by altering our perception of the canonical ones, several problems emerge from the directions and the procedures undertaken by feminist studies on James, problems that coincide with some of the issues already discussed by feminist critics and theorists in the last twenty years. Most scholarship on women and Henry James has been motivated by the political and militant need to uncover a "usable past" for feminism and, as a result, it retains a content-centered/thematic approach to the text, which selects and edits textual passages pertinent to women, examines the plot from an ideological point of view, and entertains an ontological-mimetic notion of the character as "person." Considering that James's plots are largely and undeniably about women's victimization, and that the theoretical relations between diegetic world, strategies of representation, and textual and authorial ideologies are often either suspended or ignored, these approaches can only use Jamesian texts in a rather tautological way, that is to say, to confirm a preexisting axiology on women's liberation and the critic's premises about artistic representation. When artistic representation is seen as contributing to knowledge and liberation, then James is praised as precursor or fellow traveler of feminism for his diagnosis of women's oppression. When the reading is immediately mimetic or political, then James is accused of patriarchal sadism toward his characters to whom every avenue of liberation is curtailed by plots that justify oppression.[20] Readings of a more theoretical orientation, emerging from the poststructuralist phase immediately following, avoid the impasse of a thematic reading only by shifting their interest from women as historical, concrete subjects to the "feminine" as linguistic or philosophical principle. In the first case, the referential value of the novels prevails and obfuscates their textuality. In the second case, the principle of textuality prevails to the point that any possible reference to the historical and cultural specificity of the models of femininity represented and their role in oppression becomes problematic. Paradoxically, feminist readings have little to say about James's positioning and performance as a writer concerning the woman question, about its nature and value. Instead, they end up by cautiously claiming or disclaiming James's affiliation to a possible canon of feminist literature by men and run the risk of producing, as Laura Claridge and Elizabeth Langland note in their introduction to a book on the subject, "one more celebration of the canonical male writers for their power of vision as they leapt, with superior male muscularity, over the old problems of masculine and feminine in which . . . women writers became mired."[21] As the two critics remind us, "[a] male writer may simply need the space of what he or his culture terms the feminine in which to express himself more fully because he experiences the patriarchal construction of his masculinity as a constriction. He may, that is, appropriate the feminine to enlarge himself, a process not incompatible with contempt for actual women" (4).

A like suspicion of the male writer is the premise of several influential studies of the 1980s that, moving from different theoretical perspectives, reexamine the woman question in James in relation to the process of self-construction of the artist. *The Theoretical Dimensions of Henry James,* by John Carlos Rowe, is, as I have already mentioned, the first product of a theory of literature under the guise of Jamesian criticism. In his book, Rowe devotes a few chapters to bringing into focus the woman question with an approach that intersects feminist criticism, Marxist criticism, psychoanalysis, and deconstruction. Rowe's point of departure is the "authority" about women generally attributed to James in existing criticism, an authority that, as Rowe argues, the writer ascribed to himself in response to a certain "anxiety of influence" vis-à-vis his contemporary female writers, and that is not exempt from certain limitations and ambivalences:

> What makes James's identification with women so successful . . . is his tendency to transform the social psychology of woman into the formal aesthetics as well as the psychohistory of the literary author. Even as this identification marks James as singularly sympathetic to the larger social issues of feminism, it is based on James's own inevitable defense: that process by which Henry James, the Master, *uses* feminism, uses the "other sex" as part of his own literary power for the sake of engendering his own identity as an Author. (91)

James's feminism, therefore, is severely limited, not by the ideology of the author as biographical person, but rather by its subservience to a *psycho-literary* project that does not contemplate "any effective means of social transvaluation" (91) for women and, furthermore, is functional to the author's appropriation of "femininity" as "a displaced 'androgyny' that he would identify as the protean quality of the 'modern author'" (149). Through this appropriation James is capable of neutralizing the threat that the Other in all its forms poses—from castration anxiety to anxiety of influence and social antagonism. Under such authoritarian circumstances, Tina's act of burning the poet's papers in *The Aspern Papers* is her refusal of the patriarchal fetishizing of art, the only moment of authentic rebellion that emerges "nearly against James's will" (150).

Alfred Habegger too, in his influential and widely quoted 1989 book *Henry James and the "Woman Business,"* disputes vigorously the widespread assessment of James as protofeminist. He does so by underscoring his condescension toward female characters, his appropriation and distortion of the type of fiction by women that dominated the literary market of the times, and his largely reactionary gender attitudes. Habegger situates James's work firmly within its historical context, both at the biographical-familial level (his father's opinions about women and marriage; Henry's relationship with his family members, especially with Minnie Temple) and at the literary level (the tradition of domestic and sentimental fiction, which James frequently revisits and plunders in spite of his overt disparaging comments). James's "feminism," according to Habegger, is an interpretative construct that ignores his "elusive male authoritarianism" (26). His ambivalent identification with his father, on the one hand, and with the female figure who antagonizes him, on the other, causes James to adopt, and distort, the rebellion plot of female literature so as to condemn his heroines to defeat from the very start: "Where woman's fiction was contradictory, James's fiction resolves—but in the wrong way . . . With few exceptions James's heroines would either connive at their own defeat, or their creator would weaken their powers of resistance at the critical moment. . . . Daisy, Isabel, and Verena . . . have been lamed in secret by their author"(26). His identification/disidentification with women is the trump card with which James construes and reconstrues his identity and authority as artist, while making sure to restrict his female protagonists to the role of "sublime suffering servant[s]" (235) who have to pay the price for their (conservative) embodiment of civilization.

The most interesting aspect of Habegger's work, apart from the psychological and biographical contextualizations, is the focus on James's relationship with the domestic and sentimental novel.[22] Habegger had already dealt with this aspect in his previous book, *Gender, Fantasy and Realism in American Literature*, which I will briefly discuss here, since it offers a useful context for understanding the interpretative strategy at work in his later book.[23] In his 1982 book, Habegger had presented Howells and James as the key figures in the transition from romance, the genre of the "American Renaissance," to the realistic novel: Howells and James appropriated the realistic code of nineteenth-century popular fiction by women, after clearing away the excess of sentimentalism and replacing it with a male capacity for judgment. This transition was made possible by the problematic masculinity of the two writers, who did not fit, psychologically or biographically, the definitions of American male: "Only a couple of sissies, so to speak, could perform such a balancing act" (57). What at first sight could appear as a nonessentialist redefinition of gender in writing turns into a very different construction in the chapter on *The Portrait of a Lady*. Habegger writes, in fact, that the novel's greatest fault is its "defective view of masculinity" (77), which finds expression in the refusal of male sexuality, represented in Goodwood as egotistical and aggressive. His reading ignores, not just the multiple versions of masculinity displayed in the novel, but also the overdetermination of masculinity in Goodwood, whose oppressive and possessive characterization is linked explicitly to the historical connotation of industrialist rather than to his "essential" virility. By condemning the "unbalanced femininity" (79) of the novel on aesthetic grounds, Habegger retranslates gender into an essentialist notion and regeneralizes masculinity as human and aesthetic norm. In the fourth part of the book, James's unrelatedness to codified male roles is presented teleologically as an "aborted masculine initiation" and, therefore, as "a type of deformity" (255). With the advent of James's canonization by critics as impotent and alienated as himself, this "deformity" will help eliminate social (i.e., masculine) significance from the modernist novel and ground the latter instead on the effeminate subjectivity of the alienated intellectual.

In relation to his previous book, Habegger's 1989 book appears as moving from the very opposite premise. In both, James is the object of heavy-handed criticism—in 1982 because of his lack of virility and in 1989 because of his lack of feminism. It is reasonable then to suspect that the core of Habegger's critique has little to do with the "woman business" and much more to do with James himself.

It is significant that in the scholarship examined so far, the studies that take feminism as an open or implicit point of reference are generally those most interested in acknowledging (with or without qualifications) the innovative and potentially antipatriarchal significance of James's work, since it centers on women and allows their voices to emerge and their condition to be explored. Given that the primary intent of such studies is to ask the "woman question," the authority of the author does not occupy a prominent place, and often, as we have seen, it is altogether put aside as irrelevant and replaced by a capacity for objective representation or by textuality "out of bounds." On the contrary, Habegger's book explicitly aims at "undoing James's canonical authority" (231) by reconstructing and documenting the procedures that James employed to construe his authority—procedures that are dissembled by James's own literary theory and practice. Here, as was the case in Rowe's book, the female question pivots solely on the issues of the artist's authority and its deconstruction and operates under a hidden hierarchy where women are subordinated and instrumental both in James's work, as we are told, and in the commentaries by the critics.[24] At the same time, these critics condemn the writer because he fails to "transvalue" the patriarchal value system (Rowe) or because he "lames" his heroines (Habegger), as if the only "constriction" imposed on women at the end of the nineteenth century were effected by fictional plots and as if literature could *truly* effect (against every new historicist or deconstructionist assumption) a "transvaluation" of values. It is as if, by negating James's proto- or parafeminism and claiming a more effective or militant benchmark for feminism, these critics wanted to surpass in feminism not just James but the feminist criticism that has revisited him. Thus, they build their own credibility (and perhaps their authority) on feminist grounds by deconstructing James's credibility and presenting his stance as authoritarian and instrumental. Both Rowe and Habegger criticize the *excess* of authority that James displayed toward his heroines, but, at the same time, they *negate* his authority as interpreter of women and interlocutor for today's, or yesterday's, feminism. An emblematic instance of the anxiety of influence? The woman question is, in both cases, the instrument of a deconstructive intent directed toward the canonical authority of the author. One would certainly be willing to acquit the critics of undoing James's monumental grandeur (an overdue task, to be sure), were it not that, once again, the battle over critical authority takes place between *men*, who use women as terrain and object of their contest.

To bring into sharper focus other relevant issues, I will now turn briefly to Carolyn Porter's reading of *The American*. Published in 1987, the essay centers on the relationship between female characters and authorial authority, with particular attention to women's specific textual and ideological functions. Porter here develops in terms of gender some of the arguments she had put forth in the James chapter of her previous book *Seeing and Being* (1981), where she had established the thematic and narratological figure of the "detached observer," who ends up interacting and cooperating with the world he observes, as the response to the increasing reification and alienation brought about by rapid industrial transformations in nineteenth-century America.[25] In her essay, the problem of reification is revisited and connected to the female character as emblem—for both James and the diegetic universe—of a value that is transcendent and nonmarketable: James is forced to confine Claire de Cintré in a convent to protect her value as emblem from the relentless progress of market forces. Newman too, however, searches for values that are not commodities and therefore is destined to suffer when he faces society; thus, from the very beginning of the novel, he is "feminized" at the connotative level. Porter argues that it is in this distancing of values away from the market that Jamesian heroines are born: James is "committed to a moral economy of loss," the only safeguard against market forces, and, starting from *The Portrait of a Lady*, he regrounds value in the consciousness of a female character. In so doing, "he appropriated the right gender for a protagonist doomed to victimization . . . Isabel Archer's demonstration of moral superiority through loss does not threaten her gender identity. It confirms it."[26] In Porter's view, female victimization is not the author's *choice* as much as it is a cultural *fact* that he adopts to communicate, and give veracity to, the "antieconomic" valuation of consciousness (with a gesture that could hence be defined as conservative but not punitive). James, according to Porter, takes up the role of the patriarchal father (whose absence was seen in *The American* as the root cause of women's commodification) "who uses his authority both to protect and to control his daughter" (126). His protection and control are expressed by framing Isabel into the *Portrait*, which, like a museum, removes her from the marketplace and places her in the fixed realm of artistic, unmarketable values.

Porter's essay is extremely stimulating and cogent; it would certainly be rewarding to analyze each premise, first of all the divergence between the *critical* relation that James established with the social phenomenon of reification and his mere *acceptance* of patriarchal oppression as a given. It is difficult to support the idea that the author assumes the protective and positive role ascribed to Claire de Cintré's father (who, as is the case in fairy tales, is benevolent and dead), taking into account the sinister aspects of the paternal "protection" offered by Gilbert Osmond or Doctor Sloper. Moreover, the value James invests in his character as *subject* and/or as *subject to* his authority is not gender-specific; rather it is tied, as Porter argues in her book, to a more general reformulation of subjectivity (of the individual as character and as artist) on the eve of the twentieth century.[27] As confirmed by *The Ambassadors* and the innumerable short stories with a male protagonist, James's "bid for authority" (Rowe) does not take place only in reference to female characters, in the same way as James's practice of plundering or concealing (at least partially) his sources did not involve only fiction by women, as many studies have proven.[28] One could argue that it was only *the critics'* unawareness of nineteenth-century fiction by women, deemed unworthy of critical attention and hence unknown until recently, that created the impression of concealment of intertextual presences, which were undoubtedly clear to James's contemporary public. In conclusion, gender-specific is not the ways in which James employs women as characters or as authors, but the *forms* of their reification and their oppression *as* women in the society that James represents in his narratives and of which he was a biographical actor.

The critical works examined so far, whether inspired by a political or a deconstructive interest, are generally premised on a preexisting set of theoretical assumptions that, whether acknowledged or not, determines a curiously tautological and repetitive critical process. Critical analysis centers, implicitly or explicitly, on the relationship between the ideology in the text, the ideology of the text, and the ideology of the author. The relationship between these aspects of ideology is variously played out in terms of complicity, superposition, or divergence. This alternating movement is to be found also in both British and American Marxist criticism, which displays an increased self-awareness about the crucial theoretical implications of ideology for its interpretative strategy. John Goode, Terry Eagleton, and Carolyn Porter herself credit the artistic form with a certain measure of autonomy from ideology, since it sheds light on its "margins," according to Goode, or since as an "ideological production to the second power" it is capable of "invert[ing] itself back into an analogue of knowledge" and "forc[ing ideology] up against the wall of history," according to Eagleton.[29] From this point of view, then, Jamesian texts appear capable of manifesting critically some contradictions of ideology. Jameson, on the other hand, sees James as employing a strategy of containment rather than resistance; thus, Jameson's view of the author, notwithstanding the differences between his Marxism and New Historicism, ends up resembling Mark Seltzer's stimulating, provocative, and extremely influential approach.[30] Seltzer's book investigates the Foucaultian theme of knowledge/power, appropriation, supervision, and surveillance in the social world represented by James and suggests the "criminal continuity" between those themes and the representational techniques that James adopted—even if, it must be added, these techniques are more taken for granted through generalizations than examined as textual practice. Therefore, James's art displays a complicity with the structures of power even though it would like to present itself as exempt from any involvement with the political sphere.

Taken together, these critical works are invaluable in redefining the terms of James's historicity and positioning his work within the context of advanced capitalism and within a perfected modern version of a microphysics of power. Even though they do not confront the woman question directly, they supply an opportunity for relating it to other social and economic phenomena. On the other hand, while their modeling premises are strongly theoretical, they are hardly viable as a safe foundation for practical criticism, since they diverge considerably in the way they posit the relationship between literature and ideology and in the consequences this relationship entails on the level of evaluation. Unless, of course, one avoids the question altogether by transposing it elsewhere: such is the case with Seltzer, when he evidences that the "criminal continuity" between the world represented by James and his representational techniques also prevails in the relation between these techniques and James's critics. The "politics of interpretation," which have presided over James's canonization on the basis of a radical opposition between aesthetics and politics, also give rise to "the subversive hypothesis" about art as antagonistic and liberating, in and by itself. Literary discourse, Seltzer argues in the wake of Foucault, fully qualifies as one of the practices of regulation that operate in modern society; its claim to an oppositional, external status is nothing but a homeostatic strategy of power, which is capable even of turning opposition into part of its functioning. From this vantage point, then, considering that power is pervasive and all-inclusive, the question on where to position Henry James in relation to patriarchal power becomes completely devoid of sense.

I will not avoid the issue of James's relation to women by subscribing to Seltzer's position, which, in my view, is rooted in a fairly univocal reading of Foucault at the expense of an examination of James's textual procedures. I will move the question to another terrain. My book does not posit itself, let it be clear, as capable or desirous of transcending divergent opinions and answering all the questions that preexisting critical evaluations leave unanswered. By registering some collective impasses, my intention is not to capitalize on the critical or theoretical limitations of previous critics, but rather to examine what ground has already been covered so as to change, as much as possible, the rules of the game—that is, the questions that I intend to put to Jamesian texts and the way those questions will be posited.

I choose to suspend, for the moment, the biographical question: whether James was personally in favor of or against women's liberation. Women have been able to find their own empowerment and liberation on their own, with or without James's novels. To make the Master subscribe to their cause today makes sense only in relation to the canonical status of the Master and not in relation to the critical or political cause of women. Similarly, I will suspend the deconstructive question about the author, that is, the way in which James employs women to construe for himself a gendered authority—whether as male or as narrative cross-dresser, is irrelevant here.[31]

These questions cannot be suspended with any ease, and they will come back, to a certain extent, in my conclusions. By temporarily suspending them, however, I hope to arrest the critical drift that tends to transfer the discourse about woman to another topic, of which she is the instigation and the occasion—author, authorship, social arrangements, textuality, language.

At the same time, I will also strive to put aside the notion of "female character." The strong mimetic and humanistic connotations of character, so vigorously enhanced by James's ability in construing the "character-effect," draw the critics relentlessly over to the "realistic" domain of psychology, where actions, motivations, choices, triumphs, rebellions are reconstructed.[32] My "resistance" to character will contribute, I hope, to depsychologizing the Master of psychology: I will isolate, instead, the suprapersonal traits (significant from a cultural and historical point of view) that are at play in characterization and in the dynamics of relationships instituted by the plot. I will then try to read "character" only as an instrument to analyze the process of subject construction and not as mimetic of reality or role model. This is one of the reasons why I have chosen as object of my investigation the short stories: their relative lack of complexity as compared to the novels and the abstract situations they represent allow this escape from psychology by making it easier to isolate from the mimetic simulation of *identity* those traits which constitute *subjectivity*.

My critical focus will distance itself both from the terrain of deconstruction, where the "feminine" is drawn back into the closed circuit of metatextuality, and from the mimetic terrain, where representation is based on the actual historical conditions of women and consequently confined within the polarities of victimization/utopia. I prefer to position it in the middle ground of gender, as a category that is *both* abstract *and* rooted in the historical experience of men and women. Specifically, I will read James's texts as representation of the construction of gender at a precise historical junction (bourgeois Anglo-Saxon society between the end of the nineteenth century and the beginning of the twentieth century) and as representation of the "technologies of gender" that contribute to this construction.

In mentioning the notion of "technologies of gender," I have already made clear the horizons of my analysis: Foucault's work on the construction of the subject and of sexuality, as revisited and reutilized by feminists such as Teresa de Lauretis in her book by the same name.[33] In her definition, or, one should say, in the series of incrementing definitions that account for each stage of her argument, de Lauretis does not reduce gender to something emanating from sexual difference but relates it to a sociocultural construction and to a semiotic system that assigns meaning and value to different positions within that construction: "The construction of gender is both the product and the process of its representation" (5). As representation, gender displays affinities with Althusser's theory of ideology. It operates by engaging the subjectivity of the individual, by addressing the individual through the binary language of sexual difference and thereby producing the individual as man/woman: "The construction of gender is the product and process of both representation and self-representation" (9). The mode of operation and the social function of this (self)representation are ensured by the "technologies" that Foucault described, which allow its production and reproduction within and by way of institutional discourse, social practices, and the microphysics of daily life.

By defining gender as "technology" in the sense intended by Foucault, de Lauretis has provided literary criticism with a functional conceptual category that is, at the same time, powerful and flexible. Gender cannot be reduced to its biological foundation (which, as I have mentioned, provides strong incentives for the mimetic reduction of the narrative text); as social representation and technology, it has the capability of unifying, under a single issue, the discursive procedures *of the* text, the discursive practices *in the* text, and the microscopic/macroscopic social practices represented *in* and *by* the text. De Lauretis notes that the construction of gender is a work in progress that takes place, not just in institutional discourse and in macro- and micropolitical practices, but also in each discourse centered on gender, including artistic representations, radical theories, and feminism itself: "Paradoxically, therefore, the construction of gender is also effected by its deconstruction; that is to say, by any discourse, feminist or otherwise, that would discard it as ideological misrepresentation" (3). This approach helps us understand the inherent complicity between literature and this system, *even* and *exactly* when literature confronts it to demystify it, and helps us explain the ambivalence of scholarship on the question of feminism of/in James.

Althusser, let us remember, postulated no "outside" with respect to ideology, and Foucault posited the homeostatic pervasiveness of a power that is capable of containing its own opposition. De Lauretis' theory, on the other hand, moves from the premise that women have historically existed in a place that is inside *and* outside ideology/gender. This place is occupied by what the author calls "the subject of feminism," not to be confused, she points out, either with the Woman of patriarchal idealization or with actual women, imbricated as they are in the technologies of gender and the relationships they define: "the subject of feminism, much like Althusser's subject, is a theoretical construct (a way of conceptualizing, understanding, accounting for certain *processes*, not women)" (10). This subject is born out of the contradiction, proper to our culture, between Woman as representation and women as historical subjects, who see themselves as objects of representation and are aware of the distance between Woman as representation and their own existence. Women, therefore, are "both inside *and* outside gender, at once within and without representation," "and conscious of being so, conscious of that twofold pull, of that division, that doubled vision" (10). This is the "elsewhere" produced by feminist self-awareness, the "space-off" that delimits the margins of hegemonic discourse: these margins then can be assumed as points of departure, not to exit gender, but to predicate a different construction of gender, a "de-re-construction" (24) in different terms and to different ends.

The "doubled vision" that de Lauretis theorized at the end of the 1980s is the product of a feminist approach capable of producing theory and abstract categories that are still rooted in the political and existential specificity of women (or better, with a qualification employed explicitly by the author, of white women in industrialized societies). In my view, it is still the most effective theoretical means to investigate the feminine in literature from a nonessentialist point of view and to perceive the condition of women in their historical specificity. This "doubled vision" is the perspective inscribed in Henry James's short stories that I am about to examine: a "movement in and out of ideology, that crossing back and forth of the boundaries—and of the limits—of sexual difference(s)" (25), which de Lauretis ascribes to "the subject of feminism" and to its cultural production.

It is not my intention to attribute this doubling/redoubling of vision to art's idealistic ability to transcend the ideological and temporal limitations of its production, nor to ground it—as it would be easy and perhaps fair to do—in the personal subjectivity of the artist, in his own positioning in that "space-off" made invisible by the hegemonic nature of heterosexual discourse. As I mentioned, I wish to avoid the inevitable drift toward author and authorship, as if these were the ultimate "truths" and causes of the text, and keep my analysis, at least temporarily, on the question of gender as representation and of gender representation in relation to female subjectivity.[34] Therefore, I will adopt an approach in some way similar *(si parva licet componere magnis)* to Foucault's "interpretative analytics," as Dreyfus and Rabinow have defined it: that is, a "superficial" description and analysis of the texts, which pays attention to their conditions of possibility and to the relations that the texts entertain with each other, rather than a search for a historical or biographical causality, or for "truth" as deep meaning, in a hermeneutic sense.[35]

Instead of focusing on the author's ideology, I will concentrate on the modes of representation; not on the ideological meaning and function of the text (intended as univocal), but on its *productivity*, that is, on its internal relationships, in their multiple and dialogical nature, and on the complexity of the negotiations it entertains with several aspects of the dominant patriarchal ideology. I will test the text's willingness to answer my questions on gender and its ability to posit new ones.[36] This notion of productivity as variable interaction between the text and my use of it (its formal strategies, its linguistic resistance to an immediate ideological translation, its degree of compliance to the conceptual premises of my questions) is an avowedly tactical tool that I will employ to suspend, at least momentarily, the ultimate questions stubbornly posed by the critical theories from which I will draw, with a certain degree of self-conscious eclecticism, approaches and suggestions. My own approach to the text posits itself as an explicit "history of the present," to borrow another Foucaultian expression: that is, a questioning of conceptual cores and favorite patterns, established in relation to the theoretical debate and issues of today. Thus, my revisiting the Jamesian text is not prompted by a wish to anachronistically project those cores and patterns onto it but is inspired by an awareness of its "genealogical" value, that is, of the continuity between the cultural practices embodied in the text and those that produce today a gendered reading of the text, and the questions this reading raises and poses to the text.

My questions are framed by feminist criticism and gender studies; my method is primarily textual analysis, as derived from structural narratology and semiotics, integrated by what might be termed a "new historicist" attention to the intertextual relations between James's texts and contemporary cultural products. Let me offer a further clarification. The narratological methodology to which I refer is not the rigid taxonomic system, closed and objective, we encountered in the 1970s. Rather I intend the recent work by Mieke Bal, her extraordinary ability to read different semiotic systems as integrated.[37] Bal's "critical narratology" claims for itself the status of "critical theory," in Habermas's sense, and defines its object as "ideology at work in narrative subjectivity."[38] Moving from a nonhumanistic notion of the semiotic subject derived from psychoanalysis and post-Althusserian theories of ideology, Bal focuses on the analysis of representational structures as symptom and expression of a "subjectal semiotic network" (47). This network articulates different narrative positions and roles (narration, focalization, action) and produces different subjective positionings in the act of reading, which are inscribed in the process of rewriting and interpreting texts. In other words, my use of narratology is meant to be analytical and critical rather than purely descriptive; and formalist in the sense evoked by Bal, whose claim for a "formalist rigour" is qualified by an awareness that such a notion can only be employed *sous rature*, since "formalism is not the opposite of contextualization, but part of the semiotic enterprise the latter concept evokes" (9).

As the place where individual artistic purposes converge with preexisting language and discourses, narrative representation offers, in the linguistic materiality of the text, a firm point of departure to criticism. Narrative technique is the tool used to produce it. Critical narratology, therefore, promises to be the most suitable approach for unraveling the multiple threads of James's narrative discourse and its complex orchestration, in contrast to other approaches that assume its significance and direction as a whole through a comprehensive definition, such as interpretations that give the impression of confronting Percy Lubbock rather than Henry James. Confronting, instead, the plural and conflictual positionings inscribed in the text, critical narratology is the most suitable tool for reading the signs of James's "doubled vision" from and on patriarchal ideology, and of the "doubled vision" he offers to our readings.

This "doubled vision" is displayed in the short stories that I examine here, through a variety of textual phenomena. Before presenting them briefly, let me explain the premises upon which I have built my corpus. It is, at the same time, homogeneous, representative, and tendentious. For the reasons I have already explained, I favor the short stories for their relative straightforwardness; I will reduce to a bare minimum any reference to the better-known novels. Since they are experimental products generally revolving around a single situation and a small number of effects, the short stories construe their characters in a less complex and layered manner, thus offering greater opportunities to the antipsychological analysis I am proposing. Furthermore, they are by and large less well known and have rarely been the object of critical studies; they afford, as a result, a useful occasion to revisit and read noncanonical texts, and to examine the causes and the criteria of their noncanonicity.[39] At the same time, they are connected by a multitude of technical, thematic, and situational motifs to the novels: their analysis, in conclusion, may offer suggestions and directions to possible macrotextual projects.

My first selection criterion was the presence of a female protagonist or at least of a conspicuous female deuteragonist. Once selected in this fashion, some of these short stories seemed to present a certain degree of "grammaticality" and to arrange themselves around some conceptual cores, which I started to limn and interpret under the influence of contemporary theoretical texts, whose relevance to James's stories became clearer and clearer after my initial surprise. These I have consequently used as co-texts, in a sort of "parallel reading," which produced fruitful critical collusions and collisions.

The most obvious conceptual core immediately emerging from a reading of the tales is, of course, the "international theme"—one that, for this very reason and for lack of space, has not been examined here. Let me then briefly sketch its relevance. The theme is a recurrent investigation of the relationship between America and Europe through the cultural conflict between two models of femininity, used simultaneously as benchmarks for each system and as separate objects of investigation. The problematic nature of the American girl, apart from its denotative value as social fact, reveals the relative and arbitrary quality of the codes of feminine behavior that each culture transmits as sacred and natural and offers a preliminary occasion for analyzing the construction of gender models. "Daisy Miller," the most famous short story about the American girl, is in many ways the matrix of the gender structure variously explored in later stories. The female character is both central, as the title shows, and virtually deprived of a voice of her own. All characters discuss her and evaluate her behavior all the time, but the reader is never offered direct access to her consciousness and motives. A male "reflector" acts as point of view, constantly assessing and judging her according to patriarchal norms and categories by which she is framed. Finally, an ironic but unobtrusive narrating voice frames in its turn the male character's point of view and undercuts his authority, exposing its interested partiality, its culturally determined categories, and its contradictions, and even foregrounding—in the extraordinary opening paragraph of the tale—the very ideological operation whereby culturally relative judgments are transformed into allegedly neutral description.[40] All these elements, as will be seen, variously recur in the stories I examine.

The first, less widely explored conceptual core on which I have chosen to concentrate here relates to the nexus gaze-woman-beauty-objet d'art: I have investigated it with the help of feminist work on art history, film theory, the gendered economy of the gaze, and reification. Through the recurrence of thematic motifs and narrative strategies that play on the attribution or denial of the gaze, James's short stories repeatedly display a politics of the gaze in which women are positioned as art objects, objects of material possession and aesthetical fruition through the category of "beauty," which simultaneously enhances their material value and subsumes them under an aesthetic domain. Painting, collecting, and museums are also recurring motifs that connect the "aestheticization" of women to artistic production and to the commodification of art in the modern world.

The second conceptual core is the nexus woman-speaking-silence-sexuality: my reading of this nexus is primarily based on Foucault's categories in *La Volonté de savoir*, the first volume of his history of sexuality, and on the feminist investigation of the Victorian codes regulating female sexuality. The words with which women speak of their desire—a ritual of submission and, at the same time, the point in which the self is constituted as subject—are the paradoxical locus where women-as-subjects can reveal or lose themselves or else, through reticence, escape the asymmetrical power relationship that self-revelation establishes. The issue of speaking–keeping silent relates the situation of the characters to problems of textual communication, adding a metaliterary significance to the short stories that places them in direct relationship to the words spoken or unspoken by women.

The short stories examined here cover almost the whole span of Jamesian production, from 1873 to 1909. It seemed natural to organize my analysis of each conceptual core along chronological lines (with only one exception). However, the recurrence of motifs, and their different treatment and development in different texts, ultimately provided this chronological arrangement with an added significance of its own: the sense of an investigation that develops over time and possesses the continuity of a leitmotif that construes, through the individual stories, *another* story, with a recognizable plot and an inner and perceptible narrative logic of its own.

The short stories I have chosen to analyze also share other features, which involve their representational mode. And here I anticipate, in part, my conclusions. All the texts in question play on narrative distance, through the manipulation of points of view and narrative voices and of the mutual relation between these two categories of narrative discourse. Thus they present a variety of solutions that alone would disprove the presumed normativity of James's "art of fiction." One would argue that this is a characteristic of all his work. However, in the tales in question this variety is functionally connected to other textual aspects that, I claim, display a great degree of coherence.

The first of these aspects is the "extreme" quality of their situations, all revolving around some form of "pathology" or exaggeration: the painter who does not paint, the man who loves a dummy, the woman whose refusal to wear glasses makes her blind, the girl who dies after declaring her love, the woman who dies without declaring it. The antirealistic excess undermines the mimetic illusion that regulates the confirmation and acceptance of the status quo as inevitable, and displaces the level of discourse from things-as-they-are to the aberrant potentialities that are nevertheless inherent in them: a reductio ad absurdum, properly speaking, that forces the immanent logic of the system to produce abnormal outcomes.

The second aspect is the foregrounded metatextuality of the short stories, where the process of representation is constantly underscored and made problematic through the interference between the discourse of the text and the artistic, visual, verbal representations represented and discussed in the text. Metatextuality marks the complex relation—of collusion and distance, at the same time—that the text establishes with the world represented, offering itself as other than that world but simultaneously acknowledging its involvement with it, as in a mirror image. The framing of the text, which, according to some critics, should guarantee an aesthetic closure assumed as absolute distance, triggers, instead, a *mise en abyme* whose primary effect is to turn the opposition between internal and external into a relation of reciprocity. Meanwhile, this mirroring produces telescopic effects that draw the reader into the representation and offer her or him a paradoxical positioning both *inside* and *outside* the dynamics that are the object of representation—that is, a "doubled vision."

This, then, is my thesis: the center and the object of representation in the short stories examined here are the ideology of gender, in a specific and crucial historical instantiation. The logic that these stories question and bring to its extremes through the excess of their plots is the inner logic of patriarchal society, its gender arrangements, and the historical categories of feminine identity that are derived from them. By laying bare their underlying mechanisms, inscribed both in social rituals and in subjectivity, these short stories reveal their historical specificity and the oppressive and abusive role these mechanisms play. By making a spectacle of this function at a metatextual level, they put it at a distance, as it were, while acknowledging, at the same time, their (and our) entanglement in it. Through the plurality of narrative positions that their technical articula-tion allows, these texts present inscribed within themselves, intertextually, the cultural discourses and the representations of gender they circulate, relativized and denaturalized in the dialogical textual process. Thus they are both *producers* and *critics* of gender representations, investigated and destabilized by their "doubled vision"—a "doubled vision" that is further capable of turning upon itself and self-consciously questioning the role that artistic and literary productions play in construing and circulating gender images. In other words, as Elizabeth Allen has already argued, moving from the acknowledgment that women are construed cultural "characters" even before they accede to literary representation, these stories define gender as representation; on this category they build a narrative investigation that represents the role gender plays in the construction of subjectivity, along the same lines and with the same outcomes of the theoretical co-texts with which I have interpreted them.

Two comments are necessary at this point. The first concerns the relation woman-gender. Having set forth to undertake a study of women and to engage the existing scholarship on James and women, I then opted for a strategic displacement toward the category of gender to avoid being entrapped in a mimetic reading. The risk, though, is to "dilute" once more the specificity of the "woman question" within the problem of the construction of the subject in terms of gender, thus reproducing the generalizing move that I have just decried. But this is true only to a certain extent. My insistence on the notion of gender is motivated, not just by the premise I have already discussed, but also by my conviction that in some of his short stories James succeeds in presenting the category of gender in all its performativity, à la Judith Butler, through the ironic interplay of feminine and masculine stereotypes. At the same time, I believe that in the tales here examined (and more generally in James's fiction and essays) there is a space of and for women *as women*: not just an investigation on the cultural construction of women, but also a focus on the *specific* forms of their oppression and even, at least at the embryonic stage, an attempt to give shape to their possible liberation. In this regard, I believe, James's women are neither reified and congealed in their submission and/or in their voiceless aestheticization, nor are they transitional objects that express the personal or suprapersonal dynamics of the psyche. Rather, they are autonomous figures, insofar as the categories they variously embody and negotiate are the historically specific categories of Victorian womanhood in both the English and American version—categories, it seems appropriate to remember, that still confront the female imagination.

The second comment has to do with authorial control, a problem that I suspended only temporarily. In this introduction, I have attempted to adopt scrupulously a "neutral" point of view that would only take into account textual evidence and my interaction with such evidence, without evoking other agendas except my own and without presupposing a self-conscious and programmatic codification of texts on the part of the author along the lines of my inquiry. Here I find myself, though, using the name of the author as subject and using verbs that connote or imply an intentional intellectual operation. It must be the (uncanny) return of the repressed Master, which I cannot escape.

Let me then say that these short stories' concern with gender and women is not just the outcome of my interpretative mediation. It is there, inscribed in the texts in a systematic and consistent way. How is one to interpret the origin of this consistency, on one hand, and its directions, on the other? Let us start from the second point.

The critical ambivalence on the relationship between James and women is, it must be said, totally justified. His plots are fully consistent with the Victorian images of women who are submissive, silent, reified, victimized, sacrificed, and of girls who are punished for daring to assert their independence. There is enough there, if we focus on the mimetic level of representation, to justify the charges of patriarchal sadism, which are surely more widespread than my review of the critics would lead one to believe, considering that they have currency especially among women who do *not* write books on Henry James. However, a reading that would privilege the different modes in which discourse distances history and the effects of foregrounding and foreshortening, of *mise en abyme* and *téléscopage* produced by the narrative discourse, reaches very different conclusions, as we have seen. Is this the usual difference—of class and sensibility— between the "discriminating reader" and the uneducated public, inscribed in the double reading of the text and in its implied hierarchy of "highbrow" and "lowbrow" readers? I am not convinced, if only because this double level is present both in the earlier texts and in the later ones, in an earlier James who was still aspiring to a large readership and in the later one who had given up on his aspiration. Nor were the contents of his representations of such an import as would have justified concealing them from the less educated part of the public, especially if one considers that in the same years, sensation novels and the "New Woman" fiction were conveying all sorts of transgressive and "scandalous" contents to any and all. My impression is, rather, that instead of thinking of stratified and hierarchical levels of reading, we should envision a Janus-like strategy of representation, where each face is functional and interconnected to the other. A strategy that could aptly be defined as *Sadeian* rather than as sadistic, in the sense in which Roland Barthes reads Sade as a writer, not of mimesis, but of semiosis, who assumes the practice of sexuality and the social relations of domination "not as an image to be portrayed, but *as a model to be reproduced*":

the social novel maintains social relationships in their original place (society as a whole) but anecdotizes them for the sake of individual biographies . . . ; the Sadian novel takes the *formula* of these relationships, but transports them elsewhere, into an artificial society (as did Brecht in *The Threepenny Opera*). In the first instance, we have *reproduction*, in the meaning that word has in painting, in photography; in the second instance, there is, one might say, *re-production*, repeated production of a practice (and not of an historical "picture").[41]

Let me briefly pursue this Sadeian association. Would James perhaps be the equivalent of the "moral pornographer" discussed in *The Sadeian Woman*? A "moral pornographer," writes Angela Carter, who would use pornography "as a critique of current relations between the sexes," would no longer be "the enemy of women, perhaps because he might begin to penetrate to the heart of the contempt for women that distorts our culture even as he entered the realms of true obscenity as he describes it."[42]

Such a representational practice, which finds its own potential of criticism, not in open refusal, but in the congealed and distanced reinscription of social mechanism, is linked in Western culture of the twentieth century to the theater of Bertolt Brecht, whose name emerges also in the quotation by Barthes and elsewhere in the book by Carter. James as Sade, James as Brecht? What I am arguing, in the end, is that many of these short stories could be read in a Brechtian key: accordingly, the "obscenity" of women's victimization and the indirect, "formal" nature of the representation would not be alternative readings but would be interconnected, as part of the same project. As was the case with Brecht's "beaten hero," James's sacrificial heroines are functional to the audience's perception of oppression: they are capable of producing an unsentimental, paradoxical effect through a strategy of intellectual, "cold" presentation (in that it prevents identification and is framed and distanced on the narrative level), which brings to mind the "defamiliarization" of Brecht's "epic theatre."[43]

I do not wish to push the analogy too far nor to offer these short stories, significant as they are in my view, as a valid model for the work of Henry James as a whole: their general heuristic significance should obviously be tested through specific case studies. Nevertheless, I believe that a more "Brechtian" reading of Henry James, that is, one less concentrated, for good or for bad, on the critical fetish of "consciousness," would discover many interesting suggestions in the "frail vessels of *un*consciousness" of these short stories. If the relevance of consciousness in James is an undeniable fact, one should not forget that he was also theorizing the dialectics of "awareness" and "bewilderment" in the literary character. And to my mind it is precisely the characters' *un*consciousness, as the site for the inscription of regulation and ideology, that affords a perception of the "space-off" situated beyond the limits of representational "naturalness."[44] James is often charged with refusing to represent women's agency and to offer freedom as an outcome to their situations. This refusal may be read, then, not as dictated by ideology or by the will to discipline and punish, but rather as a diagnostic approach that leaves open all complicities, including the complicity of women in their own victimization, and all contradictions, without translating or resolving them at the level of the plot—a procedure that would undeniably be open to the charge of being aestheticizing and ideologically suspicious. *Representing* women's subjection to patriarchal power and discipline, one should remember, does not necessarily imply *defending* that power and discipline.[45]

The productivity of the text in this respect can also be found in its pragmatic effect. In the opening of her essay on *The American*, Carolyn Porter relates the reaction of an unnamed woman colleague: " 'I have never read a James novel that I did not want to hurl across the room when I finished' "(99). Although this is just an anecdote, I wonder whether the violence of this and similar reactions would not attest to a rather destabilizing pragmatic effect: not the aesthetic resolution of contradictions, not the Aristotelian catharsis, not the acquiescence to the inevitable necessity of the status quo, but the vicarious experience of an unacceptable injustice, which is experienced without any comforting rationalization and produces an act of rebellion.

It would seem that I end up siding with the champions of the "subversive hypothesis," according to the ironic term coined by New Historicism. I would agree only after a few clarifications. It is not my intention to claim for James, either on the theoretical or on the critical level, a capacity or willingness to subvert the patriarchal order. As Mao Tse-tung, undoubtedly an authority on the subject, used to say: the good revolutionaries are those who *make* a revolution. Measured with this stick, Henry James is not the only writer, canonical or otherwise, who would be found wanting. Nevertheless, James's work as a whole, positioned as it is along a truly crucial historical watershed, appears to me an extraordinary moment of self-awareness in the patriarchal bourgeois world and in the ideology of gender. Self-awareness does not make this world automatically less oppressive, nor does it entail or advocate an immediate upheaval within or without the diegetic boundaries. At most, it offers some moments of utopia. It does, nonetheless, represent and lay bare the *apparatus*, that is, the imbrication of material and discursive mechanisms, of that world with critical rigor and intelligence unsurpassed by his contemporaries, and underlines the historical, hence alterable, nature of that world. I would not go so far as to attribute to James and his writing an ability to demystify completely patriarchal ideology by reducing it to what Marxist criticism would call its ultimate determinants. Undoubtedly, though, he represented with extreme perspicacity both the phenomenology and the operational modes of that ideology. And the connections he established between the representation of women and other aspects of the economic and social spheres were not just an intuition. How else would one explain that in the sample of short stories presented here the only woman who resists and voices explicitly a resistance to the appropriation of her self as aesthetic object and angel figure is Serafina in "The Madonna of the Future"? As an Italian embroiderer, a non-Anglo-Saxon woman, she is virtually the only character untouched by the Victorian cult of the angel in the house. An artisan who is a worker and a producer, profitably involved in a mode of production that antedates the reclusion in the domestic sphere, which, in the more industrialized countries, had already turned bourgeois women into expensive and nonproductive fetishes, Serafina is, not accidentally, the only woman character who can afford to denounce and reject her lover's aestheticizing move.

The Master has become at this point more invasive than ever. I have attributed to him a degree of intentionality in the codification of the text, of artistic superawareness, of demystifying intelligence, which are difficult to digest at the theoretical level and seem to contradict my initial premise about avoiding a hermeneutic and causal reading of the texts. I could invoke the "intentional fallacy" or my heartfelt indifference to James as a *person* beyond the authorial figure that the texts construe for us; but this would obviously be just a strategy of evasion. The truth is that I have no answers to this question, neither at a critical nor, for lack of any orthodoxy, at the theoretical level.

Neither the consistency of the texts under examination here nor their elaborate formal construction offer any answers: they could equally be interpreted as the outcome of omnipotent control or as the inscription of the unconscious, which displays its consistent logic independently of the author's will. In the same way, the authorial statements presented in the *Notebooks* or in the prefaces (which I have occasionally used to support my readings) would seem able and willing to offer some extratextual grounding; in reality they do not escape textuality and actually thematize it constantly, with a resulting effect of self-deconstruction. The changes effected in the transposition of the notebooks into the finished texts, James's recurring acknowledgment of having betrayed his own intentions, the untrustworthiness of the prefaces as retroactive commentary are all eloquent proof that the author himself did not claim absolute control over texts that were in fact uncontrollable.[46] On the theoretical level I can only mention that, beginning with Althusser's view of ideology as rooted in subjectivity, many scholars (Žižek, Silverman) have theorized on the social character of the unconscious, revisiting Deleuze and the Lacanian basis of Althusser's theory and working on the divided nature of the subject. The idea of ideology as psychic function posits the author not just in his role as proprietor, as intelligent and conscious controller of the production of meanings, but also as the unconscious bearer and playground of identifications and investments. In principle, then, it would be possible to offer the hypothesis that the "critical" and subversive significance of the texts that an author produces is to be found in her or his particular unconscious positioning in relation to what is dictated by a collective "dominant fiction" (Silverman) and not in her or his superior and transcendent clarity of vision.[47]

Establishing a clear relay between the author and the text would mean mastering a comprehensive psychoanalytic theory—something I cannot claim, as evidenced by my cautious use of psychoanalytic instruments in my readings as co-texts for comparisons, not as hermeneutic levers. But then even the numerous and recent sophisticated readings of James and gender based on psychoanalytic categories constitute a motley body of works, which engage in an internal dialogue and produce divergent critical outcomes. Kaja Silverman writes that "James's authorial subjectivity . . . is determined less by the refinements of his consciousness than by the imperatives of his unconscious fantasy"; "an almost hyperbolically marginal male subject" (158), the internal "author" reconstructible from the textual fantasmatic is positioned at the intersection between the negative and positive Oedipus complexes in relation to a primal scene, which surfaces under the sign of passivity, of masochism, of identifications that defy the binary language of sexual difference; the "external" author, instead—that is, the Master—cannot be read other than as compensatory construction.[48] Sedgwick disagrees with Silverman and posits the anal metaphor inscribed in Jamesian writing as conscious linguistic exhibitionism: "When we tune in to James's language on these frequencies, it is not as superior, privileged eavesdroppers on a sexual narrative hidden from himself; rather, it is as an audience offered the privilege of sharing in his exhibitionistic enjoyment and performance of a sexuality organized around shame. Indeed, it is as an audience desired to do so—which is also happily to say, as an audience desired."[49] Hugh Stevens too discusses intentionality in his recent work on this subject, where he examines James's resistance to the Victorian "ontology of sexuality" and the inscription in his texts of daring representations of marginal sexuality and transgressive desires, all under the protection of his self-conscious reticence. Stevens concludes with the image of Henry James, who "fashions himself in the spirit of camp affirmation" both through his explicit affirmation of himself as the subject of (homo)sexual desire and through his narcissistic, hedonistic, and erotic prose.[50] Many other essays besides those discussed here examine the psychological, aesthetic, and theoretical relations James entertains with his own sexuality, the psychic economy of masochism, the categories of male identity, the heterosexual arrangements, and the homosexual suggestions in his society.[51]

Let me then evoke again the notion of "doubled vision," not as a shortcut to avoid the contradiction I cannot resolve, but to launch it again in another direction and connect it to another outcome of my readings. De Lauretis presents the notion, not as a personal "gift," but as a theoretical category that describes the potential positioning of subjectivity in relation to gender—a positioning allowed by the contradiction of the subject as, simultaneously and consciously, both object and subject of representation and self-representation. This doubling *and* redoubling between the subject and the object, the inside and the outside of representation, acts as a catalyst of different possibilities. First, it relates to the psychoanalytical attempt to define the relation between subject and ideology and to the reopening of a space for political action by a subject who would otherwise be totally contained and conscripted by the power of ideology. Second, it refers to the classical mise en scène of desire in which, as Laplanche and Pontalis propose, the subject is always simultaneously observer and part of the scene, as well as to Foucault's notion that "[w]here there is power, there is resistance, and yet, or rather consequently, this resistance is never in a position of exteriority in relation to power."[52] These critical paths, which contemplate the deconstruction of the binary status of inside/outside, control/abandonment, intentionality/unconsciousness, power/subjection, seem to me the most fruitful means to describe the positionings implied and produced by Jamesian texts. I have in mind the "ambivalence" of the critical readings already quoted here, which mirror perhaps not the famous Jamesian "ambiguity" but, as I have argued, the *interdependence* in his writing of the divergent effects polarized by the act of reading. But I am also thinking of Ross Posnock's recent claim of a Foucaultian "intellectual style" for James, which draws inspiration from the value and the practice of "nonidentity," as refusal of categorizations and of leverage points allegedly situated outside the framed domain and as pragmatist practice of a "thirdness" suspended between traditional oppositions.[53] I also have in mind certain strategies of *écriture,* which, as I will argue in relation to the last short stories examined in this book, seem to descend from the acknowledgment that words are entangled in power and to defuse such an entanglement by practices attempting to suspend authorship: dramatization (which amounts to a self-effacing of narratorial function as reference authority) and a prose style capitalizing on metaphorical density and obscurity, which communicates the unsaid and negates the communicability of what it says, leaving to the reader the task of coauthoring the text and reconstructing its semantical and structural relations.[54]

In his complex reading of the interconnections between textuality and theatricality in James, Joseph Litvak proposes "scene-making," in its double meaning of aesthetic will of self-representation and "embarrassment" caused by the judgments and condemnation of others, as the recurring and crucial place that partakes of consciousness and unconsciousness, of concealment and self-revelation, of control and subjection to the control of others. To "catch myself in the act," as James puts it in his *Autobiography,* is both concealing and revealing, doubling the subject in agent and spectator, controller and object of control; it relates, on one hand, to James's "highly theatrical, inside-outside, now-you-see-me-now-you-don't, *écriture gaie*" and, on the other, to a dialectic of power à la Foucault, played out performatively with the reader:

> I would like to propose that, instead of reducing these relations between author and reader to a question of who's duping whom, we see them as local effects of the general structure of power and pleasure defined by Foucault: as an especially articulate instantiation of that structure, what I have been calling James's theater of embarrassment shows both author and readers moving back and forth across the footlights. In subjecting James to one's analytic gaze, one tends, that

is, to expose oneself as well, repeating the author's double role as spectator *and* performer.[55]

The "other" Henry James of my book is still a figure whose traits are left undefined willingly and inevitably. My only possible reconceptualization of him is, perhaps, as paradoxical Master, who, like Prospero in *The Tempest*, finds his apotheosis in the (hyperconscious?) act of renouncing the marks of power. This outcome was already foreshadowed in the image of himself as "queer monster"—an identity that is not amenable to categories, with uncertain and destabilizing sexual connotations.

What is left is "the author effect," that is, the performative effect of a textuality that, by abdicating any univocal control over its enunciations, forces readers, as Litvak suggests, to expose themselves in turn across the footlights of the textual scene: the reader herself and himself, inside and outside the text, "caught in the act," made responsible for each of her and his positionings, gender identifications, complicities, and presuppositions. In relation to the world as narrated and in relation, each one, to one's own "Henry James."

PART ONE

The Gaze:
In the Museum of Women

Women and portraits: a well-known motif to Jamesian critics, who have always been aware of James's interest in visual arts.[1] Women, however, also relate to statues, carvings, dolls, furniture, dummies, and bric-a-brac in James's stories. What is the common feature that connects such disparate objects to one another and that connects them all to the representation of woman?[2]

The predicate shared by both woman and this collection of artifacts is beauty. As a fundamental category in artistic experience and simultaneously as a crucial value in the historical construction of femininity, beauty draws woman into the aesthetic sphere; it makes her hold on the existential dimension problematic and her relation to temporality a conflicted one. The Jamesian stories I examine all revolve around women, art objects, beauty, and time—a thematic cluster whose components they relentlessly analyze and combine into ever-different plots over a forty-year span. In a recurring textual dynamic, a woman character is connected to an artifact; the relation ranges from opposition ("The Madonna of the Future" and "The Sweetheart of M. Briseux") through equivalence ("The Last of the Valerii" and "Adina") to substitution: the substitution of a woman with her simulacrum, as is the case with "Rose-Agathe" and "Glasses." Only an artifact, it would seem, can ensure the unalterable permanence of aesthetic value: woman in her actual existence is nothing but a contingent and hence finally inadequate symbol of beauty. The overall shift is from the representation of woman to woman as representation: the "*mise-en-scène* of that absence of the 'real' woman that is the necessary support of the attribution of beauty."[3]

While beauty is the ground authorizing such an iconic reduction of woman, the gaze is the axis along which this dynamic operates. Beauty is only perceived in the visual sphere: as a shared and sought for cultural value, it makes woman into a privileged visual object, thus positioning her at the passive, receiving end of the gaze. While these visual dynamics dramatically intensify the customary visual dimension of James's narrative universe, they also take on strong gender overtones.[4] The women protagonists of these tales function as instances of the gendered economy of the gaze such as the feminist work on cinema and the visual arts has described it; indeed, in being the target and repository of the male gaze, which allows no reciprocity and acts as a one-way vehicle of sexual desire, these characters seem all too literal embodiments of Laura Mulvey's, Jacqueline Rose's, and Griselda Pollock's theories.[5] In the work of these critics—on which my own analyses are based—women are characterized by their "to-be-looked-at-ness" (Mulvey), which posits them as the spectacularized object of a male spectator's gaze, whose role is defined in terms of voyeurism and scopophilia.

The equivalence between woman and art object, however, works in a twofold direction. While focusing on the reifying and aestheticizing quality of man-woman relations in this cultural universe, James simultaneously questions the reification and aestheticization of *art*, presenting the two phenomena as related and exploring their connections. As Jonathan Freedman has conclusively shown, throughout his career James was in constant if subterranean dialogue with both British and American aestheticism, whose opposite polarities of aesthetic idealization and commodification he equally confronted and whose icons he incorporated into his own writings as signs and objects of a complicitous critique.[6] By having the aesthetic sphere interact with gender, James uses each as a connotative cultural context for the other: he allows woman and art object to question each other and to denaturalize each other as both effects of representation. The aesthetic idealization of *both* woman and art is made to reveal its kinship with the commodification and fetishization typical of consumer society—a spectacularized society, where everything is commodified, but the commodity is in its turn constructed as cut off from its material and cultural production and displayed in its separateness as object for consumption and contemplation (a process, incidentally, that is explicitly staged in some of these tales).[7]

A number of recurring textual presences foreground the interpenetration of the aesthetic, the economic, and the gender dimension. First among these is, of course, the objet d'art, invariably connected to the woman character by varying homological relations, be it modern or ancient, crafted or mass-produced, rich in cultural or monetary value. Another one is the painter or collector—in other words, the aesthete, the professional of the aesthetic sphere, which he simultaneously creates and validates through his expertise. A topical figure in British, Continental, and American culture from the 1870s onward, the aesthete is a key figure both in congealing woman as object of aesthetic contemplation and consumption by transforming her into a portrait or displaying her along with china cups and bibelots and as representative of the complex historical nexus linking the idealistic attempt to purify the aesthetic sphere, its professionalization, and its commodification (as scholars from Benjamin to Bourdieu have pointed out).

The third haunting presence is the museum, a recurrent backdrop in most tales, from the early "The Madonna of the Future" through "Julia Bride" to "Mora Montravers," James's last completed tale and the final one I examine. The museum stands as an emblematic signifier pointing to the public and, as it were, institutional quality of the aestheticization of woman into an object for collection and exhibition; while making use of its existing connotations, though, James interrogates the museum itself and the notion of art it embodies and circulates, thus displaying his lucidity as a cultural critic engaging the contemporary cultural debate. By staging private and public collections side by side, James reveals their deep affinity, since both embody the mystified status of art in an era dominated by the marketplace. In its decontextualized and dehistoricized juxtaposition of "masterpieces," the museum reproduces the collector's heterogeneous bric-a-brac on a gigantic and sublimated scale. As the repository and guarantee of all that is *priceless* and therefore withdrawn from economic circulation, the museum is an important instrument of the idealization and hypostatization of art as absolute and transcendent value. The marketplace, though, is never too far removed: indeed, it grounds the whole enterprise, as witness the origins of modern museums in European aristocratic maecenatism, imperial expropriation, and—more recently—the purchasing power of American capital.

In staging and exploring these connections, James's tales enact a number of strategies of resistance against aestheticization—both woman's and their own as artistic products. These certainly include the defamiliarizing use of such characteristic tropes of the aesthetic movement as *ekphrasis*, as Freedman has noted; but to my mind, James's strategies go beyond his dialogue with aestheticism and take on an autonomous self-reflexive value. Taking my cue from Freedman's remark that "James's allusion to . . . decadent icon[s] places, as it were, quotation marks around itself" (204),

I would argue that James's practice in these tales is a constant *exhibition of representation* through narrative device: a complex *mise en abyme* of the kind exemplified in Foucault's analysis of *Las Meninas* with which he opens *The Order of Things*, whereby the *process* of representation is simultaneously staged and pointed at from an unstable position within the text—a position neither complicitous nor transcendent, yet inevitably both at once, which the text's producer and its reader problematically share.[8] Such an unstable place and point of view can possibly be described in James's words on May Bartram in "The Beast in the Jungle": "[S]he achieved, by an art indescribable, the feat of at once—or perhaps it was only alternately— meeting the eyes from in front and mingling her own vision, as from over his shoulder, with their peep through the apertures."

Chapter 1
Women, Portraits, and Painters:
"The Madonna of the Future" and
"The Sweetheart of M. Briseux"

The Muse's Betrayal: "The Madonna of the Future"

Dramatis Personae: Theobald, an American painter in Florence, elated by the close contact with classical art but also overwhelmed by the unattainable paragon of perfection it represents; Serafina, a woman whose once unsurpassable beauty is slowly but inexorably fading, and who is loved platonically and revered by Theobald as the perfect model of a Madonna yet to be painted—the epitome of all former Madonnas, rivaling those of Raphael and Michaelangelo; her lover, a clever and prolific sculptor of commercially successful, obscene zoomorphic statuettes; the circle of American expatriates, lovers and patrons of the arts, who despise Theobald for his inability to bring forth the promised masterpiece; and an occasional friend of the painter's, a young American recently arrived in Florence. An ironic and puzzled observer at first, the latter becomes more and more sympathetic with Theobald and involved in his story: after involuntarily causing him to realize his failure (Serafina is now too old to be a Madonna, and the painter is unequal to the task he has been setting himself for twenty years), he becomes the deeply affected witness to his despair and death and the posthumous defender of his memory and of the actual existence of the masterpiece, which, in fact, has never been painted. These are the outlines—teeming with literary reminiscences—of the story, as told many years later by H., the painter's friend, whose first-person narrative is in turn framed by that of a nameless narrator, a guest at the same dinner party.[1]

"The Madonna of the Future" owes much of its renown to Theobald's passionate plea for art in America, a veritable collection of memorable and oft-quoted sentences: " 'We are the disinherited of Art! . . . An American, to excel, has just ten times as much to learn as a European. . . . We poor aspirants must live in perpetual exile' " (733). It hardly comes as a surprise, then, that "The Madonna of the Future" has always been read as a tale of the artist, as a metafictional treatment of the problem of art for Americans and, more generally, of the role of art in the modern age, when everything has been touched by the vulgar hand of commerce and the great ideals of classical art are no longer viable. Such an interpretation is also supported by a comparison of James's tale with its literary sources: Balzac's "Le Chef-d'oeuvre inconnu," Alfred de Musset's *Lorenzaccio*, and two poems by Browning, "Pictor Ignotus, Florence 15—" and "Andrea del Sarto." Each of these sources is scrupulously cited in the text, and from each, as critics have noted, James has drawn themes and situations.[2] Browning's poems stage different versions of the artist's failure: Pictor Ignotus shuns the world for fear of contaminating his art; Andrea del Sarto has extraordinary technical skills but does not possess "the soul," that ideal quality that makes Raphael's painting sublime. In Musset's play, Tebaldeo is a minor character, a painter, a pupil of Raphael, and an admirer of the old masters, whose technical achievements, however, he cannot hope to emulate: "There is small merit in my works. I know better how to love the arts than practise them;" in James's tale, Theobald's description of his secluded life is taken literally from Tebaldeo's in the play.[3] In "Le Chef-d'oeuvre inconnu," old Frenhofer's failure is because of his maniacal perfectionism: in pursuit of an unattainable ideal of absolute truth to nature, he keeps adding layer upon layer of finishing touches to his masterpiece, thus turning it into a chaos of colors and lines whose only definite feature—a relic of masterliness submerged in madness—is a woman's perfect, "living" foot.

It is not my purpose, however, to read "The Madonna of the Future" as a canonical stage in James's metafictional treatment of the artist as character. Rather, I wish to shift my focus from the painter to the subject of the painting—if only to ascertain that, even in this respect, a comparison of James's tale with its intertexts can be revealing.

Even while foregrounding art and the artist as their main theme, James's sources are all haunted by female presences. Tebaldeo rejects Lorenzo's request that he paint the portrait of a famous Florentine courtesan, alleging his inability to paint anything but Florence, which is like a mother to him. Lorenzo's reply is that Florence is a whore, and the image of the city as a whore, accompanied by a lament over its decline, runs through the whole play. Andrea del Sarto blames his incapacity to attain the sublime on his wife and model, Lucrezia, an exceedingly beautiful but soulless woman, whose greed prompts her to betray him as both husband and artist by inducing him to vilify his art in a quest for money rather than for glory. The psychological pathos and drama in his monologue lie precisely in the ambiguous link connecting Andrea's artistic failure and his relationship with his wife. On the one hand, Lucrezia's greed and moral emptiness are the motive for her husband's failure; on the other hand, she represents the painter's alibi and scapegoat for that failure and thus hints at a deeper psychological causality: the antithesis of woman and art, which is implied in creativity, conceived in Freudian terms as sublimation. Andrea is unable to make a choice and thus wavers between claiming and regretting his allegiance to his wife. He alternates between extolling his physical possession of her as compensation enough ("Let my hands frame your face in your hair's gold / You beautiful Lucrezia that are mine! / 'Rafael did this, Andrea painted that; / The Roman's is the better when you pray, / But still the other's Virgin was his wife—' / Men will excuse me") and making invidious comparisons between the "wifeless" masters' work and his own—"Why do I need you? / What wife had Rafael, or has Angelo?" He ends up simply confronting his failure once again, simultaneously blaming it on Lucrezia and claiming it as his own: "So—still they overcome / Because there's still Lucrezia,—as I choose."[4] In Balzac's tale, woman plays a threefold role: abstract, as the subject par excellence of pictorial representation and, therefore, the touchstone for truth to nature in rendering and execution, in the long opening discussion; concrete, as the flesh-and-blood woman Gillette, the artist Poussin's lover and model, an object of love but also of barter (Poussin offers her as a model to old Frenhofer, thus jeopardizing both her modesty and their mutual love, in the hope of gaining a glimpse of the mysterious masterpiece he is finishing); and finally, symbolic, as a woman-picture complete with name and citizenship—Catherine Lescault, "la Belle Noiseuse," an object of passionate and jealous love for Frenhofer, who, unlike Poussin, shelters her from the gaze of other men ("It would be an awful prostitution!"), regarding her as "my creature, my spouse" and as quite human: "I have been living with this woman for ten years, she is mine, mine only, and she loves me. Hasn't she smiled to me each time I touched her with my brush? She has got a soul, the soul I bestowed on her."

James's sources, then, offer a wide range of women's roles: whore and symbol of a city, blank soul and perfection of forms, wife and Virgin Mary, lover and marketable object, betrayer and scapegoat, love object *as* art object and love object *versus* art object. In James's tale all these roles overlap and melt into a single complex character that is the one original, unprecedented creation in "The Madonna of the Future." Apart from any more superficial analogies, the interplay between the artist's creative failure and a female figure is the specific thematic core that James's tale shares with its sources. In its openly displayed intertextuality, which builds up a rich, polysemic connotative context for the tale, "The Madonna of the Future" is a rewriting of, and an attempt at thinking anew about, a tangle of issues bearing less on the generic problem of the artist than on the problem—or rather, the problematic quality—of woman as inspiring muse and as object of artistic representation.

This assessment of the story allows us to apprehend more fully the most powerful implication of the title. The word "Madonna" is a locus of exceptional semantic concentration, for here an artistic and a religious paradigm coalesce into a single image—an image of a *woman*. Whenever Madonnas are under discussion, women are under discussion, as Lynne Pearce remarks while discussing another Madonna—*The Girlhood of Mary Virgin* by Dante Gabriel Rossetti. Only by taking a deliberately perverse stand in the face of critical tradition, therefore, can one attempt to understand fully what is being said about women in instances that ostensibly deal with Madonnas: "Rossetti's *The Virgin* is interpreted as a religious painting by a cultural consensus that extends from the nineteenth century to the present day; it is a painting *about women* only through ignorance . . . , or at the point we start breaking the rules."[5]

At the point we start breaking the rules, "The Madonna of the Future" too, like Rossetti's painting, becomes a statement about women as well as one of James's first serious metanarrative reflections upon the terms of the cultural and artistic representation of women. The confrontation staged in this text is not so much that between the American artist and European art as a confrontation between divergent versions of femininity: a confrontation, in other words, between the Virgin Mary and Serafina.[6]

From an artistic point of view, the Virgin Mary dominated European iconography for centuries. Through Raphael, she became the very emblem of painting, just as the Mona Lisa would come to be considered through the influence of Walter Pater: a paradigm of classic art as compositional balance, harmony, and formal perfection. From a religious point of view, she embodied the mystery of virginal motherhood, a paradox transcending both natural law and human reason; mediatrix between God and mankind, she was the emblem of a simultaneously powerful and submissive femininity, unattainable transcendence and loving mother at one and the same time.

Culturally, she was the sublimated image of purity and chastity as feminine ideals of perfection, while at the same time embodying the archetype of motherhood. The Madonna functioned as the key figure for women's education, a model for women to identify with. The influence of this model was felt not only in Catholic countries but found realization in the Protestant world as well in that secularized Victorian version, the Angel in the House, an image combining virginal purity with maternal dedication.[7] Cultural history and art meet if one remembers that in Victorian England Raphael was regarded primarily as a painter of sweet Madonnas and became the object of a para-aesthetic cult that led in turn to the Pre-Raphaelite reaction. An involuntary ally and an objective accomplice of Victorian sentimentalization, Raphael is the perfect signifier of an idealizing and simplifying use of classical art and, at the same time, of the ideological version of femininity that it is made to express.

A single signifier, then, is made to convey a whole cluster of associations, amounting to an exceptional cultural synthesis: woman and cult object, art object and role model. As soon as one begins to sort out and expound the implications of the term "Madonna," the "Madonna of the Future" no longer appears simply as the result of an iconographic tradition, nor can its impossibility be reduced to the artist's defeat vis-à-vis the unattainability of that tradition. The unresolvable contradiction lies elsewhere; its name is the name of Theobald's faded muse, Serafina.

A Muse—"the active memory of a tradition which is voicelessly voiced through her, . . . the source of creativity as locus and object for the male gaze"—Serafina is the living synthesis of the tradition Theobald is eager to attain: a real woman, but idealized in such terms as to make her the object of a simultaneously aesthetic and religious cult.[8] " 'Can you look at a beautiful woman with reverent eyes?' . . . When at last I had assured him that I could undertake to temper admiration with respect, he informed me, with an air of religious mystery, that it was in his power to introduce me to the most beautiful woman in Italy—'A beauty with a soul! . . . This woman's beauty . . . is a lesson, a morality, a poem! It's my daily study' " (747).

The reason for such a twofold cult stems, as we later learn, from the striking effect of their first meeting:

"You should have seen the mother and the child together, seen them as I first saw them,—the mother with her head draped in a shawl, a divine trouble in her face, and the bambino pressed to her bosom.

You would have said, I think, that Raphael had found his match in common chance. . . . She, too, was a maiden mother, and she had been turned out into the world in her shame. I felt in all my pulses that here was my subject marvellously realised. I felt like one of the old monkish artists who had had a vision. I rescued the poor creatures, cherished them, watched them as I would have done some precious work of art, some lovely fragment of fresco discovered in a mouldering cloister." (751–52)

Serafina's apparition before Theobald renders her forever in his eyes as both a living picture *and* the Virgin Mary; it produces an aesthetic ecstasy that utterly submerges any dissonant implications present in being a "maiden mother," not in supernatural experience, but in the ordinary world. Despite her name, a reminder of angelic choirs, and despite the adjectives Theobald constantly lavishes on her (" 'the divine Serafina' " [751]), Serafina is not simply a paragon of beauty and spirituality. She mingles spirit and matter, the church and the marketplace, from her very first appearance: "She had been that morning to confession; she had also been to market, and had bought a chicken for dinner" (748). Even though she is embroidering an ecclesiastical vestment in gold and silver and wearing a silver cross, and even though her head has a "sanctified bend" (749) and her hair makes "a covering as chaste and formal as the veil of a nun" (749), the disenchanted narrator immediately suspects this "*bourgeoise* Egeria" of betraying "a rather vulgar stagnation of mind" (749) and of being not just "decidedly an elderly woman" but "simply coarse" (749). Despite the impression she gives of being "some pious lay-member of a sisterhood, living by special permission outside her convent walls" (750), the narrator thinks her likely to be a mere kept woman, profiting from the painter's "Platonic ecstasy" (748) and ready to make a fool of him, taking the situation "rather less seriously than her friend" (749). Serafina's dignified, undecipherable behavior makes such inferences impossible to prove at the first encounter; they seem to be verified, however, when the narrator, on going to her house again for news of Theobald, finds her in the company of "a gentleman,—an individual, at least, of the male sex" (755), and in a far from Raphaelesque attitude: "With one hand she held in her lap a plate of smoking maccaroni; with the other she had lifted high in air one of the pendulous filaments of this succulent compound, and was in the act of slipping it gently down her throat"(755).

The Madonna is eating macaroni; in her lap, instead of the Holy Child, rests a steaming dish. This dissonance, worthy of a Duchamp, elicits from the narrator a sharp reproof: " 'Prove at least that one old woman can be faithful' " (764) are the words he will later address to Theobald's old landlady, thus implicitly contrasting her solicitude with Serafina's "unfaithfulness." Interestingly enough, the narrator's accusations have continued to resound in the gratuitously strong feelings and abusive language of some critics who, even while "officially" dealing with the artistic theme of the story, manage to place the blame for Theobald's artistic failure wholly on Serafina: "a woman of too philistine and materialist a stamp to understand or appreciate the exceptional qualities of her admirer," "a rather coarse and shopworn townswoman," "capable . . . of betraying her artist's devotion by keeping up a vulgar liaison with another man."[9] Such reproofs are, quite evidently, a vehemently misogynistic response to the perception of female prominence in the text and represent a reductionist way of dealing, in terms of moral responsibility, personal inadequacy, and "betrayal," with what is instead an *objective* and *structural* impediment.

The reason why the "Madonna of the Future" will never be painted is that it is conceived in mutually exclusive terms: both as the consummation of a time-honored tradition—with its accompanying cultural models of femininity—and as a *portrait*, that is, the picture of a *real* woman. Woman in her actual reality, woman in her physical form, is the element *in excess*, which irrevocably explodes the idealistic crystallization of woman both as an aesthetic object and as a sacred one. The hypostasis of woman as a Madonna—timeless beauty and spotless purity—taking no account of her sexual identity, of her material existence, and of the passing of time, is just as much a reason for the artist's failure as is the unequal confrontation with the classics. The structural impossibility of a "Madonna of the Future" lies in its being grounded in the idealization of a woman who refuses to be idealized but demands instead to be recognized and accepted for what she *is*: a creature of the real world, with multiple and even conflicting dimensions. James's story makes a statement about women in Serafina's voice, giving her a memorable remark that is both a rebuttal of the accusatory critical readings to come and a denunciation of all kinds of idealization and male projections, which would impose on women a rule of conduct and a standard to be judged by: " 'And I can tell you this, signore—I never deceived him. Who put it into his head that I was made to live on holy thoughts and fine phrases? It was his own fancy, and it pleased him to think so' " (765).

Theobald's failure, then, is as much the result of idealizing classical art as of idealizing woman: " 'Lovely Madonna, model at once and muse, I call you to witness that I too am an idealist!' " (738). But Raphael's

Madonna, taken as a timeless paradigm, is an unrealistic model, life denying both on the artistic and on the cultural plane and destructive for anyone who embraces it. Beauty, whether in an art object or in a woman, when hypostatized in such an abstract manner, regardless of actualities—be they of history, of the marketplace, or of daily life—becomes unattainable. Sealed in an irrecoverable past, it is deprived of all present and of all future: the "Madonna of the Future," thus envisaged, becomes an oxymoron. Raphael's aesthetic harmony was itself historically contingent, the product of an age when "'people's religious and aesthetic needs went hand in hand, and there was . . . a demand for the Blessed Virgin'" (739). Painting Madonnas was no heroic deed then: all one needed to do was conform to the law of supply and demand. But anyone who tries to reproduce Raphael's art today can only make a sterile gesture: time, while canonizing it, has also unredeemably reified and commodified it. The only possible reproduction of the *Madonna of the Chair* at this point is the "huge miniature copy" bedecking Mrs. Coventry, the American patroness and "high-priestess of the arts," whose Florence apartment, thanks to the power of money, is "a sort of Pitti palace *au petit pied*" (743). In similar fashion, Serafina's beauty, which has been slowly fading as "one by one, the noiseless years had ebbed away and left him brooding in charmed inaction, for ever preparing for a work for ever deferred" (753), survives now only as the irrecoverable memory of a fleeting moment that Theobald was unable to grasp because he was too occupied with the momentous preparations required to immortalize it, all too slowly: for haste in the presence of beauty is blasphemy, and eternity is what a painter has to aim for.[10] So that Theobald's miserable cry—"'I must make up my Madonna out of *de beaux restes*! What a masterpiece she'll be! Old—old! Old—old!'" (753)—applies equally well to the human model as to the artistic one, foreshadowing a condition that might be termed a "painting of exhaustion" *ante litteram*.

Theobald's double failure stages James's parallel confrontation with the temporal dimension of art and with woman as an object of cultural as well as iconographic representation. As several critics have remarked, the contrast between the Virgin Mary and Serafina, which I have been tracing so far, has its counterpart in the contrast between Theobald's impotent aesthetic idealism and Serafina's lover's clever naturalism and artistic prolificness. His statuettes, portraying cats and monkeys "'studied from life'" (760) that reproduce life at a level of mere sensuality, owe their durability, not to the eternity of an Idea, but to the solidity of a new patent material— "'as durable as bronze—*aere perennius*, signore'" (760). Whereas Theobald, as evidence of the purity of his intentions, prides himself on having never sold a single picture, the sculptor offers to produce customized subjects and hands out visiting cards and price lists (" 'my prices are moderate. Only sixty francs for a little group like that' " [760]).[11] A perfect witness to Benjamin's later theories, he displays the products of his ingenuity " 'in Paris, on the Boulevard, in a shop of which they constitute the specialty. There is always a crowd about the window' " (759).

It would be a mistake, however, to read such an antithesis in the light of Theobald's metaphysical idealism.[12] While the painter, on the one hand, is engaged in a relentless defense of the ideal lest it be polluted by however diminutive a particle of reality, James's story, on the other hand, radically questions any such reductionism or simplification. Structured as it is around a series of sharp antitheses plentifully offered and openly displayed, "The Madonna of the Future" actually negotiates such antitheses in the same way that it negotiates the antinomy of realism and idealism, Madonnas and spaghetti.[13] Its strategy is not to choose either of these alternatives but rather to stage their confrontation, thus opening the path, within its own texture, for a dialectical tension of opposites. Theobald's "transcendent illusions and deplorable failure" are still held in suspension at the very end of the story with the Shakespearean "cats and monkeys" (766). Even Raphael's Madonnas, it is said, were possibly nothing but " 'pretty blondes of that period, enhanced by the Raphaelesque touch' " (739) and made into Madonnas to meet the demands of the local market. As for the antinomy of flesh and soul, which leads Theobald to extract the Virgin Mary from the maiden mother and to keep the diurnal, fleshy dimension separate from the silver glimmer surrounding the embroideress at night, the recurrent use of images lending Theobald's passion sensual overtones reveals the mutual implication of the would-be separate spheres: paintings are "chaste" (737), Florence is a city one can have "a very old affair"(741) with, or describe, "like a lover" (741), as "some beautiful older woman with a 'history' " (741) one falls in love with. Such a self-delusion, incidentally, is unwittingly played out again in certain critical readings of the story that explicitly ignore the element of gender underlying it, only to displace it onto the well-worn, transparent metaphor of creative "impotence," thus reaffirming a link between manhood and creativity that is already ironically underscored in the tale through the small, wiry, dark, hairy "individual of the male sex," the fecund sculptor, Serafina's lover.

However, it is above all Serafina who defies polarization and simplification: both Virgin Mary *and* maiden mother, both nun *and* lover, both embroideress of silver vestments *and* eater of succulent spaghetti. An avatar of all her literary ancestresses, whose multiple ambivalent overtones she compounds, Serafina does not idealistically transcend oppositions; rather, she *contains* them and literally *embodies* them. Her coherence is that of her life story; it is that of her body—beautiful but marked by the passing years; it is, finally, that of her full voice, claiming her own identity and her right to exist on her own terms rather than simply to conform to cultural stereotypes and other people's projections. Her voice is appropriated by James's story, which stages a confrontation between woman and her representations and denounces through her the terms of such representations, thus functioning simultaneously as a critique of ideology and as a metafictional statement—a manifesto for an art that will critically confront the opposites of idealization and commodification and keep them suspended in an unsolved dialectic, which is in itself a staging of the dilemmas of modernity.[14] "The Madonna of the Future," as Guido Fink has noted, is achieved, not in the painting, but in the tale, which is neither a beastlike statuette nor a stylized Madonna, but the real-life portrayal of a woman whose wrinkles show on the canvas and whose name is Serafina.

The Betrayed Muse: "The Sweetheart of M. Briseux"

In Henry James's multifaceted world, each situation has its own mirror image. "The Sweetheart of M. Briseux," published a few months after "The Madonna of the Future," makes use of many of the same basic elements— woman, painter, portrait, time, immortality—but inverts their operation and their function, thus exploring the other side of the coin.[15]

The story, as usual, is framed by the narrative of the visit that the nameless narrator, an American, makes to the diminutive museum of the small French town where the celebrated painter Pierre Briseux was born. Hanging on the wall is the masterpiece, exhibited about thirty years before in the 1836 Salon, which had made him famous overnight: the *Portrait of a Lady in a Yellow Shawl* or *Portrait of Mademoiselle X—*. The amazed narrator recognizes the original of the portrait in an elderly American spinster, the only other visitor to the gallery. This woman later meets the narrator and tells him the whole story, which he reports "literally," as he declares, keeping her first-person speech and only premising "a single absent clause: she must in those days have been a wonderfully charming girl" (772).

A young woman of twenty-one, poor and with no relations, the young woman had become engaged to Harold Staines—as rich, handsome, and socially faultless as he was conceited, pedantic, and untalented—and had followed him and his mother to Paris, where he meant to become a painter. Once in Paris, having ceased to regard him as a paragon of perfection, she had kept postponing the date for the wedding, notwithstanding its advantages for a woman in her position. Finally, she had promised that she would name the day once Staines had painted her portrait. While she was alone in the studio, disappointedly gazing at the portrait her fiancé was unable to achieve, a stranger rushed in—a Bohemian with a "prodigious shock of thick black curls" and "eyes really of fire" (787). It was Briseux, then a penniless and obscure young painter, come to the studio to borrow the money for the canvas and color needed to express his genius. Indignant at the ugliness of Staines's work—a waste of canvas and color—he grasped the palette, draped the young woman in a yellow shawl that Staines had discarded as a "meretricious ornament" (785), and started painting his masterpiece. When Staines came in and asked the woman to follow him at once or give him up forever, she immediately made her choice: to stay and allow Briseux to finish his picture. She then went back to the States alone: she was never to see either the painting or the painter again.

Two painters, two portraits, and a woman faced with a choice: a choice, apparently, between two opposite men and worlds, following Jane Austen's tradition of female *Bildungsroman*, usually culminating in marriage. The text sets up the contrast between the two men in the most explicit manner: the one is handsome and blond, distinguished and impeccable, stiff and frigid, dignified and sententious; the other is dark, "shabby," "meagre and vulgar" (787), unconventional and agitated, rash and passionate. The former utters only a few laconic lines, the latter pours forth a passionate speech. The former is a "decorous young Apollo" (774) as flawless as "a beautiful statue" (777), the latter is quick and feverish, "flushed and dishevelled" (792).[16] Staines is compared to "a musical symphony, of which only certain brief, unresonant notes were audible" and whose "grave notes were the beginning and end of his character" (780); Briseux is like "some ardent pianist, plunging deeper into a passionate symphony and devouring the key-board with outstretched arms" (792). Staines is a static object, Briseux is a creative subject. Finally, the former has an adolescent quality (he is forever accompanied by the protective wing of that cumbersome mother figure, Mrs. Staines) and takes on effeminate connotations ("'Monsieur Staines? Surprising! I should have sworn it was the work of a *jeune fille*'" [782], an observer exclaims while perusing one of his paintings), whereas the other has precociously consumed the inexperience of youth ("'*Il faut que jeunesse*

se passe! Mine has passed at a rattling pace, ill-mounted though it was'"
[787]) and emphatically declares himself a man: "'Now I only ask to do a
man's work with a man's will'" (787). This strongly gendered identity is also
connotatively reinforced by lexical choices explicitly evoking his manhood,
such as his eyes' "penetration" (787) or the "penetrating authority" (788)
of his way of speaking, "forcing" (788) the young woman to respect his
opinion.

Both as men and as painters, then, Staines and Briseux can be said
to embody opposite social and cultural patterns: sexual immaturity vs.
prepossessing manhood, bourgeois respectability vs. Bohemian freedom,
academic vs. romantic painting.[17] What the young woman chooses to
give up by giving up Staines is the preordained fate of a bourgeois wife:
the world of economic security and respectability but also of flatness,
convention, self-denial, and dependence. In the description she gives of
him, Staines is the perfect embodiment of a superficially faultless but
inherently void respectability: the reductio ad absurdum of a patriarchal
system too evidently grounded in mere convention, whose claims for
authority and respect go hand in hand with an utter lack of personal value:

> I could fancy him a trifle too absolute, too imperturbable, too prolific
> in cut-and-dried opinions. . . . Yes, he had certainly made the most
> of his time, and I could only admire his diligence. . . . [H]e was not
> a man of genius; and yet, to listen to him at times, you would have
> vowed at least that he might be. He dealt out his opinions as if they
> were celestial manna, and nothing was more common than for him
> to say, "You remember, a month ago, I told you so-and-so;" meaning
> that he had laid down the law on some point and expected me to
> engrave it on my heart. (782)

In sharp contrast, art becomes the touchstone and sum of all those
values, not related to the social sphere, in which both Harold Staines
and his philistine world are equally lacking. It is hardly by chance that
the ground the young woman chooses for Staines's premarital trial is art:
Staines's conceit gives way here, for it is now his turn to be on probation.[18]
Artistic failure occasions a reversal of roles—the ultimate offense, not to
love but to self-image: "the sore point with him was not that he had lost
me, but that I had ventured to judge him" (797).

For better or for worse, what the young woman is giving up is clear
enough; less so what she gets in exchange. "'You give up the man who has
offered you an honorable affection, a name, a fortune. . . . What you get

the Lord knows!'" (795), Staines cries out at the climactic moment, thus summing up—correctly, for once—the terms of the question. The young woman's alternative turns out to be a lame one: although she forgoes the opportunity of becoming Mrs. Staines, nevertheless, she will never become "the sweetheart of M. Briseux." The expectations raised by the title of the story and repeatedly reinforced in the opening scene by commonplaces and insinuations on the scanty morality of "'*Ces artistes!*'" (769), are, as we find out, misleading: the transgressive love story set in a romantic bohemia never even begins to take shape, and the implications of the title appear in retrospect to be pointing ironically to its *absence*. Possibly this is to be read as a concession on James's part to Victorian morality, forbidding him to make a "fallen woman" into the heroine of his story. The denial of a romantic plot also could be seen as James's earliest attempt to sketch a poetics of the "non-story," to be fully developed in such a later work as "The Story in It." The young woman's choice, it is true, can be regarded as the germ of a subdued and submerged love story. All the same, the manifest denial of the expectations manifestly raised by the ironic choice of "sweetheart" explodes the carefully constructed symmetry of the contrast between the two men, thus undermining a reading of the story as sentimental education, with the heroine teaching herself to choose between two contrasting men, loves, and ways of life. Once the alternatives are perceived as asymmetrical, the reader's attention is readjusted from the sentimental plot to what is, after all, the first literal object of the young woman's choice: a choice, not between two men, but between two *portraits*.

In the plot of this story, as I have tried to show, the portrait works as a test both of truth and of manhood, following a time-honored tradition that links man's potency and creative power: "'Could you ever have finished my portrait?'" (796) is the young woman's implicitly accusatory, unanswered question, which seals her fiancé's final departure from her. Painting a portrait has affective, intellectual, and cultural implications as well as technical ones: it means grasping, understanding, and rendering the portrayed subject's identity, selecting and discriminating its traits, and reproducing them according to codes that are not merely aesthetic but cultural as well. It means, in other words, to perform an act of *representation*, in the widest and most meaningful sense. The young woman's demand that Staines paint her own portrait, instead of a copy of Mona Lisa as he had intended, points to a twofold implication. On the one hand, by projecting herself onto Leonardo's subject, she is explicitly offering herself as one more avatar of that complex, ambiguous femininity that Walter Pater had mythologized at the time of the composition of this story (although, of course, it is set thirty years earlier): " 'Paint my portrait. I promise to be difficult enough' " (784).[19] On the other hand, by setting herself as an alternative to such a canonized painting, she demands to be confronted and comprehended for what she is, regardless of academic rules and misleading "copying": " 'Why then copy a portrait when you can copy an original?' " (784). But copying an original—*coping* with an original—is just what Staines, a nonentity outside the grid of convention, cannot and will not do: if his portrait is "slight and crude . . . unpromising and unflattering" (786), it is so, not merely because of the painter's lack of technical skill, but because of an inadequacy that is more ideological than technical. He is unable to confront a real woman— "an original"—in all her intensity and richness of nuances, for which he would substitute, through the agency of the portrait, a set of limited and limiting norms. His choice of dress, color, and attitude is not the result of aesthetic or expressive needs but springs from a repressive will to control, from a notion of decorum limiting the range of woman's potentialities and confining her, with the complicity of commonplace and stereotype, within the strictest conventionality:

> I brought with me a number of draperies, among which was the yellow shawl you have just been admiring. We wore such things then, just as we played on the harp and read "Corinne." I tried on my scarfs and veils, one after the other, but Harold was satisfied with none. The yellow shawl, in especial, he pronounced a meretricious ornament, and decided that I should be represented in a plain dark dress, with as few accessories as possible. He quoted with a bow the verse about beauty when unadorned, and began his work. (785)

Stiff with ideology and social convention, Staines's portrait represents less the woman portrayed than his own codes of representation: it is expressive, not of its subject, but of the painter himself: " 'Is it weak— cold—ignorant?' 'Weak, cold, ignorant, stiff, empty, hopeless! And, on top of all, pretentious—oh, pretentious as the *façade* of the Madeleine!' " (788).

The portrait painted by Briseux is in comparison something more than a great artist's original masterpiece. The long ekphrasis in the opening paragraphs does not simply describe the outline of the painting, the chromatic contrast the bright yellow makes on the dark background, the vividness and energy of the artist's touch. What it also emphasizes is that, true to the transitive nature of portraiture, this painting goes beyond the pictorial surface and hints at something outside itself—an intense and complex personality, which, rather than annihilating it, the painting manifests and reveals:

> As I continued to look, however, I began to wonder whether it did not contain something better still—the reflection of a countenance very nearly as deep and ardent as the artist's talent. In spite of the expressive repose of the figure the brow and mouth wore a look of smothered agitation, the dark gray eye almost glittered, and the flash in the cheek burned ominously. Evidently this was the picture of something more than a yellow shawl. To the analytic eye it was the picture of a mind, or at least of a mood. (769)

There are, it is true, obvious traces in this description (as well as in the story that follows) of a mystique of portrait-painting—the myth of the painter who can, if he is truly a great artist, go beyond appearances and grasp the very essence of the person being portrayed.[20] James had already experimented with this theme in 1868, in a story that figures in his oeuvre as the prototype of the portrait motif: "The Story of a Masterpiece." Here the rich widower Lennox discovers the superficial and heartless nature of his beautiful fiancée Marian Everett through the agency of a portrait of her, painted by Baxter—a talented artist who had formerly been in love with Marian and whom she had deserted. Lennox is so upset by the discovery that, although he cannot back out of the wedding, he stabs the portrait repeatedly. Indeed, a plot such as this seems an acritical acceptance of the myth of the artist, even though there is a mitigating hint that Baxter achieves his masterpiece, not simply through supernatural artistic intuition, but through his actual acquaintance with Marian. All the same, the female character here is presented as *truly* coinciding with the representation of her that the portrait provides, with no margin for complexity or ambiguity. Even the short passage directly focused on Marian's point of view offers no alternative vantage point: quite the reverse, since its function is to confirm the judgments that other characters pass on her and to make the reader, as it were, "personally" acquainted with her lack of ethical values and her empty superficiality. The few hints that her self-justification offers ("She had cared for nothing but pleasure; but to what else were girls brought up?") are not sufficient to launch an investigation of the cultural operations whereby feminine identity is produced, as is the case later in "Julia Bride."[21]

At a few years' distance, however, "The Sweetheart of M. Briseux" represents a much less moralistic and rather more complex version of the portrait motif, in spite of the questionably emphatic treatment of

Briseux, whose characterization makes use of the whole repertoire of "genius and unruliness," with no trace of the critical and self-critical irony to be found in such a later story as "Mora Montravers." The relation connecting the woman protagonist and her portrait is here much more complicated and problematic than mere mimetic reproduction—however intuitive and faithful—of the former in the latter.

It is, first of all, a two-way relation, a matter not just of mimesis but of passionate identification: the woman *is* the portrait, and her identification is such as to make her feel the blow almost physically when Staines angrily throws a brush against the portrait: "I raised my hands to my face as if I felt the blow" (793).[22] But it is not just the artistic quality of Briseux's painting that allows this identification, just as the pictorial inadequacy of Staines's portrait does not entirely account for the young woman's rejection of it. Briseux's portrait gives momentary existence to a colorful, daring, romantic, transgressive identity: it has a liberating power, both aesthetically and culturally, for it liberates its subject from the representations of womanhood that the dark shades and stiff poise of Staines's picture implied. The yellow shawl is its conceptual as well as chromatic focus: significantly rejected by Staines, it is a symbolic cipher of transgression that, in his antiacademic choice of a bright and gaudy color, the artist shares with the woman. By draping herself in the yellow shawl, the young woman takes on a romantic, heterodox identity in sharp contrast to the literally and metaphorically dull colors that her self-representation as a bourgeois wife would impose on her.

But there is more to it than this: this daring, passionate woman, the woman in the yellow shawl, will be made to live forever in the portrait. " 'I'll make you immortal' " (795) had been Briseux's only promise—and this is finally the real stake in her choice: not love but immortality. Entrance into the aesthetic sphere is contrasted as a euphoric alternative to a future as Staines's wife that is already wholly prefigured by a set of inexorable metaphors: "I asked myself sternly whether I was ready to rise and let him lead me blindfold through life" (795)—which, incidentally, foreshadows the implications of female blindness as they will be explored in "Glasses." The opposition between the two men and their respective social worlds is finally seen in terms of woman's role, as an opposition between the different potential for expansion they offer—an opposition that will provide one of the key structural features in *The Portrait of a Lady*: "Poor little Briseux, ugly, shabby, disreputable, seemed to me some appealing messenger from the mysterious immensity of life; and Harold, beside him, comely, elegant, imposing, justly indignant, seemed to me simply his narrow, personal, ineffectual self" (794).

The choice the young woman is faced with thus occasions an explicit diagnosis of woman's condition: "We women are so habitually condemned by fate to act simply in what is called the domestic sphere, that there is something intoxicating in the opportunity to exert a far-reaching influence outside of it. . . . I seemed to be the end of an electric chain, of which the rest was throbbing away through time" (795–96).

In this view, art and its promise of immortality appear no longer as the aesthetic congealment that Theobald would have imposed on life's flow, but as a means for woman to escape the strictures of a preordained existential situation wholly enclosed within the "domestic sphere." What the story seems to be saying is that only by rejecting repression and idealization and by embracing a free, in-depth exploration of life—with all its wealth of contradictions, and regardless of the boundaries of artistic and social conventions—can art be seen no longer as an imprisoning and limiting power, but as an agent of liberation.

But the adventure of the woman in the yellow shawl does not come to an end at this euphoric moment, the transitory and delusive quality of which the adjective "intoxicating" effectively conveys. There is a gap between the bold and eager girl in the studio and the "modest spinster," "gently but frankly eccentric" (771), whom the narrator meets in the museum; a gap the text does not bridge but rather tends to emphasize: "As I sat before the picture just now, I felt in all my pulses that I am *not* the person who stands masquerading there with that strangely cynical smile. That poor girl is dead and buried; I should tell no falsehood in saying I'm not she" (772).

"I am *not*," "masquerading," signal a radical nonidentity, something that goes beyond the mere passing of time, which at any rate allows for the continuity of personal identity. "That poor girl is dead and buried," the protagonist declares, and a "musty Musée" appropriately surrounds the portrait with that "sepulchral chill which clings to such knowledge of us as posterity enjoys" (771): these images of death are in sharp contrast with the former promise of immortality. Indeed, the tale here seems to echo the polemical debates on museums frequent throughout the nineteenth century: among other things, the detractors of museums described them as sepulchral institutions, where the dead remains of something that had once been alive were juxtaposed in blasphemous and meaningless contiguity, to be admired by barren generations that could no longer produce art for themselves.[23] A tombstone as well as an imperishable art object, the portrait is the estranged objectification of a self that no longer exists—or rather, of a self whose existence lasted only a fleeting moment, the time it took for it to become transmuted into a portrait: the short time of a single sitting, at the end of which the sitter "had already passed into that dusky limbo of unhonored victims, the experience—intellectual and other—of genius" (796). Once the sitting is over, the woman in the yellow shawl sets her costume aside: "I left him the yellow shawl, that he might finish this part of his work at his leisure" (796). This marks a decisive threshold beyond which her life story will be a nonstory, which appropriately is not told. To emphasize the sense of her nonexistence, the woman has no name other than the symbol for namelessness inscribed in the label of her portrait: *Portrait of Mademoiselle X*—or *Portrait of a Lady in a Yellow Shawl*—where the yellow shawl acts as the synecdoche of an otherwise nonexistent identity.

Once again, life and art are incompatible alternatives whose temporal regimes are mutually exclusive. It is, as James would later write, art that makes life—but not quite. The identity evoked by artistic representation is fixed forever in the picture but does not succeed in providing a practicable existential course, a satisfactory life continuity. The image is (relatively) deathless, but the woman's identity it conveys is a mere visual trick, an effect of physical and psychological tridimensionality produced by a skillfully painted canvas; the person is "dead and buried," since art, while allowing her to escape a limiting and reductive self-definition, has nevertheless been unable to actualize any other. Briseux's exit from the scene is in this sense evidence of James's definite and disillusioned anti-idealism: he nips the sentimental plot in the bud so as not to have his readers confuse art with the artist. Art's liberating power exists only within the regime of artistic representation, and there is no going beyond its boundaries: a portrait, after all, is just a portrait.

Entrance into an aesthetic dimension is, finally, a cruel alternative to the repetitiveness of the domestic sphere. The doubling it implies is a loss of one's self, an act—as the narrator well sees—of radical dispossession: "How did it seem to her to find herself so strangely lifted out of her own possession and made a helpless spectator of her survival to posterity?" (771). But any analogy with the romantic and decadent motif of the "vampirism" of the portrait is only superficial: James's version is materialistic, so to speak, because it is rooted in an understanding of the economic and ideological grounds of women's subjection. It is by no means fortuitous that economic imagery, as is often the case with James, recurs with reference to the portrait, describing the young woman as "a model to make a painter's fortune" (790) and Briseux's appropriation of brush, canvas, and colors as "a loan" that will be "return[ed] with interest" (792). Even the promise of immortality is explicitly far from disinterested: it is a pawn of sorts, a pledge the painter offers as security against the opening of a credit: " 'I'll make you immortal,' he murmured; 'I'll delight mankind—and I'll begin my own career!' " (795). Significantly, the young woman's choice to sit for Briseux is presented as a substitute for the golden louis that the painter would not accept from a woman: " 'I won't go so far as to say that I'm proud,' he answered at last. 'But from a lady, *ma foi*! it's beggarly—it's humiliating. Excuse me then if I refuse; I mean to ask for something else. . . . Bestow your charity on the artist . . . Keep your louis; go and stand as you've been standing for this picture, in the same light and the same attitude, and then let me look at you for three little minutes. . . . The few scrawls I shall make here will be your alms' " (790–91).

Alms, an act of charity—that is to say, not even exchange, but an unequal transaction, a free act of dedication that will find its reward, if any, only in the realm of the immaterial. This is where the aesthetic sphere proves both contiguous and complicitous with the domestic sphere, regardless of the different spatial and temporal range of each: what they share is the deep rationale that allows women no other ground for personal identity than that of being of service to others. Selflessness, the female virtue par excellence for the Victorians, is successfully literalized in the "gift of herself" performed by a woman who is consequently left precisely with no self to speak of: with no story and no name, deprived of the fate and social identity that only a man could have bestowed on her: neither Mrs. Staines nor the sweetheart of M. Briseux, but just Mademoiselle X.[24]

Art as an alternative, in other words, is *necessarily* a delusive one: all it can do is offer the alienation of self as a free gift in opposition to the alienation of self within the marriage contract. Be it as the chance starting point for an artistic transfiguration that will change an obscure bohemian into a famous painter or as the "buoyant body" required to keep the parody of a patriarch afloat and to "float him into success" (783), woman is equally reified: in either case her identity is merely instrumental. Either as a wife enclosed in the domestic sphere—"the lawful Egeria of a cabinet minister" (773)—or as the inspiring model projected into eternity, a Muse's life is not her own and her portrait represents, not her, but the costume someone else has chosen for her: be it a black dress or a yellow shawl.

Chapter 2
Women, Statues, and Lovers:
"The Last of the Valerii"
and "Adina"

Je suis belle, ô mortels! Comme un rêve de pierre,
Et mon sein, où chacun s'est meurtri tour à tour,
Est fait pour inspirer au poëte un amour
Eternel et muet ainsi que la matière.

Je trône dans l'azur comme un sphinx incompris;
J'unis un coeur de neige à la blancheur des cygnes;
Je hais le mouvement qui déplace les lignes,
Et jamais je ne pleure et jamais je ne ris.

—Charles Baudelaire, "La Beauté"

Starting with such tales as "The Last of the Valerii" and "Adina," both written in 1874, art objects are no longer presented as extensions of actual women, as the portrait initially was, but take on an existence of their own.[1] The issue is no longer about the artistic representation of woman going on within the story: rather, the art object, now unrelated to the actual woman (at a literal level, at any rate), becomes her deuteragonist and antagonist, and the opposition thus settled is further complicated by reversals, exchanges, shifts in their respective positions.

"The Last of the Valerii" is exemplary in that sense because of the vertiginous semantic chasms hidden beneath the apparent straightforwardness of its plot, based, like "The Madonna of the Future," on the open exhibition both of "international" motifs (the marriage between a rich American girl and an impoverished Italian nobleman) and of intertextual material (ranging from *The Marble Faun* to Mérimée's *La Vénus d'Ille*, which James had translated in his twenties).[2] The unearthing of a beautiful Greek statue of Juno in the Roman villa of Count Camillo Valerio—the dumb but decorative offspring of an ancient lineage—precipitates a crisis in his happy, idyllic marriage to Martha, an American heiress. Fascinated by the statue, the count becomes more and more isolated from his beautiful wife, who is at a loss to understand her husband's attitude. After suffering in silence for a while, Martha decides to regain her husband by having the statue buried again. Only one of its perfectly shaped hands will be left to the count as a relic in the end.

What makes the story bizarre and unforgettable is the narrator's interpretation of it. The narrator—a middle-aged American painter, Martha's godfather—looks on the case as a "delightfully curious phenomenon" bearing witness to the "strange ineffaceability of race-characteristics" (817), thus following a hint dropped by Valerio himself when caught ecstatically wandering in that wonderfully appropriate emblem of the overlapping of pagan and Christian cults, the Pantheon. In the narrator's view, Valerio's is a case of atavism: a "genetic" paganism of sorts, surfacing in the count upon his confrontation with the Juno and leading him back to the faith of his forefathers.

Critics, however, have long suspected that such an *ante litteram* "call of the wild" may not be all there is to the story and have offered several symbolic readings of it, ranging from Leon Edel's rather cursory interpretation, based on the customary opposition between innocent America and corrupt Europe and climaxing in the moral that "the past can be dangerous to love and life," to Andrea Mariani's more recent and acute discussion of the tale in the light of Freud's essay on W. Jensen's *Gradiva*.[3] To Mariani, "The Last of the Valerii" represents the immature male protagonist's initiation to adult love "through the intermediation of an image, that is, through the feminine archetype of Juno, the wife goddess par excellence."[4]

However convincing the interpretive framework, as in the last instance quoted, even the most accurate symbolic readings have hitherto neglected, in their search for hermeneutic coherence, what is to my mind the most critical feature of this tale: the remarkable overdetermination of each of its elements, and the semantic instability that is thereby produced. Such an effect, as I will argue, is crucially connected to a carefully constructed instability in the representation of femininity in this tale.

Delusions and Dreams in "The Last of the Valerii"

If, in a deliberately anachronistic move, one should substitute Camillo Valerio's name for Jensen's Norbert Hanold, Dr. Freud's authoritative guide would immediately promise to shed satisfactory light on the case. The count's state is an obvious case of delusion, a morbid condition where fantasy gets the upper hand, is credited as truth, and gains control over the patient's actual behavior, as Freud makes clear.[5] The statue attracts to itself all the attention that would normally be paid to a flesh-and-blood woman.

Recovery is brought about by a revival of love for the actual woman, who is also the therapist as well as the protagonist's former and repressed love object and can therefore immediately offer—in Freud's words—to "the liberated current of love a desirable aim" (85). The suggested revival of an atavistic paganism and the pagan rituals—libations, blood sacrifices—that Valerio performs for the statue, therefore, are nothing but the conscious determinants of delirious acts, the unconscious ones being connected to repressed contents, which by definition cannot be experienced consciously: in Freud's words, "[o]ne might be described as lying on the surface and covering the other, which was, as it were, concealed behind it" (52).

Even though Freud's case study sounds so uncannily relevant to James's story (composed, it should be remembered, some thirty years before Jensen's) that it might have been actually written about it, still it leaves more than one question open. The questions, of course, concern the points where Jensen's "pompejanisches Phantasiestück" diverges from James's "Roman fantasy"; and the most prominent among them concerns the tale's ending. Can the statue's reburial be regarded in the light of a therapeutic inter- vention bringing the repressed to awareness and thereby producing the canonical coincidence of interpretation and treatment? Unless one accepts the narrator's explanation (which, it should be noted, is the protagonist's own conscious motive and consequently, by definition, cannot be the unconscious one), what is missing from this tale is exactly the eventual therapeutic clearing away of mystery that Zoe Bertgang provides in *Gradiva*. The crucial question is left unanswered: Which is the repressed psychic content that has engendered the protagonist's delusion? In Hanold's case, his former love for Zoe, buried in his unconscious, is brought to light by the Pompeii engraving in the form of a fetishistic passion for a peculiar way of walking and will find its proper object again in due time. But Valerio's passion for the statue is diverted from an actual love object that is already there: what Freud terms, respectively, the living love object and its fantasy substitute are both on stage *simultaneously*. That is to say, the statue is not the substitute foreshadowing a living woman and bound to disappear in the natural course of events, as soon as the true love object has been recovered. The order of priority has been turned around here both logically and dramatically, since Martha is the first character to be introduced, and the eventual disappearance of the statue is a deliberate act rather than the natural consequence of the count's recovery of his healthy conjugal feelings. One would almost suspect that the way matters stand in "The Last of the Valerii" is precisely the reverse of *Gradiva*: namely, that the authentic object of the count's passion is not the woman but the statue. In *Gradiva,* as Freud sarcastically remarks at one point, a reading of Hanold's obsession with feet as fetishistic erotomania would only satisfy psychiatrists with their coarse view of psychical processes, since fetishistic symptoms are only the surface manifestation of the character's delusion. In "The Last of the Valerii," on the contrary, one gets the impression that the count's fetishistic passion for an inanimate object is the very repressed content of his delusion, hiding beneath the mask of the cultic ritual paid to a pagan goddess. It is no accident that the count's premonitory dream (the persistence of which into the waking state is, to Freud, "a psychical act on its own: an assurance, relating to the content of the dream, that something in it is really as one has dreamt it" [57]) featured the statue as getting up and putting her hand on Valerio's—a gesture implying equally the initiatory call from a goddess and sexual invitation from a woman. "'His Juno's the reality; I'm the fiction!'" (822), states the countess in anguish. Perhaps her words should be taken literally, less as a complaint than as a diagnosis.

The Statue as Woman

Let us now reverse the customary direction of reading and revert from the symbolic to the literal quality of the signifier around which the story is centered: a gynaecomorphous statue, that is, the image of a woman. Count Valerio's passion for it makes him the first of a well-attended lineage of Jamesian heroes of perverted desire.

As Freud reminds us, both conscious and unconscious motives in delusions must be satisfied; therefore, "the symptoms of a delusion—phantasies and actions alike—are in fact the products of compromise between the two mental currents" (52) and simultaneously manifest both. The count's behavior displays exactly this kind of twofold consistency. On the one hand, he puts the statue on a pedestal, encloses it in a temple, and pays it manic and obsessed cultic homage, reaching its climax in the night scene, when the narrator catches him in the attitude of a "recumbent worshipper" "lying flat on the pavement, prostrate apparently with devotion" (820). On the other hand, he behaves towards the statue like the most stereotypical of possessive southern European males: he is jealous (to the narrator, "a natural incident of the first rapture of possession" [812]), he hides the statue from everybody's eyes ("'*I'm* to see her: that's enough!'" [811]), and keeps "the imprisoned Juno" (819) under lock and key—quite the reverse of his ordinary urbane attitude to his wife.

While adding to the "case study," however, the text is also lavish in unsettling touches. The count's staging of the sacred, for instance, is effected by way of an unwittingly postmodern strategy that sounds parodic behind the count's back because of its explicit assembling and refunctionalizing of spurious items: the pedestal of the statue is an upturned funereal cippus; the temple, "a deserted garden-house, built in not ungraceful imitation of an Ionic temple" (810). And apart from textual ironies, even within the diegetic world, a "cynical personage" like the excavation supervisor points out the ambiguous mixture of religious, aesthetic, and erotic implications in the count's attitude and sarcastically unveils the absurdity of eroticism in such a connection by stressing the inadequacy to its purpose of the love object the count has selected: "'So beautiful a creature is more or less the property of every one; we've all a right to look at her. But the Count treats her as if she were a sacrosanct image of the Madonna. He keeps her under lock and key, and pays her solitary visits. What does he do, after all? When a beautiful woman is in stone, all he can do is to look at her'" (812).

Still, it is precisely the impossibility of a physical consummation of love that, while denouncing the count's passion as either ridiculous or delirious, simultaneously foregrounds its abstract significance. Sheltered as it is from the mutability of moods and the contingencies of the flesh, the statue shines forth as a perfect emblem of an absolute psychic and cultural content: the "Eternal Feminine" as it was conceived and represented in the nineteenth-century male imagination—marblelike, timeless, unperishable, handed down intact through a succession of centuries. The detail of its being unearthed from previously unsounded depths is, of course, eloquent: as Freud neatly terms it, "[t]here was a perfect similarity between the burial of Pompeii—the disappearance of the past combined with its preservation—and repression" (51).

What all this amounts to is that the statue is not just the image of *a* woman, but rather an image of *woman*: an image displaying its complex and paradoxical quality from the outset:

> Then, full in the sun and flashing it back, almost, in spite of her dusky incrustations, I beheld, propped up with stones against a heap of earth, a majestic marble image. She seemed to me almost colossal, though I afterwards perceived that she was of perfect human proportions. My pulses began to throb, for I felt she was something great, and that it was great to be among the first to know her. Her marvellous beauty

gave her an almost human look, and her absent eyes seemed to wonder back at us. (808)

Defined by contradictions—shining in spite of incrustations, colossal though of human proportions, almost human because superhuman, with eyes absent but capable of looking back, her transcendent greatness producing an almost sexual response—the statue effectively blurs all distinctions between light and darkness, large and small, human and super- or unhuman. Also, between movement and stillness, or rather, between stillness as an impossibility to move and stillness as the supreme balance that is the ultimate attainment of movement: "She seemed indeed an embodiment of celestial supremacy and repose. Her beautiful head, bound with a single band, could have bent only to give the nod of command; her eyes looked straight before her; her mouth was implacably grave" (808).

As an ancient and precious object, the statue is endowed with a value that is intellectual and economic all at once: "'[T]he Juno is worth fifty thousand scudi!'" (821). Its beauty pertains as much to its form as to its content: it arises from superior craftsmanship—"'a Juno of Praxiteles at the very least!'" (809)—but also from its being an idealized image of feminine beauty and of beauty as feminine, much like Baudelaire's "stone dream." As such, it invites the onlooker to an enjoyment that is both pleasure and *jouissance*, both aesthetic and erotic. As an image of divinity, it demands worship. As a huge shape at first, later to be reduced to normal size, it suggests a mother figure. And finally, its identification with Juno connotes the statue as sexually mature and as a wife, making it the emblem of a powerful femininity (significantly endowed with the phallic attribute of an "imperial wand" [808]), but one that is nevertheless subordinate to Jupiter's superior patriarchal authority.

Simultaneously, though, the statue is a "senseless pagan block" (815), conveying through its materiality the notion of a helpless and passive femininity, a mere object for contemplation and possession. A lifeless chunk of marble propped up by stones on the edge of an open excavation and at the same time a figuration of the utmost beauty and power, the statue is a mighty oxymoron, encompassing the paradoxes of femininity as a projection of the male imagination. A woman object and a goddess object—woman as object and woman as goddess—an object for possession and an object for worship, it allows man the most extreme fantasies both of omnipotence and of submission.[6]

The Woman as Statue

Be it a goddess, a woman, or an archaeological exhibit, the statue, following a time-honored tradition, only takes on life in the onlooker's eyes. Not only its meaning and significance, but indeed its very identity depends on some-body else's designation: " 'She's a Juno,' said the excavator, decisively" (808); " 'Your new Juno, Signor Conte, . . . is, in my opinion, much more likely to be a certain Proserpine—' " (811) is a German scholar's unsolicited opinion. Which amounts to saying that the statue's conversion into a woman is only effected through the agency of a crucial rhetorical figure: prosopopoeia, the trope of personification, whereby a face, voice, or subjectivity is attributed to an absent, dead, or inanimate entity.

In his fine deconstructive reading of this story, J. Hillis Miller re-gards "The Last of the Valerii" as a fictional illustration of the risks of prosopopoeia and also of its inescapability. As a founding trope of fiction, in fact, prosopopoeia presides over the animation of characters, the necessary mediators of the ethical import of fiction. The reader of James's tale, therefore, even while learning a lesson about the perils of the figure by way of the count's error, is always already reproducing that very error by projecting a personal identity on what is in fact nothing but a verbal construct.[7] Miller's subtle and convincing reading has many details in common with the one I am developing here. Through his exclusive commitment to the rhetorical level, however, Miller totally disregards the element of gender that is crucially involved in James's deconstruction of the trope, a trope, incidentally, that plays a central and recurring role in many a Jamesian story centering on the representation of the feminine. Such a paradigmatic quality, I contend, demands that one proceed from the rhetorical to the ideological plane, performing the move implied in Barbara Johnson's pregnant question: "Rhetoric, clearly, has everything to do with covert operations. But are the politics of violence already encoded in rhetorical figures as such? In other words, can the very essence of a political issue . . . hinge on the structure of a figure? Is there any inherent connection between figurative language and questions of life and death, of who will wield and who will receive violence in a given human society?"[8] Like apostrophe—the subject of Johnson's essay—prosopopoeia is a kind of ventriloquism: onto the object are projected a voice and a subjectivity that are nothing but a projection of one's own. Through prosopopoeia, an "I" posits and positions itself as subject vis-à-vis a "You" that, nevertheless, is possessed of no voice or existence of its own, has no subjectivity, is nothing but an object, instrumental to the construction of another's subjecthood.[9] Confrontation with the Other is shunned even while a pretense of it is being staged. As soon as it takes on life, the woman image becomes, in Johnson's words, a mere "rhetorical extension" of man: a screen on which his fantasies can enjoy free play, as "Rose-Agathe" will show even more explicitly.

But let me now investigate the trope a bit further. In "Autobiography as De-Facement," Paul de Man stresses the vampiristic logic inherent in the symmetrical structure of the figure and in its blurring of the boundaries between life and death: "by making the death speak, the symmetrical structure of the trope implies, by the same token, that the living are struck dumb, frozen in their own death."[10] I would insist, however, that at least in the present case the symmetrical structure of the trope operates differently, not along the life/death, but rather along the animate/inanimate axis; and above all, that it impinges, not on the specularity between speaker and object, but on the reciprocal relationship between the inanimate object and its counterpart, the live individual that it represents. In other words: if, as I have suggested, the statue is the ambivalent emblem of a representation of the feminine that is both idealized and reified, then the humanization of the statue has its counterpart in a symmetrical dehumanization of woman. This is where rhetoric and ideology coincide: inasmuch as it creates a continuity between the person and the object, prosopopoeia is the rhetorical counterpart of the reification of woman. Such a result is achieved within the world of this tale by the woman character's identification with a system of idealizing stereotypes that I have only partly examined up to this point.

"[A] young American girl, who had the air and almost the habits of a princess" (798), Martha does not seem, at first sight, to be eligible for the role of sacrificial victim, much less of reified woman: she is young, rich, and beautiful, and she holds a position of intellectual and economic preeminence within marriage. Still, a number of textual and intertextual associations connect her to the statue and reveal her involvement at more than one level in a system revolving around the reciprocal relation of reification and personification.

The first hints come from the narrator, who repeatedly suggests that Martha's love for the count may be nothing more than a passion for his villa and his mossy ancestral marbles—or even that it may be the result of the count's resemblance to a statue: "I more than once smiled at her archaeological zeal, and declared that I believed she had married the Count because he was like a statue of the Decadence" (802).[11]

This would make the countess a symmetrical, inverted version of her husband's case: whereas he is in love with the woman in the statue, she loves the statue in the man. The count's sculptural quality is explicitly mentioned several times—"he had a head and throat like some of the busts in the Vatican" (798), "a head as massively round as that of the familiar bust of the Emperor Caracalla, and covered with the same dense sculptural crop of curls" (798–99), "his large, lucid eyes seemed to stare at you like a pair of polished agates" (799)—as well as implied in his poses, frequently evoking well-known classical and neoclassical patterns: the shepherd or faun "picturesquely snoozing" (803) while his wife ecstatically watches him slumber, thus composing a group reminiscent of some "Love and Psyche"; little Hercules strangling the snakes, a *topos* of Hellenistic sculpture employed as a simile to describe the count's hypothetical fury.[12] It should be noted, however, that the emphasis on the count's sculptural quality is almost wholly to be traced to the narrator; only in two cases does he state that he is recording Martha's own words. But I will return to the narrator's role in the story later. What I would like to discuss now is the way in which the female protagonist is affected by such an aesthetic passion for the count. To do so, however, I must first analyze the peculiar role played in this love story by an issue supposedly unrelated to erotic matters but already suggestively raised in a similar connection in "The Madonna of the Future," namely, religion.

The fundamental scenes of "The Last of the Valerii" all have places of cult as a background, be they Christian (St. Peter's), Christianized pagan (the Pantheon), or downright pagan (the Ionic temple). This is hardly surprising in itself: such a choice was consistent both with the intertextual dialogue the tale weaves with Hawthorne and with the textual necessity to provide a religious framework as a context for the protagonist's alleged paganism. Much more surprising, however, is Martha's spectacular rejection of the pattern set her by Hawthorne's Hilda. In spite of the connotations of transatlantic puritanism inherent in her very name and in spite of the narrator repeatedly defining her as a "creature susceptible of the finer spiritual emotions" (804), Martha more than once declares her readiness to abjure her own faith to embrace Camillo's, be it pagan or Catholic: " 'he's welcome to any faith, if he will only share it with me. I'll believe in Jupiter, if he'll bid me!' " (822). This declaration looks back to one of the opening scenes of the tale, in St. Peter's, when Martha expresses her intention to do something special for her lover's sake, to perform some brave, openly transgressive act that she identifies with religious conversion: " 'I want to do something more for him than girls commonly do for their lovers,—to take some step, to run some risk, to break some law, even! I'm willing to change my religion, if he bids me'" (801). Count Valerio rejects her offer, inviting her to "'keep your religion . . . If you should attempt to embrace mine, I'm afraid you would close your arms about a shadow. I'm a poor Catholic!'" (801).[13]

This verbal exchange bears a little analysis. While they cleverly evoke, through the image of embracing a shadow, a scenario of descent to Hades suggestive of the count's pagan roots (the same image, incidentally, that the narrator will apply to Valerio himself),[14] Valerio's words also imply the idea of a physical contact—or rather, to be more precise, a missed physical contact: precisely what happens immediately after this speech, when the count tries to seal his words by kissing his fiancée's hands, only to give it up, "suddenly remembering that they were in a place unaccordant with profane passions" (801).

The mention of an embrace, of a kiss, and of "profane passions" has the effect of creating a dissonant context around Martha's words, conveying hints of a different kind of "love pledge," much at variance with the religious trial she herself envisages and probably much more common—the sexual. The two dimensions, the religious and the sexual, are made to appear unreconcilable in the count's suspended gesture, while in Martha's words the religious is seen as a substitute for the sexual. Religion as sublimation: one more association, as irresistible as it is (so far) arbitrary, is brought to mind: the association of the image of woman as statue with notions of frigidity and repression. A seemingly gratuitous association when applied to this tale, to be sure, but nevertheless, one that James explored in his very next short story, "Madame de Mauves," published in *Galaxy* in February–March of the same year, 1874. Again, an American girl marries a European, having fallen in love—we are told—with his castle and his aristocratic blood; again, a contrast is set up between the American moral conscience and the merely sensual conception of life of Europeans; again, in the eyes of the American observer Mr. Longmore, "the Baron was a pagan and his wife was a Christian, and between them, accordingly, was a gulf" (853).[15] But unlike Count Valerio's forcedly Platonic love delusion, the baron's "paganism" results in very actual offenses, explicitly sexual in nature; and it is possibly as a consequence of this difference that no reconciliation can take place between the baron and his wife. Self-confined within the precincts of her inflexible virtue and her renouncement (of Longmore's devotion and love, which all characters had encouraged her to accept), Madame de Mauves will refuse to forgive her husband even after his repentance and conversion, thus leading him—so we are made to understand—to his premature death and earning for herself the title of "the charming little woman who killed her husband" (902). Here the image of the statue, earlier applied to Madame de Mauves by Longmore, in whose eyes it is merely the paragon of a melancholy and reserved type of beauty—"Her delicate beauty acquired to his eye the serious cast of certain blank-browed Greek statues" (847)—displays its most disturbing connections: "[s]he was stone, she was ice, she was outraged virtue" (903). Longmore's feelings change accordingly, from an "ardent tenderness" to a feeling more appropriate for a tremendous goddess: "a singular feeling,—a feeling for which awe would be hardly too strong a name" (903).

Martha's way to the condition of statue in "The Last of the Valerii," however, is different and somewhat more original: not through outraged virtue, but through aesthetic passion. In order to grasp its implications fully, one should once again skip back to a crucial sentence following close on her assertion of her wish to abjure her faith as a love token: " 'There are moments when I'm terribly tired of simply staring at Catholicism; it will be a relief to come into a church to kneel. That's, after all, what they are meant for!' " (801).

Underlying the protagonist's words is the issue of the relation between the aesthetic and the religious—one might even term it, the existential—sphere. The notion of the work of art as an aesthetic fetish, dehistoricized and out of context—a notion earlier explored and exposed in "The Madonna of the Future"—is here countered by Martha's desire to have aesthetic and existential value coincide: an aesthetics of religion, so to speak, is contrasted to the religion of aesthetics current in James's time. Similarly, Count Valerio opposes his wife's plans to have archaeological excavations in their villa, warning against the danger of making the ancient gods into mere aesthetic objects, cut off forever from their original fullness of meaning: " 'Let them lie, the poor disinherited gods . . . and don't break their rest. What do you want of them? We can't worship them. Would you put them on pedestals to stare and mock at them? If you can't believe in them, don't disturb them. Peace be with them!' " (806).

However, the count's and the countess's statements are less similar than they may at first appear. The count refuses to aesthetically reify objects that are, to him, *actually* endowed with meaning: what he is defending is an actual coincidence of aesthetic and religious or cultural value. (Incidentally, from the vantage point of the narrator's puritan iconoclasm such an attitude is a link between Catholicism and paganism, both idolatrous in his eyes insofar as they share a belief in cult objects as emblematic of a wider spiritual significance). Martha's words, on the other hand, imply that the problem can be solved simply by inverting priorities: that is, not in endorsing an original consubstantiality of religious vision and the cult object stemming from it, but quite the reverse, in adjusting a posteriori the religious and existential sphere to the aesthetic one, which is thus made to act as the original value of reference.

So here is at last a possible key to Martha's behavior. Canonical notions of femininity, requesting woman to be shaped by man's tastes and desires, converge in her case with her wish to substantiate an aesthetic passion by making life coincide with it, so as to change it into a totalizing existential dimension. Being in love with a statue-man (and to that extent, complicitous with an overall system of reification and aestheticization of the Other, as we shall see), Martha extends her consistency to envisaging herself as a statue-woman. A seemingly harmless role at first, as she figures with her husband in the graceful attitudes of a Dresden china shepherdess, intent on a "childlike interchange of caresses, as candid and unmeasured as those of a shepherd and shepherdess in a bucolic poem" (803); of a classical Hebe ready to "fill his glass from a rusty red amphora" (803); of a Psyche watching her sleeping Love.[16] But the tragic potential inherent in such an adjustment to an aesthetic representation both of one's self and of the other (be it intentional or unintentional) is soon made clear by the advent of the statue—an unattainable rival on this terrain, since it/she is the very archetype of such an aesthetic, sculptural pattern of femininity: " 'His Juno's the reality; I'm the fiction!' " (822).

Just as Martha's words become more and more resonant as connections multiply around them, the narrator's way of describing Martha's distress now appears pregnant with meaning: " 'Her [the statue's] beauty be blasted! Can you tell me what has become of the Contessa's? To rival the Juno, she's turning to marble herself' " (821). Far from being a mere worn-out metaphor of classical origin to designate suffering, such words are a precise, if paradoxical, description of the structural and ideological pattern enacted in the tale: a woman's confrontation with the archetypal pattern of both her own and her culture's notion of femininity. Once she has recognized the fact that " 'His Juno's the reality,' " the countess must place herself on the same plane of reality if she is to regain her husband's affections: "my goddaughter expressed the desire to go out and look at the Juno. 'I was afraid of her almost from the first,' she said, 'and have hardly seen her since she was set up in the Casino. Perhaps I can learn a lesson from her,—perhaps I can guess how she charms him!'" (823).

"Learning a lesson" from the statue (which the countess significantly refers to as "she" rather than "it"—a use shared by all characters in the story) is a perfectly ambivalent gesture: it implies the statue's humanization as a possible source of teaching, but also, simultaneously, the woman's readiness to become like it/her by learning from it/her. Just as ambivalent is Martha's decisive move, the reburial of the statue: on the one hand, it restores the Juno to the unhuman quality of an archaeological item (a transition stressed by the reappearance of the neuter personal pronoun "it"); on the other hand, it consecrates its definitive humanization—"'We must smother her beauty in the dreadful earth. It makes me feel almost as if she were alive'" (825), as the countess says—by celebrating what amounts to a veritable funerary ritual:

> By the time we reached the edge of the grave the evening had fallen and the beauty of our marble victim was shrouded in a dusky veil. No one spoke,—if not exactly for shame, at least for regret. . . . The ropes were adjusted and the Juno was slowly lowered into her earthly bed. The Countess took a handful of earth and dropped it solemnly on her breast. "May it lie lightly, but forever!" she said.
>
> "Amen!" cried the little surveyor with a strange mocking inflection. (826)

The act of burying the statue amounts to a full acknowledgment of a rivalry that only its/her physical elimination can remove. And eliminating the rival is not enough: in order to become a love object to her husband again, Martha has to put herself in its/her place. To start with, Martha's decision to have the statue buried anew has the effect of investing her, for the first time, with the connotations of power and maturity hitherto attributed to the Juno: "'The Countess has given orders. . . . Sweet-voiced as she is, she knows how to make her orders understood'" (825). Such a development would appear to be positive if other hints were not there to remind the reader that the statue, as an overdetermined, ambivalent emblem, also has different, less desirable implications.

The scene of the final reconciliation between the married couple summarizes and simultaneously keeps suspended such conflicting implications. The count's gesture—"he strode forward, fell on his two knees and buried his head in her lap" (826–27)—is perfectly canonical for the repentant husband of nineteenth-century melodrama; but at the same time, it invests

Martha with both maternal and divine connotations ("lap" is where a mother nurses her child, but it also suggests the proverbial "lap of the gods"; falling on one's knees can be a sign of worship as well as of repentance), thus confirming exactly the infantile, regressive aspects and the mixture of the erotic and the religious, which had been a distinctive trait of the count's love for the statue. But most of all, Martha now offers herself to her husband's gaze as an image: the (explicitly alienated) image of the domestic goddess that Hilda is going to become at the end of Hawthorne's *Marble Faun*, "enshrined and worshiped as a household saint, in the light of her husband's fireside."[17] This image is the Protestant and Victorian crystallized "Angel in the House," a modern and domestic but quite as imperiously paradigmatic version of the pagan goddess on her pedestal, the object of his "returning faith":[18]

> The Countess . . . pretended to occupy herself with a bit of embroidery, but in reality she was bravely composing herself for an "explanation." . . . The Countess kept her eyes fixed on her work, and drew her silken stitches like an image of wifely contentment. The image seemed to fascinate him: he came in slowly, almost on tiptoe, walked to the chimney-piece, and stood there in a sort of rapt contemplation. . . . My god-daughter's hand trembled as it rose and fell, and the color came into her cheek. At last she raised her eyes and sustained the gaze in which all his returning faith seemed concentrated. (826)

As Hillis Miller notes, it is the image, not the person, that wins the count back: the scene is described "not as a shift back to wholesome feeling, but as a shift from one illusion to another. . . . The Count's love for a real person is modeled on the fictional personification of a piece of marble, not the other way around."[19]

Appropriately enough, the curtain goes down on the count and countess's supposed marital happiness at this point, bequeathing us, as the last feminine image in the story, Martha, changed from an unwitting china shepherdess into the conscious and therefore tragic crystallized image of a domestic goddess: an accomplice but also a victim of her own fixation into an "image of wifely contentment" whose conformity to the mind and feelings of an actual person no one will think again of questioning.

Further inquiry is, on the contrary, thought necessary regarding the count: the short conclusive remarks about his still keeping, after a number of years, the statue's hand, " 'the hand of a beautiful creature . . . whom I once greatly admired' " (827). The text is again sealed by ambivalence: while the information is presented as evidence of the count's dismissing his love for the statue as a thing of the past, as behooves the faithful husband of a Victorian "household saint," the choice of words—"creature," "admired"— and the use of the relative pronoun "whom" all convey the idea that a loved woman is, after all, what the count is talking about. Furthermore, the fetishistic tribute paid to a body fragment is the first instance of a motif that James's later tales will amply develop.

The Godfather

It is, of course, the narrator—this crucial third, or fourth, party—who endorses the idea that the family scene described above is really to be taken as a happy ending and that the count will actually prove "the last of the Valerii," in the most desirable sense of the expression. Having attempted to deconstruct the ending of the tale, the moment has now come to question the narrator's role in it: a move all the more advisable, in that "The Last of the Valerii" is the first among James's stories to display ideological and textual dynamics that later tales will more fully develop—dynamics centering on the narrator's role and on the ambiguous interplay of detachment and complicity, idolatry and iconoclasm that it establishes.

Even while he poses as an external and impartial observer, continually referring to himself as an "eye," to his "posts of observation," to his "watching" the count and stressing his scientific detachment from the "delightfully curious phenomenon" (817) that he regards as "a precious psychological study" (819) endowed with "a perverse fascination which deprived me of all wish to interfere" (818), the narrator is a full participant in the "pathologies" he is relating. "[A]n unscrupulous old *genre* painter, with an eye to 'subjects'" (802), as his ironic self-definition goes, the narrator is actually the first representative of the aesthetic reification of otherness, whose effects have already been discussed in connection with the count and countess. It is his eye—"which has looked at things now so long with the painter's purpose" (798)—that performs the systematic overlapping between Valerio and an ancient statue on which he blames Martha's falling in love with the count; and it is his eye, again, that graphically fixes Martha in a number of sculptural poises, long before the countess undergoes the very "petrification" that he blames on the count: "'to rival the Juno, she's turning to marble herself'" (821). It is only natural, then, that the narrator should be delighted with Martha's final reduction to an "image" of domestic happiness and with the sway such an image holds over Count Valerio: of image worship—the image as an aesthetic crystallization of otherness in the guise of a mere representative surface—he is himself an adept follower. And he shows as much in the very first paragraph of the story, by overcoming at once all his prejudice against his god-daughter's marriage to a foreigner on the strength of his remarking that "from the picturesque point of view (she with her yellow locks and he with his dusky ones), they were a strikingly well-assorted pair" (798).

Even more significant, as Hillis Miller has noted, is the narrator's susceptibility to the suggestiveness of antiquities, since it results in an aptitude to animate the inanimate—the key motif of the tale—which precisely the narrator introduces for the first time: "The statues used to stand there in the perpetual twilight like conscious things, brooding on their gathered memories. I used to linger about them, half expecting they would speak and tell me their stony secrets,—whisper heavily the whereabouts of their mouldering fellows, still unrecovered from the soil"(802).

This narrator's susceptibility to the all-too-human appeal of statues is repeated throughout the story: from the first description of the Juno, wholly based on slippages between animate and inanimate, to the fascination that the statue exerts during the moonlight scene, when the narrator seems to discern "a sort of conscious pride" on the statue's face, eliciting from him the remark that "beauty so eloquent could hardly be inanimate"(820).

The play on personification, therefore, involves the narrator as well as the rest of the characters. Far from establishing a paradigmatic opposition between sanity and delusion, it creates a *continuum* along which the narrator finds his place side by side with Count Valerio, whose obsession is consequently redefined less as qualitatively exceptional than as a quantitative intensification of an attitude shared in various degrees by the whole diegetic world.

If this is so, however, the narrator's involvement calls into question his alleged detachment from his subject and consequently his interpretation of the whole incident, based as it is on the pretended isolability of genetic traits—"the strange ineffaceability of race-characteristics" (817)—that would account for Valerio's behavior entirely in terms of heredity: "The Count became, to my imagination, a dark efflorescence of the evil germs which history had implanted in his line. No wonder he was foredoomed to be cruel. Was not cruelty a tradition in his race, and crime an example? The unholy passions of his forefathers stirred blindly in his untaught nature and clamored blindly for an issue. . . . Such a record was in itself a curse" (813–14).

The narrator, in other words, proves a perfect example of the "rhetoric of iconoclasm" as defined by W. J. T. Mitchell:

> An idol, technically speaking, is simply an image which has an unwarranted, irrational power over somebody; it has become an object of worship, a repository of powers which someone has projected into it, but which it in fact does not possess. But iconoclasm typically proceeds by assuming that the power of the image is felt by somebody else; what the iconoclast sees is the emptiness, vanity, and impropriety of the idol. The idol, then, tends to be simply an image overvalued (in our opinion) by an other. . . . The rhetoric of iconoclasm is thus a rhetoric of exclusion and domination, a caricature of the other as one who is involved in irrational, obscene behavior from which (fortunately) we are exempt.[20]

At this point, the narrator's interpretation demands to be reexamined in the light of the American characters' involvement in those very dynamics supposedly restricted to the descendants of the ancient Romans. And if it is not to be taken at its face value as a reliable explanation of events, the narrator's interpretation demands to be interpreted in its turn.

Surprisingly enough (or not so surprisingly, after all), Anglo-Saxon critics seem never to have noticed the narrator's explicit and manifest racism. Still, his recurring judgments of Latins in general and Italians in particular are unequivocal: they are mercenary—"the pretty fortune which it . . . bothered me to believe that he must, like a good Italian, have taken the exact measure of" (799)—; dishonest—"even rigid rules have their exceptions, and . . . now and then an Italian count is an honest fellow" (803)—; incapable of spiritual refinement—"a Frenchman, an Italian, a Spaniard, might be a very good fellow, but . . . he never really respected the woman he pretended to love" (805)—; gifted with a superficial grace behind which lies an utter unscrupulousness—"with an easy Italian conscience and a gracious Italian persuasiveness" (811). In other words, apart from their value in terms of the picturesque, they are totally unreliable both as individuals and, all the more, as husbands: " 'I was a thousand times right,' I cried; 'an Italian Count may be mighty fine, but he won't *wear*! Give us some wholesome young fellow of our own blood, who'll play us none of these dusky old-world tricks. Painter as I am, I'll never recommend a picturesque husband!' " (813).

Such virulence is not without meaning. The narrator's manifest racism is possibly the most extreme sign of the connection between the self's construction as subject and the reification of the Other, a phenomenon I have hitherto analyzed with reference to the count-countess-statue triangle. By isolating the protagonist's passion as the fruit of an atavistic pathology and by marking it with the stigma of an inferior race (to such an extent that "the last of the Valerii" in an expression like " 'He has proved himself one of the Valerii; we shall see to it that he is the last' " [823] takes on the ominous connotations of a genocidal project—if nothing else, by association with *The Last of the Mohicans*), the narrator disclaims all suspicion of involvement with regard both to himself and to the "modern work-a-day world of which, in spite of my passion for bedaubing old panels with ineffective portraiture of mouldy statues against screens of box, I still flattered myself I was a member" (804).[21] The oppositions past vs. present, Europe vs. America are used instrumentally as an exorcizing, covering-up device, keeping at a distance and projecting onto an "inferior" race a set of psychic and ideological dynamics that prove in fact to be much deeper and more widespread than the atavistic interpretation would acknowledge.

Like the delusion of the last of the Valerii, the tale also simultaneously conceals and manifests a "repressed psychic content," and it stages not just that content but the very machinery of its repression. It achieves as much by exhibiting the mechanism whereby an alternative "truth" is created—a mystifying account that in its turn, rather than accounting for behavior, manifests its deep content: the aesthetic reification of the Other, be it the foreign, the antique, or the feminine.

Once again, a deeply consistent pattern underlies and connects James's discourse about art, about woman, and about the "international theme." Like "The Madonna of the Future," "The Last of the Valerii" stages a problematic reflection on the conceivable role of ancient art in the age of modernity. In the contrast between the possibility to recover a "full" cultural significance to objects from remote times and their reification into mere commodities—be it as objects for mass consumption or for detached aesthetic enjoyment—lies the potentially serious and present-time significance of the narrator's interpretation of events. His age—it is worth remembering—was, after all, one in which more and more instances of that peculiar modern institution, the museum, were being created and debated throughout the Western world.[22] The narrator himself, however, only sees Valerio's case as a *fait curieux*: his perception of the ancient and the modern is in terms of a neatly contrasted pair of opposites, with the modern as unquestionably the positive pole (" 'How can he have failed to feel . . . that you are a more perfect experiment of nature, a riper fruit of time, than those primitive persons for whom Juno was a terror and Venus an example? He pays you the compliment of believing you an inconvertible modern'" [822]), where the ancient can only find its place as an archaeological relic, exhibited for the general admiring contemplation in its unbridgeable aesthetic distance, while its substratum is rejected as nothing but the "darkness of history" (814), an unending sequel of crimes and vices.

At the end of this course lies the museum that Adam Verver will establish in American City—a museum holding Charlotte Stant as one of its most precious exhibits. As was true of "The Madonna of the Future" and as "Rose-Agathe" will show even more explicitly, the museological gaze is the common denominator associating the woman, the ancient object, and the art object, all offered to the jealous gaze of their male possessor, fixed in their role of motionless and timeless ideological representations, objects of cult of a secular nature in an age when bourgeois domesticity, on the one hand, and "culture," on the other, are more and more pervasively substituted for religion in its former function as overarching social value. Even though Martha's petrifaction into an image or statue seems to be a consummation that she has to some extent desired and pursued, it is only fair to recognize that such an issue already existed at the beginning of the text, implied in the narrator's very first words: "I had had the occasion to declare more than once that if my god-daughter married a foreigner I should refuse to give her away" (798). These words, quite apart from the (pregnant, for that matter) ritual of the wedding ceremony and from the already noted chauvinism the narrator displays in his rejection of exogamous marriage, have the effect of handing over to the reader Martha already reduced to an object that can be granted or denied. Even though Camillo's subject position is represented as economically and intellectually subordinate to his wife's, this does not mean that there is no representative of patriarchal authority in the text: the godfather—god-father!—certainly is an appropriate emblem of such an exquisitely cultural form of power.

Swappings

Having tried to unravel the significance of individual features of the tale, I would now like to highlight the significance and recurrence of its structural framework by moving my focus onto another text. "The Last of the Valerii" is not the only tale from James's early production that is based on a symmetrical relation of barter or exchange between woman and art object. Immediately after the publication of "The Last of the Valerii" and "Madame de Mauves," in May–June 1874, James wrote a bizarre story that was published in *Scribner's Monthly* and never revised or reprinted since: "Adina."[23] Once again, the tale is reminiscent of Hawthorne and plays on the contrast between Europe and America. The story, set in Rome, is narrated eighteen years after the event, on the occasion of the protagonist's death; the narrator, a friend of the protagonist and former witness to the story, tells it to a mutual friend, who is the first narrator of the tale. "Adina" is one of those early Jamesian tales, told in a fairly straightforward manner and apparently devoid of formal subtleties, that seem unrewarding to critical analysis; the oddness of its uncommon plot, though, invites cultural investigation and connects the story to both earlier and later tales as different stages in a coherent narrative project. In order to better limn the significance of the plot, I will now provide a lengthy summary of the story, whose relevance to my argument, I hope, will immediately become clear.

The protagonist, Sam Scrope, is portrayed as a young man of extraordinary intellectual qualities, but "cynical, perverse, conceited, obstinate" (904). He is also described as despising the Italians, a motif already familiar from "The Last of the Valerii": "he used to swear that Italy had got no more than she deserved, that she was a land of vagabonds and declaimers, and that he had yet to see an Italian whom he would call a man . . . that nothing grew strong there but lying and cheating, laziness, beggary and vermin" (905). Such an attitude, however, is not endorsed by the narrator, who distances himself from it, and blames Scrope's comments on the beauty of Italy, painfully affecting a man so conscious of his own extreme personal unattractiveness. During a horseback ride in the Roman countryside, Scrope and his friend meet with a "really statuesque . . . rustic Endymion" (907), a handsome young hunter who is lying asleep, his head on some remains overgrown with grass.[24] "He had the frame of a young Hercules; he was altogether as handsome a vagabond as you could wish for the foreground of a pastoral landscape" (908). A pastoral recasting of Count Valerio (and of Hawthorne's Donatello), this young man is exceptionally beautiful and—so at least the two Americans suspect—rather weak-minded. In his hand he holds a small dark stone, which immediately draws Scrope's eager attention: a keen collector (the first of a series in this group of tales), he recognizes its worth and manages to get it from the young man for a ridiculously low sum. When his friend accuses him of having taken advantage of the young hunter's ignorance and naiveté, Scrope replies in nearly Nietzschean terms, casting himself as someone who is above the ordinary morality because he has acted "in the interest of art, of science, of taste" (912). Had he offered the young man a fairer sum, he explains, this would have opened "those sleepy eyes of his," perverted his nature, and caused him to think that he could "marry a *contessina*" (912); on the other hand, with the sum he actually received, "Angelo gets a month's carouse,—he'll enjoy it,—and goes to sleep again. Pleasant dreams to him! What does he want of money? Money would have corrupted him! I've saved the *contessina*, too; I'm sure he would have beaten her" (912). Already the ownership of the precious stone, while becoming a token of cultural superiority, is connected to possession of a woman.

Actually, the stone becomes to Scrope a love object of sorts: "He went about whistling and humming odd scraps of song, like a lover freshly accepted" (913); the more so, since after scraping and cleaning it turns out to be a precious, finely carved topaz, possibly belonging to Emperor Tiberius. Scrope's elation has Faustian overtones: "'Shabby Nineteenth Century Yankees, as we are, we are having our audience. Down on your knees, barbarian, we're in a tremendous presence! . . . I've annulled the centuries— I've resuscitated a *totius orbis imperator*'" (914). Like Count Valerio, Scrope decides to keep his finding all to himself while confirming its symbolic connection to a woman figure: "'I shall show it to no one else—except to my mistress, if I ever have one'" (915). However unexpected, this acquisition of a mistress is bound to happen soon: in comes Adina, "short and slight and blonde," with an "infantine bloom," extremely unloquacious habits, and a capacity for "sweet stillness"(916); unsurprisingly, her auburn hair is arranged "into a thousand fantastic braids, like a coiffure in a Renaissance drawing" (916–17).

Set at the four ends of an invisible quadrangle, the four main characters— the American, the Italian, the woman, and the topaz—can now begin to exchange their positions on stage. The connection between the woman and the topaz is the implicit principle ruling the barter. When Angelo learns the actual value of the topaz and claims rights on it, for instance, the narrator's hope is that Scrope's happy love story will make him amenable to some concession. But Scrope is firm in his ownership both of the gem and of Adina: "He treated his bliss as his own private property, and was as little in the humor to diffuse its influence as he would have been to send out in charity a choice dish from an unfinished dinner" (924). His two belongings, however, tend to repel each other rather than melt into a harmonious whole. "[A] blonde angel of New England origin" (926) reminiscent of

Hawthorne's Hilda, Adina refuses to pollute herself by contact with the topaz, which she takes to be an emblem of pagan wickedness; she seems to be very sensitive, instead, to Angelo's wrong when she comes to know of it. Everything is thus ready for the positional exchange that will refund and avenge Angelo for his loss. After suddenly and unexpectedly breaking her engagement to Scrope, Adina elopes at night to marry Angelo, a decision whose inexplicability all the characters stress. Adina has only seen Angelo once: no one knows how they may have agreed on their elopement and arranged its practical details or whether Adina's love has been caused by Angelo's silent and patient presence, his picturesque beauty, or her own awareness of the wrong he has suffered. The incident is thus variously described as "fathomless," "impossible," "a mystery," "an enigma," "a painful puzzle": "It was a most extraordinary occurrence; we had ample time to say so, and to say so again, and yet never really to understand it" (941). When he visits Adina at her new dwelling with a view of finding out whether she regrets what she has done, the narrator finds her "pale and very grave; she seemed to wear a frigid mask of reserve" (943). Her message to her family is a request that they leave her alone: " 'I only ask to be forgotten!' " (934). The narrator (who had formerly acknowledged his own romantic and sentimental bias) interprets her words as a declaration of happiness—" 'She said she was happy' " (944)—and reads the story as one of "ardent, full-blown, positive passion" (941) worthy of a novel: "I thought it *might* be out of a novel—such a thing as love at sight; such a thing as an unspoken dialogue, between a handsome young Italian with a 'wrong,' in a starlit garden, and a fanciful western maid at a window" (938). In the final scene, Scrope throws the gem into the Tiber from the Castel Sant'Angelo bridge, possibly in an extreme attempt at recovering one of his possessions by sacrificing the other.

Once again, this story might be regarded as just one more instance of James's early imitation of Hawthorne and his use of a wide range of European literary sources (from Byron to Alfieri to Chamisso) were it not for the inexorable structural logic governing the tale—a logic that is meaningful in itself and that helps shed light (albeit a dreary one) on the heroine's mysterious behavior. " 'She's better than the topaz!' " (943), Angelo contentedly declares at the end of the story, thus making explicit the exchange logic insistently hinted at in the recurring association between woman and gem and in the recurring association of both with a lexicon of reification and ownership: " 'Oh yes; she's the right thing' " (919), Scrope had commented on receiving his friend's congratulations for his engagement.

And Angelo's exclamation on first seeing Adina, " 'He has more than his share of good luck . . . A topaz—and a pearl! both at once!' " (928), in its choice of metaphor, had already expressed the basic equivalence between the lost topaz and the woman to be won.

The lack of any dramatic or psychological motive for the heroine's behavior, her inevitable, almost automatic way of taking her own equivalence with the topaz for granted and of taking on the role of an exchange object, are significant in themselves: they bear witness to the inescapable power of a structural and cultural logic based on male ownership and on the equivalence of such different possessions as gems and women. Her acquiescence to this logic—however romantically the narrator may view it—is a joyless gesture. Although, as is the case with most heroines in this series, we have no direct access to her consciousness, Adina's mask of reserve and her request to be left behind and forgotten are definitely unconvincing as declarations of happiness and rather remind one of Mrs. Osmond's mask, of her refusal to acknowledge her unhappiness, of her burial into the "house of darkness" (foreshadowed here by Adina's marital house, overlooking the gardens of the Church of the Cappuccini, renowned for its funerary crypts). The throwing of the topaz into the Tiber, which the narrator interprets as Scrope's avowal of the lasting quality of the gem's evil influence, might be better envisaged as his tribute to this obscure symmetry—a symmetry less of pleasure than of sacrifice.

Once again, as in "The Last of the Valerii," an erotic and aesthetic triangle, by positioning the woman protagonist and the statue/gem symmetrically, foregrounds their fundamental equivalence as both aesthetic objects and objects of desire, symbolic objects to be owned and bartered. One more step and the two objects will become one: Rose-Agathe, the woman-object; Flora, the image-woman. The structural dynamics operating so far under cover of the opposition between ancient and modern, Europe and America, will be henceforth presented as wholly contained within modernity; and this in turn will prevent these dynamics being disposed of in terms either of racism or of an enlightened disclaimer and will impose them on the audience as inherent features of *their own* culture.

Chapter 3
Woman as Object: "Rose-Agathe"

"Rose-Agathe," published in May 1878 in *Lippincott's Magazine*, relates the conquest of the eponymous heroine by American collector Sanguinetti, a thirty-five-year-old bachelor, who after accidentally seeing her through a coiffeur's shop window falls in love with her so obsessively that he has no peace until he can call her his own.[1] The story is set in Paris and told by James's typical anonymous witness-narrator, Sanguinetti's friend, also an American in his thirties; the successive stages of Sanguinetti's conquest of Rose-Agathe are recorded through a series of dialogues between the two gentlemen, interspersed with the narrator's private reflections and comments.

Rose-Agathe is an unusual heroine: she is an object-woman, not just in the metaphorical sense of being an object of male desire and as such deprived of the status of desiring and speaking subject, but in the most literal sense, since—as it turns out—the object of Sanguinetti's passion is not a real woman, the coiffeur's wife, as the narrator thinks, but an inanimate female face: a revolving waxen bust, advertising the hairdresser's ability by exhibiting the fashionable arrangement of her blond hair in the shop window. At first sight, such a tale is nothing more than an odd, frivolous anecdote, wholly depending on double sense and equivocation to build up the surprise of the final revelation; apart from its usual wealth of literary allusion, there is little or nothing in it to suggest deeper implications or moral and epistemological "shocks of recognition."[2] Still, when regarded as part of a series where motifs of reification are played out again and again, "Rose-Agathe" becomes a veritable climax in James's investigation, where all the issues explored so far interact and coalesce into a grotesque, extreme, and crystal-clear representation.

Fragments of an Analysis of a Case of Fetishism

"Rose-Agathe" is, first and foremost, a story of perverted desire. As he himself declares, Sanguinetti is actually in love with the dummy: " 'You are simply in love,' I said. He looked at me a moment, and blushed. 'Yes, I honestly believe I am. It's very absurd.' " (228); "He really looked love-sick; he was pale and heavy-eyed. 'My too-susceptible friend,' I said, 'you are very far gone.' 'Yes,' he answered; 'I am really in love. It is too ridiculous. Please don't tell any one.' " (230).

The collector's passion is here amplified into passion *tout court*: this is a handbook case of fetishism as described by Freud—one of those cases "in which the normal sexual object is replaced by another which bears some relation to it, but is entirely unsuited to serve the normal sexual aim."[3] Like the protagonist of *Gradiva* and like his forerunner Count Valerio, Sanguinetti might feature as a regular Freudian case study: one might note the fetishistic tendencies inherent in his collecting, which the narrator explicitly presents as a substitute for women—"to my almost certain knowledge his affections had no object save the faded crockery and the angular chairs I have mentioned" (222)—even though he refuses to perceive anything disturbing in the kind of female company his friend prefers:

> I had a great kindness for him; he seemed to me such a pure-minded mortal, sitting there in his innocent company of Dresden shepherdesses and beauties whose smiles were stippled on the lids of snuff-boxes. . . . it amused me to see a man who had hitherto found a pink-faced lady on a china-plate a sufficiently substantial object of invocation led captive by a charmer who would, as the phrase is, have something to say for herself. (226–27)

As post-Freudian and therefore more suspicious (or less willingly blinded) readers, we might notice, instead, that prominent among the objects collected by Sanguinetti are Sèvres teacups and snuffboxes, which are as transparent female sexual symbols as Dora's purse or the matchboxes in Freud's clinical cases.[4] Matchboxes, by the way, are the very root of Sanguinetti's collecting mania, as the narrator explains: "My companion, who had several sisters, was brought up like a little gentleman, and showed symptoms even at the earliest age of his mania for refuse furniture. At school he used to collect old slate-pencils and match-boxes" (126). The mention of "several sisters" is also relevant to an interpretation of the case:

as is well known, Freud traces fetishism back to the childhood discovery of female "castration," a trauma the subject exorcises by selecting some object as substitute for the lacking female penis—the fetish, "a token of triumph over the threat of castration and a protection against it."[5] The childhood of a boy surrounded by several sisters, one can surmise, must have provided plentiful opportunities for such traumatic discoveries; and as for the choice of the fetish object (which to Freud is never accidental), it can be accounted for by another recollection: Sanguinetti's grandfather, "an Italian image-vendor" who had moved to America with "his little tray of plaster effigies and busts" (225) at the beginning of the century, there to become the founder of the family fortunes.

A phenomenon of disavowal *(Verleugnung)*, fetishism is finally an expression of fear, a maneuver exorcising that threatening alterity, women's difference. Unsurprisingly, Rose-Agathe—soothing to the end—is a bust, lacking the lower half of the body: the only reminder of the lack hidden under her velvet gown is a creak, which (unsurprisingly, again) registers as annoying: "'It is a pity she creaks,' said my companion as I was making my bow. And then, as I made it, I perceived with amazement—and amusement—the cause of her creaking. She existed only from the waist upward, and the skirt of her dress was a very neat pedestal covered with red velvet" (237).

The narrator's "amusement," promptly correcting a former "amazement," seals the story in a tone of pleasant urbanity: once again, the narrator refuses to be made uneasy and rejects any pathological implications in his friend's behavior (even though on former occasions he had playfully used such terms as "symptoms" and "mania," both current in the medical discourse of the age). To him, Rose-Agathe is finally nothing but the collector's triumph: "of all his pretty things she was certainly the prettiest" (237) are the last words in the story. But apart from my (tongue-in-cheek) reading of the story as a Freudian case history, Sanguinetti's passion is far from devoid of disturbing implications, however carefully the narrator represses them: indeed, his obsession displays traits that are culturally shared as well as psychologically meaningful.[6]

The reduction of woman's image to fetishistic object is not just the result of individual pathology: it belongs within a general negotiation of gender roles and positions in nineteenth-century culture, which saw the emergence of new notions such as "monomania" (theorized by Jean-Etienne-Dominique Esquirol in the early years of the century) and "erotomania" (the theoretical forerunner of fetishism, developed by Moreau, Charcot, and

Magnan in the early 1880s). The literary exploration of such pathologies amounted to a veritable subgenre in French turn-of-the-century fiction, as Emily Apter has shown in her precious and well-documented study of what she terms "cabinet fiction"—the fiction of the *cabinet*, in the twofold sense of the word: the inner private space within the house, reserved for the male head of the family and sheltered from women's eyes, where a private museum made up equally of archaeological relics and erotic memorabilia could be collected, but also the doctor's office, the institutional place where the analysis of pathological traits was performed and the related secrets were disclosed and collected. The increasingly museum-like quality of private inner spaces; the monomania of insatiable collectors of bibelots and bric-a-brac; erotomania and the institutionalization of voyeurism—these phenomena all interact and display their deep affinity in cabinet fiction: "a disturbing set of slippages from object mania to erotomania" makes woman into a "female collectible," "fetishized as an erotic commodity or collector's item within the fin-de-siècle Imaginary"—a slippage that Apter analyzes in Maupassant, Zola, and the Goncourts, but that James's story antedates by a few years.[7] Nor is French fiction the sole example of fetishistic strategies of representation at the time: roughly in the same years, as Griselda Pollock has argued, British painting reveled in the fragmentation of woman's image and her reduction to an isolated, disembodied face:

> In the visual sign, woman, manufactured in a variety of guises in mid-nineteenth-century British culture, this absolute difference is secured by the erasure of indices of real time and actual space, by an abstracted (some would call it idealized) representation of faces as dissociated uninhabited spaces which function as a screen across which masculine fantasies of knowledge, power and possession can be enjoyed in a ceaseless play on the visible obviousness of woman and the puzzling enigmas reassuringly disguised behind that mask of beauty. At the same time, the face and sometimes part of a body are severed from the whole. Fetish-like they signify an underlying degree of anxiety generated by looking at this sign of difference, woman.[8]

Rose-Agathe, then, is a truly exemplary character, not just as an object of love, but as the *kind* of object she is. Smiling and beautiful, voiceless and gazeless, she is a mere polished surface where an inner life can be projected from the outside according to one's desire.[9] A decorative objet d'art to be kept in one's drawing-room—"'It's just the place for her'" (129)—but also an object for worship, a Madonna, Rose-Agathe is an epitome of each woman-as-portrait, woman-as-statue we have met so far, as well as the quintessential image of femininity without subjectivity, of Otherness voided of all threatening implications and made into a mere mirror of the self, the projection and embodiment of male fantasy.[10] She is the perfect woman, an ideal, a symbol qua object—the literal version, and the reductio ad absurdum, of an archetype haunting the male imagination in the nineteenth century (and possibly beyond). " 'I have always dreamed of just such a woman as that' " (228), Sanguinetti reveals to the narrator while avowing his passion: and the word "woman" here is more than just the relay accounting for the misunderstanding on which the tale is based. The complete humanization of the dummy, to which Sanguinetti refers as possessed with feelings and sensations of her own, could not have been effected if it were not possible to think of Rose-Agathe as a real woman— that is, if it were not possible, conversely, to think of a real woman in terms of those "virtues" in which Rose-Agathe undoubtedly excels.[11]

A Politics of Looking

At the end of the story, the narrator's voice once again takes on a normalizing function, playing down both the pathological and the wider implications of the protagonist's passion and presenting it as a minor, harmless eccentricity. Through the amused, forbearing tone he employs in assessing his friend's foibles, the narrator effectively confines and isolates Sanguinetti's behavior, implicitly claiming his own normality and his own (however benignant) superiority: "I had a great kindness for him. . . . There is always something agreeable in a man who is a perfect example of a type, and Sanguinetti was all of one piece. He was the perfect authority on pretty things" (226).[12]

Despite its bland and friendly accents, the narrator's voice is once again unmistakably expressing the same "rhetoric of iconoclasm" already voiced by the narrator of "The Last of the Valerii": an "iconophobia" firmly rooted in Western, and especially in Reformed culture, as a result of which the power of images is both perceived as threatening and criticized as irrational. Another's false idols are typically attacked from one's allegedly superior, more enlightened stance.[13] In the narrator's discourse, this superiority takes on national connotations—American austerity of mores vs. Sanguinetti's Italian ancestry and "Frenchified" attitude—which in turn translates into an opposition between morality and taste (to be played out again in Lambert Strether's later Parisian adventure): "A matter of taste, indeed, this question of common morality! Sanguinetti was more Parisianised than

I had supposed, and I reflected that Paris was certainly a very dangerous place, since it had got the better of his inveterate propriety"(228).[14]

The narrator's superiority and detachment regarding Sanguinetti's whimsical adventure is reinforced by his privileged textual stance as narrator and point of view. This positional privilege is also confirmed in the diegesis, which presents the narrator as panoptical onlooker from the first paragraph:

> I had invited the excellent fellow to dinner, and had begun to wonder, the stroke of half-past six having sounded, why he did not present himself. At last I stepped out upon the balcony and looked along the street in the direction from which, presumably, he would approach. A Parisian thoroughfare is always an entertaining spectacle, and I had still much of a stranger's alertness of attention. Before long, therefore, I quite forgot my unpunctual guest in my relish of the multifarious animation of the brilliant city. (219)

Incidentally, from the very beginning Sanguinetti is presented as transgressor, whereas the narrator figures on the side of norm and authority, however mild and benevolent: "I was really very good-natured to be waiting so placidly for that dilatory Sanguinetti" (221). The main function of the opening passage, though, is to introduce the narrator as privileged observer: this is effected by the remarkably long description that follows, a veritable genre sketch, where each feature observed is described in pictorial detail and assigned its place within a spectacularized scene: the woman selling violets in the road, the restaurant complete with waiters, cashier, and patrons, Anatole's hairdressing shop, with his charming wife on the threshold and the beautifully modeled revolving heads in the window. Only after the lengthy descriptive passage and the repeated verbs of vision have established the narrator's role as privileged spectator does Sanguinetti enter the stage: he is lingering in front of the coiffeur's window, staring: "There he stood in front of the coiffeur's, staring as intently and serenely into the windows as if he had the whole evening before him. I waited a few moments, to give him a chance to move on, but he remained there, gaping like a rustic at a fair" (221).

From the very beginning, Sanguinetti is thus posited as simultaneously observing and observed. The visual quality of events is a veritable textual obsession: Sanguinetti's "courtship" mainly consists of a search for circumstances that will allow him opportunities for prolonged glances; the narrator's interest is mainly expressed and sustained through his observation. The gaze is thus both a vehicle of desire and an instrument of knowledge; its critical function is revealed in the strategic importance explicitly attributed to a search for the right point of view: "There was evidently an unobstructed space behind the window, through which this attractive person could be perceived as she sat at her desk in some attitude of graceful diligence. . . . I promised myself to look out for this point of visual access the very first time I should pass" (222).

The text construes its complex visual dynamics along multiple lines:

> The narrator watches Rose-Agathe
> Sanguinetti watches Rose-Agathe
> The narrator watches Sanguinetti watching Rose-Agathe.

Within these visual dynamics, however, the narrator keeps his privileged role, since he can both watch his friend watching his object (a recurrent situation) and watch the same object on his own: his gaze contains and controls Sanguinetti's, whereas the reverse is not true—an asymmetry further emphasized by Sanguinetti's frequently noted shortsightedness. The final agnition, though, splits the hitherto unitary gaze into two different directions: from the start, as it turns out, there had been *two* distinct objects of the gaze and consequently two distinct and parallel visual axes:

> The narrator watches the hairdresser's wife
> Sanguinetti watches Rose-Agathe

—so that the overall situation might be described as follows:

> /Sanguinetti watching RA
> We watch [The narrator watching]
> /the hairdresser's wife

The final recognition of his misunderstanding—a visual and interpretive mistake—retrospectively decenters the narrator from his privileged "post of observation" (230), that is, from his authoritative position. The reader's identification with the narrator as the reliable, superior, and detached point of view on events is now replaced by a refocusing and a perception of the narrator's role as a far from transparent filter. The spectatorial detachment of the narrator on his balcony—allegedly a mere narrative frame—can no longer hide his involvement as coprotagonist of the story and his perfect functional identity with Sanguinetti. They are both observers of women, and each is the protagonist of one of two separate, parallel visual stories: Sanguinetti with Rose-Agathe, the narrator with the coiffeur's wife (the former, as regular protagonists, both entitled to a name; the latter both appropriately nameless, since their story is an unofficial one).

The functional and diegetic parallel between Sanguinetti and the narrator is further reinforced by several recurring analogies. They are both American, both the same age (they were in school together), both bachelors; while Sanguinetti has no interest in politics and only reads the newspapers for news about auctions, the narrator is a dutiful reader of the *Débats*, but he finds it "a somewhat arduous feat" (230).[15] Repeatedly the narrator wonders if the Parisian atmosphere might not affect him as it has his friend—"Should I too come to this, if I continued to live in Paris?" (228)—and he goes so far as to acknowledge that "nothing was more possible than that I too should become equally perverted" (233). More importantly, he too has his own weakness: an immoderate passion for chocolate, which makes him as faithful an adept of the rule of "taste" as Sanguinetti, albeit in the physical instead of the spiritual sense. Indeed, the "pretty little box" (219) of chocolate he keeps in his room is in no way inferior to Sanguinetti's "snuff-boxes" and "match-boxes" in its symbolic import, thanks to the well-known association of the oral and the sexual, the more so, since the adjective "pretty" is only used elsewhere in the text with reference to Sanguinetti's collectibles— "pretty things"—as well as to the "pretty faces" of Rose-Agathe and of the hairdresser's wife.

The decentering of the narrator's authority also has other implications. The functional and diegetic parallel between the two observers creates a similar parallel between the two objects being observed, the real woman and the artificial one, both equivalent in being passive objects of the gaze. The visual universe outlined in the tale is not a universe of communication: the gazes making up its texture are all monological, allowing no reciprocity. The gaze here is unidirectional, and it conveys male desire. Women, by comparison, are emphatically gazeless: the coiffeur's wife, for instance, at whom the narrator insistently looks, "gave no sign of seeing me, and I felt that if there had been a dozen men standing there she would have worn that same sweetly unconscious mask" (230); rather than reciprocating the narrator's gaze, she turns to look at the shop window in narcissistic compla- cency, as if the window were an extension of her self-display. Conversely, the humanization of Rose-Agathe is achieved through her being endowed with a gaze, imparted by the man as a mere reflection and projection of his own: "'I shall go into the shop several times, to buy certain things. . . . Meanwhile, she will slowly move around, and every now and then she will look at me'" (228). After their "elopement," Sanguinetti confers on

Rose-Agathe "an expression of pure bliss. There was something in her eyes" (236); and finally, when the humanizing performance is at its climax, Rose-Agathe is positioned "near a window . . . with her head turned away from us, looking out" (237)—fictively provided both with the gaze and with the observer's privileged point of view.

In this voyeuristic universe, man looks without being looked at, and what he looks at is the female body, which is thereby reduced to object. This is where the deep identity between the real woman and the hairdresser's dummy lies. It is no accident that from the beginning the narrator's eye puts women and windows, shop signs and shopkeepers side by side—all equally flattened as parts of the view, all equalized by their role in the "entertaining spectacle" (219) offered to his spectatorial vocation. The narrator's scopophilia is nothing but the cultural (as well as clinical) counterpart of the protagonist's fetishism: both are equally premised on the reification of woman as object of another's gaze and desire rather than as subject of her own.[16] What this story effectively articulates is the way visual roles are distributed in modern patriarchal society—a "sexual politics of looking" built on culturally defined gender roles, where male sexuality "enjoys the freedom to look, appraise and possess, in deed or in fantasy," whereas woman is positioned in the passive role, in a dynamic of domination and subjection that a later tale like "Glasses" will display to the full.[17]

Voyeurism is to Peter Brooks the rationale of nineteenth-century realism: in the realistic novel the body—and especially the female body, an object of both sexual and cognitive desire, symbolically linked to the unveiling of the truth—becomes the focus of "an 'epistemophilic' project," and the visual dimension becomes "the master relation to the world. . . . To know, in realism, is to see, and to represent is to describe."[18] Again the division of roles is along the lines of gender: "While the bodies viewed are both male and female, vision is typically a male prerogative, and its object of fascination the woman's body" (88). Fetishism, therefore, can be taken as a metaphor of the realist project as such: in deferring the object of desire[19]—whose revealed presence would result in the end of the *récit*—"this attention, the very gaze of literary representation, tends to become arrested and transfixed by articles of clothing, accessories, bodily details, almost in the matter of the fetishist" (19). In this complex psychonarrational strategy, readers are construed as "secondary voyeurs" (53), willing to experience vicariously the pleasures available to their deputy, the observer within the diegetic world, in a dynamic closely resembling the functioning of pornography (whose implications I take up again in the next chapter).

In its elaborate *mise en abyme* of the gaze, however, by displacing the reader's identification with the narrator, the text displaces *the reader*'s voyeurism as well. In its final "surprise," the story is denaturalized: the protagonist's gaze and the narrator's gaze defamiliarize each other, thus enforcing a perception of their ideological production as well as of their phenomenological operation. Switching from fictional to metafictional discourse, the text stages a confrontation with its own ideological production and offers itself as commentary on a sexual politics of looking, whose orchestration it lays bare.

Women in the Marketplace

The narrator's equivocation is no mere misunderstanding, or rather, it is a misunderstanding that has deep roots in culture. "Rose-Agathe" is the story of *two* substitutions: Sanguinetti's substitution of the waxen woman for the flesh-and-blood one; but also the narrator's substitution of the flesh-and-blood woman for the waxen one: "What in the world was he looking at? Had he spied something that could play a part in his collection? . . . But here, suddenly, I comprehended the motive of his immobility: he was looking of course at the barber's beautiful wife, the pretty woman with the face of a Madonna and the coiffure of a Parisienne, whom I myself had just found so charming. This was really an excuse, and I felt disposed to allow him a few moments' grace" (222).

If the misunderstanding resists in the narrator's mind even longer than it does in the reader's (despite telling details like the fake jewels supposedly given to the hairdresser's wife but worn by the dummy, and notwithstanding Sanguinetti's own protestations of the absurdity of his love), it is not just because of James's magician-like ability to keep up a dialogue wholly based on double entendre; nor is it enough for the two characters never to make their reference explicit, thus providing the verisimilar motive for their mutual misconception. A deeper symbolic congruence between the two referents grounds their substitution: the equivocation works because it is *linguistically* and *culturally* possible—because a woman can be *talked about* as an object, *looked at* as an object, and *thought of* as an object. Again prosopopoeia—the founding trope of image fetishism and of idolatry—is a crucial figure: indeed, the whole tale might be envisaged as its expansion and illustration. And again rhetoric and ideology coalesce: the reified woman is the specular counterpart to the personified dummy—it belongs to the same symbolic system, it provides its substratum and condition of possibility.

What looked like a "clinical case," then, is really the physiology of patriarchal culture. Language, for one, constantly homologizes women and things, as the text repeatedly shows in the sustained duplicity of its dialogues. Examples range from the recurrence of a polysemic term like "object"—" 'My dear friend,' murmured my guest, 'she is the most beautiful object I ever beheld' " (224)—to the astute use of a single adjective to connect in a single connotative chain the protagonist's "pretty things" and women's "pretty faces." The most frequent example, as well as the richest in cultural implications, is the obsessive use of an economic lexicon, of which I will provide only a few illustrations:

> "I will make a very handsome offer."
> "What sort of an offer do you mean?"
> "I am ashamed to tell you: you will call it throwing away money."
> An offer of money! He was really very crude. . . . "Oh," I said, "if you think that money simply will do it——"
> "Why, you don't suppose that I expect to have her for nothing?" He was actually cynical, and I remained silent. (228)

> "I never see the husband," said Sanguinetti, . . . "But I am in hopes he will come round. . . . He will not be sorry, after all, to have the money." (232)

> Nothing, I answered, would give me greater pleasure, but meanwhile what did the husband say?
> "He grumbles a bit, but I gave him five hundred francs." (236)

Although the actual object of this barter is a waxen bust, the supposed one is a woman. The narrator, to be sure, is shocked by his friend's businesslike way of planning his courtship as an economic transaction; still, what he objects to is not so much its absurd or unthinkable quality as its *immorality*—which he accounts for by once more appealing to national stereotyping: "You may be sure that I felt plenty of surprise at the business-like tone in which Sanguinetti discussed this unscrupulous project of becoming the 'possessor' of another man's wife. . . . But I said to myself that this was doubtless the Parisian tone, and that, since it had made its mark upon so perfect a little model of social orthodoxy as my estimable friend, nothing was more possible than that I too should become equally perverted" (232–33).

Reduced to a matter of social orthodoxy and set in the wider frame of the relativity of national mores, the purchase of a woman no longer appears disturbing and becomes an ethnological phenomenon to be looked on from an enlightened stance. The narrator, of course, never questions the possibility of discussing a woman in terms of material possession, not just in a worn-out sentimental metaphor—"making her my own" (227), "possess her" (231), "'She is mine! she is mine! mine only!'" (236)—but literally as a commodity traded between different owners in a market economy. The reification of woman easily shades off into her commodification: 'woman' naturally overlaps with objects and commodities in the narrator's mind—a perspective that is neither abstract nor merely personal, but historically and ideologically constructed.[20] This deep symbolic identification, authorized by ideology, grounds all the double entendres in the story and reveals them as less a misunderstanding than a symptom. Beneath the manifest content of the tale, the slippage from "it" to "she" effected by the protagonist's monomania, a deeper and more meaningful slippage takes place from "she" to "it"—the real subject of the tale, what it is about without saying it, as Macherey would term it: that is, the hidden ideological premise the text makes visible by elaborating on it.[21]

There is, of course, a powerful connection between woman as fetish and woman as commodity: Marx's analysis of commodity fetishism in the opening chapter of *Das Kapital* and Luce Irigaray's reading of the latter, which underscores the precise analogies existing between the status of commodities in capitalism and the status of women in patriarchal society: both man-made objects, whose value depends on exchange; both products, whose value depends on social relations and ideological investments, which, however, appear objectively embodied and inherent in them; both puzzling and enigmatic objects, full—as Marx has it—of theological and metaphysical subtleties. Hence their power as fetishes, whose exalted status lies in the concealment of the ideological origin of their value, a value *from* man and *for* man.[22] Freud's and Marx's analyses converge, in that in both fetishism is traced back to a basic device of simultaneous concealment and exaltation, inviting a "hermeneutics of suspicion."[23] There also lies woman's fullness of meaning as fetishized object, simultaneously reified and deified, manifesting and circulating within an exchange economy the value invested in it: that is, as Irigaray writes, the power of the Phallus.

Rose-Agathe, "L'Eve Future"

Rose-Agathe's name is pregnant with meaning to anyone who cares to explore its implications. It is a woman's name—suitably double, since there are in fact two protagonists—but it is also the name of inanimate objects, like the waxen woman and like the reified woman who is her ideological double. These objects, though, are precious ones—not in themselves, but by virtue of man's ideological operation; and as such, they have become conventional literary metaphors of womanhood, culturally reinforcing the representation of femininity along the lines established by the patriarchal "encyclopaedia": woman as a flower and woman as a jewel, beautiful and precious, glittering and ephemeral.[24]

Rose-Agathe is also extraordinary for the wealth of symbolic associations she catalyzes as an object, welding into a single representation a range of culturally opposite images, whose deep complementarity she reveals: both a person and a thing; both an idealized image of femininity and a fetish exorcising a fear of female otherness; both a body for sale, a prostitute, and a Madonna, with all the implications this image carries; both traded and adored.[25]

Some of these implications deserve to be further explored. As an object and commodity, Rose-Agathe is not just the emblem of a sexual politics of gaze and desire and of the way codified gender roles and individual psychic cathexes relate to political economy and to power relations. Her connection to the marketplace is literal as well as symbolic: as a product displayed in a shop window among other products, "all b[earing] the stamp of the latest Parisian manufacture" (221), Rose-Agathe is an instance of that latest development of capitalist production at the time, advertising. More than that, as an advertisement she is expressly meant to exploit the female body's potential for seduction, playing upon the fetishistic appeal of hair in the contemporary imagination and on the explicit sexual innuendo of her gestures: "each tossed back her head and thrust out her waxen bosom and parted her rosy lips in the most stylish manner conceivable" (221).[26] The attraction this image exerts on the public—"Several persons, passing by, had stopped to admire them" (221); "'it will set the fashion for all Paris'" (234)—bears early witness to the later success of the use of commodified female bodies in advertising.

More importantly, Rose-Agathe is an automaton, a prodigy of modern mechanics. As such, she decisively shifts the issue of the representation of woman from the past to the present. Renaissance paintings and classical statues are replaced by a technological artifact, whose associations no longer pertain to the present age's relation to the past but open out toward the future. Rose-Agathe (if only from the waist upward—but what is missing is meaningful) foreshadows the mechanical woman, "L'Eve Future."

In his *Bodies and Machines*, Mark Seltzer explores the "body-machine complex" in turn-of-the-century American culture, where the tensions between nature and artifice produced by the new technology and market expansion take the form of their overlapping and interference.[27] One of his case studies is a passage from *The American* (1877) where Mademoiselle Nioche is described as "a very curious and ingenious piece of machinery" and equated with a potentially dangerous industrial appliance. The critic reads this "explicit identification of the woman and the machine" as "an extraordinarily condensed and violent registration . . . of the later nineteenth-century conflation of domesticity and consumption, and the reorientation of domestic spaces as market places of consumption" (65). Likewise, Newman's curiosity about the "mechanism" regulating the relation of nature and culture, spontaneous and culturally induced behavior in Claire de Cintré, is viewed as a manifestation of "the uncertainties about the body and its representations, about the natural and cultural body, about 'culturalism' generally, . . . here read through and displaced upon the 'compound' female body" (64–65). In other words, the female body is to Seltzer one of many potential (and potentially interchangeable) materializations of a technology-induced anxiety: "the female body, the racialized body, the working body . . . those more visibly embodied figures that, on the one side, epitomize the tensions between the typical and the individual and between the artifactual and the natural and, on the other, are the figures through which these tensions can be at once recognized and displaced or disavowed" (64).

To my mind, Seltzer's argument, however articulate and stimulating, seriously underrates gender. The identification between woman and machine is constantly present in a variety of contexts and guises (and not just in James's oeuvre). This induces me to posit it as a historically and culturally specific instantiation of a reifying and exorcising representation of woman, whose paradigmatic import overrides the discourse of technology.[28] Andreas Huyssen's reading of the machine-woman in Fritz Lang's film *Metropolis* is in my view more cogent. Taking gender as his starting point, Huyssen points out that the automaton—indifferently a man or a woman in its first eighteenth-century appearance—is increasingly gendered as female as technology, no longer experienced euphorically, is perceived increasingly as a threat and as a source of anxiety in the collective imagination: "as soon as the machine came to be perceived as a demonic, inexplicable threat and as harbinger of chaos and destruction . . . writers began to imagine the *Maschinenmensch* as woman. . . . The fears and perpetual anxieties emanating from ever more powerful machines are recast and reconstructed in terms of the male fear of female sexuality, reflecting, in the Freudian account, the male's castration anxiety."[29]

In the machine-woman, then, the anxiety about technology is expressed through, but also becomes an expression of, man's age-long anxiety about woman's otherness. This takes us back to fundamental symbolic cores of "Rose-Agathe": what surfaces in the love for the mechanical woman is, beneath sexual desire, "the much deeper libidinal desire to create that other, woman, thus depriving it of its otherness" (71). What is at stake, as Huyssen notes, is man's wish for power and domination, equally expressed in his invention and construction of technological tools suitable for serving him and carrying out his projects and in his invention and construction of woman, socially and culturally programmed to mirror his desire and serve him as her master. In the machine-woman's company, "Man is at long last alone and at one with himself" (71).

The best-known literary embodiment of this fantasy is a later and more celebrated text than "Rose-Agathe," *L'Eve Future* by Villiers de l'Isle-Adam (1886), in which the protagonist's disappointment in real women causes him to create a technological one, whose outer surface perfectly reproduces the aesthetics of its real-life model (the only part of woman that deserves to be carefully kept), whereas her words and gestures are provided by her creator and functional to his demands, needs, and desires. Starting from Huyssen's remarks, Francette Pacteau suggestively reads *L'Eve Future* (along with other key texts in James's library such as "Le Chef-d'oeuvre inconnu" and "Der Sandmann," to which I will return in the next chapter) as one of a series of "scenarios of male procreation . . . premised on the exclusion of the reproductive woman"—a technological dream that, like Frenhofer's artistic one, expresses a fantasy of omnipotence and omniscience, a wish for an unadulterated projection of one's subjectivity, and a will to simultaneously eradicate and discipline female sexuality by confining it within the constrictive void of an armor, both radically separate from and totally identified with the maternal body.[30]

As can be seen, "Rose-Agathe" and *L'Eve Future* share the same psychical and ideological dynamics. However, whereas Villiers de l'Isle-Adam invests his protagonist, Thomas Edison, with absolute authority within the diegetic and ideological universe of the novel, thus endorsing and authorizing the macabre and deeply misogynistic fantasy he enunciates and enacts, James deconstructs every position of narrative or ideological authority within

"Rose-Agathe," thus opening the way to a deconstruction of that very fantasy.

Rose-Agathe, the "Madonna of the Future"

One more link is evidenced in the object Rose-Agathe: one that connects woman, fashion, art, and the market, as foreshadowed in "The Madonna of the Future." Even though a shop window is its exhibition case and advertising its function, the waxen puppet is from the first presented as "a triumph of the modeller's art" (221); significantly, it is also more than once compared to a Madonna. While operating along the axis of cultural images of femininity, this comparison enlists Rose-Agathe within that age-long iconographic tradition of which Theobald was a belated follower— the noble art of the past, which the story's narrator, voicing Sanguinetti's opinion, emphatically contrasts with the "modern rubbish" (221) of the present age.

Should Sanguinetti's passion, then, be taken as just one more example of James's replacement of life with art? "The interior", writes Benjamin, "is the retreat of art":

> The collector is a true inmate of the interior. He makes the trans-figuration of things his business. To him falls the Sisyphean task of obliterating the commodity-like character of things through his ownership of them. But he merely confers connoisseur value on them, instead of intrinsic value. The collector dreams that he is not only in a distant or past world but also, at the same time, in a better one, in which, although men are as unprovided with what they need as in the everyday world, things are free of the drudgery of being useful.[31]

And here is the description, worthy of Benjamin's analysis, of San-guinetti's *intérieur*: "His rooms were charming, and lined from ceiling to floor with the 'pretty things' of the occupant—tapestries and bronzes, terra-cotta medallions and precious specimens of porcelain. There were cabinets and tables charged with similar treasures; the place was a perfect little museum" (237).

Shall we read such a domestic museum as an exaltation of aesthetic experience disengaged from its material conditions, or rather as a (self-) critique of the artist à la James? I am unconvinced by the notion of Henry James subscribing to such a rearguard battle to defend the purity of the aesthetic function against the assault of technology and the market at the outset of mass culture. The tales I have examined hitherto, as well as James's treatment of such later characters as Adam Verver, Gilbert Osmond, or the repentant collector Ned Rosier, seem to tell a different story and to show the writer's awareness of the ambiguous nature of aestheticism conceived as an escape *à rebours*.[32] Sanguinetti, it is true, purifies art from the marketplace as Benjamin has it—and his transfiguration of an advertising puppet into an art object belonging to a private collection is in a sense the very emblem of such an operation. But James's story irreverently establishes manifold connections between art and the marketplace: for instance, by ironically stressing the origins of the fortune allowing the collector to "ransom" art objects from the market—his grandfather's business, the plaster statuettes that the Italian "image vendor," like Theobald's rival, successfully commercialized "in the days when those gentlemen might have claimed in America to be the only representatives of a care for the fine arts" (225). Or again by emphasizing the inevitable commodification of art objects in the modern age *even* to Sanguinetti, through repeated mention of the auctions where he gets his treasures. And most of all, inextricably fusing aesthetic and commercial functions in the material object, Rose-Agathe, that once more joins problematically would-be separate or even opposite polarities—both dummy and Madonna, both advertisement belonging to the ever-new world of fashion and art object related to the enduring temporal dimension of art.

A further twist: as is well known, in Benjamin's cultural theory fashion is art's substitute in the modern age; and as Angelika Rauch notes following Benjamin, woman plays the same role in both as the crucial catalyst where historical and ideological dynamics coalesce with visual and psychological ones:

> Fashion uses woman just as art had used her before, as an image surface behind which the body disappears—dies, so to speak. This death is, however, equally the result of the dominance of looking in modernity. Look(ing) compensates for the loss of experience and the debilitation of agency in an industrialized environment. And by extension, fetishism signifies the atrophy of sensuous experience even in the sexual realm, where experience is reduced to scopophilia.[33]

Sanguinetti's Rose-Agathe, then, is no viable metaphor for modern art—but James's possibly is. A prized artifact enclosed in its museum as an object of worship, the agent of a cheap kind of bliss, the former is the metaphor of an art equally incapable of confronting woman's otherness and the weight of history—art reduced to fetish in its alleged purity. The tale, though, also bears witness in its narrative texture to art's capacity for critical self-awareness and to its willingness to become a crossroads for the discourses of its culture. As an overdetermined object welding together some of the major symbolic issues of modernity, Rose-Agathe certainly is a worthy candidate for a "Madonna of the future."

Chapter 4
Woman as Image: "Glasses"

Le langage (des autres) me transforme en image.
—Roland Barthes

"Rose-Agathe" explores women's objectification in a grotesque and slightly surrealistic key, in the guise of a brilliant anecdote. When the same issue is investigated in the modes of realistic and psychological fiction, however, it results in tragedy: this is the case with a later and longer tale such as "Glasses" (1896).[1]

The story was suggested by James's accidental and undramatic meeting with "a very pretty woman in spectacles the other day on the top of an omnibus," as recorded in his *Notebooks* on June 26, 1895.[2] The plot centers on an exceptionally beautiful girl, alone in the world and not very well off, faced with the alternative of either losing her sight or of disfiguring her perfect face with a particularly ugly and cumbersome pair of glasses. Flora Saunt (another floral name) refuses to wear glasses until it is too late and tries to conceal her infirmity so as not to jeopardize her prospective marriage to rich Lord Iffield. After the latter discovers the secret and forsakes her, Flora—by now totally blind—agrees to marry her faithful but ugly suitor Geoffrey Dawling, whom she had formerly rejected and who will take care of her from now on.

Narcissists and Idolatrists

What we would seem to have here is a specular and complementary pathology to "Rose-Agathe": an extreme case of narcissism—to Freud, "the type of female most frequently met with, which is probably the purest and truest one" whereby woman, reveling in her own beauty, acquires "a

certain self-contentment," which establishes her as her own love object—
"[s]trictly speaking it is only themselves that such women love with an
intensity comparable to that of the man's love for them."[3] This is clearly the
case with Flora from her first appearance in James's *Notebooks*: "A very pretty,
a very beautiful little woman, devoted to her beauty, which she cherishes,
prizing, and rejoicing in it more than in anything on earth" (125). The
text constantly underscores Flora's solipsistic self-sufficiency through the
remarks of the other characters—prominent among these, the nameless
narrator, a portrait painter: "Her beauty was as yet all the world to her, a
world she had plenty to do to live in" (529).

Beauty is to Flora the very essence of her identity—" 'her idolatry of
her beauty, the feeling she is all made up of' " (545). It is the premise of
her every social transaction: an aesthetic object completely identified with
her role, Flora self-consciously offers herself as such—"she was a beauty
of the great conscious, public, responsible order" (526–27)—automatically
positioning others as spectators (one would almost say, paying spectators)
of her self-display: "Was this by reason . . . of a subtle acknowledgment that
she contrived to make of the rights, on the part of others, that such beauty
as hers created?" (527). This situation is outlined from the first in one of a
number of memorable tableaux:

> [S]he was at the far end of the cliff, the point at which it overhangs
> the pretty view of Sandgate and Hythe. Her back however was turned
> to this attraction; it rested with the aid of her elbows, thrust slightly
> behind her so that her scanty little shoulders were raised toward her
> ears, on the high rail that inclosed the down. Two gentlemen stood
> before her whose faces we couldn't see but who even as observed from
> the rear were visibly absorbed in the charming figure-piece submitted
> to them. (531)

Like Stevens's jar, Flora polarizes the surrounding space by her mere
presence; occupying the foreground of the scene, she reduces a celebrated
view to the rank of mere pictorial background that nobody—she least
of all—any longer cares to look at. She is both protagonist and director
of a mise en scène of herself as spectacularized object, both officiant
and cult object in the idolatrous worship of her own beauty. And to
this narcissistic self-sufficiency played out in the aesthetic sphere, Flora
sacrifices all actual self-sufficiency in practical life: " 'Those wonderful eyes
are good for nothing but to roll about like sugar-balls—which they greatly
resemble—in a child's mouth. She can't use them . . . not to read or write,

not to do any sort of work. She never opens a book, and her maid writes her notes'" (530).

Flora's blindness, then, is perceived in the story as a result of her own choice, the logical consequence of an identity consistently embraced and stubbornly defended to the end. Paradoxically, it is "the best thing for her happiness": "The question was now only of her beauty and her being seen and marvelled at: with Dawling to do for her everything in life her activity was limited to that. Such an activity was all within her scope: it asked nothing of her that she couldn't splendidly give" (569).

In the story, blindness is both punishment and prize—both the extreme fulfillment of Flora's self-image and the tragic penalty for an aberrant behavior. In the text it is the iconic equivalent of a false conscience, the literalization of the character's incapacity to look beyond the boundaries of her own self, the metaphor of the excess inherent in her sterile self-contemplation. Indeed, Flora's attitude is madness, and as such it is condemned unanimously by all other characters: "'What, at any rate, if she does look queer? She must be mad not to accept that alternative.' 'She *is* mad,' said Geoffrey Dawling" (547). But though this be madness, it must be acknowledged that there is method in it. Flora's attitude is nothing but an extreme instance and a reductio ad absurdum of the cult of feminine beauty, which is, in fact, the shared value of the whole diegetic world—and notably of men, however apt to condemn such excesses they may seem to be.

I am using "value," here, first and foremost in its economic sense, as marketable value. Beauty is the only valuable asset for an "English gentlewoman" (527) like Flora. As a bourgeois Victorian woman, Flora is radically impaired, not just by her blindness, but by her lack of emancipation, that is, by her socially sanctioned incapacity to live from her own work, which makes the investment on the marriage market her only social and economic opportunity. Once again, Flora's pathology is an extreme version of the physiology of the social order, where the safeguard of one's beauty may be a matter less of personal vanity than of economic survival. Significantly, this feature is crucial to the story from its conception, as witness the *Notebooks*, where James tentatively experiments with plots and situations, finally getting hold of the economic factor as the most promising (and, one might add, most culturally representative) motive: "She must have been a married woman—separated from her husband. Or she may marry—THIS IS BETTER—a rich man from whom she keeps the secret of her infirmity. May it not be *in order* to catch him, nail him, that she so keeps it? She is in dread of losing him if she lets him know how she may be afflicted and disqualified in the future" (126).

Significantly, Flora's economic situation is carefully described in the tale: she is an orphan, she has a small and dwindling fortune inherited from her parents, and she has a "pecuniary arrangement" with a family of parasites, who officially accompany her for the sake of propriety (the inevitable duenna preserving the respectability of the unmarried "English gentlewoman"), while in fact they "had their hands half the time in her pocket":

> She had to pay for everything, down to her share of the wine-bills and the horses' fodder, down to Bertie Hammond Synge's fare in the "Underground" when he went to the City for her. She had been left with just money enough to turn her head; and it hadn't even been put in trust, nothing prudent or proper had been done with it. She could spend her capital, and at the rate she was going, expensive, extravagant and with a swarm of parasites to help, it certainly wouldn't last very long (529).

Flora's decision to prize beauty more than sight, then, can be seen as a speculation ("'she has been speculating on her impunity'" [554]) and a calculation ("in our young lady's calculations the lowest numbers were now Italian counts" [563])—that is, as a hazardous but necessary financial investment: "her precious reasoning was that her money would last as long as she should need it, that a magnificent marriage would crown her charms before she should be really pinched. She had a sum put by for a liberal outfit; meanwhile the proper use of the rest was to decorate her for the approaches to the altar, keep her afloat in the society in which she would most naturally meet her match" (539).

As a shrewd manager, Flora even experiments with some later techniques of mass communication, using an exhibition of the narrator's portraits of her as a form of self-advertisement and the exhibition catalog as an opportunity for a very specialized kind of mail trade. The advertising campaign is an effective one, as witness Dawling's falling in love from a distance: "A letter from him had expressed to me some days before his regret on learning that my 'splendid portrait' of Miss Flora Louisa Saunt, whose full name figured by her own wish in the catalogue of the exhibition of the Academy, had found a purchaser before the close of the private view" (535). The narrator repeatedly emphasizes the transitive quality of the portrait, thus confirming what Flora's insistence to appear in the catalog with her "full name" had suggested—that the object for sale in the exhibition is not the painting but its original: "He [Dawling] was like the innocent reader for whom the story is 'really true' and the author a negligible quantity. He had come to me only because he wanted to purchase, and I remember being so amused at his attitude . . . that I asked him why, for the sort of enjoyment he desired, it wouldn't be more to the point to deal directly with the lady" (536).

Flora's adoption of overt business strategies betrays the presence of an economic rationale behind her narcissistic madness—a rationale that the occurrence of commercial metaphors elsewhere in the text confirms. Of Lord Iffield, for instance, it is said that on discovering Flora's secret "he had conducted himself like any other jockeyed customer—he had returned the animal as unsound" (562). Such a brutal simile, laying bare the nature of the barter underlying the broken marriage transaction, recalls the fundamental law of supply and demand regulating all market economies. Be it regarded as cynicism, shallowness, or despair, the use of one's beauty as a marketable commodity would be unnecessary if there were no demand for that commodity on the market. Women's beauty only becomes a valuable asset inasmuch as it possesses an ideological value for men.

The extreme personification of this ideological assessment of beauty in the story is not so much brutal and practical Lord Iffield as sensitive and generous Geoffrey Dawling. The faithful, undaunted suitor, and later kind and considerate husband, starts his career in the story as worshiper of a purely iconic, impersonal image of beauty, like Sanguinetti in "Rose-Agathe": "[H]e . . . had on the mere evidence of my picture taken, as he said, a tremendous fancy to her face. . . . He had fallen in love with a painted sign and seemed content just to dream of what it stood for. He was the young prince in the legend or the comedy who loses his heart to the miniature of the outland princess" (536).

The counterpart of feminine narcissism is, once more, men's fetishism. The object of man's desire is not woman as an actual individual but her representation—that which *stands for*, that is, *substitutes for her*. In Dawling's eyes, Flora and her portrait are one: "I ought doubtless to have been humiliated by the simplicity of his judgment of it, a judgment for which the rendering was lost in the subject, quite leaving out the element of art. He was like the innocent reader for whom the story is 'really true'" (536). For this reason Dawling's love overcomes his awareness of Flora's shortcomings and even takes her dishonesty for granted—"He was a lover who could tacitly grant the proposition that there was no limit to the deceit his loved one was ready to practise: it made so remarkably little difference"

(550)—and for this reason his "passionate pity" is "ever so little qualified by a sense of the girl's fatuity and folly" (550). The object of Dawling's love is not a real woman but a symbol, the iconic emblem of a Platonic idea of beauty. A "painted sign," Flora is to him literally an idol—and idolatry is by definition uncritical and unconditional.[4]

It is hardly surprising, therefore, that an apparently incongruous simile appears when Dawling heroically declares his readiness to accept even a bespectacled Flora: " 'I would take her with leather blinders, like a shying mare!' cried Geoffrey Dawling" (547). Such a dissonant image marks the deep congruence between Iffield's crude rejection and Dawling's warm-hearted acceptance of Flora: for both, their love object is less than human— it is a marketable commodity that can be taken or left, purchased or sold, like a mare or a painting. Iffield, it is true, is described as a jockeyed customer at a livestock market; but Dawling, to be sure, has *already* purchased Flora—in effigy:

> He was of course bewildered by my sketches [of Flora] . . . but for one of them, a comparative failure, he ended by conceiving a preference so arbitrary and so lively that, taking no second look at the others, he expressed the wish to possess it and fell into the extremity of confusion over the question of the price. I simplified that problem, and he went off without having asked me a direct question about Miss Saunt, yet with his acquisition under his arm. His delicacy was such that he evidently considered his rights to be limited; he had acquired none at all in regard to the original of the picture. (536)

The narrator's emphasis on Dawling's "delicacy" underscores the un-spoken assumption underlying the transaction: that is, the symbolic in-terchangeability between woman and portrait. To Dawling, Flora *is* her portrait—so much so that, as will be seen, when the woman rejoins the portrait in his possession, she becomes herself dehumanized into an abstract representation of quintessential beauty rather than the other way round.

If Flora's besetting sin is an "idolatry of beauty," she is certainly not the only sinner: "She *adores* her beauty, and it has other adorers," as James laconically stated in the *Notebooks* (126). All characters at one point or another figure as "worshipper[s] at the shrine of beauty" (535), like Dawling; and a recurrent religious imagery presents "divinely conceited" (529) Flora first as a Greek goddess equipped with Cupid's bow, then as a Christ figure "playing her light over Jews and Gentiles" (529), and later—when she has to wear spectacles—as an old bigot and as a Magdalene (an appellation commonly used as a euphemism for prostitutes at the time): " '[s]he went into goggles as repentant Magdalens go into the Catholic Church' " (561).[5] The cult of beauty is a shared cult in the story, as established as an institutional religion, foreshadowing the subsequent debate on feminine beauty as "New Religion" in the magazines and guidebooks of the early twentieth century.[6]

Women's beauty is here presented as an aesthetic, ideological, and economic value all at once. But *whose* value? Within this system, woman only *represents* value; she does not establish it. "Glasses" is one more version of Luce Irigaray's "marché des femmes": "*A commodity—a woman—is divided into two irreconcilable 'bodies'*: her 'natural' body and her socially valued, exchangeable body, which is a particularly mimetic expression of masculine values".[7] And if women's beauty represents and circulates *masculine values,* Flora Saunt's narcissism needs to be reexamined and reassessed.[8]

The Gaze of the Other

"Each woman, lost in her reflection, rules over space and time, alone, supreme. . . . At once priestess and idol, the narcissist soars haloed with glory through the eternal realm, and below the clouds creatures kneel in adoration; she is God wrapped in self-contemplation."[9] Simone de Beauvoir's description of the narcissist woman's triumph in *The Second Sex* bears a striking resemblance to James's representation of it in this story. It is of course a false triumph, as de Beauvoir lucidly shows, a response to a confining existential situation:[10]

> The reality of man is in the houses he builds, the forests he clears, the maladies he cures; but woman, not being able to fulfill herself through projects and objectives, is forced to find her reality in the immanence of her person . . . It is because they are nothing that many women sullenly confine their interests merely to their egos and inflate them so greatly as to confound them with Everything. . . . Ineffective, isolated, woman can neither find her place nor take her own measure; she gives herself supreme importance because no object of importance is accessible to her.
>
> If she can thus offer *herself* to her own desires, it is because she has felt herself an object since childhood. Her education has prompted her to identify herself with her own body, puberty has revealed this body as being passive and desirable. (630)

Simone de Beauvoir's existentialist reading clearly outlines the context for this pattern of feminine subjectivity, entirely contained in the *en soi* of her own body, a historical determinant lived out as an intrapsychic constraint. Positioned as an object with respect to both the exercise of power and symbolic exchange, woman *experiences herself* as an object and thereby becomes herself an instrument of male domination: her alienation is twofold, since—as Sandra Lee Bartky effectively puts it—"[t]he beings we are to be are mere bodily beings; nor can we control the shape and nature these bodies are to take."[11] Apart from the material advantages they can offer in a given historical situation, the pleasures of narcissism are "repressive" pleasures; they do not liberate the subject but increase her dependence on false needs, that is, needs whose satisfaction benefits, not the subject, but the social order that controls and produces those very needs.[12]

Identifying with one's body or with part of one's body as a beautiful object means seeing oneself from the outside with another's eyes, interiorizing the other's gaze. This phenomenon is to Lacan constitutive of subjecthood, as marking the transition from primary narcissism (the child's, bound to disappear with the child's entrance into the social world) to secondary narcissism, which takes place when a self-image is established as an introjected ego ideal. Through this secondary introjection, as Jacqueline Rose explains, "the image returns to the subject invested with those new properties which, after the 'admonitions of others,' and the 'awakening of his own critical judgment' are necessary for the subject to be able to retain its narcissism while shifting its 'perspective.'"[13] The Other plays a decisive role in the creation of the ideal image. The locus of secondary narcissism, as Lacan illustrated in his well-known experiment of the inverted vase, is a virtual image—that is, not the real image the vase produces in the mirror, but the reflection that image produces in a second mirror placed in front of the first one. The introjection of the image of an ego ideal (the basis for the future formation of the superego, regulating the subject's subsequent identifications) is "invariably accompanied by the speech of the Other," while the gaze of the Other constitutes the subject in the scopic field: "in the scopic field, the look is outside, I am looked at, that is to say, I am a picture. It is this function which lies at the heart of the subject's institution in the visible. What fundamentally determines me in the visible is the look which is outside."[14]

In the construction of women's subjecthood, this visual dynamic takes on gender implications: since woman has no access to the symbolic order, the gaze she internalizes is a male one: "In contemporary patriarchal culture, a panoptical male connoisseur resides within the consciousness of most women: They stand perpetually before his gaze and under his judgment. Woman lives her body as seen by another, by an anonymous patriarchal Other."[15]

Between the two extremes of individual pathology, on one hand, and universal psychic development, on the other, women's narcissism is a cultural, historical, and gender-specific phenomenon: women's simultaneously constitutive and alienating interiorization of the discourse of the Other—those "masculine values" according to which she is defined and assessed and according to which she defines and assesses her own self, as "Glasses" shows:

> "What *she* says is that she'll put on anything in nature when she's married, but that she must get married first. . . . Then and then only she'll be safe. How will any one ever look at her if she makes herself a fright? How could she ever have got engaged if she had made herself a fright from the first? It's no use to insist that with her beauty she can never *be* a fright. . . . 'My face is all I have—and *such* a face! I knew from the first I could do anything with it. But I needed it all—I need it still, every exquisite inch of it. It isn't as if I had a figure or anything else. Oh, if God had only given me a figure too, I don't say! Yes, with a figure, a really good one, like Fanny Floyd-Taylor's, who's hideous, I'd have risked plain glasses. *Que voulez-vous?* No one is perfect.'" (554)

This self-assessment, both dreadful and pathetic (incidentally, one of the very few lines directly spoken by Flora in the text), is exemplary of Flora's interiorization of the male gaze: "how will any one ever look at her" is a vital issue to her, not just for financial reasons, but in psychological and existential terms.[16] Her self is so identified with the notion of "being looked at" that she accepts her own reduction to a single fetishistic fragment as natural: "'My face is all I have.'" James's choice of the face here is far from meaningless. The face is the fetishistic image par excellence: to the potential for fetishistic "phallicization" (that is, for exorcising castration anxiety) it shares with all other decontextualized woman fragments, it adds a number of other connotations. As a part of the body inaccessible to the subject's gaze, it is an emblem of subjectivity as revealed to others; as the mother's face, the first mirror image in the child's identification process, it is to Lacan the quintessential lost object; as a Medusa mask, it acquires in Freud's theory threatening symbolic connections to the female genitalia; as a bright surface, it is to Bataille a receptacle of beauty whose function is to draw men's gaze away from the animal nature of sex; and for all of the above reasons, today it is enlarged to giant size and made into a favorite image in cinema, photography, and advertising.[17]

In spite of its being presented as Flora's self-absorbed gaze upon herself—"The only moral she saw in anything was that of her incomparable countenance" (540)—narcissism conveys, in fact, the all-important gaze of the Other. This is repeatedly suggested in the text through its play on the polysemy of the word "glasses" and on all images associated to glass. Glass objects normally used for looking are constantly reversed into objects for *being looked at*: glass panes and shopwindows display Flora to the beholders' gaze rather than being looked through or looked at by her; spectacles and opera glasses function less as optical instruments for Flora than as filters through which she is seen by others. Significantly enough, of all possible "glasses" mentioned at one point or another in the text, the only kind consistently and conspicuously missing is the one most obviously associated with narcissistic self-contemplation, the looking glass. The woman with the looking glass was a veritable topos both in literature (a single example: Zola's Nana) and in the visual arts of the age.[18] In discarding this traditional iconographic portrayal of woman in terms of self-sufficient self-contemplation, even while dealing with a narrative version of feminine narcissism, James evidences his intention to distance himself from the conventional representation of narcissism and to attempt a critical analysis of its cultural and suprapersonal implications.

The gaze of the Other with its paradoxical effects—both objectifying and grounding subjectivity—is ever present in this story; indeed, it is marked by a spectacular excess. Flora's being-looked-at is dramatic and magnificent: "people who had followed her into railway-carriages; guards and porters even who had literally stuck there; others who had spoken to her in shops and hung about her house-door; cabmen, upon her honour, in London, who, to gaze their fill at her, had found excuses to thrust their petrifaction through the very glasses of four-wheelers" (538). But she is not the only woman character to whom a visual lexicon is applied: of the girl who had rejected Dawling before Flora, for instance, we learn that "no one had looked at her since and no one would ever look at her again" (540).

In other words, Flora Saunt is an extreme instance of women's identity as "to-be-looked-at-ness," in Laura Mulvey's effective definition.[19] Consequently, her blindness too has implications that go beyond her individual case—the diegetic punishment for her folly and the metaphor for her false conscience in becoming a willing accomplice of her own reification.

A complex and polysemic metaphor when framed in the context of the construction of the gaze in the tale, blindness becomes another extreme representation of a sexual politics of looking.

Femininity = beauty = being looked at: this is the unseverable nexus epitomized by narcissism as a cultural phenomenon. The tale explodes its implications by pushing these assumptions to their ultimate consequences. One way in which it does so is by expanding the semantic import of the notion of looking through an obsessive use of visual lexicon in a variety of figurative senses (a recurrent stylistic feature in James, all the more meaningful here in that it is connected to the thematic and symbolic core of the text). The visual is thus made to appear coextensive with the intellectual, the communicative, and the existential dimension—"my mother, who had not much left in life but the quiet look from under the hood of her chair . . ." (532)—a semantic shift that makes Flora's blindness a form of virtual death.

Another textual move might be described as an exploration of the implications of an unspoken syllogism, the hidden rationale of the diegetic world: if woman = beautiful, then not beautiful = not woman; if woman = being looked at, then looking = not woman. This textual function is performed by a character who is Flora's real antithesis in the story: Mrs. Meldrum, "the heartiest, the keenest, the ugliest of women, the least apologetic, the least morbid in her misfortune" (525). Her misfortune, as we immediately learn, "consisted mainly of a big red face, indescribably out of drawing, from which she glared at you through gold-rimmed aids to vision, optic circles of such diameter and so frequently displaced that some one had vividly spoken of her as flattening her nose against the glass of her spectacles" (525–26).

Despite her intelligence and generosity, which all characters acknowledge, Mrs. Meldrum's ugliness makes her grotesque: the otherwise polite narrator deals with her as with an old pal—a liberty he would never take with Flora; the notion that she might be an object of love is systematically discarded; her possible unrequited love for Dawling is discussed lightly, as if it could not be taken seriously; she is so consistently denied as a possible object of desire, that, as critics have noted, readers are apt to picture her to themselves as an old woman, in spite of the narrator's explicit statement that she is much younger than his own mother.[20] In other words, Mrs. Meldrum is a nonwoman: to further deny her femininity, she is constantly accompanied by military imagery. In the spectrum of possible feminine identities, Mrs. Meldrum and Flora represent two opposite extremes: like the pair of sisters in fairy tales, one is ugly and wise, the other is foolish and beautiful. Still, the difference between Mrs. Meldrum's "big red face" and Flora Saunt's perfect countenance would seem to be very flimsy indeed in view of the fact that they immediately become indistinguishable to the narrator once Flora has taken to wearing glasses. Glasses are the main token of Mrs. Meldrum's identity, just as their absence is the main token of Flora's.

Glasses are referred to by an amazing variety of synonyms and periphrases in this tale—"aids to vision," "optic circles," "spectacles," "goggles," "eye-glasses," "pince-nez," "nippers," "glasses," "her great vitreous badge," "those things of Mrs. Meldrum's," "what you wear"—as well as spectacular, hyperbolic metaphors: they become in turn shopwindows against which one can flatten one's nose, melon-frames, cell bars, ship rigging, a muzzle, a mask, a cage, and an ecclesial shelter to a repentant Magdalene. Such an unusual emphasis reveals that they are not just crucial to the plot of the story, but as optical instruments for looking, they lie at the core of a symbolic conflict whose stake is the power of the gaze as connected with gender roles.[21]

Looking—that is, positing oneself as an active subject vis-à-vis the world—amounts to abdicating one's identity as woman: Mrs. Meldrum's glasses, tied as they are to her ugliness, deny her femininity even while they affirm her subjecthood; they deny her the role of an object of desire to others and deny her, in particular, the self-contemplative introversion that is typical of narcissism: "Blessed conveniences they were, in their hideous, honest strength—they showed the good lady everything in the world but her own queerness" (526).[22] Likewise, when Flora is wearing glasses she undergoes a metamorphosis that does not just alter her features but takes over her whole person and lends her a new, dehumanized identity:

> All I saw at first was the big gold bar crossing each of her lenses, over which something convex and grotesque, like the eyes of a large insect, something that now represented her whole personality, seemed, as out of the orifice of a prison, to strain forward and press. The face had shrunk away: it looked smaller, appeared even to look plain; it was at all events, so far as the effect on a spectator was concerned, wholly sacrificed to this huge apparatus of sight. (557)

The "deep grey eyes" that shortsightedly "brushed with a kind of wing-like grace every object they encountered" (526) are now staring at her companion—"She stood solemnly fixing me with her goggles" (557)—who is thereby placed in a position of inferiority: "I felt . . . as if she were watching my nervousness with a sort of sinister irony" (558).[23] This is the first time Flora has positioned herself as subject of the gaze (as well as of speech: significantly, this is where most of Flora's direct speech in the text is concentrated). At that very moment, though, she has ceased to exist as an object to be looked at—"I had been keeping my eyes away from her" (558), "she was so changed that one hated to see it" (563)—indeed, she has ceased to exist at all: "Flora plain and obscure and soundless was no Flora at all" (558).

In their hyperbolic and monstrous connotations, pointing to their symbolic import, glasses function as a metaphor for the incompatibility between looking and being looked at; they are the divide that keeps apart two distinct and irreconcilable notions of identity. If being a woman is tantamount to being looked at, being a woman also implies giving up looking, that is, positing oneself as subject. Woman = not looking: this is the last proposition that completes the syllogism acted out in the story as well as the deep symbolic logic requiring Flora's blindness. Again, Flora's infirmity is the pathological intensification of an allocation of visual roles along the lines of gender, inherent in the physiology of patriarchal culture.

This is the rationale underlying Flora's final apotheosis. In annihilating the intentional, directional, and reciprocal quality of the gaze, blindness is the perfect accomplishment of woman's role. The passive receptacle of the gaze of her spectators, she is now relieved from all function but the exhibition of her beauty to the ecstatic admiration of the beholders in that most appropriate setting, a theater:

> The question was now only of her beauty and her being seen and marvelled at: with Dawling to do for her everything in life her activity was limited to that. Such an activity was all within her scope: it asked nothing of her that she couldn't splendidly give.... Yes, Flora was settled for life—nothing could hurt her further.... For herself above all she was fixed forever, rescued from all change and ransomed from all doubt. Her old certainties, her old vanities were justified and sanctified. (569)

The internalized gaze of the Other is by now the only possible gaze, a reduction that is both penance and perfection: "in the darkness that had closed upon her one object remained clear. That object, as unfading as a mosaic mask, was fortunately the loveliest she could possibly look upon" (569). Transfigured into a pure aesthetic object, Flora has become another Rose-Agathe, whom art has rescued from the slavery of commerce. Whereas she had formerly been described, in a scene tellingly set in a department store, as an object on sale among other objects—"an exhibitability that held its own even against the most plausible pinkness of the most developed dolls" (543)—Flora has now acquired the priceless, timeless fixity of a Byzantine mosaic in "Sailing to Byzantium." But whereas Rose-Agathe became humanized by acquiring a fake gaze, what we are faced with here is a real woman reduced to an animated puppet, whose "glass" is no longer an instrument of vision but a stage prop feigning "the parody of a look" (569). Her motions belong to a state-of-the-art mechanical doll that sightlessly reiterates graceful but meaningless gestures: "Flora after a while again lifted the glass from the ledge of the box and elegantly swept the house with it. Then, by the mere instinct of her grace, a motion but half conscious, she inclined her head into the void with the sketch of a salute, producing, I could see, a perfect imitation of a response to some homage" (569).

Condemnation and Complicity

The final scene of "Glasses" is, to my mind, both memorable and infuriating as an extreme representation of woman's "narcissistic self-sufficiency," pushed to its ultimate reifying and alienating consequences, metaphorized at its most impairing, and reduced ad absurdum. Of course, this does not apply to the inner logic of the story, where the final scene figures as the triumphant if pathetic achievement of Flora's career—the exalted, meaningful moment that retrospectively illuminates her life as forcefully as God's grace might have illuminated a saint: "Her old certainties, her old vanities were justified and sanctified" (569).

The disturbing, perverse quality of blind Flora's glorification and sanctification, however, induces me to interrogate the inner logic, not just of her *story*, as I have done so far, but of the *telling* of her story, that is, of its representation. Consequently, I now will shift my focus to the narrator in his twofold role as character in the story and producer of the tale.

As a character, the narrator would seem to be a secondary one, a mere witness and observer. Still, his seeming detachment from the Flora-Iffield-Dawling triangle is no more than the usual deceptive appearance that James's nameless narrators cultivate: even if we choose to give no credit to his casual, ironic suggestion that he too may be one of Flora's rejected suitors—a fact that would make his whole tale appear in a light of spite and retaliation—the detached witness is still indisputably an actor in the drama.[24] He is the one who finds out about Flora's secret and by abstaining from interfering allows Lord Iffield to find her out in his turn. He tries to dissuade Dawling from loving Flora; and Dawling is the first to cast a doubt on his claims for disinterestedness and impartiality, denouncing the narrator's interference when he relates the scene in the toy store: " 'It's the girl's own affair.' 'Then why did you tell me your story?' I was a trifle embarrassed. 'To warn you off,' I returned smiling" (550).[25]

One salient aspect of the narrator's relation to Flora is undoubtedly the intellectual one: like the protagonist of *The Sacred Fount*, whom he in some ways foreshadows, he is playing a detective game, whose stake is the discovery of Flora's "secret" (a recurrent word, along with an amazing inventory of terms belonging to the same semantic field: "mystery," "deceit," "disguise," "conceal," "subterfuge," "clandestine," "surreptitiously," "dissimulation"). Like many morally ambiguous Jamesian narrators, he combines, in Peter Brooks's words, epistemophilia and scopophilia: through his gaze, knowledge becomes equivalent with a voyeuristic intrusion into another's privacy, and "spectatorship is made complicit with a violation of intimate space."[26] This is nowhere more evident than in two crucial scenes of "Glasses," the scene at the theater, which I have already examined, and the one in the department store in section 6; in both, Flora's privacy within a public space is violated by the narrator's gaze, the vehicle of a will to knowledge and disclosure. The dialectic of public vs. private is particularly apparent in the scene at the theater, where Flora is tellingly described as belonging to the category "lonely loveliness in public places" (565) and the narrator positions himself as the super-spectator of an object who is already "the aim of fifty tentative glasses" (564–65), while the box where Flora is sitting alone is explicitly connoted as private. The narrator's intrusion is physical as well as visual: "I dropped into a chair just behind her and, having . . . noted that one of the curtains of the box would make the demonstration sufficiently private, bent my lips over [her hand] and impressed them on its finger tips. . . . [A]ll the privacy in the world couldn't have sufficed to mitigate the start with which she greeted this free application of my moustache . . ." (566–67).

The same dynamics prevail in the scene at the department store, in which Flora's furtive attitude conveys the idea of privacy, and the narrator observes both Flora's surreptitious maneuvering to watch a toy with the help of a pair of glasses and Lord Iffield's perception of it and violent intervention, which leaves Flora "blushing, glaring, exposed, with a pair of big black-rimmed eye-glasses, defacing her by their position, crookedly astride of her beautiful nose" (544). The narrator's curiosity here explicitly gets the upper hand on every other impulse:

I felt at that instant the strangest of all impulses: if it could have operated more rapidly it would have caused me to dash between them in some such manner as to give Flora a warning. In fact as it was I think I could have done this in time had I not been checked by a curiosity stronger still than my impulse. There were three seconds during which I saw the young man and yet let him come on. Didn't I make the quick calculation that if he didn't catch what Flora was doing I too might perhaps not catch it? (544)

And his voyeurism is coupled with an intellectual taste for hypotheses and interpretations, as it will be in *The Sacred Fount*: "I had thought it all out; my idea explained many things.... I hesitated to let him hear as yet all that my reflections had suggested. I was indeed privately astonished at their ingenuity" (546).

The second and more important characteristic of the narrator's relation to Flora is the aesthetic aspect. The narrator's constant denunciation of Flora's "idolatry of her beauty" as well as his ironic stance vis-à-vis Dawling's naive worship of it should not make us forget that he is the professional representative and hence the true minister of that cult in the diegetic world.[27] As a painter, he produces and circulates—both in the economic and in the ideological sense—the eidola, the images/idols. His studio is a "shrine of beauty" (535), the "tabernacle" (537) for Flora's face; when she is humbled and made ugly by her spectacles, the narrator plays the parson to her old church-going woman.

The intellectual aspect of the narrator's relation to Flora reifies her as a mystery to unveil; the aesthetic one reifies her as an art object. In the painter's eyes, Flora exists so that she may be transmuted into an image. "This was a little person whom I would have made a high bid for a good chance to paint" (526), he comments at their first meeting, thus immediately envisaging her, in a striking combination of aestheticism and economic imagery, as both painted image and auctioned lot. A professional regarding pictorial value, the narrator, while blaming Flora for her desperate defense of a "purely superficial charm" (553), systematically reduces her to that very surface, extolling her purity of line and plasticity of form as explicitly disassociated and inconsistent with all other aspects of her personality. A comparison of his attitude toward Flora with that toward Dawling is revealing. In portraying the former, he resorts to a purely decorative, superficial pictorialism; her beauty is mere exteriority, whose reproduction requires no depth, no search for an inner life: "by the time I had mastered her profile and could almost with my eyes shut do it in a single line I was decidedly tired of her perfection. There grew to be something silly in its eternal smoothness" (537). Soulless, superficial Flora is bound to become unrepresentable once she has lost her beauty: "I had studied her face for a particular beauty; I had lived with that beauty and reproduced it; but I knew what belonged to my trade well enough to be sure it was gone for ever" (563). Dawling's ugliness, on the other hand, is a very different source of inspiration: "My relation to poor Dawling's want of modelling was simple enough. I was really digging in that sandy desert for the buried treasure of his soul" (542–43). This aesthetic double standard translates a more general law of man-woman relations: whereas all characters agree that Flora could not marry advantageously if she lost her beauty, all unanimously condemn her for her incapacity to go beyond appearances and appreciate Dawling's good qualities in spite of his ugliness. Dawling's ugliness and awkwardness, though, are repeatedly underscored in the text, thus throwing the double standard into relief. The rule of gender is once again emphasized: beauty is all-important to women—and to women only.

While revealing his involvement in the ideological assessment of beauty as coextensive with femininity (the logic by which Mrs. Meldrum is unsexed), the narrator's aesthetic relation to Flora points to his complicity in her reduction to a fetishistic fragment. From her very first appearance, she appears to him, not as a woman, but as beauty personified as a face—a face that, through the successive stages of a spectacularly baroque metaphor, becomes completely autonomous, severed from the person to whom it belongs:

> In the course of a walk with [Mrs. Meldrum] the day after my arrival I found myself grabbing her arm with sudden and undue familiarity. I had been struck by *the beauty of a face that approached us* and I was still more affected when I saw *the face*, at the sight of my companion, *open like a window thrown wide. A smile fluttered out of it as brightly as a drapery dropped from a sill—a drapery shaken there in the sun by a young lady* flanked with two young men who, as we drew nearer, rushed up to Mrs. Meldrum. (526, my emphasis)

The rest of her person can be remorselessly ignored: "The figure from the neck down was meagre, the stature insignificant" (526): the portrait painter's professional eye anticipates Flora's later self-assessment. Already Flora's reduction to her face is an accomplished fact: an obsessive lexical presence in the text, "face" (enlarged, at most, to include the "head") is not so much a synecdoche epitomizing the protagonist as it is a decontextualized fragment excluding all the rest of her person, discarded into the trash can of parceled womanhood.[28]

As usual, the narrator's "rhetoric of iconoclasm," while denouncing the irrational power of the idol and distancing himself from its cult "by assuming that the power of the image is felt by somebody *else*," betrays his deep complicity with the system he denounces: he is as much of a fetishist as Dawling, even though his fetish is not a "painted sign," but a disembodied and dehumanized human face, reified as an abstract emblem of beauty.[29] Not only do the intellectual game and the aesthetic approach converge in reifying their object; they also spring from the same source, as Laura Mulvey points out:

> Ultimately, the meaning of woman is sexual difference, the visually ascertainable absence of the penis. . . . Thus the woman as icon, displayed for the gaze and enjoyment of men, the active controllers of the look, always threatens to evoke the anxiety it originally signified. The male unconscious has two avenues of escape from this castration anxiety: preoccupation with the re-enactment of the original trauma (investigating the woman, demystifying her mystery) . . . ; or else complete disavowal of castration by the substitution of a fetish object or turning the represented figure itself into a fetish so that it becomes reassuring rather than dangerous . . . This second avenue, fetishistic scopophilia, builds up the physical beauty of the object, transforming it into something satisfying in itself. The first avenue, voyeurism, on the contrary, has associations with sadism: pleasure lies in ascertaining guilt (immediately associated with castration), asserting control and subjugating the guilty person through punishment or forgiveness.[30]

What we are finally faced with is a coherent strategy of repression of female sexuality, involving both Mrs. Meldrum's masculinization and Flora's reduction to either an icon of beauty or the keeper of a guilty secret. Another important feature in this strategy is the narrator's constant upholding of filial love and his reverence for his often cited mother. An important third woman in the story (indeed, the first to appear on stage), she is the only known object of the narrator's affections as well as possibly his earliest feminine ideal.[31] She is another synecdochic image of womanhood—"there was one dear chair, creeping to its last full stop, by the side of which I always walked" (525)—but one that is desexualized by her age and maternal role. She is presented by way of bodily details ("caressing her stiff hand, smiling up into her cold face" [532]), but these details pertain to the mortuary rather than to the erotic paradigm; she is neither enterprising nor threatening, but reassuring and needing care. Should it be regarded as quite accidental that a tale sealed by the image of a blind young woman is opened by the figure of an old invalid in her wheelchair?

Telling a Portrait: Art and Pornography

If Flora's narcissism, as I have argued, is her interiorization of the gaze of the Other and of culturally valued representations of femininity, the nameless but far from impersonal narrator is the true bearer of that gaze and representative of that ideology. One might even surmise that he is the real Narcissus in the tale, following a Romantic tradition of the artist's narcissism ranging from Rousseau's *Narcisse* to Schlegel's *Lucinde*. Whereas after her ecstatic self-contemplation Flora is forced to know herself and to "die" of the knowledge ("I had . . . left poor Flora for dead" [565]), the narrator, like Ovid's Narcissus (bound to live a long life "si se non noverit," "if he shall himself not know") seems destined to thrive forever, since he never seems to recognize his specularity with Flora, the mirror of his own notion of beauty and his own desire.[32]

So far I have examined the narrator as character and his interaction with Flora within the diegetic world. I will now examine his specific function as fictive narrator of the tale, instrumental to the production and circulation of its ideological significance. Indeed, a major feature in the ideological framework of the tale is the mutual positioning of two narratively and culturally dissymmetrical polarities: the male narrator, posited as subject and endowed with the authority of interpreting, judging, and relating— with the power of representation; and the female character, posited as object, subjected to other people's evaluation and interpretation (most of the story is made up of other people's comments on her), and virtually voiceless (although the tale is based on dialogue, only a few lines are spoken by her in direct speech). The former holds the narrative point of view; the latter is both textually and literally sightless.

Indeed, in focusing my attention on the narrator's ideological production of the tale, I am doing no more than following a lead offered by the narrator himself. "He was like the innocent reader for whom the story is 'really true' and the author a negligible quantity" (536), he ironically comments on Dawling's naive identification of the portrait with the person being portrayed, regardless of the artistic medium. I read this as a metafictional caveat for would-be "innocent readers" and as an invitation to concentrate on narrative mediation—that is, on the narrator's representational strategies and on the author's own.

The narrator's representational strategies are all deeply consistent with the motifs examined so far. Prominent among them is Flora's metaphorical animalization, which most of the time is linked to the narrator's verbal activity.[33] Images such as those the narrator applies to Flora wearing spectacles— "something convex and grotesque, like the eyes of a large insect" (557); "She was as quiet as a mouse" (559)—evidence his deep linguistic and ideological complicity with the values circulating in the narrated world.

A subtler and more meaningful strategy might be termed "flattening." The narrator's verbal portrayal of Flora, like a bidimensional portrait on canvas, refuses to take on depth.[34] Both as a painter portraying Flora as a perfect but blank surface and as a storyteller, the narrator systematically flattens his subject, excluding all ethic and human implications from the story and insisting on intellectual coherence, completeness of reconstruction (hence the constant emphasis on the question of the reliability of memory), and stylized formal rendering. This is nowhere more evident than in the metaphor opening the tale: "Yes indeed, I say to myself, pen in hand, I can keep hold of the thread and let it lead me back to the first impression. The little story is all there, I can touch it from point to point; for the thread, as I call it, is a row of coloured beads on a string. None of the beads are missing—at least I think they're not: that's exactly what I shall amuse myself with finding out" (525).

The beads on a string, while prefiguring Flora's pearls in the last scene— her reward for blindness—are a suitable metalinguistic description of the structure of the tale, which does not aim at architectural effect and subordination of the individual parts to an overall interpretive design or at in-depth psychological investigation, but points to a purely compositional logic, based on the ranging and combination of individual elements, a logic reinforced in sentence construction by recurring modular phrastic structures and in narrative arrangement by the juxtaposition of individual scenes in succession. Both techniques, it should be noted, are far from frequent in James and hence all the more indicative of a deliberate stylistic decision; and both contribute to voiding the anecdote of any deep or disturbing implication. Indeed, the whole story is presented as diverting and entertaining—"what I shall amuse myself with finding out"—providing opportunities for self-satisfied intellectual exercise and even for sensual enjoyment, as shown in the second occurrence of the same image: "I have spoken of these reminiscences as a row of coloured beads, and I confess that as I continue to straighten out my chaplet I am rather proud of the comparison. The beads are all there, as I said—they slip along the string in their small, smooth roundness"(555).

Another decisive representational strategy is the convergence between narrative language and the language of visual arts. In the narrator's eyes, Flora exists as *already* part of an artistic representation: a "charming figure-piece" (531), a still silhouette in a series of tableaux vivants, a character in a theatrical *pièce* (where, however, Dawling rather than she is featured as "the interesting figure in the piece" [541]).[35] The climax of this strategy is, of course, the last scene, where a perfect convergence of the verbal and the pictorial is effected by means of Flora's transmutation into her own portrait, which the narrator admiringly describes in a sort of paradoxical ekphrasis: "The expression of the eyes was a bit of pastel put in by a master's thumb; the whole head, stamped with a sort of showy suffering, had gained a fineness from what she had passed through" (569).

The narrator's triumph here is the narrator's defeat. He is defeated as a painter, reduced from active creator to passive beholder of images, and forced to acknowledge his failure: "the annoyance of having happened to think of the idiotic way I had tried to paint her. . . . I hadn't touched her, I was professionally humiliated . . ." (566). But he triumphs as a storyteller: whereas his portraits of Flora have never been described, his verbal portrayal of her is graphic and vibrating. Flora's portrait is finally achieved, and it does justice at last to her celebrated beauty. This perfect act of representation, however, can take place when the gap between image and object has been bridged, not by the perfect adherence of the image to its object, but by the reverse, by the object's conforming to its own representation. Flora's perfect portrait is no portrait: it is Flora herself.

The narrator's verbal portrait of Flora is not just the narrative fulfillment of a decadent project for a totalizing art form (explicitly evoked by the mention of Wagner's *Lohengrin*, staged in the background and providing both the soundtrack for the theater scene and another opportunity for the narrator to confirm his respective ranking of the human and the aesthetic: "the music was supreme, Wagner passed first" [568]). The overlapping of the verbal and the visual definitively congeals Flora in a synchronic and two-dimensional image, lacking either depth or a margin for development and change: the end of a coherent process, it seals the crystallization of woman into an art object.

While fulfilling the narrative logic of the tale, the last scene of "Glasses" openly displays the deep cultural logic that the tale itself obeys. The same logic is also manifested, as W. J. T. Mitchell points out, in the trope employed:

> [T]he treatment of the ekphrastic image as a female Other is a commonplace in the genre. One might argue, in fact, that female Otherness is an overdetermined feature in a genre that tends to describe an object of visual pleasure and fascination from a masculine perspective. Since visual representations are generally marked as feminine (passive, silent, beautiful) in contrast to the masculine poetic voice, the metaphor goes both ways: the woman is "pretty as a picture," but the picture is also as pretty as a woman.[36]

A figure of the overcoming of Otherness, the final ekphrasis translates in terms of representational technique the voyeuristic arrangement of man-woman relations and all its implications ranging from the dissymmetry of the gaze to the punitive control of woman's difference. Such implications are almost stereotypical in connection with the artist in Western culture, where from the beginning, as Lynda Nead reminds us, "the practice of applying paint to canvas has been charged with sexual connotations": the artist—a male, active, productive subject—is "a man whose sexuality is channeled through his brush" (or in this case another tool, just as traditional, since the first line of the tale presents the narrator "pen in hand"); the sexual element, therefore, however apparently absent in the representation, is displaced "through the metaphorical language of connoisseurship."[37]

This is exactly what feminist analysis identifies as the pornographic structure of representation: "not the presence of a variable quality of 'sex,' but the systematic objectification of women in the interest of the exclusive subjectification of men," in Susanne Kappeler's classic definition, which sees pornography in this wide sense as a crucial structure in all art and literature.[38] This view is also shared by Peter Brooks, who links the violation of private and especially bodily space in modern visual arts to the original alliance of pornography and the novel.[39]

This association might seem gratuitous enough with reference to "Glasses" were it not for a peculiar feature evidenced in the narrator's representation of Flora that provides a specific link to the world of pornography: Flora's *pleasure*. This element is repeatedly underscored in the final scene much more explicitly than any perception of its tragic implications and in terms directly alluding to the erotic sphere: "her excitement broke into audible joy," "she . . . gleefully cried," "It gave them almost equal pleasure," "a gratified passion" (567–68). According to the rationale of this representation, Flora's final apotheosis is not just in her being reified, but in her *desire* to be reified and in her *pleasure* in being reified. This is represented as her supreme fulfillment, just as in traditional pornographic representation the woman's pretense of pleasure is of strategic importance as evidence of her collusion with her own objectification, reinforcing the notion that she has no desire of her own and is not an end to herself but an instrument to satisfy man's desire. Flora's pleasure is the extra feature that completes the representation of her narcissism as contingent and individual perversion and misleads the reader into forgetting that "the bizarre may stand as a confirmation of the normal," and the perverse is nothing but an intensification of the ordinary.[40]

While providing a further perspective that links vision, gender, and representation, Flora's pleasure is also the most explicit index to the narrator's ideological manipulation. His insistence on Flora's pleasure and fulfillment ignores the subjective costs of her infirmity, dilutes tragedy by reducing it to pathos, and subverts the tragic catastrophe into "the best thing for her happiness," thus reproducing in his storytelling the same censorship that Flora's blindness undergoes within the diegetic world:

> I recognised that this was as near as I should ever come, certainly as I should come that night, to pressing on her misfortune. Neither of us would name it more than we were doing then, and Flora would never name it at all. Little by little I perceived that what had occurred was, strange as it might appear, the best thing for her happiness. . . . [Dawling] would exist henceforth for the sole purpose of rendering unnecessary, or rather impossible, any reference even on her own part to his wife's infirmity. Oh yes, how little desire he would ever give *me* to refer to it! (569–70)[41]

The tragic import of this denouement is literally silenced, made unspeakable, and excluded from representation. Flora's glory originates in this suppression: purified from agency and conflict, her blindness becomes the inevitable fulfillment of a destiny.[42] As such, it forecloses analysis and investigation, supersedes individual responsibilities, and works a smooth transition from the individual to the universal, leaving out the social and the historical. The last image of Flora that the narrator bequeaths us possesses the same polished self-evidence and falsifying effectiveness as Roland Barthes's myth:

> Myth does not deny things, on the contrary, its function is to talk about

them; simply, it purifies them, it makes them innocent, it gives them a natural and eternal justification, it gives them a clarity which is not that of explanation but that of a statement of fact . . . In passing from history to nature, myth acts economically: it abolishes the complexity of human acts, it gives them the simplicity of essences, it does away with all dialectics, with any going back beyond what is immediately visible, it organizes a world which is without contradictions because it is without depth, a world wide open and wallowing in the evident, it establishes blissful clarity: things appear to mean something by themselves.[43]

Telling Tales

Meaning, however, does not accrue to things of its own accord. The textual resources of *mise en abyme* suggest as much, laying bare the ideological operation producing representation and offering the reader new and different positions from which the tale can be perceived and interpreted. The questioning of representation in the text is effected through several devices. I have already examined the narrator's metalinguistic allusions to his own recollections, stage directing, and compositional decisions, which foreground his narrative and ideological mediation, thus opening the way to its possible deconstruction. Another important way of undermining the mimetic neutrality of representation is intertextuality. "Glasses" is, among other things, a sustained interrogation of both the traditional and the contemporary imagination as well as, to some extent, a "coded" text that invites its readers to reconstruct the logic underlying its deviations from and convergences with its intertexts.

As might be expected, the scene at the theater is once again the main catalyst of allusions and citations. Many allusions are to the field of visual arts, thus adding to the interplay between the verbal and the visual that provides one of the richest *mises en abyme* in "Glasses." The situation in the final scene is a verbal rendering of a veritable topos of Impressionist painting, of which Renoir's *La Loge* (1874) is possibly the most famous example: a woman at the opera, looking through opera glasses or keeping them in her hands. While playing her social part with the help of useless binoculars, Flora is not just being perceived and described as a painting: in a further metafictional twist, she has been *codified* as a painting. This enhances the spectacularization of her image (a marked effect in Renoir's painting) and reinforces the visual quality of the reader's experience, positioned, like the narrator, as the beholder of the painting; but simultaneously, it denaturalizes the whole scene, tracing back the mutual positioning of woman as spectacle and man as spectator to preexisting artistic and cultural patterns. A striking and precise analogy exists between this Jamesian scene and a specific painting, *At the Opera*, by Mary Cassatt (1879). A woman in black, foregrounded in profile, is watching through her opera glasses in a direction that cuts across the plane of the picture; a man in the background is watching her unseen through his opera glasses, and his position within the picture is symmetrical with the position that the viewer occupies outside the picture.[44] I am citing Cassatt's painting not so much to suggest an actual or possible pictorial source for "Glasses" as to highlight the fact that James's tale, like Cassatt's picture, analyzes and represents the triangular dynamics placing the reader/viewer in simultaneous relation with two figures: a female figure who, even while actively looking (or pretending to do so), is doubly an object for the gaze, both inside and outside the boundaries of representation; and an actively looking male figure, whose positioning offers to the viewer a mirror image *en abyme* of *the viewer's own gaze*, which is thereby distanced and laid open to a denaturalizing recognition.

Apart from its allusions to the figurative arts, the final scene of "Glasses" recalls the most obvious and immediate literary referent of James's tale, Edgar Allan Poe's "The Spectacles" (1844).[45] The two tales share a number of thematic motifs and narrative situations—among them, a scene at the opera. Poe's narrator stares for some time at a fascinating unknown woman in an opera box, who after a while intentionally and intensely returns his glance through her opera glasses. The rest of the tale develops this situation in a comic and grotesque key: the protagonist and narrator, an extremely myopic young man who refuses to wear glasses out of vanity, falls in love with the beautiful stranger, Madame Lalande; he succeeds in winning her love and marries her, even though he has to promise to keep their marriage secret and to start wearing glasses. Putting on his new glasses immediately after the wedding, he discovers that the paragon of beauty he has been wooing is his eighty-two-year-old great-great-grandmother, complete with wrinkles, wig, and false teeth: she had agreed to take part in a practical joke that some of the protagonist's friends organized to convince him of his need for glasses. In the inevitable happy ending, the young man becomes rich Madame Lalande's heir, and he marries the old woman's beautiful young companion.

The coincidences are too numerous and significant to be wholly ac-cidental: James's "Glasses" is in all probability a rewriting of Poe's "The

Spectacles"—a practice to which, as is well known, James frequently re-
sorted. It is, of course, a rewriting in the female gender: indeed, one of the
most striking results of a comparison between the two tales is the realization
that their respective divergences—in plot development, narrative presentation, key, tone, and ending—all descend from the different gendering of
their protagonists. The vanity of Poe's male protagonist is a mere personal
eccentricity, devoid of culturally representative value; given the codified
gender roles in courtship that prescribe an active role for the man, the
protagonist's foible could only bring about a comedy of errors, inevitably
bound to lead to a happy ending. Even though "The Spectacles" plays on
some of Poe's thematic obsessions (ranging from the deceptiveness of senses
to dismemberment of the body), it does so in a comic key because its starting
point, in its improbability, is a comic one. A single change, however, has
a fateful impact. Once the protagonist is gendered as female, the whole
situation becomes culturally representative, socially grounded, perfectly
verisimilar, and consequently liable to be treated within a realistic narrative
code, which in turn brings about a tragic ending. The dialogue between the
two stories once again foregrounds the inexorable logic—literary as well as
cultural—of gender difference.

A powerfully evocative set of similarities links "Glasses" to another
possible source, which critics, to the best of my knowledge, have never
connected either to "Glasses" or to "Rose-Agathe": "Der Sandmann," a
novella belonging to E. T. A. Hoffmann's *Nachtstücke* (1817). Although
James never openly mentioned Hoffmann in his writings (Goethe being
the only German author to whom he ever devoted an essay), he is likely
to have read him: Hoffmann's fantastic tales enjoyed enormous popularity
both in Britain, where they were translated by Carlyle, and in the United
States, where they provided a source of inspiration for Irving and Poe and
where several editions of Hoffmann's tales were published over the years.[46]

Both "Der Sandmann" and "Glasses" share a number of thematic motifs
that trace a common coherent symbolic texture. First and foremost is, of
course, the motif of eyes and glasses, evocatively connecting the different
narrative strains in Hoffmann's tale: the protagonist's anguish as a child
(which Freud, as is well known, reads as castration anxiety in his essay on
the uncanny); Coppelius/Coppola's evil magic plots as alchemic creator
of eyes, Sandman threatening the child's eyes, and peddler of artificial
"eyes"—that is, the glasses he pours on Nathanael's desk and the telescope
he sells him, thus causing him to fall in love with the beautiful neighbor he
watches from a distance; and the magic/mechanical eyes of Olimpia, the

beautiful animated puppet with whom Nathanael falls in love, whose eyes—
disturbing to others in their lifelessness and sightlessness—are perceived by
him as full of meaning and love.[47] Olimpia is also the final object of the
violence that Nathanael anticipated in anguish as a child: in the end, her
empty eye sockets, torn eyes, and dismembered body reveal to Nathanael
her true nature, actualize his terrors, and draw him to madness.

Both tales revolve around an optical device. The telescope in "Der
Sandmann" casts a sinister spell on both the subject and the object of
vision and effects the confusion between automaton and woman: while it
naturalizes the former, endowing it in the distance with the motion and
appearance of a real woman, it denaturalizes the latter, transmuting in the
protagonist's eyes Klara, his angel-like fiancée, into another mechanical
puppet, thus drawing him to an access of final insanity and destruction. In
both tales, man is positioned as active viewer and as voyeur (Nathanael
watching Olimpia from his window), while woman is emblematically
figured as a wax face with a fictitious gaze. Like Rose-Agathe and like the
final avatar of Flora Saunt, Olimpia is the quintessential woman-as-object,
devoid of subjectivity and will, capable of fulfilling her decorative social
function (she can dance and sing), and incapable of self-expression: all she
can utter are meaningless sounds like " 'Ah-Ah!' " and pleasant platitudes
("Good night, my darling"), which her male interlocutor can invest with
meaning according to his desire, deluding himself that his narcissistic self-
mirroring is in fact prompt and complete sympathy on her part and that
her eyes—glittering from the reflection of his telescope—are in fact shining
with love.

In "Glasses" too optical devices perform a sort of evil spell. Flora's
glasses effect her dehumanizing metamorphosis into a huge insect; her
binoculars emphasize in their uselessness the empty, mechanical quality of
her automaton-like gestures. The reader's realization of Flora's blindness
in the last scene of "Glasses," for all its apparent urbanity, is the symbolic
equivalent of the violent climactic scene in Hoffmann's tale, where the doll's
two bloodstained eyes are lying on the floor, and Olimpia's vacant eye-
sockets in her waxen face contradict the implication of humanity inherent
in the mention of blood and reveal her to be an inanimate doll. On both
occasions, sight is a token of humanity, whose loss reduces the former and
returns the latter to the status of object.

What is truly uncanny about both stories, in the last analysis, is exactly
the interchangeability between woman and puppet—a motif Hoffmann's
tale plays out both in the fantastic mode (the interpretative uncertainty

between Nathanael's personal psychic obsession and Coppola's supernatural and demonic intervention) and, through the narrator's voice, in the satirical mode.[48] The "fraudulent introduction of an automaton into human society" was generally reproved, but since Olimpia had successfully attended the "philosophical tea parties" of the best society, the deception had proved very easy: "In order to be absolutely sure that he had not fallen in love with a wooden puppet, more than one lover demanded from his loved one that she sing and dance slightly out of time, that she stitch, knit, or play with her poodle during reading, etc., but most of all that she not limit herself to listening, but speak every now and then in such a way as to imply that she could also feel and think."[49]

Here lies the heart of the paradox: if a real woman must make show of her imperfection in order to prove herself real, then the requirements of perfect womanhood, which Olimpia successfully fulfils, are both inhuman and dehumanizing.[50] The interchangeability between woman and puppet is the underlying assumption of both Olimpia's social success and Flora Saunt's final apotheosis (as well as Rose-Agathe's enthronement as mistress of Sanguinetti's house). Hoffmann's "fraudulent introduction of an automaton into human society" (a phrase equally applicable to his peculiar mixture of realistic and fantastic modes in the story) is reproduced in James's "Rose-Agathe," likewise centering on a literal automaton, and transposed to a metaphorical plane in "Glasses." The plot and the symbolic texture of each story articulate a complex cluster connecting psychic events, gender identities, and visual roles in modern Western culture. All coalesce in that peculiar modern phenomenon, parallel with industrialization: the eroticization of the machine and the development of "an erotics of the human 'other'—the doll."[51] Both "Der Sandmann" and "Rose-Agathe" reestablish the distinction between human and machine in the end. The process, though, is reversed in "Glasses," where human and unhuman finally converge in a single sign, woman. The *unheimliche* no longer results from the fantastic defamiliarization of the ordinary but, quite the opposite, from the realistic familiarization of the extreme and from the defamiliarizing effects this exerts on ordinary social experience within a strictly realistic literary code. The repressed content that bores through layers of censorship and silence and surfaces by way of Flora Saunt's grotesque dehumanization is the outcome, not just of psychic, but of social repression: a well-known, commonplace, ordinary event—and hence, all the more uncanny.

Epilogue 1
Woman as Museum: "Maud-Evelyn"

Published in 1900, "Maud-Evelyn" tells the story of young Marmaduke's increasing involvement in the obsessive cult that an elderly couple, the Dedricks, pay to the memory of their adolescent daughter, Maud-Evelyn, dead for fifteen years.[1] In a literal version of memory's capacity for endurance—"She *is* with them in the sense that they think of nothing else" (188)—the Dedricks create a whole imaginary life for Maud-Evelyn, where time categories overlap in a sort of virtual past-future. Drawn into their fiction, Marmaduke becomes Maud-Evelyn's fiancé, then her husband, and finally her unconsolable widower: through him, the dead girl will have lived, loved, and enjoyed "*all* her young happiness" (201). The backdrop of this fiction is the young couple's home—a domestic museum lovingly filled with exquisite objects, the relics of a nonexistent past. Its spectators are two women: Lavinia, Marmaduke's faithful friend and confidante, to whom he had proposed before meeting the Dedricks and who, while rejecting him, had exacted from him the promise that he would never marry another woman; and Lady Emma, an older lady, their mutual friend and advisor. Lady Emma tells the story to the first, nameless narrator of the tale during a social occasion that provides an opening frame (the embedding is not complete, for the frame is not closed in the end). After a short prologue by the first narrator, however, Lady Emma's words are reported in the first person, so that she is virtually the true narrator of the story. In her turn, though, she mostly reports events as told by Lavinia; and the latter never directly meets the Dedricks or sees their house, her only contact with the story being Marmaduke's confidences. At his death, after many years, she becomes his heir, the owner and keeper of the museum-house with all its treasures.

Just as "The Last of the Valerii" and "The Madonna of the Future" have been read with respect to the international theme, "Maud-Evelyn" has been critically read through its obvious reference to some well-known Jamesian themes that have provided the lines for its interpretation. Leon Edel classified it among the ghost stories, but because of its delicate balance between the fantastic and the psychological, it has also been read as a story of obsession foreshadowing "The Beast in the Jungle." It anticipates the absolute, abstract value of the cult later to be performed in "The Altar of the Dead," but it also provides a sociopsychological representation of necrophilia as a peculiarly Victorian neurosis.[2] Finally, in Tzvetan Todorov's well-known definition, it is the perfect illustration of James's work as the staging of a quest for an absolute and absent cause—in this case, death as the absolute and absent determinant of life.[3]

I will take Todorov's reading—to my mind, the most seductive and semantically effective overall interpretation of James's short fiction to date—as my starting point. As a general interpretation of the stories, Todorov's essay is both fascinating and necessarily generic: in its identification of absence with death in "Maud-Evelyn," it fails to do justice to the very articulate "presence" of absence in the story and consequently to its connection to the central paradigm of my investigation of James's tales.

Absence is indeed a pervading mode in this tale, which is built as a set of Chinese boxes where each narrator undertakes to narrate an event he or she has never witnessed, and narrative attention is focused in turn on different characters, who are each absent from the stage. First comes Lavinia, an "unknown," "obscure," and "lonely . . . personage" (178) in the first narrator's frame. Second, in Lady Emma's storytelling, comes Marmaduke, who becomes an object of interest from the moment communication with him ceases—"his letters stopped, and that naturally was one of our signs" (183)—and whose central role in the conversations between Lady Emma and Lavinia is marked by his absence: "we avoided with much intensity the subject of Marmaduke" (186); "he dropped out of my talks with Lavinia. We were conscious, she and I, of his absence from them; but we clearly felt in each quarter that there are things after all unspeakable" (196). Attention then shifts to Maud-Evelyn, who is of course "absent" by definition—the more so, since no one among those who discuss her has ever met her. Finally, after Maud-Evelyn's "second" death, Marmaduke takes center stage again, ready to die in his turn.

Absence also prevails in the plot in typical Jamesian fashion. Lady Emma (whose interest in Marmaduke, incidentally, springs from the nonrelation created when she refused to marry his father many years before: "I was conscious of a pleasant link with the boy whose stepmother it had been open to me to become" [179]) opens her tale with an unanswered question, referring to the main *nonevent* and pivotal point of the story: "'Then why on earth don't you take him?'" (178)—that is, Lavinia's unexplained rejection of Marmaduke's proposal, despite her apparent love for him. This rejection in turn brings about a negative promise, which, however, is presented and meant as the ultimate form of assertion: "'Well, how can a man say more? . . . I swore to her that I would never marry. Oughtn't that to be enough?'" (180–81).

Another form of absence concerning traditional narrative categories is the lack of effective communication both in the story and in the text. The frequent doubles entendres among characters, which narrative discourse regularly highlights, point to a world where the ungraspable quality of referents translates as impossibility of univocal communication. Examples range from short and harmless occasional misunderstandings to long dialogues entirely revolving around what is unsaid and unexplained, such as Lady Emma's long attempt to understand from Marmaduke's words the precise status of the Dedricks' daughter, without realizing that she is dead:[4]

> "Their daughter?" I had supposed them childless.
> He partly explained. "Unfortunately they've lost her."
> "Lost her?" I required more.
> He hesitated again. "I mean that a great many people would take it that way. But *they* don't—they won't." . . .
> . . . I wondered what she had done: had it been anything very bad? However, it was none of my business, and I only said: "They communicate with her?"
> "Oh, all the while."
> "Then why isn't she with them?"
> Marmaduke thought. "She *is*—now." . . .
> . . . "Then why do you say they've lost her?"
> "Ah," he said, smiling sadly, "*I* should call it that. I, at any rate," he went on, "don't see her."
> Still more I wondered. "They keep her apart?" (185–86)

The ambivalence of discourse in the diegetic world is mirrored in narrative discourse. An unanswered question, concerning the reason and meaning of this shared cult, underlies the tale—a question critics have successfully repressed by that infallible strategy of hermeneutic recuperation, "allegorizing" the absence of motives and answers by transposing them onto a different (metaphorical, metaphysical, metafictional) plane. While the Dedricks' cult of their lost daughter can be accounted for as a manic and obsessive way of elaborating their grief, Marmaduke's attitude is the true mystery and cause for ambiguity in the tale. "Was he altogether silly or was he only altogether mercenary? I felt my choice restricted for the moment to these alternatives" (190), Lady Emma wonders in her perceptive, matter-of-fact way. The question runs throughout the story; although at one point Lady Emma seems to have decided that Marmaduke is mad, the recurring economic imagery manages to balance that hypothesis, keeping the option of interest constantly open. From the beginning—when the Dedricks' bourgeois respectability is described in terms of their being "as safe as the Bank of England" (184)—to the end of the tale, when the waning of Mrs. Dedrick's and then of Marmaduke's vital energy is described as their " 'little sum of passion, as Marmaduke calls it, [being] spent' " (202), Marmaduke's involvement in the cult of Maud-Evelyn is a career of sorts, where spiritual and material motives are perfectly undistinguishable: "He had grown like a person with a position and a history. Rosy and rich-looking, fat, moreover, distinctly fat at last, there was almost in him something of the bland—yet not too bland—young head of an hereditary business. If the Dedricks had been bankers he might have constituted the future of the house" (196).

The only unequivocal feature in Marmaduke is the blankness that precedes the moment when he embraces his "career." When he first appears on stage, "his handsome empty young face" is mentioned, looking "as if, in spite of itself for a little, it really thought"(180). We are also told that "he had, after all, no great things to offer" (180); his only good quality, ever so indefinite, is his being "taking": "I had meanwhile leisure to reflect . . . on what to be taking consisted of. The upshot of my meditations . . . was that it consisted simply of itself. It was a quality implying no others. Marmaduke *had* no others. What indeed was his need of any?" (183).

We are by now familiar with this type of "man without qualities" and are possibly in a better position to read his involvement in the Dedricks' game as related less to grief than to eroticism—that is, as another instance of a recurrent and culturally significant "perversion of desire." Sexual implications are in fact suggested rather directly from the very first time his meeting with the Dedricks is mentioned: " 'Then whom has he picked up?' I asked; but feeling sorry, as soon as I had spoken, to have made Lavinia blush. It was almost as if he had picked up some improper lady, though in this case he wouldn't have told her, and it wouldn't have saved him money" (181). What this tale is staging—behind, beneath, or beside the metaphysical quest or the metatextual allegory—is another peculiar love story, operating through what might be termed a kind of subtractive eroticism. The pattern structuring the triangular relation Marmaduke-Lavinia-Maud-Evelyn is a negative one: a pattern of desexualized possession through nonpossession, befitting Marmaduke's "atrophied, asexual personality," as one critic has defined it, and working according to a principle that Lavinia clearly states: " 'It wasn't that he might have had "me"—that's nothing: it was, at the most, that I might have had *him*. Well, isn't that just what has happened? He's mine from the moment no one else has him. I give up the past, but don't you see what it does for the rest of life? I'm surer than ever that he won't marry' " (195).[5]

Being "nothing" herself, Lavinia—insistently described in terms of mutually excluding couples of opposites—is the appropriate partner for a hollow man like Marmaduke.[6] An epitome of the Victorian woman, she is willing to find her identity and fulfillment in the triumphant selflessness of the "angel in the house": " 'Well,' she replied, 'if they do run after us I'm not likely to suppose it will ever be for me. It will be for *him*, and they may do to me what they like. My pleasure will be—but you'll see.' I already saw—saw at least what she supposed she herself saw: her drawing-room crowded with female fashion and her attitude angelic" (181–82). Her deference to Marmaduke is complete, and so is her submissive acceptance of his decisions and of her own ancillary role: "an acceptance so deep and a patience so strange that they gave me, at the end, even more food for wonderment than the rest of the business" (187). In her heroic practice of angelic self-denial, Lavinia is not the alternative to Maud-Evelyn, as Lady Emma seems to think; rather, she is her inadequate copy, since for all her self-denial, she cannot hope to emulate the perfection of a woman who is *literally nonexistent*. Traditionally read as a tale of absence, "Maud-Evelyn" is, to my mind, first and foremost a tale of *the absence of woman*.

The genesis of "Maud-Evelyn" confirms its link to the thematics of gender representation. In a note of May 7, 1898, James records the "germ" of the tale:

Gualdo's story of the child *retournée*—the acquisition, construction (by portrait, etc.???) of an ANCESTOR, instead of *l'Enfant*. The setting up of some one who must *have lived*: *un vrai mort*. Imagine old couple, liking young man: "You must have married our daughter."

"Your daughter?"

"The one we lost. You were her fiancé or her *mari.*" (169)[7]

He then proceeds to sketch a detailed outline for the tale, which, however, he did not actually write until 1900. "Gualdo's story" (James is probably referring to Italian writer Luigi Gualdo) was taken up again on September 11, 1900, a few months after "Maud-Evelyn" had been published: "a young childless couple come to a painter and ask him to *paint* them a little girl (or a child *quelconque*) whom they can have as their own—since they so want one and can't come by it otherwise" (192).[8] The motif of the dead girl's fiancé, in other words, was from its inception connected with the portrait motif—the portrait of an absent and nonexistent person, that is, the portrait as *substitute* for the portrayed subject.

From woman to portrait, statue, puppet, image, and then nothingness. "Maud-Evelyn" is the consummation of the absence of woman in her representation: it eliminates her physical existence, and it even does away with the material prop of a painted or sculpted image, which still point back to a woman's body, whose shape and existence they mimic. The only concrete token of Maud-Evelyn's bodily existence is a "little photograph" that "represents a young loveliness" (189)—a trace whose appeal "unenlightened" Lady Emma, proof against the satisfactions of the invisible, fails to understand: " 'Is her little photograph his fun?' . . . I had never supposed him to be *that* sort of fool" (189). But the photograph, after all, is itself redundant: in a further turn of the screw to nineteenth-century necrophilia, Maud-Evelyn is an ideal woman, not just because she is dead, but because to Marmaduke she *never* existed.[9] This makes her a pure creature of the mind, as G. A. Santangelo notes in his analysis of consciousness in the story: "The value of Maud-Evelyn is not her having once lived and died, but her actuality in the present. She has been made an object of consciousness by Marmaduke, her identity depending upon the content which Marmaduke and her parents decide to give it. Her existence or non-existence makes no difference, just as her personal qualities are a function of Marmaduke's conscious needs."[10] Maud-Evelyn is the ultimate emblem of femininity as a product of man's mind. A mere imaginary projection, she offers no resistance, sets no limits, and allows of complete, because immaterial, possession.

Woman's absence, though, is compensated by the erection of a museum/mausoleum. Whereas in former instances woman and/or her representation figured as an exquisite object framed in a gallery or collection, here the image of woman has disappeared, and a customized décor has taken its place, simultaneously feigning her presence and signaling her absence: objects, "the few small, cherished relics, . . . the fondest figments and fictions, ingenious imaginary mementoes and tokens, the unexposed make-believes of the sorrow that broods and the passion that clings" building up a "temple of grief and worship"(191) for the Dedricks. To Marmaduke, though, this temple is no mournful trace of a loss; rather, it is the self-complacent fiction of a presence that has never been and of an erotic and emotional possession that is only realized through displacement in the materiality of objects:

> "There are our rooms—the whole set; and I don't believe you ever saw anything more charming, for *her* taste was extraordinary. I'm afraid too that I myself have had much to say to them. . . . And the things——! . . . Oh, selected with a patience that makes them almost priceless. It's really a museum. There was nothing they thought too good for her. . . . All *my* things are there."
>
> I thought a moment. "Your presents?"
>
> "Those I made her. She loved each one, and I remember about each the particular thing she said. Though I do say it," he continued, "none of the others, as a matter of fact, come near mine. I look at them every day, and I assure you I'm not ashamed." Evidently, in short, he had spared nothing, and he talked on and on. He really quite swaggered. (199–200)

Temple, museum, and love nest all at once, Marmaduke's "house," like the collector's *cabinet*, is a place where erotic, aesthetic, and religious dimensions overlap. But here only the paraphernalia of the cult are left: its former object has disappeared, dispensed with altogether. The displacement of woman—both as body and as simulacrum—is by now complete: where she should or might have been, *objects* reign alone.

Epilogue 2
The Memoirs of an Objectified Woman: "Julia Bride"

Introducing Julia Bride

Julia Bride is a young woman belonging to the New York demimonde, who lives with her mother in a "horrible flat . . . so much too far up and too near the East Side" (683).[1] Her main peculiarity is that she is extraordinarily beautiful; her problem is that she has been engaged several times, following in the steps of her mother, also very beautiful, who has been married and divorced more than once. This undermines Julia's respectability and jeopardizes her great opportunity in life—getting married to Basil French, "quiet, cultivated, earnest, public-spirited, brought up in Germany, infinitely travelled, awfully like a high-caste Englishman," as well as possessed of a "notoriously enormous wealth and crushing respectability" (668). Marriage being her "measureless prize" (665), Julia tries to counteract the Frenches' negative prejudice by asking her potential allies to lie for her and put her in a favorable light, but she is disappointed. Mr. Pitman, one of her mother's former husbands, refuses to take the blame for their divorce: instead, he asks Julia to testify in his favor with Mrs. Drack, a rich widow he hopes to marry, who is against divorce and will only accept him if she gets assurance that his divorce was not his fault. Murray Brush—one of Julia's former fiancés, a penniless, fascinating social climber—enthusiastically agrees to deny their former relation in hope of thus getting in touch with Basil French and the exclusive social circle he represents. Even while talking with him, Julia realizes that Brush's interested and tactless interference will definitively alienate French, "incapable of taking her from the hands of such patrons": such awareness, however, while plunging her into despair, only "made her supremely proud of him" (696).

Some New Developments

"Maud-Evelyn" had been the ultimate consummation of a well-rehearsed triangular relation between man, woman, and art object, now dispensing with woman altogether; "Julia Bride" (1908) resumes that relation on new terms and launches it in new directions. New with regard to the plot, since for the first time in this group of tales ("The Sweetheart of M. Briseux" is a partial exception), the story has a female protagonist rather than centering on a man and his passion, which positions the real or artificial woman as an object. And new with regard to narrative technique, since the narrator is no longer a male character and witness, ideologically involved in the dynamics he narrates, as has been the case in most of the stories, but an impersonal extradiegetic narrator, whose disembodied voice is for the first time focused on the female protagonist's mind. This amounts to a complete reversal of both textual strategy and meaning production: the woman's point of view, unvoiced so far and only conveyed indirectly through the text's visual, metaphorical, and metatextual orchestration, takes center stage and becomes the true subject of the tale. Apart from dialogue, the whole plot unravels within Julia's consciousness: her awareness of past events, her perception of the present, her analysis of motives, feelings, and situations, her anticipation of the future make up the story. As a result, narrative condensation is extreme: the whole story is presented in three sections and as many scenes, covering a couple of days in Julia's life and taking place respectively on the steps of the Metropolitan Museum (Basil French waving Julia good-bye in the opening scene), in one of its rooms (Julia's conversation with Mr. Pitman and later with Mrs. Drack), and in a secluded corner of Central Park (Julia's meeting with Murray Brush). The last paragraph, in a flashlike summary, features Julia in the street and then at home, flung on her face in her room.

As if wishing to avenge so many mute protagonists congealed into icons, James offers Julia Bride an interior monologue in the third person, rich with all the nuances of free indirect speech and all the stylistic resources of the major phase: a floating, abstract, and oblique prose, resonant with echoes and thick with markedly physical and visual images; a prose that in its signifying density lends the character an articulate inner experience, where perceptions and feelings, self-analysis and self-deception, lucid reasoning and passionate obnubilation are in constant interplay. This inner experience is in turn shared by the reader, who is both identified with and detached from the character by virtue of the textual play on narrative voice and point of view.

The impact of this reversal of perspective amounts to a retrospective defamiliarization of former textual and diegetic dynamics. Woman, hitherto constantly reified by another's gaze, discourse, and desire, is now represented as a thinking, looking, and desiring subject and as painfully and desperately aware of her own predicament. At her time of disillusion and self-deprecation, Julia Bride is like a later and more self-conscious Flora Saunt: even while she is experiencing them, she can lucidly analyze those social and ideological operations whose effects Flora suffered in complete, tragic identification. For this reason "Julia Bride"—in spite of its being in many ways the story of her defeat—reads as a feminist denunciation echoing the arguments of eighteenth- and nineteenth-century feminism and anticipating our own. For this reason also I will let the text speak for itself as far as possible, highlighting its relevant points and reading it as retrospective comment on and clarification of the common thematic kernels of all previous tales.

Beauty

Women are everywhere in this deplorable state. . . . Taught from their infancy that beauty is woman's sceptre, the mind shapes itself to the body, and roaming round its gilt cage, only seeks to adore its prison.
—Mary Wollstonecraft, *A Vindication of the Rights of Woman*, 1792

She could have worked it out at her leisure, to the last link of the chain, the way their prettiness had set them trap after trap, all along— had foredoomed them to awful ineptitude. When you were as pretty as that you could, by the whole idiotic consensus, be nothing *but* pretty; and when you were nothing "but" pretty you could get into nothing but tight places, out of which you could then scramble by nothing but masses of fibs. And there was no one, all the while, who wasn't eager to egg you on, eager to make you pay to the last cent the price of your beauty. What creature would ever for a moment help you to behave as if something that dragged in its wake a bit less of a lumbering train would, on the whole, have been better for you? (667)

Once again, beauty epitomizes and devours all possible identities for woman. Julia's tone, though, is consciousness-raising: her realization is a radical one in that for the first time it explicitly describes beauty as a social and ideological, rather than fatally destined, phenomenon. One is not born beautiful; one becomes such less by virtue of personal qualities inherent in one's being than through the operation of a historically grounded *doxa*—"the whole idiotic consensus"—and of the socially conditioned behavior it produces:

> [E]very one had thrust upon them, had imposed upon them as by a great cruel conspiracy, their silliest possibilities; fencing them in to these, and so not only shutting them out from others, but mounting guard at the fence, walking round and round outside it to see they didn't escape, and admiring them, talking to them, through the rails, in mere terms of chaff, terms of chucked cakes and apples—as if they had been antelopes or zebras, or even some superior sort of performing, of dancing, bear. (668)

There is no room for idealization or aesthetic self-delusion here: the gilt fence is nothing but a cage, and what lies inside is no statue on its pedestal or icon displayed for worship, but a circus animal, an attraction exhibited at a fair.[2]

The Gaze

Still, beauty—a psychic phenomenon as well as a social one—provides its satisfactions:

> Julia had practised almost to lassitude the art of tracing in the people who looked at her the impression promptly sequent; but it was a singular fact that if, in irritation, in depression, she felt that the lighted eyes of men, stupid at their clearest, had given her pretty well all she should ever care for, she could still gather a freshness from the tribute of her own sex, still care to see her reflexion in the faces of women. Never, probably, never would that sweet be tasteless—with such a straight grim spoon was it mostly administered, and so flavoured and strengthened by the competence of their eyes. Women knew so much best *how* a woman surpassed—how and where and why, with no touch or torment of it lost on them; so that as it produced mainly and primarily the instinct of aversion, the sense of extracting the recognition, of gouging out the homage, was on the whole the highest crown one's felicity could wear. (679)

No less an accomplice than a victim of a perfectly internalized patriarchal machinery, whose every detail she has dutifully mastered—from narcissistic complacency for the admiration of others to rivalry among women—Julia can nevertheless lucidly reflect on those processes of which she herself is an obvious personification: "Julia Bride could, at the point she had reached, positively ask herself this even while lucidly conscious of the inimitable, the triumphant and attested projection, all round her, of her exquisite image" (668). This twofold quality of women's consciousness (recalling de Lauretis's "double vision," which I earlier took as my guideline) has been described in similar terms by twentieth-century feminism: "The gaze of the Other is internalized so that I myself become at once seer and seen, appraiser and the thing appraised. . . . Such a person wants to retain sufficient awareness to enjoy her own finished and perfect thinghood."[3]

The gaze of the beholder is the permanent mirror where Julia can find herself by being reduced to an image: "her reflexion in the faces of women" (679), "unmistakeably the most dazzling image Mrs. Drack had ever beheld" (680), "the glare—what else could it be?—of the vast and magnificent attention of both her auditors, hushed, on their side, in the splendour she emitted" (681). This is not a light of knowledge or transcendence, but rather the glare (recurring throughout the tale) of footlights: a false light, trapping the subject in the specular play of her reflection in another's eye, a reifying identification that ceaselessly reiterates the mise-en-scène of the self as other. Or else, to term it differently, it is the Lacanian logic of "photo-graphy," whose definition exactly describes the visual and psychic dynamics represented in this tale: "What fundamentally determines me in the visible is the look which is outside. It is through the look that I enter into the light, and it is from the look that I receive its effect. From which it emerges that the look is the instrument through which the light is embodied, and through which . . . I am *photo-graphed*."[4]

The Picture

If a man select a picture for himself from among all its exhibited competitors, and bring it to his own house, the picture being passive, he is able to fix it there: while the wife, picked up at a public place, and accustomed to incessant display, will not, it is probable, when brought home stick so quietly to the spot where he fixes her; but will escape to the exhibition-room again, and continue to be displayed at every subsequent exhibition just as if she were not become private property and had never been definitively disposed of.

—Hannah More, *Strictures on the Modern System of Female Education*, 1799

"In the scopic field, the look is outside, I am looked at, that is to say, I am a picture," writes Lacan.[5] If "Maud-Evelyn" tries to eliminate the first term of the equation woman = art object, "Julia Bride" experiments with the opposite path: painters, paintings, and statues are removed from the story as actual diegetic presences. But the picture remains as an abstract cipher of the visual dynamics that Lacan describes—dynamics Julia Bride perfectly carries out in that she consciously experiences herself as an image. In a tale such as this, where events are mostly internalized and scraped clear of the merely anecdotal, the picture figures only as a trope: "it was an extraordinary situation for a girl, this crisis of her fortune, this positive wrong that the flagrancy, what she would have been ready to call the very vulgarity, of her good looks might do her at a moment when it was vital she should hang as straight as a picture on the wall" (666–67).

In an eloquent abatement of idealistic delusions, the picture is no longer a synonym for beauty; indeed, this tale subverts its former exalted connotations. Degraded here from symbol of aesthetic excellence to mere material object, the picture now openly manifests its stillness, its silence, its rigid and passive conformity to pre-established positions—those reifying implications that the protagonists' aesthetic passion had previously kept in the background of representation.

The Museum

A "museum story" in Adeline R. Tintner's definition, "Julia Bride" is for two-thirds of its narrative set in the Metropolitan Museum of New York, which had recently (1902) been enlarged and enriched with its monumental façade and staircase.[6] Indeed, all the stories I have examined so far are "museum stories," if one recalls the Uffizi Gallery in Florence, with its unattainable and crystallized treasures of art; the small provincial museum, a prototype of Adorno's museum as the tomb of art, where the lady in the yellow shawl is buried; the public gallery where Flora Saunt's portraits are displayed like an advertising portfolio; the private collections—small temples, houses, *cabinets*—where women and their simulacra are ranged and exhibited for private consumption. The Metropolitan Museum both continues and varies this coherent sequence: its textual and contextual connotations, as will be seen, make it both structurally homologous to and qualitatively different from all previous museums.

The museum figures here as a meeting point, a mere succession of rooms and galleries, which characters scurry through without a glance at the art objects it exhibits. It is no longer the frame and décor that, from the vantage point of a hegemonic male onlooker, contributes its aesthetic prestige toward transmuting woman into an art object. In Julia Bride's view, its significance has remarkably changed: "She saw the great shining room, with its mockery of art and 'style' and security, all the things she was vainly after, and its few scattered visitors who had left them, Mr. Pitman and herself, in their ample corner, so conveniently at ease" (675).

Paradoxically, the museum has become a place where the aesthetic function is annihilated. The metaphor of woman as painting, as I just argued, is reduced here to its mere reifying materiality; similarly, in Julia's view of the museum the aesthetic is traced back to the economic. Reversing the process whereby beauty is changed into material value on the marketplace, the museum declares a thing of beauty "priceless" and removes it from economic circulation, sheltering it from the vagaries of the marketplace. This is why in Julia's eyes it is a synonym less of aesthetic value than of social and financial security—"all the things she was vainly after." James himself had described the Metropolitan Museum in similar terms in *The American Scene*:

> Acquisition—acquisition if need be on the highest terms—may, dur-ing the years to come, bask here as in a climate it has never before enjoyed. There was money in the air, ever so much money—that was, grossly expressed, the sense of the whole intimation. And the money was to be all for the most exquisite things—for *all* the most exquisite except creation, which was to be off the scene altogether; for art, selection, criticism, for knowledge, piety, taste. The intimation—which was somehow, after all, so pointed—would have been detestable if interests other, and smaller, than these had been in question. The Education, however, was to be exclusively that of the sense of beauty; this defined, romantically, for my evoked drama, the central situation. What left me wondering a little, all the same, was the contradiction involved in one's not thinking of some of its prospective passages as harsh.[7]

The museum in America is a monument to "conspicuous consumption" established as a national institution: originating as it does in purchasing power rather than in cultural tradition, it betrays the marketability of beauty—a dramatic departure from both Theobald's radical idealism and the yearning for eternity of the woman in the yellow shawl. Rather, what stands out is the link connecting such an institution with the commodification of female beauty as exchange value on the marriage market. A word like "mockery" presents Julia's confrontation with the exhibits in the museum as a competition, a fact that has an almost unbearably pathetic impact: like a picture unable to get herself bought, Julia is envious of the "security" of other pictures, safe in the status they have acquired.

The Stock Exchange

The definitive reduction of aesthetic value to economic value—leaving no residue, either in the form of idealistic fictions or of narcissistic self-sufficiency—is sanctioned by the unusual crudity of economic language in the tale. In this world no one scruples to acknowledge his or her interested motives in the most explicit fashion:

> If he was after a future financially assured, even as she herself so frantically was, she wouldn't cast the stone. . . .
>
> [H]e had been looking at her now so pathetically hard. "Julia, she has millions."
>
> Hard, at any rate—whether pathetic or not—was the look she gave him back. "Well, so has—or so *will* have—Basil French. And more of them than Mrs. Drack, I guess," Julia quavered.
>
> "Oh I know what *they've* got!" (674)

Money figures here as a universal signifier (along with another recurrent isotopy revolving around the notion of measuring, the mercantile counterpart and necessary premise of all financial transactions). "Cost," "credit," "interest," "value," "worth," "count," "figure" constantly occur both in the literal and in the figurative sense, thus making up a whole economic lexicon that describes the characters' feelings and relations: sacrifice, "what he was costing her" (674); sincerity, "it took them but three minutes to turn out, on either side, like a pair of pickpockets comparing, under shelter, their day's booty, the treasures of design concealed about their persons" (670–71); satisfaction, "the cost of her action already somehow came back to her with increase" (681); generosity, "he turned on her the large warmth of his charity. It was like a subscription of a half a million" (689). It comes as no surprise, then, that the market value of women's beauty, which had been only suggested in "Glasses," has here become brutally explicit:

> Never had she so exulted as on this ridiculous occasion in the noted items of her beauty. *Le compte y était,* as they used to say in Paris— every one of them, for her immediate employment, was there; and

there was something in it after all. It didn't necessarily, this sum of thumping little figures, imply charm—especially for "refined" people: nobody knew better than Julia that inexpressible charm and quoteable "charms" (quoteable like prices, rates, shares, or whatever, the things they dealt in downtown) are two distinct categories. (682)

Beauty is here capital to be profitably employed according to the logic of financial capitalism—an image that, incidentally, updates the technological imagery linked to the mechanical woman, adjusting it to the most recent developments of capitalism. Or else woman's beauty is a luxury item offered to a particularly demanding class of customers, according to the dictates of incipient consumer society. Julia's anxious search, after all, is nothing but an entrepreneurial strategy—an advertising campaign based on the use of testimonials and aimed at beating competitors like Mrs. Maule's daughters, "kittens—four little spotlessly white ones, among whom she'd give her head that Mr. French should make his pick" (676).

Lies

In such a world as this, where everyone makes use of everyone else (as witness the frequent occurrence of "use" and related terms) and where everybody's right to exploit everybody else is tacitly acknowledged, the one sphere of life subjected to rigid control and censorship is sexual behavior. This is where the arts of reticence, omission, and lying must be practiced:

"But she has every name, every date, as you may say, for my dark 'record'—as of course they all call it: she'll be able to give him, if he brings himself to ask her, every fact in its order. And all the while, don't you see? There's no one to speak *for* me." . . .

"But can't you—lovely as you are, you beautiful thing!—speak for yourself?"

"Do you mean can't I tell the lies? No then, I can't—and I wouldn't if I could. I don't lie myself you know—as it happens; and it could represent to him then about the only thing, the only bad one, I don't do." (676)

This would seem to be a bizarre enough personal ethics, urging others to lie while proudly defending one's right to truthfulness. Where is the rationale underlying this contradiction?

Significantly, the text explicitly states, during Julia Bride's conversation with Murray Brush, that there is no question of Julia's having lost her virginity; Julia is no "fallen woman," and no act that current Victorian morality would condemn as final and irrevocable has taken place. This is not just a concession to the contemporary readers' prudish refusal to identify with a woman guilty of major improprieties, such as could at most be forgiven at death's door. Indeed, I would argue, this is where the semantic and ideological kernel of the tale lies. The texture of lies that Julia tries to weave around herself is not meant to hide a sensational and shameful secret, but the simple fact of her sexuality. This is what her engagements, as well as her mother's marriages, stand for: they are shocking not because they are illicit, but because they point to a manifest and conscious search for pleasure—"the fact of their having so shockingly amused themselves together" (666).[8] Julia openly acknowledges this fact, even though she wavers between claiming and regretting it: " 'I *did*—"lovely as I am"!— have my regular time; I wasn't so hideous that I couldn't!' " (676); " 'To have our reward in this world we've had too sweet a time' " (674).

Women's desire is unacceptable *in itself* unless it is perverted into socially sanctioned forms—search for status and financial security. Herein lies the scandal of Julia's relation to Murray Brush, despite its "technical" innocence: in its being impracticable " 'practically, financially, on the hard worldly basis' " (688) and openly grounded instead in the physical appeal "of his inordinate romantic good looks, those of a gallant genial conqueror . . . involving so glossy a brownness of eye, so manly a crispness of curl, so red-lipped a radiance of smile, so natural a bravery of port" (685)—to which, of course, might be added the pictorial and phallic connotations of his name. This truth Julia can neither avow, since it is socially unacceptable, nor deny, since it is coextensive with her individual identity. Tellingly enough, the hiding of one's past is metaphorized as a need to produce "a cleaner slate" (687): a woman with a history ("history" is another recurring word), Julia is not the tabula rasa that the patriarchal code prescribes, which is personified instead by Mrs. Maule's immaculate but undistinguishable daughters (" 'He could [make his pick among them] with his eyes shut—you can't tell them apart' " [676]). Julia's story is her identity, and the truth of the self cannot be disclaimed: " 'Besides, do you imagine he'd come and ask me?' 'Gad, I wish he would, Julia!' said Mr. Pitman . . . 'Well then I'd tell him!' And she held her head again high" (676).

"The thing that one hides, we are told. But what if, on the contrary, it was what, in a quite particular way, one confesses? Suppose the obligation to conceal it was but another aspect of the duty to confess to it? . . . For us, it is in the confession that truth and sex are joined, through the obligatory and exhaustive expression of an individual secret."⁹ Julia's demand that others lie for her is the counterpart of her own inevitable confession or else of the silencing of women's sexuality in the stories I examine in the next few chapters. An exemplary instance of Foucault's "incitement to discourse," it constitutes its object as par excellence the secret of the self. Woman's sexuality is thus represented as the unspeakable core of her self; and the taboo forbidding its revelation exorcises the threat it poses—that is, the threat of women positing themselves as subjects.

Guilt

> "Don't you seem to take the ground that we were guilty—that *you* were ever guilty—of something we shouldn't have been? What did we ever do that was secret, or underhand, or any way not to be acknowledged? . . . What harm, in the sight of God or man, Julia," he asked in his fine rich way, "did we ever do?"
>
> She gave him back his look, turning pale. "Am I talking of *that*? Am I talking of what *we* know? I'm talking of what others feel—of what they *have* to feel; of what it's just enough for them to know not to be able to get over it, once they do really know it." (688)

The interiorization of the Other as moral standard could hardly be more explicit or complete: it is not an absolute ethical system or an intimately shared principle that is in question here, but the obligation to conform to the judgment of others: " 'It's as if we had but just waked up, mother and I, to such a remarkable prejudice' " (688). What accepting the morals of others involves is disavowing one's past—"It was a queer service Basil was going to have rendered her, this having made everything she had ever done impossible" (682)—and ultimately one's very identity as "the freeborn American girl who might, if she had wished, have got engaged and disengaged not six times but sixty" (689). Julia Bride manages to outline a critique of the social character of beauty as an outer cage created by the categories of others, but she cannot afford to be as critical of the bourgeois morality, revolving around the notion of saving appearances. She is no New Woman ready to fight for her sexual and civil liberties, but someone who, lacking a new and different moral framework, allows the patriarchal definition and assessment of woman to become her own. She is condemned, like Daisy Miller, for transgressions that she had not recognized as such; but unlike Daisy Miller, she never questions the rationale of her judgment and conviction: she is like a Daisy Miller who, instead of challenging Mrs.

Walker, asks Giovanelli to bear witness to her innocence in order to marry Winterbourne.[10] For one moment, it is true, she grasps and denounces the contradiction between individual liberty and social constraint: confronted with Brush's patronizing attitude, she discovers anew her individual rights as "the freeborn American girl." But apart from this one proud moment, her subjection to the morals of others is complete: her financial and existential stake is too high for her to pursue her moment of awareness to its ultimate consequences—unlike Daisy Miller, again, whose status as a rich heiress (possibly, as it turns out, a matter more of disenchanted realism than of romance) allows her to speak for herself and puts her in the position of having nothing to lose—nothing but her life.

Julia Bride is, in other words, a classic instance of what traditional Marxism would define as "false consciousness": being incapable of analyzing the real terms of her subjection and the universal character of her oppression, she blames her predicament on her own faults and on contingent circumstances. Typically enough, she insistently blames her mother—her *alter ego* and accomplice—for the rash behavior of both and for her own trouble: as is well known, the Oedipal conflict between women is the first psychical and social form of male power.

"She spoke as with her head held well up both over the shame and the pride" (671). Apart from the occasional emergence of pride, the dominant logic of Julia's thoughts and decisions is the logic of shame: to Sartre, "in its primary structure shame *before somebody*," "shame *of oneself* before the Other," "judgment on myself as on an object, for it is as an object that I appear to the Other."[11] If female narcissism is the interiorization of the patriarchal gaze, shame is the interiorization of the patriarchal *norm*.[12] Significantly, a judicial paradigm unravels throughout the story, starting from the literal court where her mother's divorces are sanctioned ("Julia had always heard, from far back, so much about the 'Court'" [662]) and leading to the metaphorical tribunal where Julia anticipates being judged— "'do you see me breaking out to him, unprovoked, with four or five what-do-you-call-'ems, the things mother used to have to prove in Court, a set of neat little 'alibis' in a row?'" (676)—knowing that she has nothing to produce in her defense: "she hoped nothing, as it were, from any other *alibi*—the people to drag into court being too many and too scattered" (687). The morality on whose ground Julia convicts herself even before she has undergone any judgment—"the clearness and harshness of judgement, the retrospective disgust, as she might have called it, that had of late grown up in her" (663)—is another, censorious, and judgmental version of the gaze of the Other.

Alienation

Beauty and chastity are both normative abstractions, which equally deny the subject's individual identity. Caught in-between, Julia can only be lost: as Sartre writes, interiorizing the gaze of the Other—that is, abdicating one's point of view and completely identifying with the other's view of oneself— implies experiencing oneself as an *object*. The imagery employed in this tale conveys the increasing self-alienation of Julia's consciousness: she can only perceive her own self in the ecstatic vertigo that the admiration of others produces or else in the unarrestable tidal wave of their instrumentalizing her. Images of flight prevail in the first two sections:

> [S]he had no free attention for them and was only rising and soaring. She was rising to her value, she was soaring *with* it—the value Mr. Pitman almost convulsively imputed to her, the value that consisted for her of being so unmistakeably the most dazzling image Mrs. Drack had ever beheld. . . . It was relevant to do what he wanted—it was relevant to dish herself. She did it now with a kind of passion, to say nothing of her knowing, with it, that every word of it added to her beauty. She gave him away in short, up to the hilt, for any use of her own . . . She measured every beat of her wing, she knew how high she was going and paused only when it was quite vertiginous. Here she hung a moment in the glare of the upper blue; which was but the glare—what else could it be?—of the vast and magnificent attention of both her auditors, hushed, on their side, in the splendour she emitted. (680–81)

In this ambiguous moment of self-transcendence, the narcissistic satisfaction offered by the admiration of others becomes undistinguishable from the moral need to transcend the utilitarianism ("any use of her own") that Julia recognizes as her own, mirrored along with her beauty in the gaze of others. It would be hard to decide whether the protagonist's exaltation is more the result of the ecstatic admiration of her interlocutors or of the satisfaction that comes from fulfilling the requirements of one's ethical conscience. In any case, abstaining from using others for one's purposes means agreeing to become instrumental to their own: "the value Mr. Pitman imputed to her," "to do what he wanted." This mixture of self-transcendence and false consciousness already involves a loss of control on the self: "She had at last to steady herself, and she scarce knew afterwards at what rate or in what way she had still inimitably come down—her own eyes fixed all the while on the very figure of her achievement" (681).

The loss of control undergoes a dizzy acceleration in the last section, and the images of flight are replaced by water images, creating a crescendo of descent, fall, and sinking. While at the end of her conversation with Mr. Pitman and Mrs. Drack, Julia had "floated even to her own sense swanlike away" (682) in her delusive triumph, her resorting to Murray Brush is metaphorically rendered as a "plunge" (684) caused by "the fascination of the abyss" (686). In her insecure position, Julia is like someone who, "feeling herself slip" (686), needs somebody to "make use of the spade with her for the restoration of a bit of a margin just wide enough to perch on till the tide of peril should have ebbed a little" (688). And a tide is the metaphor for her discovery of Brush's designs: "the cold swish of waters already up to her waist and that would soon be up to her chin" (691). In its devastating rush, the tide translates the self's overwhelming discovery of its own complete subjection: "And as she took it all in, as it spread to a flood, with the great lumps and masses of truth it was floating, she knew inevitable submission, not to say submersion, as she had never known it in her life; going down and down before it, not even putting out her hands to resist or cling by the way" (691).

Coherently, when the triumphant conclusion of the previous scene is recalled, its effect is to underscore Julia's present loss of control of her image—that is to say, her loss of her own self:

On her having had a day or two before to meet Mrs. Drack and to rise to her expectation she had seen and felt herself act, had above all admired herself, and had at any rate known what she said, even though losing, at her altitude, any distinctness in the others. . . . At present, however, as everything was for her at first deadened and vague, true to the general effect of sounds and motions in water, she couldn't have said afterwards what words she spoke, what face she showed, what impression she made. (691–92)

Julia's alienation is thus fully achieved. An object in that she is a reified image of beauty, mortifying her wholeness as an individual; an object in that she is an instrument to others rather than an end to herself; an object in that her own perception of herself is filtered through the perception and the categories of the Other, she has now become an object to herself, as she watches herself live from an estranged, distanced point of view: "she had still to see herself condemned to allow him this" (692), "she felt herself do it, she heard herself say" (695), "desperately, fantastically passive" (695). Even her mind is now objectified and estranged, as conveyed in the wonderfully apt image of a mechanical music box—a passive instrument, unable to produce music by itself, and only capable of automatically playing the tunes that others have programmed:

> [H]er consciousness had become, by an extraordinary turn, a music-box in which, its lid well down, the most remarkable tunes were sounding. It played for her ear alone, and the lid, as she might have figured, was her firm plan of holding out till she got home . . . There was something her head had been full of these three or four minutes, the intensest little tune of the music-box, and it had made its way to her lips now; belonging . . . to the two or three sorts of solicitude she might properly express. . . . She would propose it to Mr. French, propose it to Mr. French: that hummed in her ears as she went—after she had really got away; hummed as if she were repeating it over, giving it out to the passers, to the pavement, to the sky, and all as in wide discord with the intense little concert of her music-box. (693–95)

Renunciation

The very last sentence of the text resumes the musical metaphor: "It was a high note, too, of Julia's wonderful composition that, even in the long lonely moan of her conviction of her now certain ruin, all this grim lucidity, the perfect clearance of passion, but made her supremely proud of him" (696). Given the exquisite Jamesian polysemy of "note" and "composition," where the musical and the psychological dimension coalesce, how should we read Julia's final "high note"—as the authentic voice of her inner self or as another tune mechanically played by her music box?

The inherent logic of James's stories, as several critics have noted, is frequently a logic of renunciation, involving defeat in the practical realm experienced as victory in the moral sphere. In a sense, Julia's prospective defeat is a moral achievement, marking her accession to an antieconomic and antiutilitarian attitude that redeems her from the surrounding world— a brand new moral dimension, where values are based on being rather than on having, and even Basil French becomes an emblem less of wealth than of supreme decorum. Such an option had been prefigured already at the outset, when Julia was confronted with a choice between Mr. Pitman's interests and her own:

> Everything else was against her, everything in her dreadful past . . . ; but was that going to be the case too with her own very decency, the fierce little residuum deep within her, for which she was counting, when she came to think, on so little glory or even credit? Was this also going to turn against her and trip her up—just to show she was really, under the touch and the test, as decent as any one; and with no one but herself the wiser for it meanwhile, and no proof to show but that, as a consequence, she should be unmarried to the end? (673)

The inner demand for a morality transcending the horizon of personal interest is here posited as the potential kernel of an identity that the individual can call her own, for it is the only thing about her that escapes the beholders' gaze—which amounts to saying that only renunciation can grant accession to subjecthood.

The only possible ground for constitution of the self, thus, would paradoxically seem to lie in selflessness and self-denial. The only options open for women's identity are negative options, all equally implying self-obliteration: either the denial of one's self through one's reification as object of another's perception or the denial of one's self by repudiation of one's self-interest. I wonder, then, whether the ending of Julia's story should really be taken as a new departure or rather as a symmetric repetition of the conclusion of her talk with Mr. Pitman, where her attempt at self-transcendence ambiguously wavers between yearning for authentic values and narcissistic self-exaltation, true ethical urge and sacrificial ecstasy—the last resource when everything else has failed. Similarly, in the last paragraph, despite her resentment at being used by Brush and his fiancée, Julia anticipates a possible future when "she . . . might even live to take comfort in having done for them what they wanted" (696); while on the other hand, her pride in Basil French, her now unattainable object of desire, is not exempt from the old instinct of self-preservation, conveyed by her bitterness at "missing a connexion, missing the man himself, with power to create such a social appetite," and by the "long lonely moan of her conviction of her now certain ruin" (696). Still accepting as a natural phenomenon her own reduction to an object of transaction—Basil French "as incapable of taking her from the hands of such patrons as of receiving her straight, say, from those of Mrs. Drack" (696)—Julia passionately identifies with the very values that condemn her and deny her the status of a person.

One might surmise, then, that Julia's "high note" is yet another sign of alienation, a supreme moment, not of awareness, but of false consciousness: the tune performed by a conscience that does not truly succeed in playing its own music and remains a mechanical music box to the bitter end.

America

Lies, guilt, alienation, renunciation are not abstract operations of the psyche; they do not take place within an indistinct scenery or else in one of those private and intimate spaces that supposedly qualify them as individual pathologies rather than as cultural dynamics. Quite the reverse: both settings of this tale visibly display a definite historical and geographical identity, and both share features that are uncommon in James's fiction. They are both urban public places, whose strong modern and democratic connotations descend not just generically from their being American but also specifically from the public debate that had accompanied them. Central Park in New York had been planned by Frederick Law Olmsted as a space where the working class would be able to enjoy their Sundays and benefit from the healthy air, the beauty of Nature, and the inspiring vicinity and example of the upper classes.[13] Such socioaesthetic implications were not lost on James, who in *The American Scene* (where, incidentally, he insistently metaphorizes the park as feminine) describes Central Park as "a field for the unhampered revel, the unchecked *essor*, material and moral, of the 'common man' and the common woman" (502–3), pervaded with an "intention of beauty everywhere too insistent" (501). A similar pedagogic function of democratization of aesthetics was initially performed by the great museums, as Tony Bennett recalls in his Foucaultian reading of their establishment and of the debate accompanying it.[14] This function was also clear to James's eyes during his stay in New York: "Education, clearly,—he writes about the Metropolitan Museum—was going to seat herself in these marble halls . . . and issue her instructions without regard to cost" (513).

How do such sociological remarks relate to the life and adventures of Julia Bride? Or rather, what is the significance of the shift from Count Valerio's garden and the European collector's *cabinet* to Central Park and the Metropolitan Museum, two emblematic places of modern American democracy?

When commenting on "Julia Bride," critics have frequently insisted on what James wrote in his preface to volume 18 of the New York Edition about "foreshortening" as his privileged technique in this tale.[15] Since the world of finance characterizing contemporary American life was to him an incomprehensible mystery, James had decided to represent it through foreshortening, thus portraying the world of "downtown" by way of its reverberation on a more familiar "uptown," equally saturated with economic values. Julia Bride, in other words, would be the *means* rather than the subject of representation: an expedient of sorts, a minor object to fall back on, given the impossibility of attaining a larger—and implicitly worthier and weightier—aim. This would, of course, account for the insistent "Americanization" of the setting and circumstances of the tale—a connotation to be interpreted with reference to the author's mimetic intent rather than to the protagonist's story.

I cannot help wondering, though, whether this interpretation is the most fruitful way of reading a tale that so evidently exhibits a woman's name in its title—as if the condition of a woman or the condition of *woman* is not a weighty enough subject for a writer at the acme of his possibilities.[16] The more so, since to read the story this way one has to ignore James's rather explicit irony in the same preface, for instance, when he solemnly endorses the primacy of the "huge organised mystery of the consummately, the supremely applied money-passion" (1275), or when he emphatically deprecates his own ignorance of such mysteries, associating it with his memory of a childhood condition characterized by the "absence . . . of a serious male interest" (1274). Indeed, after thus making his case, James immediately proceeds to upturn this perspective by denouncing the hypertrophy of the economic dimension in American life to the detriment of all other and by revaluing the artist's concentration on "uptown" (that is, on culture and society) as capable of incorporating the economic dimension, in homage to a search for complexity that exclusive concentration on business would inevitably sacrifice. This is, to my mind, what Jamesian "foreshortening" means: it is not a technical device to bypass his ignorance of mightier things through representation of smaller and more accessible ones, but a contestation of the very relevance and rationale of the opposition through what New Historicists would call, in Clifford Geertz's unwittingly Jamesian expression, "thick description." James's way of expressing the same notion is "full-fed statement": "the picture of as many of the conditions as possible made and kept proportionate," "the surface iridescent, even in the short piece, by what is beneath it and what throbs and gleams through" (1278). Foreshortening is James's way to reconcile narrative economy with an awareness that "a human entity, a situation, a relation, an aspect of life, however small, . . . strains ever, as it were, toward the uttermost end or aim of one's meaning or of its own numerous connexions" (1278).

It is no accident, then, that one page earlier James had ironically defined the "international young ladies" as his "appointed thematic doom" and voiced his need to treat them "at an angle and from a quarter by which the peril and discredit of their rash inveteracy might be a bit conjured away" (1277). "Julia Bride" is not James's way of dealing with the unknown through the well known but the reverse, a new way of dealing with an old subject, whose full dignity James claims even while ironically deprecating its compulsive quality. Expressly presented as a "companion-study to 'Daisy Miller'" (1276), "Julia Bride" resumes the same ideological issues and investigates them anew in a deeper and, as it were, more materialist fashion, after what James himself terms "[a] whole passage of intellectual history" (1276). The result is a "full-fed statement" of the condition of women in its full historicity—that is, in its specific time, place, and class (all emphasized as never before) as social product and ideological process.

At this point the implications of the New York scenery begin to make new sense. Compared with previous settings, they convey a sense both of coherence and of an epochal transition, a veritable paradigm shift: from aesthetics to economics, from private to public, from past to present, from aristocratic to democratic. Pointing to a democratization of beauty, both the park and the museum are not just the past and present setting for Julia's vicissitudes but a metaphor for her predicament, highlighting the specularity between the individual and the social processes that constitute her as such. Julia's beauty, so showy and so shared, has the same "public" quality of the "too insistent" beauty of Central Park and is consequently just as incompatible with an elitist form of private fruition. Her anxious desire to cancel the past as the only way to build up a future recalls the demolishing frenzy that James stigmatized in his New York notes as marking America's failure to achieve maturity (a theme possibly echoed in the images of building and architecture pervading the text).[17] Her identity, like American identity in the early twentieth century, is exclusively rooted in money rather than in the accumulation of life experience.

This interpretation might seem to contradict my previous argument and induce us to read "Julia Bride" as an allegory of sorts, representing the United States in the Gilded Age, just as Daisy Miller was an epitome of American innocence at an earlier stage of its history. This is probably to some extent true. Still, this allegory is gendered as female, and as such, it belongs in what is possibly the richest paradigmatic series in James's works.

If "Julia Bride" focuses on the *American woman*, then, it is possibly less to represent *the American as woman* (lacking the power and competence to tackle the "real thing," man) than to represent *woman as an American*, that is to say, women's condition in the first modern democracy in the world.

This condition, we find out, is a paradoxical one. The "freeborn American woman," entitled to life, liberty, and the pursuit of happiness, is subjected— as *woman*—to the norms of a different time and place: the codes of honor and chastity, dictates of aristocratic and European origin unscathed by the American Revolution.[18] The preserver of these aristocratic remnants is significantly called Basil French, a name reverberating with associations to ancien régime monarchy and the Old World; he is described as "awfully like a high-caste Englishman" (668) and connected to images of noble architecture—"the palace of wedlock" with its "grand square forecourt" and its gate opening on "stiff silver hinges" (669)—and highly ritualized movements as in "the gravest of minuets" (669).[19]

In "international" tales such as "Daisy Miller" and many other from all stages of James's career, the clash of cultures provides an opportunity to unveil the relativity of the would-be absolute codes that prescribe women's behavior and define their identity, disclosing the ideological character and oppressive function of such prescriptions. Here the emphasis on the peculiarly American quality of Julia's story explodes the contradiction of woman's identity, simultaneously modeled, on the psychical as well as on the social plane, on two historically and ideologically divergent sets of requirements. The modernizing and democratizing processes under way within American society are as yet unable to grant women the right to subjecthood. The phrase "freeborn American woman" is not an alternative paradigm for female identity; rather, it is an oxymoron of sorts, marking a contradiction that Julia Bride is unable to solve on her own.

PART TWO

The Voice:
Discourses of Silence

Let me define, first, the silence I wish to discuss here. It is not the silence of linguistics, rhetoric, philosophy—silence as the foundation, limit, or margin of language, silence as the ineffable, as absence, as absolute negation.[1] It is not even the silence that Jamesian critics cherish, as an instance of metaphysical void, absence, the unsaid as the concealed core of his work, which words can only skim over. It is not silence as lack of communication or indirection, the most recognizable and recognized feature of James's work, which the critics paraphrase and appraise in several ways: as the poetics of ambiguity, the style of absence, the heritage of symbolism, the void as center and impulse of James's imagination; as the removal and concealment of the social relationships underlying the world he represents or else as the musical space offered to a Lacanian emergence of the unconscious in language.[2]

What interests me here is silence as cultural prescription and permission—in other words, *what* can be said and *who* can say what, who restricts or does not restrict the power to speak in a given culture. As Pierre Bourdieu reminds us, in his classic study of language and power, linguistic exchange is par excellence a symbolic power relation, where the power relations between speakers and groups are enacted.[3]

This silence has strong gender connotations. It relates, on one hand, to the "silencing" of homosexuality ("The love that dare not speak its name," in Lord Alfred Douglas's famous words) into the "epistemology of the closet."[4] On the other hand, it relates to the well-established tradition that prescribes silence for women, from St. Paul to Dr. Johnson and Lacan. Hence, thirty years of feminist criticism have investigated this silence in depth, from Tillie Olsen to Adrienne Rich, from Luce Irigaray to Barbara Johnson, from Deborah Cameron to Sandra Gilbert and Susan Gubar. With Virginia Woolf pointing the way, they have investigated the silence induced by culture, textual silence as omission and repression, silence as a deliberate strategy of oblique representation that protects women's writing from external and internal censorship.[5]

Surprisingly, though, and perhaps because it is so pervasive and so openly linked to the author's poetics, Jamesian silence has never been explicitly connected to the representation of the feminine, even though James is renowned for his female characters.[6] The following chapters address this connection, which appears to me extremely clear in some of the short stories. Again I use as parallel texts James's instances of silence and what feminist criticism has brought to light about the silence of women—literary and otherwise. For me, both varieties of silence intersect on the terrain explored by Foucault's well-known theses in the first volume of his incomplete *History of Sexuality*.

La volonté de savoir—the original title, which translates as "the will to knowledge," is much more telling than the title of its English version, plainly called *An Introduction*—has offered to gender studies of the last few years its most trenchant conceptual tools: the redefinition of sexuality as a category defined, not by natural, but by cultural constructs, the critique of the so called "repressive hypothesis," the study of the production of sexuality through the "incitement to discourse," that is, through the proliferation of regulatory and prescriptive discourses that deal with it.[7]

I will not dwell on these concepts, which have a wide circulation among critics. What interests me here is to draw attention to the crucial connection that Foucault's analysis established—especially fruitful in relation to the short stories under study—between expression and repression. The cipher of sexuality is not silence, prohibition, or censorship; rather, it is a sort of highly regulated *obligation to speak*. Sexuality is thus placed at the center of the paradoxical double activity of concealment-disclosure, which Foucault describes with extraordinary synthesis: "[w]hat this actually entailed . . . was using these tenuous pleasures as a prop, constituting them as secrets (that is, forcing them into hiding so as to make possible their discovery)" (42).

A central place in this connection is occupied by the dynamics of the "aveu," that is, both avowal and confession: the ritual, codified since the Middle Ages, in which truths are produced. The avowal works as a process of individuation, one so crucial in the constitution of the subject in Western culture "that we no longer perceive it as the effect of a power that constrains us; on the contrary, it seems to us that truth, lodged in our most secret nature, 'demands' only to surface" (60). It is through confession, as we have already seen in "Julia Bride," that the realm of sexuality is constituted as the domain of subjectivity and personal truth:

> The thing that one hides, we are told. But what if, on the contrary, it was what, in a quite particular way, one confesses? Suppose the obligation to conceal it was but another aspect of the duty to confess to it . . . ? What if sex in our society, on a scale of several centuries, was something that was placed within an unrelenting system of confession? . . . For us, it is in the confession that truth and sex are joined, through the obligatory and exhaustive expression of an individual secret. (61)[8]

A power structure underlies this ritual of discourse: confession is predicated not just on the self-awareness of the self, which guarantees the constitution of subjectivity, but also on the presence of the other, not a mere interlocutor, but "the authority who requires the confession, prescribes and appreciates it, and intervenes in order to judge, punish, forgive, console, and reconcile" (61–62). The relation of power, therefore, is asymmetrical: power is held, not by the speaker (as is the case in many other linguistic transactions), but by the person who questions, listens, and does not speak. It is not a question of acquiring some knowledge, since the person who hears the confession already possesses that knowledge; rather it is a question of self-revelation, which acknowledges implicitly both the authority of the listener and the paradigm of truth that motivates and supports the confession.

The dynamics of what Foucault terms "l'inavouable-avoué," that is, "what [is] unmentionable but admitted to nonetheless" (64), played out in several keys, are central to the short stories I examine in the following pages.[9] By connecting Foucault's analysis with and moving it onto the specific terrain of feminine sexuality, these stories explore the codes that produce and regulate it in Victorian culture and constitute it as a "secret" in Foucault's sense, that is, as a minutely codified prohibition, an omnipresent and potentially subversive "unsaid."[10] If sexuality, then, is the "inavouable-avoué" locus of the truth of the subject, where subjectivity is constituted (and becomes subjected), the "confession" of women's sexuality is an ambivalent act: it entraps women under the net of patriarchal power and its codes but, at the same time, constitutes them as subjects, thus rescuing them from the reifying economy of men's gaze.

In the context of feminine sexuality and subjectivity, silence too appears under a different light once it is connected to the "aveu," which is its implicit or explicit correlative. The repressive injunction of the "aveu," which subjects women to highly codified speech acts, is now reversed into a self-aware evasion of the power structure underlying the confession and even into a paradoxical retaliation, where the relations of power are turned upside down by the refusal to verbalize and share a knowledge that is thereby transformed into a "secret."[11]

Chapter 5
Of Shame and Horror:
"A London Life"
and the
Theatricals of Femininity

The Story and Its Contexts

The theme of the "inavouable-avoué" supplies a common ground for two short stories prompted by James's conversation with Paul Bourget, reported in the *Notebooks* under the date of June 20, 1887.[1] Aggrieved by the suspicion that her mother may have several lovers, a well-to-do girl wants to distance herself from the situation. Unable to envisage a solution other than marriage, she tries to induce a potential suitor into declaring his love. His surprise reveals to her that her assumptions were wrong; overwhelmed by shame and convinced she has no way out, the young girl kills herself.

In the same *Notebooks* entry, James immediately develops Bourget's suggestion into what will later become the plot of "A London Life." Once more he exploits the international framework by placing the story in London and by transforming the mother and daughter (a mother committing adultery under her daughter's eyes, James writes, would be unacceptable to the American public) into two American sisters: the elder, more beautiful, extroverted, and frivolous, is married to a British gentleman and has a lover, about whom there is no mystery. The younger sister, serious and naive, is a guest at her sister's home; she is also her dependent after their father's bankruptcy and their parents' death. James outlines in detail the psychological drama he develops in the story and adds the character of an older confidante, absent from Bourget's tale. The plot adheres to the original anecdote except for the suicide, which James replaces with the younger sister's making her escape and returning to America.

"A London Life" thus becomes a novelette, over 120 pages long, published by *Scribner's Magazine* the following year.[2] The events are narrated in the third person by a heterodiegetic narrator and filtered most of the time through the point of view of Laura Wing, the younger sister and protagonist. The thirteen sections of the story faithfully follow the original plan by presenting the situation through Laura's meditations and her dialogues with Lady Davenant, the elder gentlewoman who comforts and supports her, employing irony and disenchantment to put Laura's apprehensions into proper perspective. Laura's brother-in-law, Lionel Berrington, is the typical representative of an aristocracy that is superficial, frivolous, and fashionable rather than truly evil. Selina, the elder sister, is very able at dissimulating and makes the most of Laura's admiration for her. Mr. Wendover, the American traveler who is a frequent visitor at the Berringtons', is the suitor whose declaration Laura is soliciting in order to escape disgrace. In the end, during a secret meeting, Lady Davenant reminds him of his duties as a gentleman and perhaps offers him a better understanding of himself and his predicament. Wendover runs after Laura to America, leaving the door open for a possible, and utterly hypothetical, happy ending.

"A London Life" has often been placed by the critics (the few who have given it any extended attention) with the short stories dealing with the "international theme," a placement that takes into account the geographical origins of the characters rather than the structural relevance of the Europe/America dichotomy to the textual strategy. James himself had already lessened this story's pertinence to the international theme; in point of fact, the New York Edition presents "A London Life" in a series with *The Spoils of Poynton* and "The Chaperon," whose common denominator is not the international conflict, but the conflict between a young female protagonist and the written and unwritten laws of a rigidly codified social life.[3]

Such conflict, I am convinced, is the central issue of "A London Life," and the social codes that the protagonist confronts are specifically those that define and regulate feminine sexuality in the Victorian age.

As Heath Moon reminds us in a well-documented essay, when James wrote "A London Life," the British newspapers were still talking about the Campbell scandal, a divorce case that had shaken London's high society and given new currency to the question of divorce after the difficult approval of the Matrimonial Causes Act in 1857.[4] The Campbell divorce became a cause célèbre because of the social standing of the protagonists: one was the Earl of Marlborough, a close friend of the Prince of Wales, whose entourage James mentions explicitly in the *Notebooks* as the model background for the story. The daily press contributed an extensive coverage of the proceedings without leaving out any of the more sordid details, including the servants' testimony to fleeting intimacies between their employers. Once the trial was over, the case was kept in the eyes of the public by a debate on whether the press should give so much space to morally objectionable events.

Even if Moon finds analogies between some of the facts in the Campbell case and some details in the story, what interests me here is not so much whether the story makes reference to the case, of which James was aware and about which he wrote in a letter. What is worth noting here is that such a public and noisy divorce case resurrected the whole debate about the nature and the social position of women, a debate that had accompanied the Matrimonial Causes Act. With its double standard, the divorce act solidified into an institution all the ideological assumptions that defined women as property and as instruments for the transmission of property: not subjects entitled to rights, but symbolic objects of the subjectivity of men as owners of property and entitled to rights. Women were, therefore, defined exclusively in terms of reproduction, of dependency and passivity.[5] By absolving, for all intents and purposes, the adulterer, the act reaffirmed the idea of male sexuality as active and irrepressible and condemned women, at the same time, to a role of resigned acceptance and protection of the domestic sphere. Husbands, in contrast, could obtain a divorce on the basis of just one adulterous encounter on the part of their wives. Women's sexual initiative, as a result, was banished outside the boundaries of normalcy: as Lynda Nead writes, "Woman as victim could be accommodated within the code of sexual respectability but woman as offender transgressed that code and was defined as sexually deviant."[6]

The issue of divorce and adultery, therefore, was immediately related to the problem of the representation of feminine sexuality. Victorian medical discourse, exemplary *scientia sexualis* à la Foucault, discusses it incessantly by analyzing it in minute detail while simultaneously negating it. The dominant and widespread opinion (even within the emerging feminist movement and in most of the "New Woman" fiction) was that sexual desire was totally unknown to women. Opinions to the contrary existed but were relegated to an eccentric and marginal position as the entire sexual sphere was reorganized on the basis of the scientific authority of medicine. Suffice here the example of a doctor as well known as William Acton, whose treatise *The Functions and Disorders of the Reproductive Organs, in Childhood, Youth, Adult Age, and Advanced Life, Considered in their Physiological, Social and Moral Relations* claimed, by its title alone, to be the definitive theoretical synthesis and practical guide on sexual matters. William Acton is a case in point of the "incitement to discourses" that conferred on the medical caste the authorization and the power to speak about feminine sexuality, which at the same time was being taken away from women by negation of its very existence. His treatise, published in 1857, reprinted and enlarged several times in just a few years—the fourth edition came out in 1865— was one of the most influential factors in the definition and dissemination of a notion of woman as intrinsically pure, sexually passive, and naturally devoid of desires other than those related to the domestic and maternal sphere: "The majority of women (happily for them) are not very much troubled with sexual feelings of any kind. . . . As a general rule, a modest woman seldom desires any sexual gratification for herself. She submits to her husband, but only to please him. . . . The best mothers, wives and managers of households, know little or nothing of sexual indulgences. Love of home, children, and domestic duties, are the only passions they feel."[7]

Within such a discourse, the adulteress is defined as a doubly aberrant figure according to both the laws of society and the laws of nature. In order to save the premise of the absence of an active and original sexual impulse in women, popular culture gave ample circulation to the idea of seduction and mistreatment on the part of the husband as motivations for the adultery, giving men once more exclusive claim to an active role.

The *verso* of the adulteress' deviance is the innocence of the young woman, an emblem of femininity in its natural and untainted purity, a crucial image for the cultural representation of woman and, as such, the object of public debate. A variety of parental guidance books, conduct books, morally uplifting tracts, and magazine articles contributed to defining the characteristics of young women and delimiting the behavior of the "modest young girl," foreshadowing, as we will see in the next chapter, the paradox of an innocence represented as innate and intrinsic yet needing attentive and detailed regulation.

Knowledge

"A London Life," then, stages the confrontation between two culturally codified representations of femininity: the adulteress and the young woman. Such a confrontation does not take place solely at the symbolic level, through the dramatic structure of the plot or the attribution of roles to the characters: the story openly displays it, in its texture and in the dialogues, through recurring quotations of the assumptions and the behavioral codes that embodied the Victorian debate about feminine sexuality. This debate is the backbone of "A London Life": Laura's and Selina's characters and behaviors are analyzed in detail throughout the story from the point of view of a minute and rigid set of norms, the same defining stereotypes that abounded in the middle and late Victorian popular culture. A rich sample can be found in chapter 1 in the dialogue between Laura Wing and Lady Davenant, which introduces the situation:

> She herself [Lady Davenant] had been a good woman and that was the only thing that told in the long run. It was Laura's own idea to be a good woman. (440)

> "And how is your sister going on? She's very light!" (441)

> "It's a bad house for a girl. . . . it isn't the business of little girls to serve as parachutes to fly-away wives!" (441)

> "[S]he's worse than I thought. I don't mind them [adulteresses] so much when they are merry but I hate them when they are sentimental." (442)

> "And the worse she is the better she looks."
> "Oh my child, if the bad women looked as bad as they are——! It's only the good ones who can afford that," the old lady murmured. (442)

> "It takes courage to marry for such a reason."
> "Any reason is good enough that keeps a woman from being an old maid." (443)

"Good women"/"bad women," "fly-away wives"/"little girls," adulteresses whether "merry" or "sentimental," "light women," "old maids": these are the categories of the "girl's lesson in philosophy" (446), as this scene is significantly called at the end of the chapter. The other topical character of bourgeois femininity—the governess—is also summoned to be first summarily dismissed by Lady Davenant as another abstract category ("'You know they are always crying, governesses—whatever line you take. You shouldn't draw them out too much'" [439]), then evoked metaphorically in relation to Laura ("she might very well have been a young person in reduced circumstances applying for a place" [446]).[8] The governess is not just a character in the story (Miss Steet, who attends to the young Berringtons), but her avocation is also considered an avenue of respectability in comparison to being a dependent in a household threatened by disgrace: "she herself would have found courage to become a governess" (448).

The array of stereotypes continues in the following chapters, where Selina's behavior is analyzed and evaluated: "It was bad taste and bad form, it was *cabotin* and had the mark of Selina's complete, irremediable frivolity—the worst accusation (Laura tried to cling to that opinion) that she laid herself open to. . . . She hoped she should get a letter from Selina the next morning (Mrs. Berrington would show at least that remnant of propriety) . . ." (459). And where the nuances of Selina's demimonde acquaintances are examined: "She was not ready to say that the companion was any worse, though Lionel appeared to think so, than twenty other women who were her sister's intimates. . . . It was new work for our young lady to judge of these shades—the gradations, the probabilities of license, and of the side of the line on which, or rather how far on the wrong side, Lady Ringrose was situated" (459).

All through the story, the quantity and quality of Selina's "improprieties" are accurately weighed and commented on by husband, sister, and confidante up to the final act, when she runs away with her lover, an event described with a verb whose "technical" quality the text ironically foregrounds: "'Selina has bolted, as they say.' 'Bolted?' Mr. Wendover repeated. 'I don't know what you call it in America'" (529).

The young girl is no less an object of discussion than is the adulteress, since Laura's condition and situation expose her to judgments and categorizations. That these pronouncements are often openly instrumental underlines their regulatory rigidity, their existence as "objective" categories independent from the individual's good intentions. The brother-in-law, for example, tries to find the correct codes to communicate to her his intention of petitioning the court for a divorce. On the one hand, he wants to respect her codified condition of innocent young girl: "'I never know how to talk to you—you are so beastly clever,' he said. 'I can't treat you like a little girl in a pinafore—and yet of course you are only a young lady. You are so deuced good—that makes it worse'" (461). On the other hand, he wishes to implicate her and have her take his side, on the premise that her innocence has already been stained: "'Oh I say, Laura, don't put on so many frills, as Selina says. You know what your sister is as well as I do!'" (461); "'You know all about her—don't make believe you don't . . . You see everything—you're one of the sharp ones. There's no use beating about the bush, Laura—you've lived in this precious house and you're not so green as that comes to'" (463).

As to Selina, she responds to her sister's recriminations and admonitions by throwing back at her the accusations, exploiting the verbal and behavioral codes of virginal innocence: "'I never heard of such extraordinary ideas for a girl to have, and such extraordinary things for a girl to talk about! My dear, you have acquired a freedom—you have emancipated yourself from conventionality—and I suppose I must congratulate you'" (470); "'My dear, you do indulge in a style of innuendo, for a respectable young woman! . . . You have ideas that when I was a girl——'"(470).

When Laura visits the Soane Museum with Mr. Wendover, unaccompanied, as was the American custom, by any other chaperon, she meets Selina, who is supposed to be visiting a sick friend, with her lover. Again it is Selina who accuses her sister of disgraceful behavior: "'I didn't ask you to be indecent! If Lionel were to know it he wouldn't tolerate it, so long as you live with us . . . . It's different for a married woman, especially when she's married to a cad. It's in a girl that such things are odious—scouring London with strange men. . . . it was not your finding me that was out of the way; it was my finding you—with your remarkable escort!'" (498–99).

Laura, on her part, is very self-conscious about etiquette: she is well aware that even though, as a young American girl, she has the right to be alone with a man in public, her behavior runs counter to London rituals, and she takes pains to explain all the international precedents of the case:

In the carriage she anticipated the inquiry that she figured to herself he presently would make and said, laughing: "No, no, this is very exceptional; if we were both English—and both what we are, otherwise—we wouldn't do this."

"And if only one of us were English?"

"It would depend upon which one."

"Well, say me."

"Oh, in that case I certainly—on so short an acquaintance—would not go sight-seeing with you." (490–91)

Similar examinations of "matters of conduct" (150) are the very texture of this story. The sample offered here, though extensive, does not fully account for all of them. Certainly, the international situation justifies such an insistence on social conventions, which would otherwise have been taken for granted. However, the metalanguage of behavior is employed to such an extent as to exceed any requirement of verisimilitude, any hypothetical necessity of explaining to the American public the main categories of London's social life.

Rather, the obsessive presence of categories and behavioral norms explicitly named and discussed can be read more productively from a Foucaultian point of view as that "incitement to discourse," which characterizes, as much as do repression and suppression, Victorian discourse on sexuality. The proliferation of discourses illustrates the process, described by Foucault, of constituting sexuality as *knowledge*: that is, a domain structured and constituted on the basis of definitions and regulatory statements, of accepted and deviant behaviors, predicated on notions of respectability where gender and class, as Nancy Armstrong has shown, intersect.[9]

The recurring notion of "knowledge" further shows the remarkable degree to which this story is in harmony with Foucault's description. From the very beginning, and with an emphatic frequency, it develops a notion of knowledge that is not indistinct but is meant as a cogent and specific expertise, of which one may or may not be cognizant: "A year ago she knew nothing, and now she knew almost everything" (436); "She knew so many things to-day that when she was younger—and only a little—she had not expected ever to know" (458); "Laura Wing felt the want of proper knowledge to explain such anomalies" (496).

Furthermore, as in *What Maisie Knew*, Laura's partial lack of knowledge traces from the outside the boundaries of a homogeneous and coherent system of knowledge: her "I don't know" and "I don't understand" recur in the dialogue from the beginning to the end of the story (with a peak of five instances in half a page) as a counterpoint to the induced acquisition of "knowledge" that she laments.

At the center of this domain of knowledge there is, of course, sexuality and especially the definition and practice of female sexuality, accurately repressed and diligently codified. And what interests me now is precisely the expression of this knowledge.

To Say

The taboo here is, in full accordance with Foucault, what everybody speaks about throughout the story: Selina's (and to a lesser extent Lionel Berrington's) sexual life is the unseen center of everyone's thoughts and the engine that drives conversations. A whole domain, which is officially repressed and removed from expression and whose divulgation in public is feared the most, is constantly at the center of attention and discussion. Selina's misbehavior is illustrated in detail—how many lovers, what they are called, where they meet—perhaps in a satire of the reports in the famous Campbell case. Divorce—"that horrible word" in pronouncing which "Laura's voice almost failed her" (471)—is a widely debated possibility: "She had heard it . . . often enough on the lips of others; it had been bandied lightly enough in her presence" (471); at times in their dialogues, the couple seem to show off how well versed they are in the rules of procedure.

In this case as well, the verbal expressions are accompanied by ample metalinguistic commentary: to say or not to say, what to say, how to say it, what to say to whom, with a disconcerting recurrence of *verba loquendi*. Naturally, Laura is the main target of this metalinguistic overabundance, either as addressee or as producer of communication: her condition of young girl, who must by definition be kept in the dark as to the whole question of sexual behavior, and her actual immersion, at the same time, in a universe of discourse full of sexuality make her simultaneously the subject and the object of a verbose conspiracy of silence. On the one hand, what can or cannot be said in her presence is explicitly codified: "the anecdotes were mostly such an immense secret that they could not be told fairly if she were there" (478); "of that Laura was unable to judge, not knowing what was said, because of course it was not said to *her*" (495). On the other hand, this codification cannot prevent, under the circumstances, the saying of that which should not be said. This adds to discourse an overtone of explicit and self-aware transgression, both when Laura is the producer of the discourse (as in the exchange with Selina, already examined above: "'Don't pretend to be shocked, Selina; that's too cheap a defence. You have said things to me—if you choose to talk of freedom! What is the talk of your house and what does one hear if one lives with you? . . . I'm very glad if you understand that I don't care what I say. If one talks about your affairs, my dear, one mustn't be too particular!'" [470]) and when she is the addressee, as in the dialogue with her brother in law:

> "[Y]ou're so good yourself that you needn't give a shriek if one is obliged to say what one means. . . . I don't know what I said to you before dinner—I had had too many brandy and sodas. Perhaps I was too free; if I was I beg your pardon. . . . I'm sorry to have to say it to you, but he's her lover. I mean Selina's. And he ain't the first. . . . I haven't told you the fiftieth part—you will easily understand that I can't. They are not nice things to say to a girl like you—especially about Deepmere, if you didn't know it." (463–65)

The unsayable so explicitly defined as such produces the effect of summoning the object it wants to conceal, of making it conspicuous even when it is not mentioned: "She had a horror of the name, the name that was in her mind and that was apparently on his lips . . . [She was] infinitely relieved that the name was not the one she had feared" (458). In relation to sexuality words are always in excess or defective; they are marked either by reticence or by the redundancy of overdetermination. The discourse of sexuality is pervasive and under the sign of a painstaking preterition—a mode of communication of which the text itself offers an extraordinary and ironical *mise en abyme*: "Nothing had been said yet in the house, of course . . . ; but the servants pretended so hard not to be aware of anything in particular that they were like pickpockets looking with unnatural interest the other way after they have cribbed a fellow's watch" (532).

Confession

The universe of discourse in "A London Life" illustrates to the highest degree Foucault's connection between repression and expression: sexuality is construed by the proliferation of discourses that define it as prohibition and, as such, open it to investigation, giving it legitimacy as an object to be addressed by the *volonté de savoir*.

This will to knowledge is manifest from the very first scene: the dialogue between Lady Davenant and Laura Wing opens with a question, " 'And what's going on *chez vous*—who is there and what are they doing?' " (438). The question is only apparently of a general and benevolent nature; in fact, it immediately shifts the subject of conversation to the irregularities of the Berrington household. In the same way the dialogue proceeds with a crescendo of question marks so that the situation that engenders the plot is presented in the highly connotative form of the cross-examination. Should any doubt be left as to the pertinence of this reading of the story, consider what Lady Davenant exclaims almost at the closing of the scene: " 'I feel as if I were cross-questioning you, which God forbid!' " (446).[10] She then adds a couple of questions that are put as a doctor or a confessor would: " 'But I have to know, you know.' " To which Laura answers (her final words in the scene): " 'Oh, don't try to know any more shames—any more horrors!' " (446), thus establishing from the beginning the key words of her experience and the terms of the Foucaultian alternating movement between the "obligation to conceal" and the "duty to confess" which will develop in the rest of the story.[11]

"A London Life" is patterned by scenes of "confession." The first takes place in section 5, when Laura, after the revelations by her brother-in-law, faces Selina, hoping to redeem her and to avoid disgrace. The section begins in medias res, intensifying the tone of the preceding cross-examination, and places the scene unequivocally within the (again, Foucaultian) framework of confession as "ritual of truth": " 'And are you telling me the perfect truth when you say that Captain Crispin was not there?' " (467). Yet confession as a means to producing truth is immediately disavowed: "the girl's earnest, almost barbarous probity" (467) is impotent vis à vis Selina's deliberate capacity for deceit:

> "The perfect truth?" Mrs. Berrington straightened herself to her height, threw back her head and measured her interlocutress up and down; . . . then, after an instant's reflection, she . . . exchanged her expression of scorn (of resentment at her veracity's being impugned) for a look of gentle amusement; she smiled patiently, as if she remembered that of course Laura couldn't understand of what an impertinence she had been guilty. . . . "My poor child, the things you do say! One doesn't put a question about the perfect truth in a manner that implies that a person is telling a perfect lie. However, as it's only you, I don't mind satisfying your clumsy curiosity." (467)

By reducing the inquisitor to the status of "only you," the search for truth to a "clumsy curiosity," and the "barbarous probity" to a lack of "certain pleasant little forms" (467), Selina avoids her sister's "will to knowledge," thus turning confession into a mundane parody of a ritual of truth and the oath into a caricature: " 'Will you swear—will you swear by everything that is most sacred? . . . By our dear mother's memory—by our poor father's?' 'By my mother's, by my father's,' said Mrs. Berrington, 'and by that of any other member of the family you like!' " (472–73).

This scene should shake up Laura's faith in confession as an instrument of truth. However, it does not: "Even while Selina spoke Laura had a cold, horrible sense of not believing her, and at the same time a desire, colder still, to extract a reiteration of the pledge. Was it the asseveration of her innocence that she wished her to repeat, or only the attestation of her falsity? One way or the other it seemed to her that this would settle something" (473). Paradoxically, even as it produces lies, the ritual continues to function: what matters is that truth and deceit may be clearly separated, so that the discovery of deceit may in itself produce truth. Truth, however, is produced, not by the person who is uttering the confession, but by the person who receives it, and it can emerge only if, and inasmuch as, the inquisitor *knows already*. The ritual, therefore, is not a ritual of truth: rather, it is a ritual of subjection, an acknowledgment of the authority of the ritual as legitimate means to produce truth. Laura, however, does not and cannot know all this yet.

A confession is also staged in section 10 after the chance encounter in the museum has proven to Laura how real is the liaison she dreaded. The scene again opens *ex abrupto* on a verbal exchange: " 'What do you intend to do? You will grant that I have a right to ask you that.' 'To do? I shall do as I have always done—not so badly, as it seems to me' " (500). Laura's claim to legitimacy is juxtaposed once more to Selina's ability to avoid her sister's compelling "demand for truth," as Foucault terms it (77), by moving away from the level of profound self analysis to that of the most engaging superficiality. This time, however, Selina's attitude changes abruptly: embraces, requests for help, a torrent of tears accompany what is explicitly defined as a "confession":

> She besought her to save her, to stay with her, to help her against herself, against *him*, against Lionel, against everything—to forgive her also all the horrid things she had said to her. Mrs. Berrington melted, liquefied, and the room was deluged with her repentance, her desolation, her confession, her promises and the articles of apparel which were detached from her by the high tide of her agitation. Laura remained with her for an hour, and before they separated the culpable woman had taken a tremendous vow—kneeling before her sister with her head in her lap—never again, as long as she lived, to consent to see Captain Crispin or to address a word to him, spoken or written. The girl went terribly tired to bed. (506–7)

The irony of the narrative voice is evident in the emphatic crescendo of the sentences, in the watery hyperbole, in the casual commingling of promises and articles of clothing. Placed under the banner of excess, confession is once more only the parody of a moment of truth: a self-conscious imitation of a painting by Egg or Watson or of the agonizing denouement of a melodrama, interpreted according to the rules, with the "culpable woman" in the sanctioned pose of repentance, complete with hair hanging loose, tears, and a "tremendous vow."[12] It is Laura's *expectation of truth* that induces her once again to perceive the scene literally as an authentic confession and to view her sister's repentance as authentic. Bent on reforming her sister, Laura spends the following month taking her to concerts and to the National Gallery—efforts eliciting from Lady Davenant an ironic and world-weary comment: " 'My dear child, you are too delightful! You are trying to reform her? By Beethoven and Bach, by Rubens and Titian?' " (508). In her blind determination, Laura is getting ready for the third and last confession of the story, in which she is the protagonist.

The locale of the scene in section 11 is a box in an opera house (I will come back to the relevance of this background) where Laura and Selina are Mr. Wendover's guests and are watching *The Huguenots*. When Selina leaves her alone with Mr. Wendover, against the rules of etiquette and chaperonage, Laura realizes that Selina has betrayed her and has run away with Captain Crispin. The scandal is about to become public knowledge and disgrace the entire family. It is at this point that, as in Bourget's anecdote, Laura thinks of Mr. Wendover as an escape route from dishonor: "There was a certain chance in life that sat there beside her, but it would go for ever if it should not move nearer that night; and she listened, she watched, for it to move. . . . To-morrow he would know, and would think sufficiently little of a young person of *that* breed: therefore it could only be a question of his speaking on the spot" (518). Laura, however, waits in vain for Mr. Wendover to speak and in her despair—"She felt as if she were running a race with failure and shame" (518)—she breaks into a series of questions that are meant to produce yet another moment of truth and to induce the presumed suitor to declare himself: " 'Why have you come so often? . . . To see *me*—it was for that? Why have you come? . . . And is it because you like me that you have kept me here?' " (519). Mr. Wendover is surprised and disoriented: perhaps it is only his sense of chivalry that induces him to reply at one point with " 'I love you.' " And all seems lost to Laura:

> Then an unspeakable shame and horror—horror of herself, of him, of everything—came over her, and she sank into a chair at the back of the box, with averted eyes, trying to get further into her corner. . . .
> For many minutes she was perfectly still—she was ashamed even to move. The one thing that could have justified her, blown away the dishonour of her monstrous overture, would have been, on his side, the quick response of unmistakable passion. It had not come, and she had nothing left but to loathe herself. (520–21)

What has happened then? The ritual of confession once again has not functioned according to expectations; it has not provoked a profession of love that perhaps did not exist or was unable to manifest itself in the expected forms. Yet from another point of view, there *has* been a confession: because it has found no correspondence, Laura's solicitation has transformed her from inquisitor into "inquisitee," and has forced her to the very confession she has been unable to elicit from Mr. Wendover (whether a confession of love or of the socially induced need to find a husband is of no import here). Significantly, Laura relives the episode in terms of *self*-revelation: "monstrous overture" (520), " 'I asked him to marry me!' " (524), " 'I asked him, I couldn't help it, it was too hideous—I offered myself!' " (524). Unlike Selina's confessions, in which she is able to manipulate every word and gesture, Laura's own confession has provoked the unexpected eruption of a "truth of the self"—a revelation whose content is not just the violation of the social codes that prescribe that it should be a man to take the first step, but rather a symbolic trauma of sorts. The "shame and horror" that define this experience for Laura are not shared by all. Lady Davenant's comments, as usual, are an attempt to keep it in perspective, and Mr. Wendover does not seem to have understood the tragic implications of the scene.[13] When Lady Davenant summons him, unbeknown to Laura, in order to understand what happened and rebukes him for not having thrown himself at the feet of the young girl as he should have, he utters a rather pedestrian reply: " 'You must remember where we were—in a public place, with very little room for throwing!' " (527), a remark whose quasi-comic import effectively deflates Laura's tragic perception of the scene.

"Shame and horror," then, would seem to be Laura's personal reaction to the experience rather than its inevitable and objective outcome. In order to interpret the origins of her response, it is now time to look at Laura's role as point of view, as optical and moral device through which the events are presented.

Judgment

The sparse critical debate on "A London Life" has been devoted mainly to the reliability of Laura's point of view as final moral standard offered to the reader. According to Leon Edel, she is moralistic, puritan, "rigid and meddlesome," and James is criticizing her moral inflexibility, whereas for the first time in his career, he is apparently showing an "indulgent, though not altogether approving" attitude toward the adulteress Selina.[14] In Gorley Putt's view, Laura is "as socially perceptive as her creator," but her reaction to the scandal is that of "a poor hysterical girl" who, in her excessive moral rigor, ends by appearing "the least charitable" of all the characters.[15] More recent criticism, however, tends to give credit to Laura's moral position and to consider the text as a critical representation of the immorality typical of London high society.[16]

These polarized evaluations would seem to reflect faithfully the complex treatment of Laura as character and in general the problem of judgment in the text. Incidentally, this effect was noted and criticized by the anonymous reviewer who in 1889 condemned without exception all the characters in the story as "for the most part repellent, and certainly most unloveable." Though accepting the unpleasant world represented in it as a "picture of a certain phase of modern social life," he attacked the author for his lack of reliable standards for judgment: "This dim groping in the minds and sayings and doings of his personages for an explanation of their characters and actions, which seems to place author and readers on a common level of inquiry, tends to give an air of intense reality to Mr. Henry James's books; but we have generally found it aggravating, especially at the end of a tale, when, to gain a clear idea of what the author means, we would often dispense with our share in the responsibility for following up the clue."[17]

Unable to find a stable vantage point from which to judge, the reader is forced to the "dim groping" lamented by this reviewer. The contributing factor to this instability is the full-blown irony, which does not leave any room for a completely reliable point of view the reader may trust. On one hand, Laura's insightful eye leaves the other characters no escape; on the other, Laura's point of view is itself limited, as the text clearly shows.

First of all, Laura is presented as a reliable interpreter of the qualities of the other characters, major and minor. Her perception of them is supported by the text as a whole, and the other occasional points of view (Lady Davenant and the narrative voice) tend to confirm her evaluation: Selina as the insincere woman who is one with her role of "professional beauty" (484); Lionel as a "good-natured but dissipated boy" (461) whose mental strivings are limited to hunting and horse riding (which provide him with his only idiolect); Mr. Wendover as a good man but rather ignorant (he believes Lady Davenant to be a contemporary of Garrick) and too sluggish "to emulate her own more rapid processes" (485). As to minor characters, Miss Steet, the governess, is aptly epitomized by her "drooping, martyr-like air" (447), as is Lionel Berrington's elderly and placid mother by the image of "a tablet of fine white soap—nothing else was so smooth and clean" (438).

Furthermore, Laura's point of view is much more complex, and self-consciously so, than her critical reduction to puritanical morality would lead one to believe. Upon closer inspection of her moral standards, one discovers that though the opposition "good"/"bad" recurs in her cogitations with sufficient frequency to justify the critical pigeonholing, her consciousness is not guided solely by a moral criterion or by such a restrictive one. One could almost say that for the most part Laura's difficulties and the text's instability emerge from the continuous necessity of negotiating morality with different sets of standards, which do not always coincide—that is, social and aesthetic standards. "Duplicity," a frequently recurring word in the text, alludes to the discrepancies in a picture that does not lend itself to cohesion. Selina is, of course, the most duplicitous character of all and a fit embodiment of the discrepancy between aesthetics and morals. On the one hand, she is so beautiful that she looks like a photograph of herself ("[h]er photographs were not to be purchased in the Burlington Arcade—she had kept out of that; but she looked more than ever as they would have represented her if they had been obtainable there" [477]) or else like a sculptural image of spiritual femininity ("she might have passed for some grave, antique statue of a young matron, or even for a picture of Saint Cecilia" [469]). These images, it goes without saying, look back to the reification of feminine beauty into an artistic object, which I analyzed in part 1. On the other hand, her beauty is not consistent with either rectitude or intellectual substance. Nor is Selina an exception in this regard: in society, as Laura has to recognize, even "good women" adhere to the social criterion of "proper" vs. "improper" rather than to the moral one of "good" vs. "bad." The beauty and antiquities of England lead Laura to perceive every place and scene from an aesthetic point of view, as a picture, but they exist side by side with institutions (another recurring word) that give to "iniquity" the authoritative sanction of tradition, thus making every judgment unstable: "her condemnation of this wrong forgot itself when so many of the consequences looked right . . . : which was the fate sooner or later of most of her unfavourable judgments of English institutions. Iniquities in such a country somehow always made pictures"(435–36). The English picturesque does not always manage to conceal with beauty either its own vacuity—"she marveled at the waste involved in some human institutions (the English country gentry for instance) when she perceived that it had taken so much to produce so little" (450)—or the discrepancy between its symbols and its values, as in the case of the delicate eighteenth-century decorations of the Berringtons' country house: the "slim festoons, urns and trophies and knotted ribbons, so many symbols of domestic affection and irrevocable union" (472), which ironically overlook the unfaithful couple from the ceiling.

But if through Laura Wing, English society becomes an object of obser-vation and satire, Laura herself is often the object of explicit irony. Lady Davenant's secular, illusionless, and at times cynical point of view acts as a constant counterpoint to Laura's by putting into less dramatic perspective her exalted views ("'I have no patience with the high-strung way you take things'" [446]) and by making fun of her idealism and naiveté, although she respects her fundamental aspirations: "'She exaggerates the badness of it, the stigma of her relationship. Good heavens, at that rate where would some of us be? But those are her ideas, they are absolutely sincere, and they had possession of her at the opera'" (531). And more importantly, even the narrative voice maintains toward her an almost constant ironical distance, expressed through abundant references to the "poor girl," through recurring stylistic choices that run counter to Laura's feelings, through the relentless underscoring of her partial vision (not to have any divorce in the family "struck Laura as in itself almost sufficient to constitute happiness" [447]), unrealistic and literary longings ("The governess's evening hours in the quiet schoolroom would have suited Laura well—so at least she believed" [449]), and limited culture ("it is to be feared that the poor girl's notions of knowledge were at once conventional and crude" [488]). The narrator even intervenes explicitly in section 6 by appealing directly to the reader in a way that reminds one immediately of a similar intervention in chapter 6 of *The Portrait of a Lady*:

> She drifted on, shutting her eyes, averting her head and, as it seemed to herself, hardening her heart. This admission will doubtless suggest to the reader that she was a weak, inconsequent, spasmodic young person, with a standard not really, or at any rate not continuously, high; and I have no desire that she shall appear anything but what she was. It must even be related of her that since she could not escape and live in lodgings and paint fans (there were reasons why this combination was impossible) she determined to try and be happy in the given circumstances—to float in shallow, turbid water. (476)

Such an open distancing is rather unique in this story. Yet, one is inclined to ask whether the primary object of the irony here is Laura or the reader's expectation of a "continuously high standard" on her part. Such expectations, as the phrase "it must even be related" underscores with false compunction, are likely to be based on that kind of fiction where, in order to protect their innocence from the proximity of sin, the immaculate heroines are ready to undertake a variety of dignified but unrealistic occupations. After all, Laura's projects are no more idealistic and unrealistic than the expectations of the potential readers: the fact that this ironic treatment involves the "hypocrite lecteur" suggests that Laura's point of view may represent, as point of view always does in James, not just her personal naiveté or a worn-out cliché of American Puritanism, but a set of suprapersonal standards of judgment, less visible because they are more commonly shared. These standards of judgment are really prejudices, that is, representations that pertain to ideology and hence come *before* judgment and provide the preliminary and unexamined assumptions grounding the kind of judgments that I have examined so far.

Prejudice

The poor but honest young girl who supports herself by painting fans is not the only literary and stereotypical representation offered in "A London Life." The culturally sanctioned categories of Victorian femininity, as we have seen, constitute the "knowledge" of the story: their persistent use is accompanied by a profusion of clichés that, though difficult to perceive as such from today's vantage point, faithfully reproduce the terms of the contemporary debate about women, women's role, and women's function. Around Laura's "maidenly bonnet" (478) revolve the most canonical topoi of Victorian femininity through the stages of life: from adolescence—the "nice girl" (496) as opposed to "fastness" (515) as the stereotypical behaviors open to young women—to old age as a dignified and reassuring point of arrival, through an intermediate age that is identified, of course, with motherhood as woman's supreme mission and duty.[18] Motherhood is evoked throughout the story: through the maternal care that Lionel Berrington's mother provides in the nursery (449); the "access of maternal tenderness" (469) that transforms Selina into an icon of motherhood; the love with which Laura observes Selina's children asleep in their beds "as mothers and maids do alike over the pillow of rosy childhood" (502); and the admonition to the adulteress—"'think of your children!'" and, if necessary, "'[d]ie for them'" (506).

As is to be expected, most of the stereotypes are occasioned by the adulteress. Laura's reactions are grounded in the moralistic or sentimental representations common in the middle and late Victorian popular culture. For example, it was a widespread opinion that, given their sexual passivity, women's adultery was caused by their husbands' neglect or unworthy acquaintances—an opinion echoed in Laura's comment, "Such the husband such the wife" (503), and in her holding Mr. Berrington responsible for his wife's "fall": "'You haven't given her an example!'" (462). As to Laura's view that, after her sister's elopement, nobody will want to marry her, Gorley Putt reads it as a sign of hysteria and offers the ironic comment "as if anyone would think of associating so very different a pair."[19] The *scientia sexualis* of the times, however, actually expounded the premise, so authoritatively put by Dr. William Acton, that "the sin of unfaithfulness is often inherited, as well as many other family diseases"—a premise voiced in the story several times, both by Lady Davenant ("'*c'est de naissance* . . . I daresay there was some improper ancestress'" [442]) and by Laura ("To-morrow he would know, and would think sufficiently little of a young person of *that* breed" [518]; "Laura felt the dishonour of her race" [538]).[20]

The fate of the adulteress was compounded by disgrace, social dishonor, no possibility of redemption, and death by suicide or extreme poverty, according to a codified mythology, expressed in countless poems, newspaper articles, sensational novels, illustrations, and paintings.[21] While these *idées reçues* dictate Laura's response to her sister's elopement, the discrepancy between the presumed gloom and doom and the reality of the adulteress' fate is explicitly underscored, as always, by Lady Davenant: "'In peace!' cried Laura; 'with my wretched sister leading such a life?' 'Oh, my dear, I daresay it will be very comfortable; I am sorry to say anything in favour of such doings, but it very often is'" (522). After Lionel's evocation of the other powerful sentimental icon of the adulteress' children—"He talked a great deal about the children and figured himself as pressing the little deserted darlings to his bosom" (533)—Laura herself is forced to admit how inapplicable those stereotypes are to her healthy and indifferent nephews: "It added to the ugliness of Selina's flight that even her children didn't miss her, and . . . that one could neither spend tears on the mother and wife, because she was not worth it, nor sentimentalise about the little boys, because they didn't inspire it" (536).[22]

Laura's actions no less than her emotions after her sister's elopement conform to a prepared script. "Woman's mission to women" was the slogan that subsumed the theory by which, in the second half of the nineteenth century, bourgeois women were assigned the charitable duty to help redeem their fallen sisters through the exemplary virtue and domestic values they embodied.[23] This redemptive scenario is evoked by Laura's overemphatic insistence on wanting to run after her sister and bring her back from her sinful exile: "[Laura's idea] was to go after her sister, to take possession of her, cling to her and bring her back. Lionel, of course, wouldn't hear of taking her back, nor would Selina presumably hear of coming; but this made no difference in Laura's heroic plan. She would work it, she would compass it, she would go down on her knees, she would find the eloquence of angels, she would achieve miracles" (533). Laura's final deployment of

her plan takes on even more explicit literary and sentimental connotations
through the point of view of the governess (from whom she is forced to
borrow money for her trip, in the best tradition of the imperiled heroine):

> [S]he had never before been concerned in a flurried night-episode,
> with an unavowed clandestine side; the very imprudence of it (for a
> sick girl alone) was romantic, and before Laura had gone down to the
> cab she began to say that foreign life must be fascinating and to make
> wistful reflections. . . . At the door of the cab she tried to make her
> take more money, and our heroine had an odd sense that if the vehicle
> had not rolled away she would have thrust into her hand a keepsake
> for Captain Crispin. (540–41)

Laura's consciousness, in conclusion, is inhabited by ideological presences, embodied in a repertoire of the "True Womanhood" clichés that
permeated all levels of Victorian culture.[24] This repertoire predefines her
response to experience and presents it to her in the key either of domestic
idealization (the mission of women as caretakers of children, companions
of men, and nurses to the elderly; innocence and self-sacrifice as guiding
values of feminine existence) or of dark melodrama (the castaway sinner, the
rejected and needy adulteress, the neglected children). The melodramatic
emphasis is further reinforced by Laura's modes of expression, which tend,
in the moments of crisis, to hyperbole and triplication: "'It's all black
darkness'" (522); "'It's awful, awful, awful!'" (523); "'You must tell me or
I'll kill myself—I give you my word!'" (537); "'I must, I must, I must!'"
(539). This tendency continues up to her last words in the story, the final
threat to the innocuous Mr. Wendover, who is trying to prevent her from
leaving—words that any of Richardson's persecuted damsels could have
uttered: "'If you follow me I will jump off the boat!'" (542).

I believe that within this internalized ideological repertoire of Victorian
feminine roles, Laura's shame and horror after the "confession" scene take
on a much more pertinent meaning. Her sister's elopement shatters the
pillars of Laura's domestic ideology: the image of domestic and maternal
femininity and the utopian redemption of the sinner through the beneficial
influence of purity. Indeed, even the image of innocence that Laura embodies is sullied both by public exposure and by her *avances* to Mr. Wendover.
The crisis involves not just cultural stereotypes, but more deeply the images
of the self they have helped forge. "Shame" and "horror" speak first and
foremost the language of the psyche before they address the mind and the
categories of rational judgment. They belong to the emotional rather than

to the ethical sphere and are the sign of an experience, not filtered by the intellect, but lived in the immediacy of inner life through the internalization of a symbolic order that, according to cultural psychology, is not the product of what the self thinks, but is the unconscious background *from which* the self thinks. If shame is being laid open to a gaze that, as we have seen in "Julia Bride," embodies social norms, horror is the much deeper feeling that is born out of the violation of the symbolic order. It is the threat to the symbolic order that makes the experience incomprehensible and unspeakable: precisely, an "unspeakable shame and horror" (520).

The Performance

The threat to the symbolic order is even more radical than would be implied by the shattering of the ideological categories upon which Laura has built her own identity and her notions of femininity. Indeed, the scene in the theater threatens its very foundations.

When Selina leaves the box and exacts from the second gentleman the promise not to return to the box himself, thus ensuring that Laura will be left alone with Wendover, her maneuver establishes a functional equivalence between the two sisters: as Selina elopes with her lover, Laura too is creating an involuntary scandal, thanks to her unbecoming intimacy with Mr. Wendover. It does not matter here whether Selina's intention is malicious (shaming her sister in public) or possibly benevolent (offering her the chance of a clarification with a potential suitor): in any case, the drama is internal to Laura's consciousness. She perceives Selina's move (casting her perception, as usual, in a conventional terminology) as the attempt "to bring her sister to her own colour by putting an appearance of 'fastness' upon her" (515), "to spatter her sister with the mud into which she herself had jumped" (518). As a result, in the eyes of the world both will have lost their honor, and the sweet young girl—"an honest girl, the most loyal, the most unselfish of sisters" (515)—will be brought to the same level as the acknowledged adulteress. Like a magician, Selina manages to conceal for a moment her own transgression and replace it with the spectacle of her sister's apparent one, a staging of dishonor of which Selina is the director, Laura the involuntary protagonist, and the entire theater the public: "to her troubled spirit the immense theatre had a myriad eyes, eyes that she knew, eyes that would know her, that would see her sitting there with a strange young man. She had recognised many faces already and her imagination quickly multiplied them" (515).

Through Selina's subtle maliciousness, or better, through James's subtle maliciousness by means of Selina, a play within the play is staged in an appropriate theatrical setting—a *mise en abyme* that, fulfilling its peculiar function, self-reflexively interrogates the first representation and puts into question its reality.

The fact that the roles of adulteress and innocent girl could so easily be reversed exposes the arbitrary and prescriptive character of the codes that define and regulate women's sexual behavior. Unrelated to any superior ethical dictate (as their geographical relativity confirms), they are precariously identified with purely exterior conduct. "Appearance" is their key word: "honourable women didn't (for the appearance of the thing) arrange to leave their unmarried sister sitting alone, publicly, at the playhouse, with a couple of young men" (513–14); "an appearance of 'fastness' " (515) is the consequence to which Laura is subjected.

The codes of female honor, therefore, do not refer to an essence and cannot be the foundation of identity: they are nothing but a never-ending *performance* in which both honor and dishonor can be feigned. The setting of the scene foregrounds, at a metatextual level, the theatrical character of the entire representation and retrospectively links Laura's enactment of dishonor with Selina's continuous and competent enactment of honor. Selina has been the protagonist of what Laura now unequivocally perceives as a series of "intervening comedies" (515): the enactment of the loving mother (468–69), the caring daughter-in-law and good parishioner, the faithful and solicitous friend answering the call for help of a "tiresomely ill" lady (490), the repentant and redeemed sinner (506)—all the canonical roles of contemporary womanhood, denaturalized through the exhibition of their theatrical nature.[25] Or rather, through the exhibition of their *performative* nature: whereas in the case of Selina the enactment can still be seen as predicated on the truth/falsehood opposition, Laura's exposure is *by itself* sufficient to create the identity of the "fast girl."

It would be excessive to attribute to James the radicalness and the theoretical sophistication of Judith Butler. However, the way in which this story employs some historical categories of womanhood in an antiessentialist manner is not too far from some of Butler's conceptualizations: "There is no gender identity behind the expressions of gender; that identity is performatively constituted by the very 'expressions' that are said to be its results."[26]

Here and elsewhere, James represents gender identity as continuously produced and reproduced through its expressions, through its codified staging, within the limits prescribed by norms that become one with subjectivity. "The 'performative' dimension of construction is precisely the forced reiteration of norms," writes Butler.[27] And her clarifications on the performativity of gender may help shed light on my assessment of the dynamics at play in "A London Life":

> Performativity cannot be understood outside of a process of iterability, a regularized and constrained repetition of norms. And this repetition is not performed *by* a subject; this repetition is what enables a subject and constitutes the temporal condition for the subject. This iterability implies that "performance" is not a singular "act" or event, but a ritualized production, a ritual reiterated under and through constraint, under and through the force of prohibition and taboo, with the threat of ostracism and even death controlling and compelling the shape of the production, but not, I will insist, determining it fully in advance.[28]

By metafictionally laying bare the performative quality of gender as representation, by exposing the theatrical, that is, pre-scripted quality of gender roles, "A London Life" performs vis-à-vis *cultural* representation the same critically inquisitive function that the embedding of portraits and art objects in previous stories performed in relation to *artistic* representation.

Specularity

The deconstruction of the "natural" and "essential" quality of the opposition between the "Angel in the House" and the "Fallen Woman" is effected not solely by exhibiting the reversal of roles and the performative character of identities. The "shame" and "horror" that the threat to the symbolic order and the shattering of its images of womanhood—cultural images but also self-images, it must be remembered—evoke in Laura are not unique; rather they are the culminating moment in a sequel of horrors, shames, and synonymous and related words, which appear in the text with extraordinary frequency, especially before the theater scene in reference to Selina and her behavior.[29] And this is just one of the parallels between the two sisters—two opposed poles in appearance but actually tied together by a profound similarity, as in the fairy-tale archetypes on which they are modeled.

In effect, the scene in the theater is not the only one in which an equivalence is established between the two sisters. The scene of their chance encounter in the museum, each with her own male companion, each with her own clandestine and irregular situation, had already established an evident symmetry between the two; and immediately before their meeting, Laura had thought precisely about the possibility that Selina's encounters with Captain Crispin might be, after all, as innocent as hers with Mr. Wendover. Further on, after the scene in the opera house and Selina's elopement, Lionel points out other resemblances between the two sisters: " 'That's the tone Selina used to take. Surely you don't want to begin and imitate her!' " (537); " 'Dear old girl, don't try and behave just as *she* did!' " (539).

The insistence on the symmetry obviously is not an occasional effect but the sign of a specularity that section 10 underlines and sanctions through another *mise en abyme*. Selina's second pseudoconfession, in fact, takes place in front of a mirror: "It was in the mirror that they looked at each other— in the strange, candle-lighted duplication of the scene that their eyes met" (505). The mirror is the meeting place for the two sisters: as a metaphor of the double, it duplicates a *single* scene, framing the two sisters into a reciprocal relationship of specularity; as a metaphor of the mediated nature of perception and representation, it ties them, through an indirect gaze, each to the *reflection* and to the *image* of the other. Such an image, perhaps, is but the image reflected back to women by a male gaze, which has the power of positioning them within the different pigeonholes of a single category, "womanhood." Laura discovers this during her last interview with Lionel, immediately after he has accused her of imitating Selina. Once again the parallel between the two sisters is established through a reflection, not of the mirror but of Lionel's gaze:

> [E]ven at the moment she had a sense, from the way he looked back at her, that this was in no manner the first time a baffled woman had told him that she would kill herself. . . . even in her trouble it was part of her consciousness that he now lumped her with a mixed group of female figures, a little wavering and dim, who were associated in his memory with "scenes," with importunities and bothers. It is apt to be the disadvantage of women, on occasions of measuring their strength with men, that they may perceive that the man has a larger experience and that they themselves are a part of it. It is doubtless as a provision against such emergencies that nature has opened to them operations of the mind that are independent of experience. (537–38)

With unprecedented force, the narrative voice interjects here a gener- alization to attest that, rather than the personal qualities of Laura Wing, the category "women" and the ways it is perceived and represented occupy

a central position in the story. The evasive designation of vague "operations of the mind that are independent of experience" but are capable
of redressing the balance of power in the relationships between men and
women brings to mind a famous conceptualization of the artist in "The
Art of Fiction" (published four years earlier, in 1884) and opens the way
to the alliance between the silence of women and the voice of narrative
writing, which characterizes such short stories as "The Story in It" and
"The Beast in the Jungle." What interests me here, though, is mainly how
the apparent opposition between Laura and Selina conceals and reveals,
through the mechanism of specularity, their actual congruence as members
of the repertoire of images of womanhood produced by and inhabiting the
perception of *men*. This shared position, rather than their common genetic
heritage, is the profound relationship that gives symmetry to Laura and
Selina and interchangeability to feminine roles.

The Monster

One source of Laura's "unspeakable shame and horror" is the acknowledgment of her close connection with Selina, a connection that does not just
depend on the positional symmetries created by circumstances, but is rooted
in the symbolic order that grounds them both. In effect, Laura's *avance* to
Mr. Wendover is an attenuated version of Selina's elopement with her lover:
in differing degrees, both are expressions of the same phenomenon—the
possibility made explicit that women may possess an active and original
sexual subjectivity. Her declaration to Mr. Wendover is the expression
of a desiring self in the bud—the same that openly expresses itself in
Selina's repeated adulteries; the very same self whose existence in women
the Victorian *scientia sexualis* negates and that the law, so often invoked
by Lionel Berrington, condemns and represses when it is manifested by
women.

"'I don't pretend to be better than other women, but you do!'" (500),
Selina exclaims to Laura at the conclusion of one of their verbal battles.
And the scene in the theater possibly offers yet another trauma in Laura's
acknowledgment of her own involvement with her sister and with the
sexuality Selina reveals. According to its infallible dynamics, the "aveu"
has created an "inavouable" that is thereby constituted as "the truth of the
self"—a truth revealed but unacceptable, because it violates the symbolical
boundaries constitutive of the self within that culture. Her "monstrous
overture"(520) turns Laura into a monster in Foucault's sense of the word:

a being that exceeds the existing taxonomies, that cannot be comprehended because it cannot be reduced to the existing categories and to the field of knowledge they define.[30] In the retreat of her corner in the opera box, Laura Wing can only immure herself in the silence of her unspeakable horror—as the protagonist of "The Visits," in a much more tragically conclusive way, will also do.

Chapter 6
Dying to Speak: "The Visits"

"The Visits" (1892) is definitely one of James's most obscure stories—not mentioned in *The Notebooks*, left out of the New York Edition, hardly ever quoted or examined by critics.[1] With its apparently anecdotal and bizarre character, this story is the ideal text to bring into focus the paradoxical dynamics of silence and speech and the complex interplay of prescriptions and interdictions underlying them. The conciseness, intensity, and lack of thematic redundancy of this story as compared with the thematic richness of "A London Life" allow such dynamics to emerge distilled, as it were, to their essence.

"The Visits" is the story of a young girl who literally dies *because she has spoken*: because, during her visit to the country house of friends of the family, she has impudently manifested her attraction to a young man. An unpardonable violation of the Victorian code, her declaration gives rise to a concealed and oppressive sense of guilt that, aided and abetted by a heart condition, leads Louisa Chantry to an untimely death within a few short days. The narrator, a friend and contemporary of Louisa's mother, is the astonished witness of the young girl's evident but inexplicable state. She watches with trepidation Louisa's behavior in the sequence of short scenes during her one-day visit to the country house: the intensity with which she looks at the young man; her being alone with him during innocent but discreet moments of intimacy in the house and in the garden; her deep distress as she throws herself, troubled and in tears, into the narrator's arms; and her entreaty not to divulge to her mother these tears, whose reasons are unknown. Finally, the narrator witnesses Louisa's wasting away in the second part of the story, which takes place in the Chantrys' home.[2] Only in the concluding scene, when she is at death's door, does Louisa reveal to the narrator the secret reason for her despair, in exchange for a promise never to reveal it to her mother: the girl dies soon afterward, and her secret is kept.

A melodramatic and casual anecdote? There is no trace in *The Notebooks* of how the story came to be; however, the reappearance, after only four years, of a situation already portrayed in "A London Life" would seem to exclude chance and, rather, suggest design. The deliberate re-presentation of a motif already assessed as crucial to the norms regulating Victorian womanhood brings the internal logic of the situation to its extreme consequences in what amounts to a reductio ad absurdum. The punishment is extreme, disproportionate to the apparent nature of the crime, and functions, therefore, as a denaturalizing device that foregrounds, against an essential backdrop lacking all the comedy of manners encountered in "A London Life," the symbolic stakes: the expression of an active female sexuality, coinciding with the expression of a subjectivity in woman.

As we have seen, Victorian medical discourse denied women such an active sexuality. But that denial included exceptions and paradoxes. The notion of the asexual purity of women was explicitly produced in terms of class and related to bourgeois domesticity as the hegemonic model. Within this framework, it was relatively easy and "natural" to label as deviant and discard the unregulated and frightening sexuality attributed to lower-class women and prostitutes; much more problematic to deal with was the paradox this notion entailed for the sexuality of "nice" young girls.[3] These were considered from puberty onward as troubled by dangerous emotions and disturbances that were rooted in the senses and could erupt, if improperly regulated, with irreversible results: seduction or at least the contamination of their purity of spirit—that precious and irrecoverable asset whose loss would have an equally catastrophic social outcome, as Nanda Brookenham discovers in *The Awkward Age*. This attitude gave rise to a whole system of controls, restrictions, chaperonage; a literature of guidebooks urging parents and guardians to exercise an unrelenting and lynx-eyed surveillance; countless conduct books explaining the elaborate code of feminine "modesty," which, since the eighteenth century, had prescribed, down to the minutest detail, the modes of expression and cultivation of what was yet presented as a *natural* female virtue.[4]

"True modesty" was carefully differentiated from the opposite and self-conscious attitudes of both the "prude" and the "coquette" and was seen as a natural inclination, unaware of itself and of any other contaminating reality. It was, first of all, a *mental* state, as was emphasized by such influential authors as William Cobbett and Sarah Ellis, who in the 1830s and 1840s wrote conduct books widely consulted throughout the Victorian era: "Chastity, perfect modesty, in word, deed, and even thought, is so essential, that, without it, no female is fit to be a wife. It is not enough that a young female abstain from everything approaching towards indecorum in her behaviour towards men; it is, with me, not enough that she cast down her eyes, or turn aside her head with a smile, when she hears an indelicate allusion: she ought to appear *not to understand* it, and to receive from it no more impression than if she were a post."[5]

Feminine modesty, then, implies two fundamental principles. On the one hand, it is the behavioral correlative of an identity devoid of any autonomous activity, intellectual understanding, or emotional reaction that has not been filtered through external norms established by others, so much so that its most suitable metaphor is "a post," the very image of immobility and insensibility. On the other hand, it implies that the "natural" and "instinctive" virtue, tirelessly urged and carefully cultivated, is so hard to distinguish from its opposite, simulated modesty, that its expression cannot be relied on. In her famous *Daughters of England*, Sarah Ellis even condemns embarrassment and blushing "about what a truly delicate mind would neither have perceived nor understood."[6] Only the deepest ignorance can sufficiently guarantee authentic modesty. Female modesty is unstably balanced between nature and culture (or, better, is a typically cultural representation of what is "natural"). Thus, it ends up by being defined in terms of *performance*, as the unconscious exhibition of an essence that, like every performance, however, does not exclude dissimulation. Ruth Bernard Yeazell summarizes this point very effectively: "[I]f women were essentially without erotic passion, after all, then there could be no danger that their modesty was false, their restraint affected and hypocritical."[7] The paradox of the young girl who must "appear not to understand"—that is, as Reynolds and Humble put it, "the felt necessity of conscious ignorance from women declared naturally pure"—embodies fully the ambivalence of a feminine sexuality defined, at the same time, as nonexistent and as in need of control.[8]

This is, then, the logic implied in the taboo that Louisa Chantry violates: the code of feminine modesty sets out not only the prohibition but, strictly speaking, also the impossibility of feminine self-expression, since self-expression is incompatible with a sexual identity defined in terms of unawareness and insensibility and in terms of the absence or, at any rate, the passivity, of desire. As Yeazell notes, "a woman who knows her own desires always threatens to take secret charge of the scene. But if women remain modestly unaware that they love until they are asked to marry, their desires will remain safely in the keeping of their husbands. Not until young gentlemen 'declare themselves,' as the idiom has it, will female consciousness—and sexuality—be awakened."[9]

Louisa's declaration to Jack Brandon is a scandal and has disruptive results on the person who pronounces it because it is a breach of more than just social etiquette: it violates the definition of womanhood underlying it. Unthinkable even more than unbecoming, it kills the protagonist because it explodes the irreconcilable aporia of Victorian femininity. As an expression of herself and of her own desire, it is what constitutes her as subject; and yet it cancels her out as a woman because it excludes her from any codes of femininity sanctioned by her class and culture and consequently intelligible to her. Death is not only the dramatic outcome of this conflict, but the symbolic transcription of censorship, of the compulsory *unspeakableness* and, therefore, *nonexistence* of woman as a subject of desire. This is why Louisa's illness cannot be named—"the doctor . . . could give no name to the disorder" (159–60)—and this is why her transgression, like Laura Wing's, is insistently referred to in terms of something horrific and unspeakable: "'Then she does tell you?' 'Not a bit. She only begins and then stops short—she says it's too dreadful.' 'Too dreadful?' 'She says it's *horrible*'" (158).

The entire episode of Louisa's illness is studded with acts of nonspeaking, which are all the more relevant because they are presented as the outcome of a repressed effort to speak: "She . . . [would] stretch out her hand from time to time (at intervals of very unequal length) and begin 'Mother, mother!' as if she were mustering courage for a supreme confession. The courage never came; she was haunted by a strange impulse to speak, which in turn was checked on her lips by some deeper horror or some stranger fear" (160).

The recurring emotions resulting from Louisa's declaration are, once again, horror (a term signifying, as we have seen, a strong feeling that exceeds the ethical or social level to suggest an existential or metaphysical experience) and shame in the social sense of being exposed to the gaze of others. These are both voiced in the last scene, in which Louisa finally accomplishes the "supreme confession" she had attempted and aborted so many times, again in the appropriate, ritualized form of question and answer:

"In the garden. I changed suddenly, I drove him away, I told him he filled me with horror."

"Why did you do that?"

"Because my shame came over me."

"Your shame?"

"What I had done in the house."

"And what had you done?"

She lay a few moments with her eyes closed, as if she were living it over. "I broke out to him, I told him," she began at last. But she couldn't continue, she was powerless to utter it.

"Yes, I know what you told him. Millions of girls have told young men that before."

"They've been asked, they've been asked! They didn't speak *first*! I didn't even know him, he didn't care for me, I had seen him for the first time the day before. . . . Then before he could turn round . . . it rolled over me that I was lost."

"Lost?"

"That I had been horrible—that I had been mad. Nothing could ever unsay it. I frightened him—I almost struck him." (161–62)

"First" is the key word, as the added emphasis of italics shows, which motivates the unspeakable "horror" of the situation: it is the sign of an active and original desire that, as soon as it is recognized and expressed, drags woman irreversibly ("nothing could ever unsay it") outside the boundaries codified by culture and turns her into a being who inspires horror, a frightful and wounding maenad: "'I frightened him—I almost struck him.'" This outcome is all the more significant since it goes to the heart of the system itself: Louisa is presented not as the "fast young woman" or the "girl of the period" (the negative alternative to the modest girl), but as the very epitome of the purest and most canonical Victorian innocence.[10] When she first appears, the narrator defines her as "a very pretty girl, a real maiden in her flower, less than twenty, fresh and fair and charming" (148), with a conscious use of stereotype.[11] An authentic "lily maid," one could say, like Elaine in Tennyson's *Idylls of the King*, who constitutes her correlative and probable intertext. Elaine too dies after having been the first to declare her love for Lancelot, who is unresponsive and unsympathetic. In Tennyson too the scene takes place in the garden and bears a connotation of insanity. The same verb is used to describe the revelation ("to break out," the "technical" verb of a revelation that does not proceed from premeditated decision, but from a spontaneous emotion of the heart):

> He found her in among the garden yews,
> And said, "Delay no longer, speak your wish,
> Seeing I go today." Then out she brake:
> "Going? And we shall never see you more.
> And I must die for want of one bold word."
> "Speak; that I live to hear," he said, "is yours."
> Then suddenly and passionately she spoke:
> "I have gone mad. I love you, let me die."

If the cause of Elaine's death is unrequited love, Louisa's demise is caused explicitly by the very fact that she has expressed (autonomously and not in response to male initiative) that desire that the story establishes, by framing and deferring it, as the unspeakable core of the self.

The story is embedded in a double narrative frame (the first-person tale by the main narrator is preceded by a brief introduction of another narrator who presents it, immediately after this lady's death, as the faithful transcription of one of the many anecdotes of which she had been witness and narrator) and a double time frame (the time elapsed between the events and the first narrative and between the first and the second narrative—a time period that remains unspecified but is assumed to be quite long, given that the narrator is said to have died at a considerable age). Set at a distance within this twofold frame as well as by the death of both witness and protagonist, the secret is the narrative and hermeneutic core of the tale. These structural features are reinforced by expressions that suggest, from the very beginning, the existence of something unsaid and concealed ("muffled," "secret," "discovering," "nameless," "soundlessly," "smother") and by Louisa's reiterated, emphatic entreaties not to divulge her condition to her mother.

Double secret/double confession: enclosed in the analeptic revelation—the "supreme confession" on her deathbed—the young girl's declaration of her feelings construes them as a doubly intimate secret, doubly unavowable and avowed twice. Louisa's secret is not an act but a word: following the logic of the "inavouable avoué," the confession is in and of itself a performative act that acknowledges and hence constitutes feminine sexuality, only to negate it at the same time as unacceptable, unconceivable, and unspeakable "horror." A purely symbolic transgression, Louisa's confession of love simultaneously actualizes her sexuality in the verbal sphere and removes it from the practical one: confessed and negated, female sexuality is subjected to a double removal. Woman as subject and as sexual subject is subjected to a double metaphorical displacement.

The transgression may be "purely" symbolic, but Louisa's death, merciless reductio ad absurdum of the code of feminine modesty, is there to remind us, as is always the case in James, of *the material effectiveness* of symbolic systems. And feminine silence, when displayed as the silence of interdiction and repression—the counterpart of control over expression—takes on a particular poignancy: "My hours with Louisa were even more intensely silent . . ." (160); "There was an intensity in her silence" (162). Intense silences, as intense, once interdiction is turned into deliberate choice, as those surrounding the protagonists of the stories examined in the next section.

Chapter 7
Gender Trouble: "Georgina's Reasons"

Feminine Sensations

Stories like "A London Life" and "The Visits" lay bare the violence of the symbolic system on which feminine identity is premised and implode it within the very walls of bourgeois domesticity and within the framework of the realist code that was its literary counterpart. In the 1860s, however, another genre, written mainly by and for women, found its place in the emerging gap between high literature and popular fiction as an expression of the repressed underside of bourgeois femininity. The sensation novel, as avidly read as it was publicly decried, employed *coups de théâtre* and lurid, eventful plots hinging on crimes, mysteries, seductions, bigamous relations, fires, and all types of coincidences.[1] Contemporary commentators did not fail to highlight and to condemn the culturally transgressive traits displayed by the genre. Its heroines were energetic, active, full of feelings and passion, and therefore, they threatened the ideological premise of bourgeois women's purity and passivity by suggesting that women too may harbor a disquieting potential. They moved indifferently between bourgeois or aristocratic homes and promiscuous and degraded environments and gained access to spheres deemed unbecoming for women or reserved, up to then, for men. And all this was happening, not in a remote gothic environment, but in the there and then of contemporary England, desecrating the sanctity of the bourgeois hearth, as contemporary commentators pointed out: "It is on our domestic hearths that we are taught to look for the incredible. A mystery sleeps in our cradles; fearful errors lurk in our nuptial couches; fiends sit down with us at table; our innocent-looking garden walks hold the secret of treacherous murders."[2]

The young Henry James, barely in his twenties, sized up all these elements very well in his review of Mary Elizabeth Braddon's novels, on the occasion of the American edition of *Aurora Floyd*. He named Collins as the precursor of the genre for having introduced in the novel "those most mysterious of mysteries, the mysteries which are at our own door," and cited Braddon as "the founder of the sensation novel," whose main feature was to cast as protagonist "an English gentlewoman of the current year, familiar with the use of the railway and the telegraph. The intense probability of the story is constantly reiterated. Modern England—the England of today's newspaper—crops up at every step."[3]

The article on Braddon shows James's curious ambivalence: from the tone of supercilious irony, typical of the reviews of his youth, there emerges a clear interest in the sociological aspects of the phenomenon, a sort of respect for the writer's ability to understand and interpret the needs of the public, and even a grudging admiration for her scope: "The novelist who interprets the illegitimate world to the legitimate world, commands from the nature of his position a certain popularity. Miss Braddon deals familiarly with gamblers, and betting-men, and flashy reprobates of every description. She knows much that ladies are not accustomed to know, but that they are apparently very glad to learn" (745).[4]

Notwithstanding his irony at the expense of the public in search of cheap thrills, James seems to acknowledge in the last sentence the substantial limits imposed on bourgeois women in their knowledge of reality and the utter artificiality of those same limits. This acknowledgment traces a possible connection between James's interest in the sensation novel, of which he was an avid reader, and the theme of knowledge and prohibition, which I have been examining.[5] Sensation novels, with their ready-made repertoire of active heroines and/or villainesses, recognizably endowed with initiative and (sometimes) passion, were James's first sampling of and his first means of overcoming the boundaries of femininity codified by those bourgeois *bienséances* of which both Laura Wing and Louisa Chantry were each in her own way a victim.

For this reason, it is important to turn now to a story that antedates those just analyzed but stands in a dialectical relationship to them and hence constitutes the direct premise of those later short stories in which the prohibition against women's self-expression becomes its opposite, reticence—the secret consciously experienced as complete adherence to the code and, at the same time, as a paradoxical form of power that reverses the deep logic of the code itself. By explicitly adopting sensational elements, James frees himself in this story from the obligation for verisimilitude and decorum and experiments for the first time with reversing the balance of power between men and women, using the theme of secrecy as leverage and upturning the codified relation between silence and gender identity.

Mr. Henry James Braddon

Georgina Gressie is the twenty-year-old daughter of a rich business family in New York; she is seeing Raymond Benyon, a young and promising naval officer. Her family opposes the courtship because of Benyon's limited financial means. Georgina decides to marry him secretly. First, however, she exacts from him the promise never to reveal, for any reason whatsoever, that they are married, unless she gives her permission. After some time, Georgina discovers she is pregnant; she reveals the secret to a friend of the family, Mrs. Portico, and convinces her to accompany her to Europe to conceal her pregnancy. Georgina leaves, gives birth to the child in Genoa and gives him to a peasant family, though still paying for his support. All these actions are unbeknown to Benyon, whose ship, in the meantime, has left for the Pacific. Mrs. Portico becomes ill from the tension and sense of guilt and dies right after mailing a letter to Benyon, informing him of the events. Georgina goes back to her family in New York and resumes her life as if nothing had happened. Ten years go by. Raymond Benyon has been looking in vain for his son and feels only hate and resentment toward Georgina, whom he has never seen again. His ship is now in Naples, where he meets two sisters from New England, Mildred and Kate Theory. Mildred is gravely ill, and Kate attends to her with angelic dedication. Benyon falls in love with Kate, but he cannot declare himself, since he is already married, nor can he explain the reasons why he cannot. During a visit to the Royal Palace he discovers, through the likeness of the portrait of a Bourbon princess, brought to his attention by a lady visitor, that Georgina is now married to a rich businessman. He then returns to America, convinced he finally has Georgina in his power: he intends to force her to a divorce, under the threat of revealing her bigamy to her present husband. When they meet, though, Georgina refuses to divorce him and reminds him of his promise. Benyon is equally unable to break the promise and to offer Kate a marriage that would be illegal; there is nothing left for him to do but wait for Georgina's death, which will finally free him. At his side, Kate waits, as angelic, patient, and faithful as ever.

This is the plot of "Georgina's Reasons," published in installments in the Sunday edition of the *New York Sun*, on July 20 and 27 and August 3, 1884, and syndicated in a number of papers all over the country.[6] The plot is certainly on a par with the works by Mrs. Braddon and friends: in fact, alone among all of James's works, it was presented by the *Chicago Tribune* with a sensational title: "Georgina's Reasons: Henry James's Latest Story: A Woman Who Commits Bigamy and Enforces Silence on Her Husband."[7] All the right narrative materials are there, and the reference to Mrs. Braddon is transparent from the very title, which echoes closely the more famous *Lady Audley's Secret* (1862). Like *Lady Audley's Secret*, James's story deals with bigamy discovered through the resemblance of a portrait that the betrayed husband sees by sheer chance. As in *Aurora Floyd* (1862–63), the protagonist is tall, beautiful, and insolent. Like Georgina, Aurora had fallen in love with a man of inferior class and married him in secret; thinking the first husband dead, she had remarried, only to be blackmailed by the resurrected husband until his death.[8] Literary echoes are not limited just to the work of Mrs. Braddon: the secret wedding, voluntary or accidental bigamy, and the trip to Europe to conceal the unwanted pregnancy were the topoi of the sensation novel of the 1860s. To these conventional elements are added some aspects reminiscent of the French melodrama, with its energetic adventuresses and social climbers, such as *L'Aventurière* (1848) and *Le Mariage d'Olympe* (1855) by Augier or *Le Demi-Monde* (1855) by Alexandre Dumas fils—where, it must be noted, the naive male protagonist is an officer called *Raymond* de Nanjac.[9]

Despite its obvious similarities, though, even a cursory summary of the plot reveals in "Georgina's Reasons" some glaring anomalies from the formulaic structure of melodrama and sensation fiction: these anomalies involve mainly the gender of the protagonists in relation to the conclusion of the story.

To be sure, it is not unusual—Mrs. Braddon *docet*—for the bigamist to be a woman. A compromise formation if ever was one, bigamy "keeps sexual desire within societal moral control—it is sanctioned, if illegitimately."[10] Mrs. Oliphant had already remarked that this narrative device could have been invented only by "an Englishwoman knowing the attraction of impropriety, and yet loving the shelter of the law."[11] It is absolutely exceptional, however, that such a character as Georgina, with her conscious and deliberate choice of bigamy, be unpunished: a social crime, feminine bigamy is only compatible with a happy ending (as in the case of *Aurora Floyd*) when it is not also a moral crime, that is, when it is committed by mistake and accompanied by honorable intentions. Otherwise, as with

Lady Audley, the culprit must be punished, and expelled as criminal or insane: the acknowledgment of an active and manipulative intention in women is acceptable only if it is contained within its natural channel, that is, the final reaffirmation of bourgeois marriage as moral norm. Along the same lines, Augier's and Dumas's melodramas punish the adventuress as an undesirable character who undermines the intelligibility and immutability of social relationships with her ambition and her ability to dissimulate.

Very different consequences, though, were produced by male bigamy, which was evidently much more compatible with the gender roles codified by Victorian society, with the active, irrepressible, and manipulative sexuality attributed to males, and with the man's role as the holder of patrimonial assets. In this case, the bigamous hero is entitled to a happy ending, while the heroine's self-sufficiency and self-sacrifice are emphasized, the better to allow her to be victimized. The implication is clear: women are allowed to become autonomous only if they are victimized, that is, only as a result of men's actions and decisions. The literature of the 1860s and 1870s offers several cases in point: from *Adrienne Hope* by Matilda Hays (1866), whose protagonist, throwing caution to the wind, accepts a secret marriage with a man who will then marry another woman; to "The World's Wayside," by Ernest Brent (*London Journal*, 1873), in which Kate, the protagonist, believes her husband dead in a shipwreck and manages to support herself and her son with great sacrifices, only to discover that her husband is alive and has remarried, whereupon she promises not to reveal his secret.

The ending of "Georgina's Reasons," then, manifests a gender/genre anomaly, the most glaring of many other anomalies that deserve scrutiny.

Gender/Genre Models

"He had a manner of adoring the handsome, insolent queen of his affections . . . ; indeed, he looked up to her literally, as well as sentimentally, for she was the least bit the taller of the two" (2). Thus at the end of the first long paragraph of the story, the narrator—a distanced, historiographical, heterodiegetic voice, impartially ironic to every character—positions the two protagonists in relation to each other and sanctions unequivocally the balance of power that emerges from the very first lines and is confirmed by the way the characters are initially presented.

"[A] tall, fair girl, with a beautiful cold eye . . . auburn hair, of a hue that could be qualified as nothing less than gorgeous, and . . . a stately grace" (1), Georgina "looked like a duchess" (1); she is repeatedly defined as "insolent"; she exhibits a "general indifference" and "a certain haughtiness" (3). Benyon, on the other hand, is "only a lieutenant, without a penny in the world but his pay . . . , a considerable appearance of talent, a feverish, disguised ambition, and a slight impediment in his speech" (1–2). His small build and his features, "a trifle pale, smooth and carefully drawn" (2), suggest a certain feminine element, which is reinforced by the prominent negation of any seaworthy virility ("He was neither salt nor brown nor red nor particularly 'hearty'" [2]) and by the implicit gender connotation inherent in his main behavioral traits: "He stammered a little, blushing when he did so," "his modest, attentive manner" (2). Though presented in terms of attenuated manhood, Benyon is described as having known "many types of women" and as being "fond of women" (1); this information, however, does not imply a dominant position, because we are also told that "he was a lamb with women" (2). Even a favorable comparison— "She thought the great Napoleon, before he was celebrated, before he had command of the army of Italy, must have looked something like him" (3)—does not dispel the power imbalance but rather highlights it. If he is the short officer, the image of a merely potential grandeur, she is the empress, the emblem of a fully embodied power: "she perceived a certain analogy between herself and the Empress Josephine. She would make a very good empress—that was true; Georgina was remarkably imperial" (3).[12] Right at that moment, one recalls, England was under the reign of an empress; and four kings of England (to that point) had borne the name whose feminine version was "Georgina." Strong, assertive, and haughty, Georgina is the perfect embodiment of a powerful femininity, of that "myth of ruling womanhood," which, according to Nina Auerbach, constitutes the counterpart of the victimization of women in Victorian culture.[13]

The more conventional model of victimized femininity is embodied in the Theory sisters. Mildred, the very emblem of the Victorian cult of the invalid woman, is represented as being "as beautiful as a saint, and as delicate and refined as an angel" (29)—a description that, considering how unrealistic a personal knowledge of angels and saints would be, implicitly refers to a painted model and brings us back once more to woman-as-painting. As for Kate, she is described from the first appearance in no uncertain terms:

> Her own ideas, her personal tastes, had been folded up and put away, like garments out of season, in drawers and trunks with camphor and lavender. They were not, as a general thing, for southern wear, however

indispensable to comfort in the cold climate of New England, where poor Mildred had lost her health. Kate Theory, ever since this event, had lived for her companion, and it was almost an inconvenience for her to think that she was attractive to Captain Benyon. It was as if she had shut up her house and was not in a position to entertain. So long as Mildred should live, her own life was suspended; if there should be any time afterwards, perhaps she would take it up again; but for the present, in answer to any knock at her door, she could only call down from one of her dusty windows that she was not at home. (29–30)

The image of the garments "folded up and put away," which suggests the domestic sphere; her abnegation; the closed door as image of a virginal and negated sexuality; the paradox of the explicit denial of her own existence, extraordinary image of a self who, in response to an Althusserian interpellation, constitutes its subjectivity through denial: all this sketches Kate Theory in a few traits as one of the most emblematic embodiments of selflessness as the authentic self of women: "She looked as if the habit of watching and serving had taken complete possession of her, and was literally a little sister of charity" (35). As discreet, retiring, and altruistic as Georgina is assertive, active, and self-directed, Kate Theory is her exact opposite as well from a social and symbolic point of view: Georgina comes from the rich merchant class of materialistic New York, Kate from the impoverished gentility of spiritual New England. Even their names have opposite connotations: royal Georgina is contrasted to the humble and common diminutive Kate, and Theory ("singular name, wasn't it?" [34], comments the American consul) evokes abstraction and immateriality in a way far removed from the associations of Gressie (compounded of grand, greed, gross, greasy, crass).

What we have here is, on the one hand, a deflating of the male figure, and, on the other, an extreme polarization of female characters. One of these embodies to the letter the canonical model of femininity, duly respectful (unlike Georgina, who defies her family's interdiction) of patriarchal authority, embodied in Kate's case by her brother. Subjected to man's control and initiative and, therefore, submissive and at the mercy of his choices, Kate is ready, at the end of the story, to devote her life to waiting for Benyon's word, as a prototypical May Bartram who lacks, furthermore, the gift of knowledge and understanding: "he saw that the girl only trusted him, that she never understood. She trusted without understanding, and she agreed to wait. When the writer of these pages last heard of the pair they were waiting still" (63–64). Especially canonical is her attitude toward self-expression—an attitude that abides to the very letter by all the behavioral prescriptions that Laura Wing and Louise Chantry will break, with painful results. As her sister Mildred notes: "Kate thought always that they must hide everything" (38), even the most innocent things such as their dislike for the sister-in-law, disclosed by Mildred to Benyon as "a great secret" (38). Consistent to the end, Kate does not reveal her love for Benyon even to Mildred. When Mildred suggests that she should marry him, Kate's reply is irreproachable: " 'I had better wait till he asks me' " (32). Only when she learns that Benyon is about to leave without declaring himself does she reveal her love for him to her sister and to the reader, and even then only obliquely, through an involuntary burst that has the force of a revelation: "Kate Theory turned away, with a sudden, strange violence, a movement and exclamation which, the very next minute, as she became conscious of what she had said—and, still more, of what she felt—smote her own heart (as it flushed her face) with surprise and with the force of a revelation. 'I wish it would sink him to the bottom of the sea!' " (40–41). And even when Mildred, with the special privilege of the dying, tries to induce Benyon to propose to her sister—"this poor, sick, worried lady was trying to push her sister down his throat" (39)—Kate's feelings remain undisclosed: "after all, with regard to her sister, Miss Mildred appeared to him to keep back more than she uttered. She didn't tell him the great thing—she had nothing to say as to what that charming girl thought of Raymond Benyon" (39).

Turning the Tables

In comparison to this meticulous paradigm of puritan/Victorian femininity, Georgina is an obvious anomaly. And as such she is perceived by both Benyon and Mrs. Portico (through whose points of view the story is filtered) and defined from the outset: "She was certainly a singular girl" are the first words in the tale.[14]

Georgina's singularity is deployed specifically in terms of gender, as was well understood by commentators such as Robert Louis Stevenson, who characterized her as "that far-different she," and the anonymous reviewer who spoke of her as an "ungirlish girl."[15] Her behavior, in effect, goes well beyond the codes of sensation fiction in that it contradicts, one by one, all the aspects of the canonized and culturally valued feminine model, embodied by Kate, especially, as I will show, in relation to the symbolic core of the secret.

As we have seen, the reversal of gender roles between Benyon and Georgina is apparent from the very beginning; the rest of the story fleshes out the premises outlined in the presentation of the characters. In the face of Benyon's passivity, vague intentions, and verbose sentimentalism, it is Georgina who manages the relationship, sets up their meetings and the means to effect them.[16] It is Georgina again who takes the crucial initiative of marriage, which she proposes to him despite all the codes of "modesty": "she really proposed—for that was the form it took—to become his wife without more delay. 'Oh yes, I will marry you:' these words . . . were not so much the answer to something he had said at the moment as the light conclusion of a report she had just made (for the first time) of her actual situation in her father's house" (8).

Once Benyon is out of the picture, Georgina manages the complications caused by her secret pregnancy with a practical approach and a "businesslike completeness" (25) that are the exact opposite of the bewilderment, repentance, and tearfulness appropriate to the "damsel in distress"—a sort of stand-in reference evoked by Mrs. Portico's expectations,[17] only to be contradicted by Georgina's demeanor: "Georgina came very early . . . and instantly, without any preface, looking her straight in the face, told Mrs. Portico that she was in great trouble and must appeal to her for assistance. Georgina had in her aspect no symptom of distress; she was as fresh and beautiful as the April day itself; she held up her head and smiled, with a sort of familiar challenge, looking like a young woman who would naturally be on good terms with fortune" (14).

Significantly, the reversal of the stereotypes involves the explicit negation of some of the symbolic kernels we have already encountered in "A London Life" and "The Visits." Confession is the first of these, since it appears, as the quote above already shows, quite devoid of any solemn or ritualistic formalism: "It was not in the least in the tone of a person making a confession or relating a misadventure that she presently said, 'Well, you must know, to begin with—of course, it will surprise you—that I am married' "(14).

The second and related reversed stereotype is modesty, as it appears in section three on the occasion of the first dialogue between Georgina and Benyon. Georgina is relating how her parents would like to send her to Europe so that she may forget her suitor:

"[O]f course they think that absence would cure me of——cure me of——" And she paused, with a kind of cynical modesty, not saying exactly of what.

"Cure you of what, my darling? Say it, please say it, "the young man murmured, drawing her hand surreptitiously into his arm.

"Of my absurd infatuation!"

"And would it, dearest?"

"Yes, very likely. But I don't mean to try. I shall not go to Europe— not when I don't want to." (9)

The oxymoron "cynical modesty" makes explicit reference once more to the violation of the code, by turning it upside down. The attribute "cynical" transforms modesty into a parody of itself by denaturalizing the code of virginal communication and emptying it of all its cultural implications. The reticence and hesitation signaled by the pauses do not signify the bashfulness that increases the value of concealed feelings according to the code of modesty and the "inavouable avoué" and according to the expectations betrayed by Benyon's quivering request of an explicit declaration of love. They mark simply and ironically a search for the right word to best convey the belittlement and depreciation of a feeling defined as "absurd infatuation"—a definition that one would be tempted to take as describing the point of view of her parents, but that immediately turns out to reflect Georgina's own evaluation.

Georgina's "Reasons"

It should be clear by now that Georgina's "singularity" can be ascribed to cultural expectations about gender/genre that prescribe the modalities and scenarios deemed probable and realistic—that is, culturally shared and intelligible—for these situations. It is her breach of cultural expectations that makes Georgina a hermeneutic problem for the other characters as well as for the reader, since the complete lack of narrative focalization on her denies access to her consciousness. From the very title of the story, her "reasons" are the center of narrative attention and are superimposed intertextually on the "secret" that must be revealed in the textual machinery of *Lady Audley's Secret*.

These "reasons" have a rather bizarre peculiarity. They are repeatedly explained (for a Jamesian character, Georgina is unusually willing to explain) but are as repeatedly judged unintelligible by all the other characters: "her explanation only appeared to make the mystery more dense" (17). This lack of intelligibility is only partly related to the reticence that Georgina at times displays. Rather, it circumscribes through silencing and euphemism an area of discourse that is marked as culturally taboo but, for that very reason, is clearly defined and perceived: less a secret than a tacit understanding. This is the realm of sexuality, of course, implicitly evoked when Georgina reduces her relationship with Benyon to an "absurd infatuation" (which eliminates, for good measure, the alibi of irrepressible and supreme passion) and pointed out more clearly elsewhere. The affirmed need for previous marriage is a *pruderie* that does not manage to conceal but rather explicitly reveals that the matrimonial contract here is a legitimization pure and simple of the sexual act, removed as it is from any emotional, existential, or social implication, from any maternal instinct or establishment of a family hearth:

> [P]resently she said that . . . the sooner they were married the better. The next time he saw her she was quite of the same opinion; but he found, to his surprise, it was now her conviction that she had better not leave her father's house. The ceremony should take place secretly, of course; but they would wait awhile to let their union be known.
>
> "What good will it do us, then?" Raymond Benyon asked.
>
> Georgina coloured. "Well, if you don't know, I can't tell you!"
>
> Then it seemed to him that he did know. Yet, at the same time, he could not see why, once the knot was tied, secrecy should be required. (10)

The content of this "knot" is sexual exchange, a content that remains unsaid but is nonetheless known to them both.[18] Once again, a conventional behavioral detail such as Georgina blushing is used to subversive effect, considering that she herself had made the hint to which blushing is the "correct" answer. The dialogue with Mrs. Portico, in which Georgina divulges her pregnancy to her, will later make even more clear that for her matrimony is a synonym for sexual activity: " 'I am not Georgina Gressie— I am Georgina Benyon; and it has become plain, within a short time, that the natural consequence will take place.' 'The natural consequence?' 'Of one's being married, of course; I suppose you know what that is' " (14).

I will return later to what this notion of marriage implies—something more, in my view, than a simple concession to Victorian decorum, which deemed bigamy preferable to sexual freedom. For the moment, let me reiterate that all the explanations proffered by Georgina suggest in no uncertain terms the eminently sexual purpose of marriage and proclaim the protagonist's active role, as subject of desire, in tying this knot: " 'I loved him' " (18); " 'I adored you' " (59)—language that pertains not only to feelings but to physical desire. When Mrs. Portico protests that a marriage conceived only as a " 'sanction—of the affair at the church' " is disgraceful, Georgina replies: " 'Would you have liked me to—to not marry?' " (21), thus suggesting that the alternative contemplated would have been sin rather than restraint. And it is no surprise that at this juncture Mrs. Portico's lexical choice should be strikingly consistent with what appears by now as a coherent "technical jargon," when she thinks of Georgina's revelation as a "cynical confession" (23).

Georgina's claim to an active sexual interest is connected to another of her reasons, in turn connected to the symbolic issue of feminine subjectivity: her willingness to posit herself as an autonomous and self-directed subject rather than as a docile and yielding member of the patriarchal clan. This willingness had already emerged in the dialogue with Benyon quoted above (" 'I shall not go to Europe—not when I don't want to' " [9]) and is manifested from the beginning to the end of the tale, both prospectively and retrospectively: "it afterwards became plain that he owed his brief happiness—it was very brief—to her father's opposition; her father's and her mother's, and even her uncles' and her aunts'. . . . Georgina was imperial in this—that she wouldn't put up with an order" (3–4); " 'There was one more reason,' she said. 'I wouldn't be forbidden. It was my hideous pride' " (62).

The third and last reason is financial and motivates Georgina to secretiveness. Once the initial passion was spent, Benyon opines, Georgina had fallen back on the materialistic habits of her family and had asked herself "why she should keep faith with a man whose deficiencies (as a husband before the world—another affair) had been so scientifically exposed to her by her parents" (52–53). Georgina herself supported this explanation, at least in part, when she explained to Mrs. Portico that, after Benyon's departure, when she had to live alone " 'without my husband after all, with none of the good of him,' " it had seemed pointless to face her family's reactions: " 'to go through it all just for the idea . . . I am bound to say I don't think that would be worth while' " (18–19).

Good or bad, selfish or selfless as they may be, "Georgina's reasons" are in any case explained, hypothesized, and commented on for a good part of the story, coherently and in no ambiguous terms.[19] They may be despicable— " 'You strike me as a very bad girl, my dear; you strike me as a very bad girl!' " (22)—but are certainly not mysterious. How, then, are we to account for the lack of understanding that is reiterated throughout the story almost as a refrain, from the very first sentence—"She was certainly a very singular girl, and if he felt at the end that he didn't know her nor understand her, it is not surprising that he should have felt it at the beginning" (1)—through an imposing sequel of "don't understand" and "can't understand," up to the protagonists' final dialogue: "'I have never understood you; I don't understand you now'" (59)?

To Know the Monster

It is Georgina's gender anomaly, and not her metaphysical or melodramatic mystery or even her supposed folly (a possibility that, however canonical in sensation fiction, is hardly ever contemplated in the story), that makes her unintelligible to her interlocutors.[20] Her reasons—sex, money, self-assertion—are not at all obscure: indeed, they are explicitly *declared*. What makes them impervious to a *symbolic* rather than to an intellectual understanding is the fact that they are "male" reasons, in radical contrast to the cultural definition of femininity based on purity, self-denial, and motherhood as *natural* feelings of women—precisely those feelings that Georgina's actions contradict, one by one. A prototype of the "tough" female character later to be personified by Kate Croy (with whom Georgina shares more than one element: resistance to prohibition, willpower, subterfuge, manipulation of appearances, the attempt to reconcile sexuality and money, a relationship with a promising but somewhat feminized young man), Georgina, like the Dreiserian financier, acts on the principle "I satisfy myself." Entrepreneur of herself, she uses her body at times for pleasure and at times for gain.

I suspect, then, that the title should be read, not as a question, but as a signal. The lack of understanding so profusely proclaimed is just a password: a sort of exorcism that covers up the possibility that a female subject *may* be understood according to the rules and within the domains engendered as male. The story seems to suggest it at least once, when relating Mrs. Portico's reactions to Georgina's revelations: "Mrs. Portico rose also, and, flushed with the agitation of unwonted knowledge—it was as if she had discovered a skeleton in her favourite cupboard—faced her young friend for a moment" (21). The "unwonted knowledge" is certainly "unwanted" as well: Georgina's words bring to the surface a knowledge that, like the skeleton in the proverbial cupboard, one would rather keep concealed and removed under the most respectable appearances. As Foucault points out with reference to the nineteenth-century discourse on sexuality, "there can be no misunderstanding that is not based on a fundamental relation to truth." What is embodied in the characters' paraded incomprehension is the same set of "systematic blindnesses" that are evinced in the objects of Foucault's discussion, namely, "a refusal to see and to understand . . . a refusal concerning the very thing that was brought to light and whose formulation was urgently solicited."[21]

At this point it is certainly not surprising that (for us, yet again) the symbolical offense evokes the monster, an image that all other characters apply to Georgina with a frequency and escalating verbal violence unparalleled in any of the stories examined. Here is a sample of Mrs. Portico's comments and reflections: "'My dear young woman, you are a living wonder!' Mrs. Portico exclaimed, looking at her companion as if she had been in a glass case" (19); "'Georgina Gressie, you're a monster!'" (19); "the event . . . seemed to her beyond measure strange and dreadful" (25); "This young woman's blooming hardness . . . acted upon her like a kind of Medusa mask. She had seen a horrible thing, she had been mixed up with it, and her motherly heart had received a mortal chill" (26); "Georgina came to appear to her a creature of clay and iron" (27). And this is Benyon: "[he wouldn't] have thought it possible then that a woman should be such a cold-blooded devil as she had been" (50); "he had mated himself with a creature who just happened to be a monster, a human exception altogether" (51); "she had tortured him . . . through the heart and the human vitals that she had not herself" (51); "'you're the most horrible woman I can imagine'" (62).[22]

In a chapter of *The Novel and the Police*, David Miller writes, with unsurpassed insight, that the recurrent use of madness within the sensational framework demonstrates that women are not allowed to be "criminals," that is, rationally deviant: acknowledgment of their chosen deviance would contrast with the lack of consciousness and responsibility that is culturally ascribed to them and contributes to their oppression. In the case of Georgina, monstrosity performs the same function: like madness, monstrosity "like a fate, lies ever in wait to 'cover'—account for and occlude—whatever behaviors, desires, or tendencies might be considered socially deviant, undesirable, or dangerous."[23]

The monster is by definition "against nature": as a category, it effects the expulsion and removal of what is considered deviant. On the other hand, the monster also questions forcibly the definition of "nature" by exposing how partial and limited the boundaries of this field of knowledge are. "Nature" and "natural" are inevitably the recurring terms that Benyon employs when he denies Georgina's humanity and even her being equipped with a human "heart and . . . human vitals" (51): "she was marked out by nature for so much greater a fortune" (2), "he felt that he was face to face with a full revelation of her nature" (50), "[s]he had found herself on a slope which her nature forced her to descend to the bottom" (52). How does one reconcile Georgina's "nature"—her "essential depravity" (51)—and the "natural" nature of women that the reassuring Kate Theory embodies? Georgina's "reasons" unhinge the symbolical premises of femininity (Benyon did not think that "*a woman* should be such a cold-blooded devil" [50], italics mine) and displace at the same time the whole system that rests on those premises.

Georgina 1 and 2: The Displacement of the System

Georgina 1 is a deviant figure because she is inhabited by desire and can express it; because she disobeys patriarchal authority; because she effectively manages her own life according to economic principles; because she is devoid of maternal instinct or is able to disentangle herself from it. If Georgina's story were not so completely framed by the boundaries of bourgeois women's economic dependency, it would make her a forerunner of the New Woman of the 1890s or even, with a few substitutions of the most historically specific aspects, of the sexual revolution of the twentieth century: sexual freedom instead of the secret marriage, birth control and abortion instead of the trip to Europe, economic emancipation instead of living off the family riches.

Georgina 2, on the other hand, is a faultless figure: devoted wife of a wealthy businessman, a paragon of bourgeois solidity ("William Roy had one of the biggest incomes in the city" [48]; "Mr. Roy suggested squareness and solidity; he was a broad-based, comfortable, polished man" [60]); model mother ("'I have a son, the dearest little boy. His nurse happened to be engaged for the moment, and I had to watch him'" [56]); mistress of her home, a "big modern house" on Fifth Avenue, whose sitting room (perhaps an echo of Lady Audley's) is another proof of conspicuous solvency: "an immense, florid, expensive apartment, covered with blue satin, gilding, mirrors and bad frescoes" (54). A very different background from the "topmost streets" and "sidemost avenues" (6), from the little church in Harlem's "dusty suburb" (15), and, we can surmise, from the small rented rooms where her first clandestine lovemaking had taken place. A small but crucial relational change intervenes to show that time has passed and that the codes proper to canonical femininity have now been accepted: " 'He adores me' " (62), says Georgina about her second husband; whereas she had told Benyon: " 'I adored you' " (59). The difference between Georgina 1 and 2 is all there, in the syntactical shift that declines her first as subject, then as object of love and desire. It is not without significance, then, that the first narrative signal of Georgina's new marriage is the portrait exhibited in a palace-museum. A retrospective self-quotation as well as a Braddon quotation, the portrait evokes, *en abyme*, the pattern I have already explored in this book, and that James had already thoroughly explored in his tales, of the portrait as instrument of the aestheticization and reification of women, thus foreshadowing the metamorphosis of Georgina's role.

This transformation would be thoroughly conventional, as conventional as its axiological and teleological orientation (in line with what happens in the sensation novel), if the social and legal premises of each identity were not in a chiastic relation to the identity itself.[24] The "unnatural" deviance of Georgina 1 is validated legally and morally by holy matrimony and is unimpeachable from the point of view of both law and religion. The ideal domesticity of Georgina 2, on the other hand, rests on lies and illegality and, for all legal and religious intents and purposes, is nothing but an unlawful concubinage. The first marriage is binding and lawful, even though it was motivated by pure sexual desire and disconnected from any social recognition or personal commitment. The second, bourgeois, unreprehensible marriage rests on a doubtful foundation and is devoid of legal force.[25] The feminine *Bildung* underlying the bigamous plot à la Braddon—a plot in which, as Reynolds and Humble write, "bigamy has the effect of displacing sexual desire, and replacing it with the concerns of material wealth and social position"—reveals, in the case of Georgina, that the "lawfulness" of bourgeois matrimony rests on the commodification of the female body.[26] It is an economic transaction in which exclusive possession of woman is exchanged for economic stability and respectability—exactly the opposite of what transpires in the marriage between Georgina and Benyon, where no social value changes hands, and legal sanction is only sought to allow a free woman to lend her body in an exchange of pleasure.

By separating the erotic, affective, legal, and social levels of institutional marriage, which are usually (or supposedly) linked, the story denaturalizes the institution and lays bare its deep structures. In the end, Georgina's reasons are the same unconfessed, ignored, and repressed reasons on which rests the impeccable edifice of bourgeois domesticity.

Furthermore, the separation of lawfulness, social norms, and desire is played out again and in a different key in the third union of the story, the impossible marriage between Raymond Benyon and Kate Theory. Confronted with a choice between legality and feelings, Benyon behaves as an anti-Rochester: on the altar of his promise to Georgina and of the abstract lawfulness of marriage, he sacrifices his love and his involvement with Kate. His behavior, though ethical (in the sense of a disinterested adherence to moral principles) and legal, is nominalistic and devoid of human content and supports, though for different reasons, the separation of levels displayed in the other two marriages.[27] Very telling is one of the reasons Benyon uses to justify his choice to avoid bigamy and not marry Kate: his own inability to think that "their children, if they should have any, would, before the law, have a right to exist" (63). By subordinating the right to exist to lawfulness, he quotes almost verbatim but inverts in meaning a previous statement in which Georgina explains why she abandoned their (legitimate) son: " '[he] was a complete mistake; he had no right to exist' " (56), where the right to exist was seen as depending on the requirement of subjective desire rather than of the law. Indeed, it is by no means an accident that Benyon is in love with a "Theory." To him, honor and lawfulness are the foundation of existence and literally his second nature, as witness his way of conceptualizing his promise to Georgina: "[I]t imposed itself on him *as stubbornly as the colour of his eyes or the stammer of his lips*; it had *gone forth into the world to live for itself,* and was far beyond his reach or his authority" (63, italics mine). Nowhere is the "naturalization" of ideology more clearly enunciated than here. And nowhere is ideology as clearly and ironically "denaturalized" as in the lines that almost immediately follow: "dishonour was in everything but renunciation. So, at last, he renounced. He . . . returned to Boston to tell Kate Theory that they must wait. He could explain so little that, say what he would, he was aware that *he could not make his conduct seem natural*" (63, italics mine).

The length of their waiting, mentioned in the final clause immediately following, denaturalizes even further the choice dictated by honor and further complicates any negotiation between terms that are by now irreparably divided, like law and nature, desire and society. In reference again to the Victorian sensation novel, David Miller notes that if the extremes of sacrifice and the violent and improbable expedients adopted to ensure the "correct" conclusion of the story were undoubtedly meant to signify the supreme value of the norm—a value for which no sacrifice is too high—they also have a diverging effect "that we, more laxly oppressed than they, are perhaps in a better position to specify. This is simply that, recontextualized in a 'sensational' account of its genesis, such a norm risks appearing *monstrous*: as aberrant as any of the abnormal conditions that determine its realization."[28]

Secrecy and Power

The displacement of the social system and symbolic order effected by "Georgina's Reasons" hinges entirely on one narrative device—secrecy—which is the pivotal point of the whole development of the plot. Now is the moment to examine it closely.

Georgina's secret presents a peculiar trait as compared with the secrets I examined in the previous chapters: it is entrusted to a man, not to a woman. If the symbolic content of the secret is feminine sexuality as the "truth of the self" where her subjectivity is deployed, as I have argued, following Foucault, then this story creates a new situation: the feminine code of chastity and modesty is bound by means of a promise to the masculine code of honor—*the word given*.

Masculine honor thus becomes the guarantee of a secret that, by being entrusted to a person other than the self, becomes ipso facto untrammeled by the dependent obligation of self-revelation: the "obligation to conceal" no longer coincides with the "duty to confess." The subject is no longer bound to the ritual of the "aveu," which is thus systematically reduced, as we have seen, to a "cynical" parody or even (with "unparalleled impudence" [60]) to an object of defiance and explicit denial: "'Fancy me telling such a hideous story—about myself—me—me!'" (62).

The differential allocation of the secret does not affect just the woman to whom it is usually entrusted. By exacting the promise, Georgina transforms drastically the usual distribution of gender roles with regard to silence and speaking. The promise effects a reversal of the situation whereby silence and waiting belong to the feminine domain and speaking and action to the masculine one: only Georgina can speak or authorize Benyon to reveal their secret. Forced to be reticent, Benyon is thus bound to the role usually assigned to the modest young girl, as zealous custodian of the unspoken feminine sexuality. Furthermore, in relation to Kate, the impossibility of breaking the promise makes him unable to disclose his feelings openly—a highly gender-specific situation—and confines him to the feminine role of forced sublimation and silent anticipation, thus enforcing on him that split between the domains of sexuality, on one hand, and of domestic and emotional values, on the other, a division that is typical of women's *éducation sentimentale*. What entraps him is the culturally sanctioned relation between gender and speaking: the masculine code of the *word given* binds him to the feminine condition of the *word denied.* " 'I could damn you with a word!' " (59), he cries out to Georgina in exasperation. In spite of Georgina's implicit challenge (" 'You say you could damn me with a word; speak the word and let us see!' " [60]), however, this word will never be uttered: "He asked himself whether he should be able to speak if he were to try, and then he knew that he should not, that the words would stick in his throat, that he should make sounds which would dishonour his cause" (61). Significantly, Benyon's silence is directly related to a moment of sexual intimacy in which the dynamics of gazing and blushing assign him an ambiguous "female" positioning: "his silence was after all the same old silence, the fruit of other hours and places, the stillness to which Georgina listened while he felt her eager eyes fairly eat into his face, so that his cheeks burned with the touch of them" (61). Benyon's "slight impediment in speech" (2), alluded to at the beginning of the story, has become at this point an utter impossibility.

The bond of silence alone effects a reversal of man-woman relationships. Significantly, the promise is explicitly related in the text to two crucial elements: freedom and power. "[H]e left her free while he bound himself" (22); "she had reserved herself—in the strange vow she extracted from him—an open door for retreat" (51). The promise allows Georgina to keep her freedom (" 'What in the world have I done to you but let you alone? . . . I leave you your liberty, and I can live as I like' " [58]) and almost acts as a counterweight to Benyon's masculine independence and freedom to move: " 'You could do as you pleased . . . You roamed about the world, you formed charming relations. . . . Think of my going back to my father's house—that family vault—and living there, year after year, as Miss Gressie!' " (59).[29]

As to power: from the very beginning the distribution of roles between the two characters does not follow the codes, but the question of power is still left untouched. It is addressed directly, however, after Benyon's discovery of Georgina's bigamy, which gives him briefly the upper hand in the relation: "it made a difference—an immense difference. . . . he saw it clearly—it consisted in Georgina's being in his power now, in place of his being in hers" (49–50). The war metaphor employed during their last encounter confirms that there is a power struggle going on.[30] Georgina's characterization, however, in which all the images of power attributed to her are evoked and amplified, suggests what the outcome of this struggle will be:

[S]he was magnificent, in the maturity of her beauty, her head erect, her complexion splendid, her auburn tresses undimmed, a certain plenitude in her very glance. . . . There was nothing definite about her but her courage; . . . it seemed to glow in the beauty which grew greater as she came nearer, with her eyes on his and her fixed smile . . . She was ready for anything, she was capable of anything. . . . She had carried on an intrigue before she was twenty; it would be more, rather than less, easy for her now that she was thirty. All this and more was in her cold, living eyes . . . She was a truly amazing creature. (55–56)

Benyon's euphoric sense of power will return again, but only for a moment, during the last scene: "This personage was conscious of only one thing, of his own momentary power, of everything that hung on his lips; . . . he felt his opportunity, . . . he held it there in his hand, weighing it noiselessly in the palm" (61). Having chosen to keep silent, he will revert to what the text has defined several times as "impotence"—the passive possession of a secret that, paradoxically, confers subjection, not power, on the person who keeps it.

Gender/Genre

The story presents yet another paradox. Notwithstanding the literary contrivance of the story, with its implausible plot and intertextual references, "Georgina's Reasons" was born, not out of literature, but out of life. There is a detailed entry in the *Notebooks* about its origin, an anecdote related by Mrs. Kemble, whose lack of verisimilitude James repeatedly highlights: "The story has only the *tort* to be very incredible, and almost silly; it sounds 'made up'"; "the situation as presented in the foregoing anecdote (which is impudently crude and incoherent) might be variously modified."[31] In actually developing his plot, though, James modified nothing, preserving even the detail about the child abandoned in Europe, which in his entry he had defined as "an impossible incident" (27): his story, in the end, follows closely the original anecdote with all its indecent details. Why would he follow it closely if it were not to explore, in fact, the potential of a story so out of the ordinary: the dislocation of gender connotation, the reversal of the traditional power balance between the protagonists, the central role played by the promise to keep the secret—"it is the most important point of the whole!" (27), he notes—the final confirmation of an anomalous and, to the dominant contemporary morality, offensive state of affairs, in which the woman who has violated all cultural and moral codes enjoys, unperturbed, the "wages of sin," whereas the sacrificial role of submissive custodian of social values is ascribed to an honorable but defeated male figure.

Certainly, all of these features would be best conveyed by sensation fiction. No other genre of the times, in fact, would have lent itself to such radical questioning of gender codes without totally renouncing the realist code and the representation of social mores or alienating James's traditional audience. No other genre could have "naturally" allowed the reader to perform a transgressive identification with the deviant heroine—an identification that is one of the founding devices in the pragmatics of sensation novels.[32] No other genre would have offered an ending displaying such a variety of identification options, each one cathartic in its own way, each one equally problematic because it is unwilling to offer a reassuring and culturally validated synthesis: the triumph of the nonconformist and courageous (but "evil") heroine; the triumph of canonical (but unlawful) bourgeois domesticity; the triumph of feminine self-sacrifice and love (but pointless and unfulfilled); the triumph of honor and of ethical (but ineffectual and frustrated) behavior.

In conclusion, James's use of the sensational genre, as always happens with his intertextual reference, is experimental, wary, and cognitive. In sensation fiction James finds a well-oiled literary machinery of excess, out of which he manufactures potentially disturbing and indecent material under the protection offered him by the encoded expectations of the genre. The well-known "exaggeration" of the sensational would "cover up" for the deviant elements of the plot while nonetheless exposing such "aberrations" to the scrutiny of the public. Masquerading reality as literature, the writer is free to explore its dynamics to the full and to cast them in extreme forms, through the adoption of a key he would never adopt again in such an undiluted form. For all these reasons I consider this story, not a potboiler that makes concessions to sensationalism in order to please a large audience, but rather an important experiment, a crucial development in James's textual exploration of gender and of gender as text.[33] By playing out the opposition between silence and speaking and the reversal of its cultural gender connotations, James exposes those connotations and the symbolic order underlying them, thus opening new directions to explore: on one hand, the price exacted from feminine subjectivity by the symbolic order, in the short stories examined so far; on the other hand, in the short stories that will follow, the possibility that may open to feminine characters of negotiating between self-expression and self-defense in the interstices between speaking and keeping silent.

Chapter 8
The Word Not to Say It:
"The Story in It"

Ce qu'on ne peut pas dire,
il ne faut surtout pas le taire,
mais l'écrire.
—Jacques Derrida, "Envois"

"L'honnête femme n'a pas de roman," wrote Henry James on May 8, 1898, to summarize in the *Notebooks* the germination of what would later develop into a tale, "The Story in It" (1902).[1] The story is conceived as a true drama in three acts—a three-way dialogue integrated by a narrative voice that confines itself to supplying the elements of mise en scène and to describing from the outside actions and reactions of the characters without making incursions into their interiority. It is an experimental story on more than one account: because of James's rigorous adoption of the dramatic form, recently assumed as narrative pattern in *The Awkward Age*, and because of its metaliterary dimension, revealed in the title itself, which lends this tale the character of a narrativized debate on the novel as genre. The question under discussion was much debated at the time: the comparison between the "immorality" of the French novel, with its overt representation of sexuality in love and in life, and the English novel, which lent itself to the accusation of providing an insipid and sugar-coated representation of the world because of its adherence to morality and decorum.[2]

Perhaps because of this open metadiscursive quality, "The Story in It" has always been classified as one of James's short stories about the artist. This classification is based on a *Notebooks* entry, foreshadowing an artist as male protagonist, and on James's own retrospective reading of the story in his preface. There he traces its origin to a discussion of aesthetics with a novelist friend (presumably Paul Bourget) and presents it as an expression of a truly Jamesian principle, that is, the subjective and relative quality of such a notion as "adventure": "a human, a personal 'adventure' is no *a priori*, no positive and absolute and inelastic thing, but just a matter of relation and appreciation—a name we conveniently give, after the fact, to any passage, to any situation, that has added the sharp taste of uncertainty to a quickened sense of life."[3]

The character of the story as literary manifesto and its congruence with James's poetics have thus put in the background the *"honnête femme"*—as crucial an element, in my view, as the *"roman."*[4] In fact, this story interlaces the social codes of femininity with the literary codes of the novel, revealing their interaction and their reciprocal construction as "truth"; and once more, by taking silence as its theme, it looks for new ways to articulate femininity with writing.

The Stage

Act I: the sitting room, elegantly appointed, of a country house. The afternoon of a stormy spring day. "Two ladies seated there in silence" (403), each independently occupied: Mrs. Dyott, the mistress of the house, a "fair and slightly faded beauty" (404), is writing letters; Maud Blessingbourne, younger, dark-haired, pretty, is reading a French novel. Each woman is secretly keeping a watchful eye on the other, trying not to show that she is anxiously waiting for the third actor, Colonel Voyt, dark, full of an "un-English" attractiveness, with the beard "of an emir or a caliph" (406).[5] When he arrives, Mrs. Blessingbourne, who is apparently perturbed by their imminent meeting, leaves the room for a few minutes; the behavior of the other two, alone, reveals that they are, in fact, lovers.

Act II: in the same sitting room. The three characters sit around the fire and discuss literature. The topic is French novels, which Maud loves to read, " 'for I seem with it to get hold more of the real thing—to get more life for my money' " (409). Voyt appears to be shocked but, at the same time, defends the French novel on aesthetic grounds for its realism and its power: it looks at life in its entirety and is " 'as near as art can come—in the truth of the truth' " (411); in comparison the decorum of English and American novels " 'seems really to show our sense of life as the sense of puppies and kittens' " (410). Maud also expresses her dissatisfaction with what she cannot find in French novels: " 'Well, I suppose I'm looking, more than anything else, for a decent woman' " (412). To which the colonel offers a sanctioned rejoinder: " 'Oh then, you mustn't look for her in pictures of passion. That's not her element nor her whereabouts' " (412). Maud's position, instead, is that it is possible to represent passion even in relation to a "decent woman"; in defending it, she implicitly reveals her own literary ambitions. Throughout the dialogue, Maud insists repeatedly, interrogatively, that the terms of the debate be defined: " 'Doesn't it depend on what you mean by passion?' . . . 'Doesn't it depend a little on what you call adventures?' . . . 'Doesn't it depend a good deal on what you call drama?' . . . 'Doesn't it depend on what you call romance?' " (412–13). In answer to her questions, Voyt replies with a crescendo of certainties and increasingly peremptory statements:

> "My dear lady . . . their romance *is* their badness. There isn't any other. . . . The adventures of the honest lady? The honest lady hasn't—can't possibly have adventures. . . . The adventure's a relation; the relation's an adventure. The romance, the novel, the drama are the picture of one. The subject the novelist treats is the rise, the formation, the development, the climax, and for the most part the decline, of one. And what is the honest lady doing on that side of the town? . . . What's a situation undeveloped but a subject lost? If a relation stops, where's the story? If it doesn't stop, where's the innocence? It seems to me you must choose." (413–14)

The discussion is almost exclusively between Maud Blessingbourne and Voyt, with Mrs. Dyott in the role of amplifier and supporting cast to his arguments, and ends with the rhetorical victory of the colonel, who nevertheless fails to convince his interlocutor.

Act III: after Voyt's departure, Maud reaffirms to Mrs. Dyott her ideas and refers to her own life as evidence that "decency" and "romance" may coexist: she has an illicit passion, " 'my little drama' " (416), " 'my . . . romance' " (417), which is honest because it is unrevealed and lived in the secrecy of her consciousness: " 'The romance of what? Of his not knowing?' 'Of my not wanting him to. If I did . . . where would be my honesty?' " (417). Maud denies that Voyt is the object of her passion, as Mrs. Dyott suggests: it is this very denial, as Mrs. Dyott will tell Voyt privately, that proves Maud's love for him. In the last exchanges of the text, the two lovers reluctantly admit that perhaps there is some truth in Maud's theory:

> Her consciousness, if they let it alone—as they of course after this mercifully must—*was*, in the last analysis, a kind of shy romance. Not a romance like their own, a thing to make the fortune of any author up to the mark—one who should have the invention or who *could* have the courage; but a small, scared, starved, subjective satisfaction that would do her no harm and nobody else any good. Who but a duffer—he stuck to his contention—would see the shadow of a "story" in it? (420)

The Staging of Love/Power

The immediate effect of the ironical reference to the title in the very closing of the story is to distance the reader from Voyt. As readers, we are led to acknowledge the limitation of his notion of "story" and endorse instead the Jamesian poetics of the narratability of a nonstory (along with the authoritativeness of the author, who, with Hitchcockian coyness, dares to appear *en abyme* in the role of the "duffer").

A mere reversal of the statement, however, does not exhaust its potential implications. Upon closer observation, the invitation to learn and "see a story in it" is fairly destabilizing: which story, whose story? Against the simple and unchanging background, which confers on the story its unity of place, time, and action, under the apparently abstract dialogue, a complex fabric of relationships is woven along the web of minute reactions and nuances that convey the unsaid of language. These relationships are all regulated by love and power—two rules that, in the geometrical bareness of the triad on stage, describe and seem to exhaust gender relations.

"Deep, sore, tragic"—as James describes her in *The Notebooks* (177)—Mrs. Dyott is static and often appears congealed in a passive and silent pose of waiting, imprisoned by a secrecy imposed on her from the outside as clandestine lover. Significantly, during her first dialogue with Voyt, he is shown checking whether she has burned the message with which he had announced his visit; during the literary debate, her moment of unguarded identification with the "bad" women who yield to their passion—"'Oh, they pay for it!'" (413)—betrays her soreness at being one of them.

Voyt, on the other hand, is good-humored, mobile, and active: when he first appears on stage, he is presented as "a pleasant, weather-washed, wind-battered Briton," who has just successfully emerged from "a struggle with the elements that he appeared quite to have enjoyed" (406). As well as being the arbiter of when and how he meets his lover, Voyt completely dominates the relation between the two women, as shown in the opening scene through the silent and tense watch they keep on each other and through their skirmishes about which is the woman he has come to see.[6] His centrality in the relational dynamics of the three is confirmed by the final scene, in which Mrs. Dyott sacrifices her friend Maud to him along the lines of the typical pattern of women's rivalry in patriarchal society. By betraying her secret, Mrs. Dyott aims at rendering Maud's love ineffective, thus reinforcing her own possession of Voyt: "'I see,' Voyt after a moment returned. 'Your real calculation is that my interest will be sacrificed to my vanity—so that, if your other idea is just, the flame will in fact, and thanks to her morbid conscience, expire by her taking fright at seeing me so pleased'" (419). Voyt also dominates the scene when all three characters are together, as is highlighted by the construction of the communicative situation along the lines of highly gender-specific linguistic choices.[7] Maud uses interrogative, tentative, and reticent tones, and Mrs. Dyott only speaks to echo someone else's words. Voyt, in contrast, argues in a peremptory and assertive language, which verges on the monologue ("'You'll doubtless tell me . . .'" [410]); he is condescending ("a genial derision" [414]; "his indulgent manner" [415]), overtly ironic ("'Oh, now we have you!' her interlocutor laughed" [411]), and behaves as if the conversation were a duel that triumphantly ends in self-proclaimed victory: "'They've been in long enough to point a moral. That is to point ours!'" (415). A game of love and power is under way underneath the aesthetic debate, and it is betrayed, not just by the way in which the characters argue, but by the tacit erotic implication underlying the skirmishes, as if Voyt (whose "experience" in this field is mentioned several times and whose interest in Maud is attested both by his questions about her to Mrs. Dyott and by his vague and evasive replies to her own questioning) was using the literary argument as a form of seduction to convince Maud of the inevitability of "yielding." The erotic undercurrent of the dialogue is signaled by the frequent ambivalence of the language and becomes evident in the exchanges that close both the literary discussion and section 2:

> "We've spoiled her subject!" the elder lady sighed.
>
> "Well," said Voyt, "it's better to spoil an artist's subject than to spoil his reputation. I mean," he explained to Maud with his indulgent manner, "his appearance of knowing what he has got hold of, for that, in the last resort, is his happiness."
>
> She slowly rose at this, facing him with an aspect as handsomely mild as his own. "You can't spoil my happiness."
>
> He held her hand an instant as he took leave. "I wish I could add to it!" (415)

The Staging of Literature

Underneath and through the literary debate, another story is staged: a story that deals with men and women, with love relations as power relations, and with remarkably unbalanced power relations between men and women. In

James's habitual vertiginous manner, the love story contains a defense of the novel that contains a love story that will perhaps produce a story . . . Far from offering an orderly and reassuring narrative framing, the levels of the text tend to intersect each other, because erotic liaisons are not just the occasion for the story but the object of the literary debate, which is itself an instrument of and an episode in the amorous plot.

From the conceptual point of view as well, the story presents a complex intersection of different levels of discourse. The complexity derives not so much from its "pure" metafictionality as from the inquiry into the condition of women that interfaces it and the resulting tension between the two levels. "Honest woman" and "fallen woman" are, at the same time, characters on stage, social and moral notions, and the topic of an aesthetic debate. The two terms circumscribe options that are at once literary and existential, as shown by the frequent doubles entendres in the dialogue and by the polysemic use of the term *romance*, which recurs in the story in each of its definitions in relation both to life and to literature. The interference in the text between life and literature, mimesis and metafiction is part of a larger system, since it descends from cultural patterns that simultaneously prescribe roles in life and roles in literature. In both fields, man is the point of reference, arbiter, and censor. In his double role as lover of one of the women and judge of the reading material of the other ("her fellow-guest wished to scold her for the books she read" [408–9]), Voyt is the perfect embodiment of the "double standard" and of the hypocritical nature of the current denigration of the "French novel" and its women readers.[8]

The same cultural premise, the same gender structure, preside over both the social and the aesthetic model: hence the interdependence and deep congruence of both models. Feminine sexuality, its use, and its control according to categories created by men and for men are the key elements both in the novelistic scenarios and in social codes: life and literature are twinned at the source, much more so than would be suggested by the chiastic relation between the two women characters, seemingly pointing to the well-known aesthetic opposition between art and life.[9] Life and literature, in fact, share a single system of representation, whose categories reciprocally sustain and enhance each other. If the difference between the French and the English novel is defined on the basis of the moral opposition between their women protagonists, reciprocally the very notion of "honest woman"—a moral and social notion—is culturally defined and circulated in narrative terms: "l' honnête femme n'a pas de roman."

The honest woman is a woman without history and one who consequently has no access to a story; the fallen woman is a woman with a history, whose story she herself cannot tell, although it can be told by others. In both cases, women are subjected to an interdiction or an impossibility concerning their speaking about themselves: the narrative nonexistence of the *honnête femme* implies the nonexistence of woman as the subject of her own story, that is, as subject *tout court*, considering that apperception rests on the narrativization of the self. The maxim that gives rise to the story is not just an innocent commonplace: it sanctions the nonexistence of feminine subjectivity as word spoken and word narrated.

It is not surprising that the story should originate from a maxim: as Roland Barthes wrote, it is in these sayings that the *doxa*—common knowledge and common sense—is deposited in such a way that, despite their utterly bookish origin, they end by being perceived as the very essence of "real life."[10] This is the kind of knowledge that Voyt expounds in the text, which thus internalizes and makes explicit the codes of plausibility of its contemporary culture.

With respect to this shared knowledge, though, James adopts a perspective of deliberate "demaximization," as Nancy Miller writes of *La Princesse de Clèves*, a text that is echoed in this story.[11] By openly playing with the literary conventions while at the same time thematizing his own attempt to escape them, James is not solely working on the literary codes at a metalinguistic level but is also investigating the ideological premises these codes convey and produce along the writing-reading circuit of representation.[12] Violating the maxim in the story, writes Nancy Miller, "is not merely to create a puzzling fiction but to fly in the face of a certain ideology (of the text and its context), to violate a grammar of motives that describes while prescribing" (341).

If the prescriptive maxim operates, as I have just argued, on the relation between woman-story-speaking, the "demaximization" operates, as does Maud in the story, by questioning each term of the maxim and by denaturalizing their apparent obviousness. Again: what story, whose story? By acknowledging the literary conventionality of the duality French/English, moral/immoral novel, domestic/adulterous plot, the ensuing representations of women are also unmasked as unilateral, codified, and restrictive—representations that do not welcome feminine desire but imprison it in preconstituted and deadening roles and stereotypes. Only when viewed in these terms—terms that are at once cultural and aesthetic—is the plot that Maud imagines implausible. "The blind spot here—in Nancy Miller's words—is both political (or philosophical) and literary. It does not see, nor does it want to, that the fictions of desire behind the desiderata of fiction are masculine and not universal constructs" (357).

What is at stake here then is the assertion, through the story, of one's own word. And of a desire and a narrative desire that belong to women and are not pure and simple submission to masculine desire, as in the "inevitable" adulterous script that Mrs. Dyott recites. It is the literary expression of *another* story, still invisible because it is *woman-centered*, written according to a new script that no longer obeys the rules of passion, which are still man-centered. If "the honest woman has no romance," one could say, it is also because that novel has not been written yet.

The Staging of Renunciation

In the version offered by Maud Blessingbourne—and by James's story—the novel of the "honest woman" seems to be threatened by a paradox. This instrument of reappropriation and expression of one's own story, the place in which the "lovely subject" (411) of an original plot promises to become the "subject" of an acquired subjectivity, is predicated on renunciation and silence as the necessary conditions for the advent of its premises.

According to Luisa Villa, renunciation—with its range of philosophical, historical, and psychoanalytic implications—is the defining gesture of the Jamesian subject *tout court*: "renunciation is a perfectly internalized version of 'conspicuous waste'—a sacrificial ritual aimed at establishing the victory of the self over the world by displaying the luxury of consciousness and of its impractical objects."[13] Renunciation is the answer to a historical upheaval of subjectivity when a historical divide was established between life and forms, individuality and the social system: the self hides this upheaval by claiming control over the world through the "ascetic" option. By transferring to consciousness her desire to possess, Maud Blessingbourne, like Fleda Vetch, becomes another inhabitant of that "mystified stage which . . . James's protagonists are forced to inhabit precisely at the moment when they constitute themselves as 'free' and 'great.'"[14]

Villa's rigorous analysis might offer useful suggestions regarding this story too by providing a wider background against which Maud's renunciation need not be interpreted in terms of her mere adherence to the sanctified codes of feminine behavior and of James's concession to current bourgeois morality, to which he seems to return every time one of his heroines must choose between convention and transgression. Renunciation, viewed as the last historical resort of the subject's self-assertion, does not contradict but rather supports the desire to affirm one's own "story." But add to this the variable of gender, and a much more radical question is raised. Why renunciation? Renunciation of what? To qualify Maud's choice as renunciation may mean that we have already adopted a male-centered point of view and accepted the script of passion as the only possible one. We should not make the mistake of reading Maud as abdicating a fullness of life of which man is the only guarantor and that appears, therefore, very unstable, at least based on Mrs. Dyott's example. What we call here "renunciation" is perhaps the only space for self-assertion open to the feminine subjectivity within the rigid legality and the binding categories of the existing system.

The Staging of Desire

In commenting on the ending of *La Princesse de Clèves*, Nancy Miller rereads Freud's essay on "The Relation of the Poet to Daydreaming" and develops an argument about feminine fantasies, narrative plot, and desire that is very much applicable to "The Story in It." Freud states that masculine fantasies are about power and feminine fantasies about love; if this is true, for women where lies the space of the Ego—"His Majesty the Ego, the hero alike of every day-dream and of every story"?[15] The departure of some feminine plots from the verisimilitude, based on the "maxim," of codified scripts follows a different economy, where egotistical desires attempt to assert themselves alongside erotic ones: "The repressed content, I think, would be, not erotic impulses, but an impulse to power: a fantasy of power that would revise the social grammar in which women are never defined as subjects; a fantasy of power which disdains a sexual exchange in which women can participate only as objects of circulation" (348).

Maud Blessingbourne, like the Princess of Clèves in Miller's reading, "knows herself to be without a text" (351): her renunciation, therefore, is not a refusal of love or of life but a refusal of the cultural/narrative logic that positions her inexorably as an object and denies her possession of her own self in a world in which love relations are based on an unequal exchange. The protagonist gives up the actualization of her love fantasy "not because she does not want to live happily ever after, but because she does" (351)—and in fact, in the ending of section 2, she claims a happiness that cannot be spoiled precisely because it is self-legislated and independent from the other. In this context, fantasy is "the only sexual performance she can afford in an economy regulated by dispossession" (350).

Renunciation, then, coincides in both texts with the "feminine enlight-
enment" of self-assertion: the *"honnête femme"* is not (only, necessarily)
sexually repressed by the patriarchal injunction to be chaste but is also a
self-directed and self-legislated subject, free from the reach of the structure
of power and possession. She envisions and writes her own story in which
she asserts herself as *subject* and, therefore, protagonist and *author* instead
of character in a preordained script that follows somebody else's logic.[16]

Once more, narrative and existential levels coincide: whereas the
"French" love-passion story follows an inevitable, predictable, and punitive
logic ("bad women" " 'paying for their badness' " [413]), Maud's story is
open-ended, because it is predicated on the nonsaturation logic of desire.[17]
In this respect, renouncing the option of possessing the loved one corresponds to the Lacanian principle of the absence of the object. Fantasy does
not operate on the material model of physical need but produces pleasure
through the continuous staging of desire. As in the case, analyzed by Freud
and reread by Lacan, of the butcher's wife who does not allow her husband
to buy her the caviar that she craves, Maud Blessingbourne "st[ands] in
need of an unfulfilled wish": the nonactualization of passion allows desire
to remain forever active without crystallizing in appeasement, and it allows
the subject of the fantasy to avoid identifying with the object of somebody
else's desire but to sustain the self indefinitely as *desiring subject.*[18]

The Staging of the Secret

The move that allows the protagonist to avoid the oppositions and defy the
cultural antinomy between honest woman and passion, story and nonstory,
is once more predicated on silence. More than ever, silence reveals here its
ambivalent function: a repressive injunction liable to be transformed into
an instrument of self-preservation. As a nonrequest for love, silence can
create that *epoché*, that suspension that guarantees the inexhaustibility of
desire and allows its subject to be assertive and self-sustaining.

In this story too we encounter a scene of *denied confession*—a double
scene, indeed, since Maud twice refuses to answer the others' questions:
as author, in respect to the subject of her novel (" 'It's not that she doesn't
know . . . It's only that she doesn't say.' . . . 'Tell us then at least what it
is.' . . . 'Oh, to tell it would be to express it, and that's just what I can't
do' " [410–11]); and as woman, in respect to the object of her love: " 'You
deserve that one should speak *for* you!' Her companion looked cheerful
and secure. 'How *can* you, without knowing——?' 'Oh, by guessing! It's

not——?' But that was as far as Mrs. Dyott could get. 'It's not,' said Maud, 'anyone you've ever seen'" (417–18).

Unlike the young victims of "A London Life" and "The Visits," Maud Blessingbourne knows and recognizes her own desire without naming its object: her secrecy—completely orthodox from the point of view of gender codes—allows her to be in control of her choices and removes her from the grasp of social and literary norms. The economy of secrecy—even when it is not aggressive, as in the case of "Georgina's Reasons"—implies control over inner elaboration and mastery over the self, that is, deliberate defense of the self's inner space, which is thus safeguarded from the struggle for power exemplified by the story both in the Dyott-Voyt relationship and in Mrs. Dyott's self-serving use of Maud's secret as a weapon.[19]

The use Mrs. Dyott makes of it, on the other hand, highlights the paradoxical nature of Maud's secret. It is no secret, in fact, since Mrs. Dyott has no difficulties in decoding and utilizing it: "'Why are you so sure that I'm the man?' 'From the way she denies you.' 'You put it to her?' 'Straight. If you hadn't been she would, of course, have confessed to you—to keep me in the dark about the real one'" (419). As in the case of Laura Wing with her sister, this is a domain of convention in which confession produces meaning, not directly through its easily understood truth, but through its ritualistic character. The same applies to its counterpart, the secret: even if it is understood, its function persists since it depends, not on its cognitive content, but on the pure and simple will to keep it, on the denial opposed to confession as ritual of subjection to power and social control. David Miller makes an accurate distinction between "secrecy" and "secret" and writes that the meaning of the secret "lies in the subject's formal insistence that he is radically inaccessible to the culture that would otherwise entirely determine him. I cannot, therefore, resolve the double bind of a secrecy that must always be rigorously maintained in the face of a secret that everybody already knows, since this is the very condition that entitles me to my subjectivity in the first place."[20]

In this regard, then, secrecy is not the outcome of an external injunction but *a refusal of the language in which the subject is interpellated.*

The Staging of Silence: The Story

Maud's silence is as eloquent as those that fill up the text from the opening scene—"two ladies seated there in silence." Crucial meanings are conveyed in this story through what is not said: Maud's anxiety while she waits, Voyt's interest, her love, the nature of the relationship between the colonel and Mrs. Dyott, to wit, "It was exactly the silence ensuing on the retreat of the servant and the closed door that marked between him and his hostess the degree of this ease. They met, as it were, twice: the first time while the servant was there and the second as soon as he was not. The difference was great between the two encounters, though we must add in justice to the second that its marks were at first mainly negative . . . it did without words" (406).

Throughout the story silence has a self-conscious and metalinguistic quality, as is suggested from the very first lines: "What their silence was charged with, therefore, was not only a sense of the weather, but a sense, so to speak, of its own nature" (404). Equally charged with "a sense of its own nature," the story displays the same self-awareness in confronting its own nature as literary expression of the two-fold feminine silence: the issue of keeping silent and speaking—which has, by definition, powerful metafictional implications—entangles the text in the very dynamics of speaking/keeping silent, which are its theme.

Feminine silence becomes here the voice of writing: hypothetical writing of a novel that is planned in the plot but also writing of the story of which we are the readers. This is where we can fully appreciate the importance of the change James made in his original idea: according to *The Notebooks*, the artist was to have been a man who in the end accepts the possibility of an inner adventure. In the actual story, instead, the two gender roles are unreconciled, and the artist and the literary project are identified with the feminine polarity; if man has the last word in the story—a condescending and reductive word—the story itself, with its very existence, is ironically there to reduce his authoritativeness. Maud's argument finds a literary actualization in James's story: by shifting its communicative axis from sensual to mental, from assertive to allusive, from explicit to implicit, the story enacts Maud's ethical and aesthetic requirements and claims dramatic interest for a woman's story that would not otherwise have been written. In choosing to be the nonstory of the "honest woman," "The Story in It" makes it into *a story*.

This alliance with the feminine is not exempt from a suspicion of paternalism: in line with what Habegger and Rowe maintain, James seems to want to construe his own effective and triumphant authorship through the wishful cogitation of a would-be artist. In this light, his story would be nothing but the continuation of Mrs. Dyott's betrayal who, with the false caring tone of her " 'You deserve that one should speak *for* you!' " reveals

Maud's secret to Colonel Voyt, that he may use it according to patriarchal rules. The story *about* woman is yet again a story that speaks *for* woman.

I will revisit this issue, which I deem crucial. For the moment, let me offer one last comment. The story, like Maud, speaks and keeps silent, that is, it reveals its secret to the same extent that Maud does. Whatever the atmosphere, gazes, and gestures may suggest, the truth about Maud's secret is, after all, a conjecture.[21] Because of its unusual theatrical format, which puts the narrator in the background and eliminates focalization, the text does not offer the voice of truth or of authority. Or else, and better still, the authority over the self is given back to the protagonist, who alone can choose to engage in or to deny self-revelation, to speak or not to speak, to enter into or to remove herself from, the power structure of confession. By staging her discourse directly, "The Story in It" gives woman her voice and the words not to say.

Epilogue 3
The Silence of the Sphinx:
"The Beast in the Jungle"

Silence can be a plan
Rigorously executed
The blueprint to a life
It is a presence
It has a history a form
Do not confuse it
With any kind of absence.
—Adrienne Rich,
"Cartographies of Silence"

"The Beast in the Jungle" (1903), the only fully canonical story in my corpus, has produced an imposing number of readings, from metaphorical, symbolic, metaphysical, mythic, psychoanalytic, formal, philosophical, and religious points of view.[1] Attempting to exhaust the extraordinary overdetermination of this story—one of its fascinating qualities—would exceed the scope of this book. I have chosen, then, to take the opposite direction and concentrate on those elements that relate "The Beast in the Jungle" to the issue of feminine silence and its narrative representation, making it the last piece of the puzzle I have been putting together in this book. Instead of surrendering to the strong metaphorical/abstract suggestion of the story, therefore, I will first read the letter of the text in search of its gender structure.

Sociology of an Obsession

"The Beast in the Jungle" is entirely predicated on cultural gender assumptions: they regulate the relationship between the protagonists and are the implicit but indispensable premise to the ensuing story of waiting and absence. In certain respects, the drastic reduction of descriptive, dramatic, and referential details seems to confer on the story the same quality that Marcher perceives in his own life, "the simplification of everything but the state of suspense" (514). If we resist Marcher's perspective on the story and concentrate on the background details, however, we discover that the plot of the sex-gender system is accurately constructed.

The social codes regulating the relationship between a man and a woman are openly evoked, for example: from the " 'sweet' speech" meant to gratify feminine vanity ("The vanity of women had long memories" [501]) to the love offer ("With another woman, a totally different one, he might have feared the recall possibly even some imbecile 'offer' " [501]); from marriage, negated at the very moment in which its possibility is enounced ("The real form [their intercourse] should have taken on the basis that stood out large was the form of their marrying. But the devil in this was that the very basis itself put marrying out of the question" [508]), to other forms of relationship that, though less defined, are nonetheless codified and dissemble Marcher's "diversity": " 'What saves us, you know, is that we answer so completely to so usual an appearance: that of the man and woman whose friendship has become such a daily habit, or almost, as to be at last indispensable . . . What's the most inveterate mark of men in general? Why, the capacity to spend endless time with dull women . . . I'm your dull woman, a part of the daily bread for which you pray at church. That covers your tracks more than anything' " (511–12).

May Bartram's bland tone and religious reference do not manage to change the fact that this relationship is unorthodox, even if it can be defined in such precise terms, and as such brings social disgrace to the woman: "If he had practically escaped remark . . . how could the alliance, such as it was, since they must suppose it had been more or less noticed, have failed to make her rather positively talked about? 'I never said,' May Bartram replied, 'that it hadn't made me talked about' " (516).[2] Marcher, however, is totally impervious to this social stigma, since he confines himself to his own personal reading, connected to the "beast," of such terms as "saved" and "compromised":

"Ah well then, you're not 'saved.' "
"It has not been a question for me. If you've had your woman, I've had," she said, "my man."
"And you mean that makes you all right?"
She hesitated. "I don't know why it shouldn't make me—humanly, which is what we're speaking of—as right as it makes you."
"I see," Marcher returned. " 'Humanly,' no doubt, as showing that you're living for something. Not, that is, just for me and my secret."

May Bartram smiled. "I don't pretend it exactly shows that I'm not living for you. It's my intimacy with you that's in question."

He laughed as he saw what she meant. "Yes, but since, as you say, I'm only, so far as people make out, ordinary, you're—aren't you?—no more than ordinary either. You help me to pass for a man like another. So if I *am*, as I understand you, you're not compromised. Is that it?"

She had another hesitation, but she spoke clearly enough. "That's it. It's all that concerns me—to help you to pass for a man like another." (516–17)

May Bartram's hesitations leave no doubt on how different her meaning is from Marcher's, on the implications that being "humanly right" has on each one, and on the fact that May's complicity in Marcher's secret is at the cost of her respectability.

Like the social codes underlying the relations between the sexes, the cultural stereotypes of masculinity and femininity are continuously and explicitly evoked as a pattern imposed on reality, especially in the first three sections of the story. Marcher's mental theater is gender-connoted: there he rehashes old and well-worn novelistic plots to enrich, retrospectively, his relation to May. He casts himself in the role of the chivalrous hero and May as the angelic and charitable heroine: "Marcher said to himself that he ought to have rendered her some service—saved her from a capsized boat in the Bay, or at least recovered her dressing-bag, filched from her cab, in the streets of Naples, by a lazzarone with a stiletto. Or it would have been nice if he could have been taken with fever, alone, at his hotel, and she could have come to look after him, to write to his people, to drive him out in convalescence" (499–500). In the last section, Marcher's romantic self-image is again gender-connoted, as he figures himself "in the likeness of certain little old men he remembered to have seen, of whom, all meager and wizened as they might look, it was related that they had in their time fought twenty duels or been loved by ten princesses" (536). And unequivocally gender-connoted is the fantasy about the Beast, which is obviously connected to the scenario of the masculine adventure/exotic genre and reserved for the male hero: "It signified little whether the crouching beast were destined to slay him or to be slain. The definite point was the inevitable spring of the creature; and the definite lesson from that was that a man of feeling didn't cause himself to be accompanied by a lady on a tiger-hunt" (508–9).[3] A literary fantasy for "gentlemen only," Marcher's romance of exotic adventure had its counterpart in the childish and escapist tendency of contemporary male writers, as Henry James himself branded it in his 1901 essay on Matilde Serao. Many contemporary writers, he remarked, were apt to deal with "relations with the pistol, the pirate, the police, the wild and the tame beast" rather than with the adult and self-aware theme, increasingly left to women writers, of "man's relations with himself, that is with woman"—a statement that attributes a specific gender identity to the two literary and existential procedures embodied in this story.[4]

May Bartram's image, in turn, follows scrupulously all the prescriptions regarding feminine roles: domesticity, manifested in the "immaculate order" (521) and in the "perfection of household care, of high polish and finish"(522), as well as in her regular attending to the "frugal but always careful little supper that awaited his pleasure" (516); woman's role as "man's helpmate," incessantly codified for decades by every Victorian conduct book, newspaper, painting of women, and evoked throughout the story by the obsessive lexicon of service and functionality. Once more, *selflessness* is the key word. The beneficiary can take such abnegation for granted inasmuch as it is dictated by the very definition of womanhood, as the text does not fail to underscore by contrast, highlighting the fastidious care with which Marcher tries to remember that May Bartram is, after all, "also" a person:

> There was that in his situation, no doubt, that disposed him too much to see her as a mere confidant [sic], taking all her light for him from the fact—the fact only—of her interest in his predicament, from her mercy, sympathy, seriousness, her consent not to regard him as the funniest of the funny. Aware, in fine, that her price for him was just in her giving him this constant sense of his being admirably spared, he was careful to remember that she had, after all, also a life of her own, with things that might happen to *her*, things that in friendship one should likewise take account of. . . . He never would be in the least coercive, and he would keep well before him the lines on which consideration for her—the very highest—ought to proceed. He would thoroughly establish the heads under which her affairs, her requirements, her peculiarities—he went so far as to give them the latitude of that name—would come into their intercourse. All this naturally was a sign of how much he took the intercourse itself for granted. (507–8)

Once Marcher's waiting is not immediately translated in metaphorical and allegorical terms, the background against which he awaits becomes more ideological and socialized than one would otherwise tend to notice. In the void of his "negative adventure," in that absence that characterizes an identity built on deferral and subtraction, Marcher's only recognizable foundation is his "natural" positioning in a gender system where stereotypes of virility (hunter, savior, hero, seducer) are frequently evoked, if only to be negated, and regularly left unquestioned: the man/woman dichotomy is lived as a *natural* hierarchy where man constitutes his own central position as subject and the other is relegated to a derivative, subordinated, and marginal role.[5]

Secrets and Myths

"The Beast in the Jungle" appears once more as the radical representation of solidified structures and roles. Marcher's claim to May Bartram's dedication is, in his nothingness, solely based on gender expectations; in her commitment to Marcher's self-absorption, May Bartram becomes the utmost *honnête femme* who "n'a pas de roman" and who, like Goethe's Makarie, does not even have her own story—the supreme embodiment of the perfect Victorian angel who experiences no desire other than that of comforting and serving others.[6]

Perhaps for this reason, even in those rare cases in which they have allowed her story to surface, the critics, almost without exception, have taken for granted what to me, on the other hand, seems the most problematic issue in the tale, that is, May Bartram's silence.[7] Not so much her silence about Marcher's secret, but her silence about herself: the fact that she never expresses her own feelings or desires, even in extremis, in the famous and intense scene in front of the unlit fireplace, in section 4. She keeps silent for decades, beyond any reasonable and realistic expectation, beyond death: is this not the most extreme and hyperbolic embodiment of the code of feminine modesty that James explored and exposed in a critical light? What prevents May Bartram from expressing her love fully, without limiting herself to voiceless allusions and gestures, which fall on the deaf ears of an interlocutor totally absorbed by his own question about himself? Is it not that fundamental and internalized taboo that precludes women from taking the initiative and forces them to wait, until death if necessary, for man to take the first step? Indeed, this injunction is spelled out in the text:

> So, while they grew older together, she did watch with him, and so she let this association give shape and colour to her own existence.

Beneath *her* forms as well detachment had learned to sit, and behaviour had become for her, in the social sense, a false account of
herself. There was but one account of her that would have been true
all the while, and that she could give, directly, to nobody, least of all
to John Marcher. Her whole attitude was a virtual statement, but the
perception of that only seemed destined to take its place for him as
one of the many things necessarily crowded out of his consciousness.
(511)

Critics have always taken May's silence as an obvious and unproblematic
starting point—an approach that goes to prove how lasting and naturalized
the cultural codes of femininity are. Her silence, instead, seems to me all
the more problematic, since May's scrupulous observance of this historical
code of behavior transforms it into a crucial element of the plot, together
with Marcher's obsession, which is its premise. It is only because of May's
silence, in fact, that Marcher's destiny of nothingness can be fulfilled: "The
Beast in the Jungle" is as much a story about non-doing as it is a story about
non-speaking. What is unvoiced transforms May's nonstory into the *crucial
determinant* of Marcher's negative adventure, not just its hidden underside.

In her pyrotechnic reading of "The Beast in the Jungle," Eve Sedgwick
argues that John Marcher has two secrets, the secret of his hidden fate and
the secret of keeping a secret, and that the second acts like the closet of the
first.[8] If this is true, then it is by keeping *her own* secret about her love, that
is, the secret about her desire and about her own autonomous subjectivity,
that May Bartram becomes the custodian and, indeed, the owner of John
Marcher's most intimate secret. In this respect, the "truth" about his secret
does not matter (supposing that we could, as readers, establish it beyond the
shadow of a doubt), whether it is homosexual panic—as Sedgwick argues,
on the basis of textual and contextual inferences—or solipsism, alienation,
or inability to love in an orthodox heterosexual relationship, as the great
majority of the critics have argued, paraphrasing the ending of the story.[9]
What interests me here is that in either case it is May Bartram's silence
about herself that seals John Marcher's fate and nails him to the loss of self,
either as homosexual or heterosexual man, either as man doomed by fate
or as a common human being. May Bartram's and John Marcher's secrets
become one, but it is she who controls both.

What are the implications and the consequences of this situation? From
her pedantic observance of a gender code whose main effect is the repression
and interdiction of feminine subjectivity, May Bartram derives a certain

form of power: by turning prohibition into choice, by turning silence into a secret—that is, by refusing the *aveu* as a form of submission—she becomes the owner of her own subjectivity and of the subjectivity of others. We watch this transformation live, as it were, at the end of section 2, in a scene that explicitly revives, at the end of a sequel of questions, the scenario of confession we have met with elsewhere:[10]

> He had had, all along, to-day, the sense of her keeping something back, and he still had it. As this was his first impression of that, it made a kind of date. The case was the more marked as she didn't at first answer; which in turn made him go on. "You know something I don't." . . . Her silence, with the face she showed, was almost a confession—it made him sure. "You know, and you're afraid to tell me. It's so bad that you're afraid I'll find out."
>
> All this might be true, for she did look as if, unexpectedly to her, he had crossed some mystic line that she had secretly drawn round her. Yet she might, after all, not have worried; and the real upshot was that he himself, at all events, needn't. "You'll never find out." (515)

The "mystic line" around her circumscribes and, at the same time, preserves May Bartram's subjectivity while conferring on her knowledge/power over Marcher; it is a "line" that does not infringe on the boundaries of feminine propriety but rather intensifies them to the point of effecting, paradoxically, a reversal of its function. In the extraordinary and often quoted portrait that opens section 4, James seems to be translating this reversal into visual terms by summing up all the images of aestheticized and reified femininity of his stories, only to make an abrupt change of direction:

> Her own aspect—he could scarce have said why—intensified this note. Almost as white as wax, with the marks and signs in her face as numerous and as fine as if they had been etched by a needle, with soft white draperies relieved by a faded green scarf, the delicate tone of which had been consecrated by the years, she was the picture of a serene, exquisite, but impenetrable sphinx, whose head, or indeed all whose person, might have been powdered with silver. She was a sphinx, yet with her white petals and green fronds she might have been a lily too—only an artificial lily, wonderfully imitated and constantly kept, without dust or stain, though not exempt from a slight droop and a complexity of faint creases, under some clear glass bell. . . . She

was "out of it," to his vision; her work was over; she communicated with him as across some gulf, or from some island of rest that she had already reached, and it made him feel strangely abandoned. Was it—or rather, wasn't it—that if for so long she had been watching with him the answer to their question had swum into her ken and taken on its name, so that her occupation was verily gone? He had as much as charged her with this in saying to her, many months before, that she even then knew something she was keeping from him. (521–22)

Sculpted wax bust and painting, natural and artificial flower under a glass bell, silvery object and dying woman, May Bartram is here the synthesis of all aestheticized feminine icons we have encountered in the stories examined in this book. The image of the "serene, exquisite, but impenetrable sphinx," however, introduces an element of uncertainty and dissonance: without undermining the aestheticization of the whole picture, it transforms the immobility and speechlessness of the reified impotent object into the immobility and speechlessness of authority and power derived from a knowledge that is not shared.

The sphinx (the body of a lion, the face of a woman, to underline the profound solidarity between May Bartram and the Beast, which is expressed also by the lexicon they share and by the recurring motif of the eyes) has been an image of knowledge and power since ancient times, as is the sibyl evoked in the scene that follows.[11] It appears here in a double meaning. On one hand, it recalls the Sphinx of the classical myth, arbitress of life and death through the famous riddle solved by Oedipus: it is as a riddle that Marcher repeatedly envisions his own destiny, even if, in another reversal of the heroic pattern, he cannot solve the riddle about himself. On the other hand, it is a modern Sphinx, filtered through the icons of aestheticism—Moreau's paintings, Wilde's and Swinburne's poetry, where the Sphinx does not pose questions but *is questioned*.[12] This reversal of the mythical model of question and answer becomes the emblem of a mysterious and inaccessible knowledge and of a power that manifests itself through silence and torments the interlocutor by withholding the answer. In this complex final renegotiation of the visual and verbal dynamics of all the stories, the blindness of the other women protagonists has undergone a reversal: May's gaze, throughout the story, meets, holds, and returns Marcher's gaze, and its "cold charm" (525), evoked insistently throughout section 4, becomes the very embodiment of the power conferred on her by the knowledge acquired. Simultaneously, by refusing the ritualistic abasement of confession, silence puts woman in a position of power, both when she is questioned—her knowledge detained and denied—and when she questions, as does Oedipus's Sphinx. It would almost seem redundant to mention here how pertinent and, at the same time, ambivalent is the answer to the Sphinx's riddle: "man," that is, a human being—that common humanity that Marcher, absorbed by his obsession, forgets to share with others—but also, man as male, the sexual and gender identity that Marcher exploits and, at the same time, keeps in suspension in his relation with May Bartram.[13]

It is not surprising that once more, as in "Georgina's Reasons," a secret accomplishes a reversal of roles. May's extreme respect for feminine codes transforms their meaning and function into a paradoxical form of power. This reversal entails the feminization of John Marcher. By abdicating his prerogative of active agent in life and relationships, Marcher ends up being robbed of his very subjectivity. He spends his life as a vestal virgin, who watches over a secret of unknown content and waits for his life to be defined from some external source, like the girls mentioned in chapter 7 of *The Portrait of a Lady*, who "waited, in attitudes more or less gracefully passive, for a man to come that way and furnish them with a destiny."[14] Ironically, this is exactly what happens to John Marcher when he meets a stranger in the cemetery.

To See against, to See With

Certainly May Bartram, the very opposite of Georgina Gressie and Mora Montravers, is not a feminist heroine: her strength is too submissive, her victory too ephemeral; she never attempts rebellion, never speaks with a stronger tone of voice, never makes an explicit statement.

Yet James's story does not turn her into the stereotypical sacrificial lamb; on the contrary, the text offers the basic elements of May's counternarrative. Sedgwick (virtually the only critic who has departed from the main thrust of a critical tradition that has variously praised or deplored, but unanimously taken for granted, May's role as self-sacrificing heroine) notes that "The Beast in the Jungle" allows us to perceive that the woman character cannot be reduced to her function as attending angel to John Marcher: "Of May Bartram's history, of her emotional determinants, of her erotic structures, the reader learns very little; we are permitted, if we pay attention at all, to *know* that we have learnt very little. . . . 'The Beast in the Jungle' seems to give the reader permission to imagine some female needs and desires and gratifications that are not structured exactly in the image of Marcher's or of the story's own laws" (199).

What I would like to examine now are the textual devices through which the readers are given this "permission." What is at stake here is something stronger and more decisive than a simple "permission"—an expression that implies the possibility of following a road that is still clearly defined as deviant and marginal. The overall strategy of the story pivots entirely on May Bartram's implicit point of view.

In "The Beast in the Jungle," James establishes a relationship between "reflector" and narrating voice that is among the most unstable and ambiguous of all his fiction. The place from which the story is offered to the reader is neither a rigorous internal point of view nor a detached ironic one: it is an unsituated place, at the same time *inside* and *outside* Marcher's consciousness. Through the fluidity of free indirect speech, we find ourselves immersed in the flow of his consciousness, which covers many years and is nearly uninterrupted by specific events. The vantage point from which we look at events for most of the story is often identified, often decentralized, but never openly antagonistic with respect to Marcher. This vantage point is best defined by the double positioning that the text attributes to May, in relation to the "mask painted with the social simper, out of the eyeholes of which there looked eyes of an expression not in the least matching the other features." This constitutes John Marcher's social appearances: "This the stupid world, even after years, had never more than half discovered. It was only May Bartram who had, and she achieved, by an art indescribable, the feat of at once—or perhaps it was only alternately—meeting the eyes from in front and mingling her own vision, as from over his shoulder, with their peep through the apertures" (510–11).

May Bartram's positioning is a metaphor of the unsituated duplicity of the vantage point that the story offers; through her, the narrating voice finds the opportunities to effect an ironic distancing from Marcher's point of view and to expose his egocentrism through his words in the dialogues, his actions, and his pauses, which underline his obvious inability to understand. The passage I quoted earlier, for example, explicitly refers to *her own* "account of her[self]," an account that is nevertheless described as unvoiced, not corresponding to Marcher's, and indeed "crowded out of his consciousness" (511): this is one of the clearest moments in which the narrating voice distances itself from the protagonist's point of view.

In "The Beast in the Jungle," a triangular dynamics is in place that is accomplished, not just through the usual complicitous/distanced interaction between narrative focus and narrator (that is, between the diegetic world and the discursive strategies), but through the added involvement of a third subjective positioning, which is not textualized as a "focus" but is nonetheless always present. For most of the tale this point of view is juxtaposed to Marcher's, implicit, surfacing, as it were, against the light through the orchestration of the scenes and the interventions of the narrating voice, whose positioning often coincides with it.[15]

"The Beast in the Jungle," therefore, stages not one but two points of view, not one but two stories: Marcher's *master narrative*, hegemonic and explicit, where his totalizing consciousness occupies all the space; and May Bartram's subaltern and implicit *counternarrative*, whose main form of expression is silence, which inhabits the interstices of the dominant discourse. Moreover, "The Beast in the Jungle" stages the confrontation between these two discourses and the power structure underlying them in three ways. It *dramatizes* and *textualizes* the monologic invadence of a masculine way of thinking that is unable to perceive otherness and therefore imposes itself over the existence of the other and subordinates it to itself. It dramatizes and textualizes, again, the *silencing* of woman, the *process* through which she is erased as subject of her own vision and her own desire. And finally, it dramatizes and textualizes also the existence and the resistance of this other subject and invests her with *authority*.

For this reason I believe that the notion of "permission" suggested by Sedgwick is restrictive. The textual strategy at work in this story does not simply authorize the perception of May Bartram's existence as autonomous subject but confers narrative authority on her, because it is through her that *of necessity* the reader is urged to perceive the story. In this respect, the ending is decisive: Marcher's final awareness, and the awareness acquired by the reader through him, coincides with what May Bartram had silently known *all the time*: "*she* was what he had missed," "*she* had seen it," "*[s]he* had lived" (540, emphasis in the text). By retrospectively recasting the story from her point of view, the text officially displaces the seat of narrative authority, forcing an abrupt decentering of man's self-proclaimed centrality, and imposing *her* reading as his reading of himself. In this retrospective rereading, May Bartram becomes the protagonist, not only of her own story, but of Marcher's story as well: the final agnition upsets the explicit hierarchy prevailing in the story hitherto, which coincides with the historically prevailing gender economy. The intensity of the ending, which critics have often faulted for its excess of explanation and gnomic sententiousness, is intended to effect this reversal by simultaneously turning upside down Marcher's expectations and the gender structures that dominated the story.

It would seem at this point that my reading, focused as it is on the polarity man/woman and on the heteropatriarchal scenario, contradicts Sedgwick's hypothesis about the centrality of homosexuality to the story, while bringing new elements to her critique of the tale's ending. Sealing the story with that "stylish and 'satisfyingly' Jamesian formal gesture," the assertion of absence, James then proceeds—such is Sedgwick's argument—to fill that void "to a plenitude with the most orthodox of ethical enforcements . . . 'He should have desired her'" (201), thus reinstating the heterosexual scenario as normative. To be sure, the way matters stand in this tale is even more complex than either Sedgwick's or my reading, taken individually, can account for. Everything hinges, once again, on the triangle Marcher-Bartram-narrator and on the latter's unsituability with regard to point of view. The traditional reading of the tale's "moral" is based on the notion, which even Sedgwick endorses, that in the end "James and Marcher are presented as coming together, Marcher's revelation underwritten by James's rhetorical authority" (200). It is exactly in the ending, however, that the relationship between these two aspects of narration is at its most undecidable.[16] The narrating voice in the last two paragraphs completely adheres to the conscience that is its subject and never makes itself visible as a separate narrative agent. This coincidence, though, can point to two different implications: either to the narrating voice's utmost identification with Marcher's point of view, or to its intention to represent the character's consciousness in an utterly dramatized fashion, making him—as well as the reader in her or his turn—totally accountable for his interpretation (an effect recalling the finale of *The Portrait of a Lady*, if one discounts the difference in the means employed to achieve it). The disappearance of all marks of the narrator, in other words, can be taken equally well as signifying the absence of irony toward the character or as a refusal to ratify his interpretation. Although the question cannot be decided on purely linguistic and stylistic grounds, it is certainly significant on the rhetorical plane that the concluding narrative sequence is introduced by two forceful interventions by the narrator, both of which produce an ironic and defamiliarizing effect. Marcher's final illumination on the meaning of his life, at first presented as "[t]he most extraordinary thing that had happened to him," is immediately qualified by the narrator's incidental remark, "though he had given that name to other matters as well" (539), which seems to diminish this decisive agnition to the rank of the many false illuminations that have preceded it. A couple of pages earlier, the accidental meeting with the stranger had been introduced by one of the most explicit interventions of the narrator—one that is technically ironic in its distancing effect, even while it is ambiguous in its semantic import:

> It was a thing of the merest chance—the turn, as he afterwards felt, of a hair, though he was indeed to live to believe that if light hadn't come to him in this particular fashion it would still have come in another. He was to live to believe this, I say, though he was not to live, I may not less definitely mention, to do much else. We allow him at any rate the benefit of the conviction, struggling up for him at the end, that, whatever might have happened or not happened, he would have come round of himself to the light. (537)

As reticent as it is sententious, the narrating voice refuses here either to contradict or to endorse Marcher's imminent revelation, leaving readers to interpret it as they can or will on ambivalent grounds. We are not even provided with conclusive evidence of Marcher's destiny after the final episode: is he going to die on May Bartram's tomb ("he was not to *live*"), or is he going to live on in his inert and inactive way ("to *do* much else")? Similarly ambiguous in effect, the sequence that follows can be seen as both a reversal and a continuation of the dynamics prevailing so far both in Marcher's life and in the text. On one hand, it upsets Marcher's expectations, radically accelerates the rhythm of events, and alters the register of the tale from cognitive-abstract to melodramatic; on the other hand, it fulfills Marcher's obsession, albeit in a negative way, confirms his uniqueness, and provides a highly concentrated résumé of the recurrent imagery of the tale: light, flame, chain, abyss, naming, seeing and blindness, sleeping and waking, sweet and bitter, satiety and sickness.

This effect of semantic instability involves gender relations as well. These relations are not merely reversed but rather undergo a deconstruction in the technical sense of the word. On the one hand, we are encouraged as readers to re-envision the story from May Bartram's authoritative point of view, retrospectively reviving our perception of the dissonances and suggestions scattered in the text. On the other hand, one has to note that, by accepting May's point of view and her perception of him as the truth about himself, Marcher is once again *appropriating* May Bartram's view as *his own*. While recognizing for the first time her autonomous existence as a loving and desiring subject, Marcher still reinstates the instrumental view of her that he has held all along: "so she served at this hour to drive the truth home," "[t]he escape would have been to love her; then, *then* he would have lived" (540)—a statement that reads less as recognition of the other than as one more instance of "the chill of his egotism and the light of her use" (540). As for the restoration of the heterosexual script as normative, I would maintain that the ending of the tale sounds more like a posthumous celebration of its impossibility: what better proof of the nonreciprocity of May's (supposed heterosexual) desire, than this retrospective acknowledgment of it in the past conditional, the tense of *unreality*? Whatever norm "The Beast in the Jungle" includes in its finale—be it aesthetic, human, or sexual—it is negated even while it is being stated, inasmuch as the tale *has already* disproved it.

The Rhetoric of Secrecy

"The Beast in the Jungle" is a peculiar story. It is so explicit that all comment—including the author's in his preface—sounds like mere paraphrase, but it is so provokingly hermetic that it has invited an inexhaustible hermeneutic activity. It is full of secrets and revelations, but all revelations are semantically unstable in that they are indirect, unspoken, or complicitous with the very processes they disclaim. And this is probably so, not despite, but by virtue of the unusual degree of (apparent) explanation in the ending, with its pretended finality and achievement of stable meaning.

This effect, of course, is far from accidental, but neither is it the result of some metaphysical inexhaustibility of its subject. "The Beast in the Jungle" revolves at all levels around the *impossibility of denotation*. Like many previous tales, playing around the implications of a privileged figure of speech (ekphrasis and prosopopoeia for the tales of the gaze, aposiopesis or reticence for "A London Life" and "The Visits," while "The Story in It" might be envisaged as the narrative expansion of a preterition), "The Beast in the Jungle" centers on a specific trope: catachresis, that is, a metaphoric expression that makes up for a lack in natural language.

A figure expressing what *has no name*, catachresis dominates the tale from its very title: what else is the beast in the jungle but a "pseudoname" employed to designate an experience that cannot possibly be expressed literally and requiring interpretation because it is not grounded in shared knowledge or semantic equivalence existing prior to its invention?[17] John Marcher's "beast" is no ornamental or substitutive expression: it is *constitutive* in that only by that expression can the object be mentioned; and to that extent, it has the same function as a name, which designates the thing and gives it existence. Catachresis is crucial to this tale in a twofold sense: it simultaneously *allows the expression* of what exists but has no name of its own and *bears witness to its unspeakability*, that is, to the nonexistence of a proper name for it.

This same twofold logic—of both expression *and* repression—presides over the tale in more than one sense: with regard to John Marcher's secret, "never mentioned between them save as 'the real truth' about him" (509), because it cannot be spelled out, be it on practical, philosophical, theological, or social grounds. (I think Sedgwick has a strong point here in associating Marcher's unspoken secret with "the love that dare not speak its name" and other culturally current euphemisms for homosexuality.) With regard to May Bartram, who equally lacks the (culturally acceptable) word that would spell out her truth and is confined to an indirect and oblique language made up of gestures, pauses, and silences—a "virtual statement," the only socially proper expression of an otherwise forbidden "true account of her" (511), which makes May Bartram into a sort of living metaphor of herself. And last, with regard to the text, a narrative of experiences that will not allow or be allowed more direct expression. The unprecedentedly thick (even for James) metaphoric texture of language in this tale, which involves literally each word in one isotopy or the other and organizes the imagery in coherent patterns that develop along narrative lines, seems to be offered as the only possible, tentative approach to expressing a situation that is both difficult to grasp as such (as witness the numerous occurrences of "as," "as if," "as it were") and centered on a "negative experience" of nondoing and nonsaying that traditional narrative codes are inadequate to represent.[18]

Indirection and reticence, then, are not just the socialized forms of feminine communication or the ways of alluding to the equally unspeakable facts of female sexuality and male homosexuality; they are the communicative strategy of the text, whose metaphoric language *mimes secrecy* even while expressing the secret. What are the implications and significance of this rhetoric of secrecy, which involves the characters, the narrator, and even the author himself (whose idiosyncrasies of style are here spectacularly amplified) in a general upholding of the necessity of metaphor and the inevitability of indirection?

It seems to me that the issue engaged in this tale is the problematic status and implications of talking about oneself and talking about the other, both in the diegetic world—teeming with unverbalized secrets that coincide with the kernel of each character's identity—and in narrative discourse, whose indirection and instability reproduce the characters' mode of expression, even while propounding an alternative vantage point. Expression and repression—keeping the secret while revealing it, unveiling the secret without uttering it—are the two poles of a dialectic that equally involves all subject positions inscribed in the text. The issues addressed in this tale— silence and words, revelation and self-revelation, and the relation of both to power—commit James to metafictional self-questioning, since the word of the text is inscribed and *knows itself* inscribed in the same Foucaultian dialectic between the "obligation to conceal" and the "duty to confess" and in the same power structures that the text stages and explores.

My final contention, then, is that "The Beast in the Jungle" is a powerful metafictional synthesis of the relation between silence *in* the text and silence *of* the text, gender (self)representation and fictional writing; and this hypothesis allows me to draw some tentative conclusions on the directions and implications of James's exploration of this issue. There are two distinct and interfaced questions at stake: one of representation and one of self-representation.

The first is the question Gayatri Spivak addresses in the title of a well-known essay: "Can the Subaltern Speak?"—that is, the question of those who are not entitled and authorized to speak and the question of who speaks *for* them and *of* them.[19] The question here is how to voice the other without *speaking for* the other, without reducing the other to the self, and simultaneously, without producing the other as Other, that is—as Spivak terms it—without reducing to a single reified *subject* a plural and heterogeneous subject. This question is lucidly engaged in the text, through John Marcher's monologic discourse, his nonlistening, and his culturally determined blindness to the other's individual existence. In contrast, May Bartram's silence can possibly appear, at this point, as a form of "compassionate authority," based, not on the exclusion and/or appropriation of the word of the other, but on the horizontal, nonhierarchical, listening, sustaining "connectedness" that fosters the autonomous emergence of the other's voice.[20]

The second question is memorably stated by David Miller in a chapter of *The Novel and the Police* devoted to an examination of secrecy in the novel as connected to the author-character relation. The paradoxical character of the secret, writes Miller, lies in the fact that it can only be perceived as such if its existence is hinted at: it consequently operates as a double bind, "a secrecy that must always be rigorously maintained in the face of a secret that everybody already knows, since this is the very condition that entitles me to my subjectivity in the first place."[21] The way out of the double bind is by "changing the subject": "if I cannot speak of myself without losing myself in the process, I can keep myself secret and—'so to speak'—change the subject: convinced of my indeterminability in the safety of silence, as I speak of—and seek to determine—somebody or something else" (195). Fictional writing offers this opportunity: "the Novel, where one's own secret will be kept because somebody else's will be revealed" (200).

I wonder whether the deep nexus Miller traces between secrecy, representation, and self-representation might offer a key to the tales I have been examining and to their lucid and passionate way of simultaneously engaging the issue of the representation of women as problematic and engaging themselves in a spiral of metafictional introversion that involves each tale in that very same issue. On one hand, as Spivak points out, stories about women—even when they critically examine and expose the modes of their representation and the modes of gender construction and representation in modern Western culture—are not stories where women *speak*, but stories where women are spoken *for* and *of* and, consequently, stories that extend the epistemic violence of culture, the violence of representation, the power structure underlying the use of words. On the other hand, speaking of the other is speaking of oneself, enacting the inevitable continuity between representation and self-representation as well as the cultural continuity within the gender system. In regulating sexual identities and presiding over the constitution of both the writing and the written subject, the gender system ambiguously positions the subject of enunciation as simultaneously *within* and *without* the process of representation of its *subject* (in both meanings of the word) and of woman as subject.

I wonder, then, whether James's writing—the famously intransitive and abstract writing of the later style, which goes hand in hand with the most lucid and inexorable signifying patterns—could not be envisioned as a response to the double bind of representation and self-representation, that is, as another rhetoric of secrecy. Style is a way of *déjouer*, of evading the binary opposition between saying and not saying, since *both* are equally inscribed in power structures; it is a way of avoiding both the violence of repression as silence enforced and the violence of expression as *speaking of* and *speaking for*. James's writing is, rather, a kind of *speaking with*: a writing that accompanies its subject without peremptorily defining it, that appeals to its reader to find her own paths for herself and to reconstruct relations as she may or will. It is, finally, a way of evading, while inevitably reproducing, the dialectics of secret and confession, silence and speech, whereby the subject is constituted as such but is also entangled in a structure of power and control.[22] Can a style of profuse reticence disentangle the writing subject from self-revelation and control? "A style like that seemed just the place for guilty secrets," critic F. M. Colby wrote in 1902 in an article suggestively titled "The Queerness of Henry James."[23] James's style, which in certain respects is inevitably traced back to the author's individual inner dialectic of closet and coming out, in other respects seems to be externalizing that dialectic and dramatizing it—"dramatize," a favorite Jamesian precept whose implications certainly exceed structural and formal considerations. Thus dramatized, it becomes irreducible to the secret of (his) homosexuality or to homosexuality as secret and available for the use of others: for other subject positions, and different secrets—foremost among these, as I have argued, women's—as a pattern of resistance to all injunctions of totalizing (self-)definition, be it critical or existential.

The End of the Story,
or Telling a Different Story:
"Mora Montravers"

Oportet ut scandala eveniant
—Matthew 18:7

But sirens possess an even more formidable weapon
than their song, that is their silence.
—Franz Kafka, "The Silence of the Sirens," 1917

The story I examine last is centered on the resistance to and victory over the will to definition and appropriation of others. "Mora Montravers" (1909) completes my corpus and presumably the entire corpus of James's short stories: the images and motifs of a lifelong investigation are, as it were, summed up in a final flourish of self-awareness and projected into a utopian horizon.[1]

Mora Montravers is an orphan who has been raised by her aunt and uncle, the Traffles, in the London suburb of Wimbledon. At age twenty-one, Mora leaves their home to live—presumably—with Puddick, a painter of genius with whom Mora, a painter herself, has studied. Her decision throws the respectable and monotonous existence of the Traffles into turmoil and makes them the center of a small suburban scandal. Each reacts in a different way. The philistine aunt is convinced that the niece is living in sin and offers Mora an annuity if she marries Puddick, thus putting an end to the scandal and returning to the fold of respectability. The uncle—amateur painter and frustrated intellectual—intuits that the situation may be more nuanced, is attracted by its bohemian character, and almost hopes that it may last so as to give him a vicarious "sense of life," a sense that is missing from the cold respectability of his social and matrimonial condition. The aunt's offer has its effect, though not what she expected: Mora marries Puddick—with whom, as he attests, she had never really lived; the marriage, however, is a mere formality so that he may acquire the annuity that Mrs. Traffle promised and attend to his painting without the burden of economic needs. Mora has a chance meeting with her uncle in the National Gallery and entrusts her husband to the uncle, even while the aunt at home is enthusiastically taking upon herself the task of "consoling" the abandoned Puddick. Mora, at this point, leaves the scene, free from the judgments and expectations of others, free to pursue her artistic aspirations and perhaps even her sentimental ones, which seem to be embodied, momentarily, by Sir Bruce Bagley, rich and elegant patron of young talents.

"Looking for Mora"

As is the case with "Daisy Miller," the matrix story about the representation of women, "Mora Montravers" stages the divergence between an active heroine, who is constantly the subject and the agent of her own initiatives, and the defining, interpretative, and normative activities that go on around her.[2] "Mora's own extraordinary artful action" (761) is the engine of the plot. The protagonist, however, is never presented from her own point of view, and her inner perceptions are never brought into focus. Though Mora is never on the scene (she appears only twice and says only a few lines in all), she is central and omnipresent because she represents the enigma at the center of the interpretative efforts of the others. In its entirety, the story is made up of exchanges between characters who speak about her and of reflections on her by Sidney Traffle, the middle-aged would-be intellectual, whose point of view is the focus of the story. Mora Montravers, like Georgina Gressie, is absent from the scene, has deviant behavior, and is literally "extraordinary," as she is repeatedly defined.[3] She acts but does not explain. Her behavior is unintelligible but provokes and challenges the obsessive propensity for definition of the others: "'[O]ne of the most curious of 'cases'" (762), "an extraordinary person" (763), "'a rum case'" (763), "'an awful little person'" (765), "'a monster'" (769), "their portentous inmate" (773), "the scandalous person" (774), "'a chit of a creature'" (775), "'a fiend of insolence as well as of vice'" (775), "'irreproachable and immaculate'" (783), "wonderful" (784), "'the very cleverest and most original and most endowed, and in every way most wonderful, person I've known in all my life'" (788), "'incalculable creature'" (788), "'flaunting'" (789), "an absolute incomparable value" (793), "'not respectable'" (808), "'respectable'" (811).[4] The innumerable and contradictory epithets attributed to her throughout the story signal her essential elusiveness and bring out the fact that any definition ends up defining not the object, but rather the mental framework and categories of the person who proffers it: the thirst for scandal in the small Wimbledon community, Puddick's broadmindedness and lack of social reference points, Mrs. Traffle's puritanical philistinism, and her codes of decency and respectability, which are entirely based on sex. Sex is, as in "A London Life," at once removed from consciousness and evoked all the time, as is conspicuously attested by the recurring allusions to the "vulgarity" of Puddick's "horrible" name—whose reference to the male member is thus decried and exhibited constantly—or by some dialogues centered around the most crude and yet reluctant examination of sexuality, which is forever suggested and never mentioned:[5]

> "What I want to know in plain terms, if you please, is whether or no you're Mora's lover?" . . .
>
> "It depends, ma'am, on the sense I understand you to attach to that word" . . .
>
> "I attach to it the only sense," she returned, "that could force me— by *my* understanding of it—to anything so painful as this inquiry. I mean are you so much lovers as to make it indispensable you should immediately marry?"
>
> "Indispensable to who, ma'am? . . . Indispensable to *you*, do you mean, Mrs. Traffle? Of course, you see, I haven't any measure of *that.*" (778, 779–800)

Mora's exegesis, of course, is mostly in the hands of Mr. Traffle, since his point of view, which maintains a certain ironic distance from his wife's sense of decorum, is the main agent of representation. He feels attraction and curiosity for his niece's adventure; and even though he is not scandalized by Mora, he adopts codes that are no less stereotypical than those adopted by his wife, however aesthetic, rather than moral, they may be. He thinks in terms of *romance*, which would circumscribe Mora's destiny to the exotic (and erotic?) allusions contained in her French name.[6] " 'Why the deuce did her stars, unless to make her worship gods entirely other than Jane Traffle's, rig her out with a name that puts such a premium on adventures? 'Mora Montravers'—it paints the whole career for you. She *is*, one does feel, her name; but how couldn't she be? She'd dishonour it and its grand air if she weren't' " (769).

He also thinks in terms of the romantic *vie de Bohème* and its common-place attributes of genius and disorderly life—a life, that is, that obeys only the rules of the autonomous aesthetic sphere, superior to and independent from the life of common man:

> Puddick's studio had been distinctly dirty, and Puddick himself, from head to foot, despite his fine pale little face and bright, direct, much

THE END OF THE STORY   247

more searching than shifting eyes, almost as spotty as the large morsel of rag with which he had so oddly begun to rub his fingers while standing there to receive Mora's nearest male relative; but the canvas on his easel, the thing that even in the thick of his other adventure was making so straight a push for the Academy, almost embarrassed that relative's eyes, not to say that relative's conscience, by the cleanness of its appeal. (763–64)

Traffle, the would-be artist, is not immune to the appeal of bohemian life, as might be expected. His niece's decision becomes to his eyes the occasion to live vicariously imagined literary delights: "What style of conversation . . . wouldn't he [Puddick] and Mora meanwhile be having together? If they would only invite *him*, their uncle—or rather no, when it came to that, not a bit, worse luck, their uncle—if they would only invite him, their humble admirer, to tea!" (782).

The Process of Representation

Nothing new, up to this point: the process of definition and interpretation by which Mr. and Mrs. Traffle arrive at contrary assessments is nothing but the repetition of the irresoluteness shown in "Daisy Miller" by Winterbourne, vacillating between innocence and guilt, "American flirt" and "dangerous coquette"—the same process that, in decades of short stories, had crystallized or annihilated many other women protagonists, transformed by the gaze of others into voiceless icons of beauty or into monstrous emblems of disturbing sexuality.

The qualitative difference of "Mora Montravers" is that the ideological procedure of defining and interpreting is here made explicit to an unprecedented degree and constantly highlighted by the contradictory and incessant attempts at categorizing Mora Montravers and by an extraordinary recurrence in the dialogues of the metalinguistic function of definition. With its vast array of " 'Do you mean . . . ?' " and " 'I mean . . .' " statements, which signal the need to double-check the existence of shared codes, and with its slightly surrealistic debates on the connotative meanings of the characters' names, the story foregrounds the noninnocence of language, the operation of representation, and the underlying codes (ideological and literary) that produce it.

With a complex effect of *mise en abyme*, this story is dominated by a multiple and stratified irony (not surprisingly, the word is employed and put in quotes in the very first lines of the text), which layer by layer dissolves the ground of the interpretative and evaluative operations going on in the text itself and highlights the idiosyncrasies and the ideological partiality of each of these operations. Jane Traffle is the first and most obvious target of this irony; her husband adopts toward her the constant tone of superiority of the enlightened spirit, impatient and amused at the same time, thus foregrounding her dullness ("a goose" [778], "a goose of geese" [781]); her self-complacent and theatrical morality ("Flushed and exalted, her hand on the door, Jane had for this question a really grand moment" [772]); the rigid and overbearing conformism that pervades her down or up to her hairdo ("her 'done' yellow hair—done only in the sense of an elaborately unbecoming conformity to the spasmodic prescriptions, undulations and inflations of the day, not in that of any departure from its pale straw-coloured truth" [765]). This irony, while satirically undermining Mrs. Traffle's opinions on her niece and her limited and philistine view of the world, has the added subjective function of distancing Sidney Traffle from her, thus allowing him to constitute himself as a superior and disillusioned "man of the world" able to take "the impartial, the detached, in fact—hang it!—even the amused view" (762).

Conversely, Traffle's irony is in turn framed ironically both by the textual discourse and by events. At every turn of the plot, Traffle is surprised by the behavior of the other characters, which falls short of his expectations and projections; his self-congratulatory superiority is thus undermined and leaves him at the mercy of his imagination, where he will take refuge as a last resort. With its discreet but incisive interventions, the narrating voice in turn distances Traffle's distancing and creates double effects of irony: "She lived altogether thus—and nothing, to her husband's ironic view, he flattered himself, could be droller" (779). After all, as the narrator's qualification "he flattered himself" (an ironic incidental-within-the-incidental) shows, Traffle's "ironic view" is no less partial and self-serving than his wife's: the text is orchestrated so as to denaturalize each view against the other and to underscore the partiality of the multiple subjective positionings inscribed in the story. The diverse representations of Mora Montravers are thus related less to her than to the need for self-representation and self-assertion of each interpreter, in a sort of miniaturized and grotesque rendering of their "will to power."

A further turn of the screw: as the typical representative of that "finer grain" that gives the title to the collection in which the story was published, Sidney Traffle is not confined, as are the other characters, to enacting a repertoire of stereotypes and clichés. He is the one to bring to light, through irony, the perceptual frameworks of others—his wife's moralistic approach, the scandal craving of his neighbors; but at times he also manages, in an extraordinary self-ironic twist, to be aware of his own prejudices.[7] Indeed, the codes through which Traffle perceives and organizes the situation are as numerous and heterogeneous as his sources: they range from Shakespeare ("to put an emphasis where Mora chose to neglect it would be work only for those who 'gathered samphire' like the unfortunates in 'King Lear'" [773]) to popular fiction. In "Georgina's Reasons" James had made liberal use of the repertoire provided by the sensation novel as a structural frame; here too he evokes that genre, with its extreme situations, its heroines who make wanton use of their sexuality, or, conversely, are chaste even in improbable circumstances. While nourishing his consciousness with literary stereotypes, though, from the very beginning James offers to Traffle a degree of self-awareness of his own clichés, which amounts, with a metafictional twist, to a display of *textual* self-awareness:

> They were such extraordinary people to have been so odiously stricken that poor Traffle himself, always, at the best—though it was indeed just now at the worst—what his wife called horribly philosophic, fairly grimaced back, in private, at so flagrant a show of the famous, the provokedly vicious, "irony," the thing he had so often read about in clever stories, with which the usually candid countenance of their fate seemed to have begun of a sudden to bristle. Ah, that irony of fate often admired by him as a phrase and recognised as a truth—so that if he himself ever wrote a story it should certainly and most strikingly *be* about that—he fairly saw it leer at them now. (760)

If Traffle envisions his own situation in the formulaic but self-aware key of the "irony of fate," as if it were the script of an untold but already written story, the events take place in front of his eyes in the form of a feuilleton: "she was as stuffed with supersessive answers as if she were the latest number of a penny periodical: it was only a matter still of his continuing to pay his penny" (805). Or else in the form of a newspaper account on topical events, when Traffle thinks about the possibility of visiting Mora, in spite of his promise to Mrs. Traffle not to do so: "'I've only to go, and then come back with some 'new fact,' *à la Dreyfus*, in order to make her sit up in a false flare that will break our insufferable spell'" (791).[8]

The last reference in particular is extremely relevant. The Affaire, which had begun in 1894 with the accusation of treason, had been brought to a close in 1906 with the captain's public rehabilitation. There were years of front-page coverage by French and English newspapers, and the echoes of the main *coups-de-théâtre* had crossed the ocean: court-martial, contradictory testimony, guilty verdict, deportation, new court-martial, rehabilitation. The reference to the most famous trial of the times certainly signals Traffle's familiarity with the popular press. Its main import, however, is to establish a comparison between microcosm and macrocosm so that all the connotations and the issues related to the famous case reverberate, on a smaller scale, within the microcosm of Wimbledon: the polarized opinions about the accused and the controversial debates between those who believed Dreyfus innocent and those who believed him guilty; the displacing of the existing political alliances and the creation of new ones; the inherent novelistic form in which reality sometimes unfolds; the role and responsibility of the intellectual as free spirit and/or mouthpiece of the system.[9] All these issues are reproduced, albeit on a Lilliputian scale, in the *affaire* Montravers, thereby accomplishing two contrasting and complementary effects: on the one hand, they ironically reduce the scope of the Wimbledon scandal; on the other hand, they also produce the opposite result of "socializing" the scandal, framing it in a larger, serious, and political context. The instant effect that the comparison with the Dreyfus case achieves is to focus on the motif of *judgment*, on the *prosecution* necessary to maintain feminine respectability.[10] This is an explicit motif in "Julia Bride," as we have seen, and is already tentatively explored in "Daisy Miller," where the actions of the protagonist are constantly under the scrutiny of Winterbourne, Mrs. Walker, and Mrs. Costello—not to speak of the anonymous chorus of servants, passers-by, and tourists, all united under the ideological patriarchal banner of the double standard and the morality of appearances—and where the only supporter of the girl's innocence is Giovanelli—not surprisingly, a lawyer.[11]

What is made explicit in this story, through an extraordinary metalinguistic twist, is the abstract procedure of forming a judgment and evaluation—that is, ideological representation as implementation of categories that precede the object to which they are applied as well as the subject who applies them. Having to face Mora in the key scene at the National Gallery and her quiet claim to her own identity, Traffle suddenly perceives (in a moment of confusion, exaltation, and insight, which is, stylistically and technically, one of the best in the story) how this abstract procedure works:

"You try to make grabs at some idea, but the simplest never occurs to you."

"What do you call the simplest, Mora?" he at this heard himself whine.

"Why, my being simply a good girl. You gape at it"—he was trying exactly not to—"as if it passed your belief; but it's really all the while, to my own sense, what has been the matter with me. I mean, you see, a good creature—wanting to live at peace. Everything, however, occurs to you but that . . ."

. . . [H]e was actually having the extraordinary girl's answer. What they thought of her was that she was Walter Puddick's mistress—the only difference between them being that whereas her aunt fixed the character upon her as by the act of tying a neatly-inscribed luggage-tag to a bandbox, he himself flourished about with *his* tag in his hand and a portentous grin for what he could do with it if he would. She brushed aside alike, however, vulgar label and bewildered formula. . . . (795–96)

What emerges in this moment of self-awareness is not the particular, contingent content of the social codes so much as the very functioning of the systems that determine ideological representation, exposed in all their potential for reification: the procedure of defining, rendered literally as a "luggage-tag," transforms individuals into objects of an interpersonal and impersonal transaction, like a piece of luggage (an extension of the image of the package, which appears twice elsewhere)—an image that is both visually effective and theoretically accurate, just like some of the metaphors that Marx or Althusser employed.[12]

To Be Elsewhere: Absence and Freedom

The representational procedure "packages" the object, wraps it in social and literary convention, personalizes it with the name of each sender, and moves it around until it becomes invisible. Mora Montravers is equally absent from Mr. Traffle's aesthetic ruminations and from Mrs. Traffle's normative patterns. For most of the story, the protagonist is literally *elsewhere*. She is physically somewhere else, in respect both to Puddick's house, where she is thought to have eloped, and to the Traffles' drawing room, where most of the story takes place—the counter-opposed spaces of art and middle class. And she is metaphorically elsewhere, since she turns out to be irreducible both to the nebulous Bohème of her uncle (given that she leaves the scene, not with the penniless artist, but with the rich patron, "the new, the impatient and distinctly 'smart,' yes, unmistakably, this time, not a bit Bohemian candidate for her attention" [800]) and to the binary classification, respectable/not respectable, of her aunt. Puddick swears that when she was believed to be his lover (not respectable) she was innocent and chaste (respectable), even though Mrs. Traffle suspects that Puddick himself is not very well informed about the subject (not respectable). Mora has married Puddick (respectable), but now perhaps she has a lover (not respectable). As in "Georgina's Reasons," the protagonist's behavior peels appearances away from substance and upsets the formulas of bourgeois morality, destabilizes the presumed foundations of its institutions, and highlights their arbitrariness.[13] In a typically deconstructive move, Mora Montravers stalemates the categories with which she is being tagged and creates an interpretative impasse both for the other characters and for the reader, who is left, once both Victorian Puritanism and flamboyant aestheticism are rendered inoperative through the Traffles, with Mora's very plain claim, expressed in ethical, rather than in social terms, of being "simply a good girl" and, at an even more basic level of common humanity, "a good creature" (795). Any hermeneutic attempt relying on predetermined codes is brought to a standstill, as is shown by the recurrent use by Mora's aunt of the well-known attribute of "monster" and, on the part of the uncle, of the terminology of the unfamiliar and wonderful: "portentous," "portent," "prodigious" (773), "wonderful" (784), "a wonder" (792). Furthermore, the situation is repeatedly defined as "incalculable" (762), "droll" (769), "different" (769), "defy[ing] any common catchword" (779), to the extent that "they could settle to nothing—not even to the alternative" (790). The situation is also defined several times as "queer"—the adjective that James uses insistently in his late work in relation to the unsettling of oppositions and identities, in a way that resembles today's use of the term in queer theory and may very likely portend awareness of the gender implications that the term was assuming in those years.[14]

This destabilizing effect is produced by the protagonist's victorious *resistance to definition*: significantly, she appears to Sidney Traffle's bewildered eyes in the National Gallery as "their invincible Mora" (792). A little older and much more astute than Daisy Miller, Mora Montravers does not have to die to escape from the evaluative formulas that others impose. Whereas Daisy Miller keeps asking others to acknowledge her to the very end, though she makes claims to her own identity, Mora Montravers renders classifications inoperative, null, and void, through her refusal to explain herself and to communicate and through her self-sufficient and self-directed indifference to the categories of others:

> That was a side of things, the awkward, that she clearly meant never again to recognise in conversation—though certainly from the first, ever, she had brushed it by lightly enough. . . . She was going to ignore, he saw—and she would put it through: she was going to ignore everything that suited her, and the quantity might become prodigious. . . . [G]racefully grave and imperturbable, inimitably armed by her charming correctness, as she sat there, it would be her line in life, he was certain, to reduce many theories, solemn Wimbledon theories about the scandalous person, to the futility of so much broken looking-glass. (772–74)

The final image is a pregnant one. Given the implications of the mirror in the process of woman's identification and socialization, which I have examined in previous chapters, the shattered looking glass conveys powerfully Mora's active refusal of both the allurements of narcissism and the prison house of clichés. While recalling the symbolic cracking of the mirror in Tennyson's "The Lady of Shalott" (a veritable Victorian myth, subject to countless feminist interpretations), it foreshadows Angela Carter's postmodern heroines, cracking the magic mirror to break the cultural spell binding women to their naturalized ideological roles.[15] As Traffle is finally forced to acknowledge, in the scene at the National Gallery from which I have already quoted, "She brushed aside alike . . . vulgar label and bewildered formula" (796).

The disjunction between the woman and the activity of interpretation/judgment surrounding her is at this point complete. Silent, unperturbed, absent, Mora Montravers finds in her *separateness* the measure of her own victorious autonomy: she fully appropriates that "absence of woman" involved in the process of her representation and literally and victoriously *removes herself* of her own volition. Silent, absent, remote, but definitely mistress of her own destiny, Mora appears to Traffle as an ironic and distant siren—Kafka's silent siren, a fascinating, superior, mysterious, and powerful figure:[16]

> She watched him, she saw him splash to keep from sinking, with a pitiless cold sweet irony; she gave him rope as a syren on a headland might have been amused at some bather beyond his depth and unable

to swim. . . . She dimly and charmingly smiled at him, for it wasn't really that she was harsh. She was but infinitely remote—the syren on her headland dazzlingly in view, yet communicating, precisely, over such an abyss. (794–95)

From beyond the gulf that now separates her from Traffle and his world, Mora Montravers is free to take untraveled and unknown roads: she exits the stage as authoritatively and irrevocably "as if she had just seated herself in the car of a rising balloon that would never descend again to earth" (800).

"Turning the Tables"

Did she wish above all to turn the tables—to show how the sex that had always ground the other in the volitional mill was on occasion capable of being ground?
—Henry James, "George Sand," 1897

The outcome of this feminine itinerary, perhaps consciously utopian (the balloon, let us recall, is the metaphor James adopts in the Preface to *The American* for the romance, a genre that cuts the cable of the laws of probability tying it to the earth), produces a sudden reversal not just of literary playscripts and genre/gender expectations, but also of the import and meaning of the symbolic and cultural motifs explored along his previous production.[17] In her independence and impermeability to prejudices, Mora is the embodiment of the New Woman. She plays with the expectations of patriarchal discourse by appropriating them to her own advantage and subverting them point by point: seduction (Puddick, not her, is the lover who is seduced and abandoned), money (she is the provider in the marriage), and marriage (the currency she cashes in for marriage is not her virtue, but rather the assumed loss of it). By refusing to act the part of heroine in a romantic plot revolving around the passion/fall association and by exiting the stage to undertake a metaphorical journey of freedom and ascent, Mora ridicules the patriarchal script, which envisions death or insanity as the only escape for the woman who puts herself outside the normative models. Escaping from the one-way track of a pre-scripted reality, Mora frees herself, at the diegetic level, from the moralizing conformism of her aunt and, at the textual level, from conformity to those scripts that would predefine her narrative journey.

Behind her, Henry James too is carrying on his own revision, utopian and ironic at the same time, of his own repertoire, a revision that throws retrospective light on the meaning of his representation of woman. The tragic and grotesque representation that pushes to the limits the oppressive images of the culture as a whole, and whose evidence has a denaturalized and denaturalizing effect, is here replaced, as in a liberating epilogue, by its subversive and playful reversal. The unmoving, passive, and reified woman appearing in the short stories about artistic representation is here described from the very beginning in terms of action and initiative: "she had acted, unquestionably, according to her remarkable nature," "Mora's own extraordinary artful action" (761). The gazeless woman, the object of vision, becomes an unyielding and relentless observer: "she would watch them flounder without help" (773); "her straight, clear, quiet beams sounded and sounded [his eyes]" (774). The woman whom beauty reduced to a pure aesthetic object now uses beauty as a weapon to her own ends ("the treacherous fact of her beauty . . . if it hadn't put them, as earnest observers, quite off their guard, . . . appeared mostly to have misled their acquaintance" [761]). And perhaps in the most significant reversal of them all, she is an artist, a painter "really clever with her brush" (761), placed, for a change, at the active, not the passive, pole in the act of representation; she is capable of using, with supreme contempt, the National Gallery as a meeting place, thus avenging, in one fell swoop, a long line of heroines buried alive in museums and private collections or driven by poverty to join their number.[18]

At the same time, the ambiguous satisfactions of imagination and renunciation have changed gender and are embodied by Sidney Traffle, one of the most nuanced and ironic incarnations of the Jamesian "poor sensitive gentleman." To Traffle, man of imagination and failed artist (as is confirmed by the exceedingly cerebral quality of his language and thinking, a sort of self-parody of the Jamesian style), Mora is the occasion for an adventure of the spirit, for acceding to a sense of the arts and of life, in a way resembling Lambert Strether's Parisian experience. As coprotagonist to all extent and purposes, Traffle undertakes the path of self-awareness typical of the Jamesian character.[19] Mora's story occasions an awakening of his awareness, one that throws light, retrospectively, on his life: the drabness of his marriage—"their thin ideals, their bloodless immunity, their generally compromised and missed and forfeited frankness" (765)—the foundering of his artistic aspirations, embodied in the bloodless cleanliness of his study, "the perpetually swept and garnished temple of his own perfunctory aesthetic rites" (763). The late discovery of the "sense of life," contrasted with the "sense of decency" that Mrs. Traffle upholds as the only possible standard of conduct (" 'What do we know about the sense of life—when it breaks out with real freedom? It has never broken out here, my dear, for long enough to leave its breath on the window-pane' " [766]) unhinges the constitution of his life and leaves him nothing in return. The emblem of his disappointment and defeat, at the end of the scene in the National Gallery, is an image already encountered with Julia Bride: "he had turned his back and begun humbly to shuffle, as it seemed to him, through a succession of shining rooms where the walls bristled with eyes that watched him for mockery" (800). Once Mora exits the stage, taking away his hope of a vicarious life, Traffle is left only with the ambiguous pleasures of imagination: " . . . [B]ut still more than either of these things he was asking himself . . . what would have been the use, after all, of so much imagination as constantly worked in him. Didn't it let him into more deep holes than it pulled him out of? Didn't it make for him more tight places than it saw him through? Or didn't it at the same time, not less, give him all to himself a life, exquisite, occult, dangerous and sacred, to which everything ministered and which nothing could take away?" (816).

Such a formulation may appear in many respects as the classical Jamesian exaltation of the abstract pleasures of the mind; but in the unprecedented context of a defeat in both the practical and the ideal world, and in comparison with Mora Montravers's victorious self-assertion, such a formulation appears less as the only practicable way to preserve one's own selfhood than as an alienated intellectual expedient producing makeshift adventures, split off from experience for which it is a sort of placebo.

In the face of Traffle's ineffectual intellectualism (and in the face of Puddick's reduction from virile figure, endowed with creative potency, to passive pawn, sucked back into the domestic stage of Mrs. Traffle's afternoon teas), a strong representation of feminine empowerment stands out in this story, which involves not just Mora but also, on a comical and satiric level, the other feminine character, Jane Traffle. Through a dense network of lexical parallels, the text brings together aunt and niece, separated though they may be by their social behavior and position, at Traffle's expense. The predicates that characterize Mora and are associated with her—activity, independence, novelty, prodigy, portent, but also abyss, freedom, the marvelous—take over, as it were, Jane Traffle, starting from section 3, under the astonished eyes of her husband. He notes her unprecedented insight ("He had rarely known her to achieve that discrimination before" [776]; "This was somehow, suddenly, on Jane's part, so prodigious, for art and subtlety" [781]), the unheard-of freedom of expression ("this freedom of address to him, unprecedented in their long intercourse" [775]; "This had entailed Jane's gravely pronouncing him, for the first time in her life, ridiculous . . . She used that term also with much freedom now" [778]), and, more generally, a new independence that foreshadows, perhaps, a new and unsuspected identity: "What looked out of her dear foolish face, very much with the effect of a new and strange head boldly shown at an old and familiar pacific window, was just the assurance that he might hope for no abashed sense in her of differing from him on all this ground as she had never differed on any. It was as if now, unmistakably, she *liked* to differ, the ground being her own and he scarce more than an unwarranted poacher there" (775–76).

Even the most unexpected domestic theater can be the stage of a struggle for emancipation. Deprived of even the blandest of patriarchal authority, Traffle finds himself addressed with the epithet he had used for his wife: " 'Don't be a goose, dear!' . . . it was perhaps the most extraordinary expression he had ever in his life received" (812). In the ending, Mrs. Traffle usurps the last of his linguistic prerogatives—the "fun" and "interest" he had meant to find in Mora's story are now his wife's monopoly vis à vis Puddick—and even manages to perform a deprecating gesture that relates her to Mora through lexical play, when she leaves "after *brushing* him good-humouredly, in point of fact quite gaily, with her skirts" (816, italics mine).[20]

"What Does a Woman Want?"

Mora Montravers is the mastermind of a prodigious system of metamorphoses, the director who oversees, concealed backstage, the development of the plot; she is the active subject of a story organized according to her own precise design, however unintelligible it might be to others, and carried forward toward an apparently punitive denouement that in reality corresponds exactly to what she herself had foreseen and desired.

Desire: this is what finds open expression in this story, for the first and only time in the corpus examined in this book. Repeatedly all the characters ask themselves, unwittingly echoing Freud's famous question, *what does Mora Montravers want?* " 'Our difficulty is that she doesn't ask the first blessed thing of us' " (765); " 'Then what in the world did she want?' " (767). Certainly the question is occasioned by Mora's anomalous behavior; but it is her very anomaly that lends it a much deeper import. As Shoshana Felman has written about Freud's question:

Let us pause a moment and reflect: let us try to grasp the creatively outrageous, visionary, revolutionary imagination that it must have taken to historically articulate this question as a *serious* question. Let us listen to the question. Let us listen to its unheard confession and to its unheard of challenge.

What does a woman want? Doesn't everybody *know* what a woman wants? Doesn't what a *woman* wants go without saying? In a patriarchal society, what *can* a woman want except—as everybody knows—to be a mother, daughter, wife? . . . And yet, Freud asks. (73)[21]

What does Mora Montravers want? Sidney Traffle seems to intuit it during their meeting at the National Gallery, and for a moment a word that recurs throughout the story in its most futile and hackneyed meanings—*freedom*—recovers its full significance: "That was it; they had given her, without intending it, still wider wings of freedom; the clue, the excuse, the pretext, whatever she might call it, for shaking off any bond that had still incommoded her" (796).[22]

The most outstanding element of this story is that here, for the first time, a woman herself says, in her own voice, what she wants. She says it in a direct and simple way, inexorable in its simplicity: "'I want to be free'" (799). And right afterward, with a few other words, she exits the stage to seat herself in the rising balloon.

Perhaps this is the reason why such a rich story, from James's celebrated "major phase," has always lived at the margins of his canon: Mora Montravers is a heroine who knows and who wills, and she is a winner, who hardly embodies the stereotypical supreme value (cherished by Jamesian critics and not just by them) of renunciation and self-sacrifice. And for this reason I find it extraordinary that this should be the last story James wrote—the final seal to his representation of the feminine: a point of arrival and a point of departure, which casts a retrospective light over the long road traveled that far and projects forward the utopian beam of its explicit program: "'I want to be free.'"

Notes

Introduction

1 I refer here also to the deconstructionist readings of the 1980s whose linguistic-literary focus brings them into line with the modernist vision of Henry James as man of letters, canonized by the New Critics and rejuvenated by structuralism.

2 Stephen Donadio, *Nietzsche, Henry James, and the Artistic Will* (New York: Oxford University Press, 1978); Richard A. Hocks, *Henry James and Pragmatistic Thought* (Chapel Hill: University of North Carolina Press, 1974); Ross Posnock, *The Trial of Curiosity: Henry James, William James, and the Challenge of Modernity* (New York: Oxford University Press, 1991); G. L. Hagberg, *Meaning and Interpretation: Wittgenstein, Henry James, and Literary Knowledge* (Ithaca: Cornell University Press, 1994); Paul B. Armstrong, *The Phenomenology of Henry James* (Chapel Hill: University of North Carolina Press, 1983); Merle A. Williams, *Henry James and the Philosophical Novel: Being and Seeing* (Cambridge: Cambridge University Press, 1993).

3 Fredric Jameson, *The Political Unconscious: Narrative as a Socially Symbolic Act* (Ithaca: Cornell University Press, 1981); Mark Seltzer, *Henry James and the Art of Power* (Ithaca: Cornell University Press, 1984); Richard Salmon, *Henry James and the Culture of Publicity* (Cambridge: Cambridge University Press, 1997); Marcia Jacobson, *Henry James and the Mass Market* (Tuscaloosa: University of Alabama Press, 1983); Anne T. Margolis, *Henry James and the Problem of Audience* (Ann Arbor MI: UMI Research Press, 1985); Michael Anesko, *"Friction with the Market": Henry James and the Profession of Authorship* (New York: Oxford University Press, 1986); William Veeder, *Henry James— The Lessons of the Master: Popular Fiction and Personal Style in the Nineteenth Century* (Chicago: University of Chicago Press, 1975); Adeline R. Tintner, *The Pop World of Henry James* (Ann Arbor MI: UMI Research Press, 1989); Pierre A. Walker, *Reading Henry James in French Cultural Contexts* (DeKalb: Northern Illinois University Press, 1995); Posnock, *Trial of Curiosity*; John Carlos Rowe, "Henry James and Critical Theory," in *A Companion to Henry James Studies*, ed. Daniel Mark Fogel (Westport CT: Greenwood Press, 1993); Alfred Habegger, *Henry James and the "Woman Business"* (New York:

Cambridge University Press, 1989); Sara Blair, *Henry James and the Writing of Race and Nation* (New York: Cambridge University Press, 1996); Eve Kosofsky Sedgwick, "The Beast in the Closet: James and the Writing of Homosexual Panic," in *Sex, Politics, and Science in the Nineteenth-Century Novel,* ed. Ruth Bernard Yeazell (Baltimore: Johns Hopkins University Press, 1986), now in *Epistemology of the Closet* (Berkeley: University of California Press, 1990); Leland S. Person Jr., "Henry James, George Sand, and the Suspense of Masculinity," PMLA 106:3 (May 1991): 515–28; Eric Savoy, " '*Hypocrite Lecteur*': Walter Pater, Henry James, and Homotextual Politics," *Dalhousie Review* 72:1 (1992): 12–36; Eric Savoy, " 'In the Cage' and the Queer Effects of Gay History," *Novel* 28:3 (spring 1995): 284–307; Kaja Silverman, *Male Subjectivity at the Margins* (New York: Routledge, 1992); Michael Moon, *A Small Boy and Others: Imitation and Initiation in American Culture from Henry James to Andy Warhol* (Durham NC: Duke University Press, 1998); Hugh Stevens, *Henry James and Sexuality* (Cambridge: Cambridge University Press, 1998).

4   John Carlos Rowe, *Henry Adams and Henry James: The Emergence of a Modern Consciousness* (Ithaca: Cornell University Press, 1976), and *The Theoretical Dimensions of Henry James* (Madison: University of Wisconsin Press, 1984).

5   Curiously, this is exactly what Rowe had not intended to do in his previous book, where each successive theoretical transcodification was offered not as "the systematic elimination of 'mystified' approaches and theories for the sake of some more authentic theory of interpretation" (257) but rather as "a history" of the dialectical relationship between past and future.

6   In this respect, the new Jamesian criticism would appear as a case in point of what Žižek has wickedly called "solidarity-in-guilt," typical of "today's 'progressive' cultural critique communities," whose founding gesture is "a fetishizing elevation of an author (typical candidates: Alfred Hitchcock, Jane Austen, Virginia Woolf . . .) all of whose 'politically incorrect' misdeeds are pardoned in advance or reinterpreted as subversive-progressive in an unheard-of, hidden way . . . which suspends the symbolic efficiency of what obviously does not enter this frame," from Slavoj Žižek, *The Metastases of Enjoyment: Six Essays on Woman and Causality* (London: Verso, 1994), 58.

7   This functionality and approach, I believe, are to be found in another recent product of the new Jamesian criticism, the *Cambridge Companion to Henry James*, edited by Jonathan Freedman for Cambridge University Press, published in 1998.

8   Edward Wagenknecht, *Eve and Henry James: Portraits of Women and Girls in His Fiction* (Norman: University of Oklahoma Press, 1978).

9   Lisa Appignanesi, *Femininity and the Creative Imagination: A Study of Henry James, Robert Musil and Marcel Proust* (London: Vision, 1973).

10   Judith Fryer, *The Faces of Eve: Women in the Nineteenth-Century American Novel* (Oxford: Oxford University Press, 1976); Paul John Eakin, *The New England Girl* (Athens: University of Georgia Press, 1976).

11   Mary Doyle Springer, *A Rhetoric of Literary Character: Some Women of Henry James* (Chicago: University of Chicago Press, 1978).

12   Judith Fetterley, *The Resisting Reader: A Feminist Approach to American Fiction* (Bloomington: Indiana University Press, 1978); Nina Auerbach, *Communities of Women: An Idea in Fiction* (Cambridge: Harvard University Press, 1978).

13 Virginia C. Fowler, *Henry James's American Girl: The Embroidery on the Canvas* (Madison: University of Wisconsin Press, 1984); Joyce W. Warren, *The American Narcissus: Individualism and Women in Nineteenth-Century American Fiction* (New Brunswick NJ: Rutgers University Press, 1984).

14 Carren Kaston, *Imagination and Desire in the Novels of Henry James* (New Brunswick NJ: Rutgers University Press, 1984), 15. The book does not deal exclusively with women, since its object is a study of imagination as authorial instrument of control of one's own life and the life of others in fiction, and of the negotiations attempted by characters for control and realization of their own existential fiction. The problem of female submission to external "imagination" and, therefore, to cultural stereotypes is discussed repeatedly, even if the author confines herself to the notion of an autonomous, whole, and free self as the natural and possible point of arrival of a "correct" and unimpeded psychological subjective development. Ultimately, this reductionist approach turns the problem into a simple question of psychological and individual *Bildung*. This limits the critical impact of a book that presents many interesting and stimulating interpretations.

15 Mary Suzanne Schriber, *Gender and the Writer's Imagination: From Cooper to Wharton* (Lexington: University Press of Kentucky, 1987), 120, 155.

16 Elizabeth Allen, *A Woman's Place in the Novels of Henry James* (London: Macmillan, 1984), 7. The book still infers a distinction between women as "self" and "semiosis," predicated on the potential divisibility of the two identities deemed inseparably one by the theoretical works of the last fifteen years. This notwithstanding, Allen's is the only work to examine the question of woman in semiological rather than psychological terms, as an issue of *representation* and not just of material oppression. In this regard, I owe much to her approach.

17 Lynda S. Boren, *Eurydice Reclaimed: Language, Gender, and Voice in Henry James* (Ann Arbor MI: UMI Research Press, 1989).

18 Peggy McCormack, *The Rule of Money: Gender, Class and Exchange Economics in the Fiction of Henry James* (Ann Arbor MI: UMI Research Press, 1990), 32.

19 Priscilla L. Walton, *The Disruption of the Feminine in Henry James* (Toronto: University of Toronto Press, 1992).

20 This is seldom the case in essays about Henry James, as should be expected, since they almost always move from a "favorable" premise; it happens more often in feminist critiques that examine literary history from a more general point of view: see, for example, Patricia Stubbs, *Women and Fiction: Feminism and the Novel 1880–1920* (Brighton UK: Harvester, 1979). Sandra Gilbert and Susan Gubar's critique of Fetterley's reading of *The Bostonians* (in *The War of the Words*, vol. 1 of *No Man's Land: The Place of the Woman Writer in the Twentieth Century* [New Haven: Yale University Press, 1988]) presents James as perfect example of the modernist male literatus who harbors suspicion and fears towards his female literary rivals.

21 Laura Claridge and Elizabeth Langland, introduction to *Out of Bounds: Male Writers and Gender(ed) Criticism*, eds. Laura Claridge and Elizabeth Langland (Amherst: University of Massachusetts Press, 1990), 3.

22 Veeder, in his *Lessons of the Master*, had explored this vein with unparalleled perception, moving from the premise that James showed great ability in *transforming* stylistically his sources.

23 Alfred Habegger, *Gender, Fantasy and Realism in American Literature* (New York: Columbia University Press, 1982).

24 Another reading in this key is provided by the Dutch scholar Duco van Oostrum in his more recent book *Male Authors, Female Subjects: The Woman Within/Beyond the Borders of Henry Adams, Henry James, and Others* (Amsterdam: Rodopi, 1995), where the appropriation of the feminine in order to construe the writer's male identity is discussed in a detailed and interesting reading of *The Wings of the Dove.*

25 Carolyn Porter, *Seeing and Being: The Plight of the Participant Observer in Emerson, James, Adams, and Faulkner* (Middletown CT: Wesleyan University Press, 1981). Robert Weimann too relates the technical and narrative developments of the later James to the crisis of liberal ideology and the author's isolation from social movements in "Realism, Ideology, and The Novel in America (1886–1896): Changing Perspectives in the Work of Mark Twain, W. D. Howells, and Henry James," in *Revisionary Interventions into the Americanist Canon,* ed. Donald E. Pease (Durham NC: Duke University Press, 1994). Another interesting, albeit not as systematic, attempt at "repoliticizing" James's writing, fostering a perception of its historical construction and of the arena of social relations from which it emerges, is the collection of essays edited by Ian F. A. Bell, *Henry James: Fiction as History* (London: Vision; Totowa NJ: Barnes and Noble, 1984).

26 Carolyn Porter, "Gender and Value in *The American,*" in *New Essays on* The American, ed. Martha Banta (Cambridge: Cambridge University Press, 1987), 124.

27 On this issue, the most analytical and convincing study is still Luisa Villa's book, *Esperienza e memoria: Saggio su Henry James* (Genoa: Il Melangolo, 1989), where the conceptual dimension of James's fiction is examined in relation to the contemporary philosophical investigations about the relationship subject/world.

28 I refer here to the many books by Adeline R. Tintner on Jamesian sources: *The Book World of Henry James: Appropriating the Classics* (Ann Arbor MI: UMI Research Press, 1987); *The Museum World of Henry James* (Ann Arbor MI: UMI Research Press, 1986); *Pop World of Henry James*; to Philip Grover's book, *Henry James and the French Novel: A Study in Inspiration* (New York: Barnes and Noble, 1973); to the book by Pierre A. Walker, already cited, which addresses James's use of French popular culture; and to the many essays on James's relationship to Hawthorne, especially Richard H. Brodhead, *The School of Hawthorne* (New York: Oxford University Press, 1986).

29 John Goode, "Woman and the Literary Text," in *The Rights and Wrongs of Women,* eds. Juliet Mitchell and Ann Oakley (Harmondsworth UK: Penguin, 1976); Terry Eagleton, *Criticism and Ideology* (London: New Left Books, 1976), 85, 96. For an impassioned criticism of the residual idealism present in Eagleton's theory, see Tony Bennett, *Formalism and Marxism* (London: Methuen, 1979). By Goode on James, see also " 'Character' and Henry James," *New Left Review* 40 (November-December 1966): 55–75 and "The Pervasive Mystery of Style: *The Wings of the Dove,*" in *The Air of Reality: New Essays on Henry James,* ed. John Goode (London: Methuen, 1972).

30 "Jamesian point of view, which comes into being as a protest and a defense against reification, ends up furnishing a powerful ideological instrument in the perpetuation of an increasingly subjectivized and psychologized world, a world whose social vision is one of a thoroughgoing relativity of monads in coexistence and whose *ethos* is irony

and neo-Freudian projection theory and adaptation-to-reality therapy," from Jameson, *Political Unconscious*, 221–22.

31 Interesting hypotheses on cross-dressing by male authors of the end of the nineteenth century, as a strategy of construction of a male subject through the expression and/or containment of oedipal conflict, with all its economic and social implications, emerge in the book by Luisa Villa, *Figure del Risentimento: Aspetti della costruzione del soggetto nella narrativa inglese della "decadenza"* (Pisa: ETS, 1997). The book offers interesting suggestions for a possible analysis of James's fiction.

32 Even Rowe's reading of *The Aspern Papers*, for all its theoretical acumen, is not completely exempt from this inescapable effect: he reads the end of the short story in terms of Tina's "choice" and "rebellion" through her "triumphant refusal" of the papers and their implications.

33 Teresa de Lauretis, "The Technology of Gender," in *Technologies of Gender: Essays on Theory, Film and Fiction*, (Bloomington: Indiana University Press, 1987); I quote from the British edition (London: Macmillan, 1989).

34 The category of gender, to be sure, is not restricted to the construction of *women*; and indeed, an examination of gender construction to include the representation of masculinity in James would be a fascinating task and one that is under way in many recent critical contributions. However, as I hope I have made clear, my study—centered as it is on the representation of women—aims at dealing with gender less as an object of representation per se than as the theoretical lens through which the woman question, one hopes, can be more clearly focused.

35 "Interpretative Analytics" is the title of chapter 5 in Hubert L. Dreyfus and Paul Rabinow, *Michel Foucault: Beyond Structuralism and Hermeneutics* (Chicago: University of Chicago Press, 1982).

36 I take the useful notion of "productivity" from Lynne Pearce, *Woman/Image/Text: Readings in Pre-Raphaelite Art and Literature* (Toronto: University of Toronto Press, 1991). In her introduction she discusses the usefulness of Marxist approaches, from Althusser to Macherey and Williams, for a gendered reading and describes a procedure of "symptomatic reading" very similar to what I am offering here. She touches on the different "productivity" of texts on the basis of such readings, according to the degree of complexity with which the texts negotiate the dominant ideology.

37 See also her biblical readings of the 1980s (especially *Femmes imaginaires: L'ancien testament au risque d'une narratologie critique*, Paris: Nizet, 1986), as well as the essays devoted to the interaction between text and spoken word and their cultural function: *Reading "Rembrandt": Beyond the Word-Image Opposition* (New York: Cambridge University Press, 1991); *Double Exposures: The Subject of Cultural Analysis* (New York: Routledge, 1996); *The Mottled Screen: Reading Proust Visually* (Stanford CA: Stanford University Press, 1997).

38 I refer here to the essay "Narratology as Critical Theory" in *On Storytelling: Essays in Narratology*, ed. David Jobling (Sonoma CA: Polebridge Press, 1991), from which I quote.

39 An investigation in this regard has been launched by Jamesian critics under the influence of new interpretative approaches. Up until recently, there have been only a few critical essays, rather limited in scope, on the short stories, except on those stories, perhaps ten

in all, that have been canonized by success and their adherence to the modernist canon: "Daisy Miller," "The Turn of the Screw," "The Beast in the Jungle," "The Figure in the Carpet," and some others centered around the theme of the artist. Some studies of the short stories are Richard P. Gage, *Order and Design: Henry James' Titled Story Sequences* (New York: Peter Lang, 1988); George Bishop, *When the Master Relents: The Neglected Short Fictions of Henry James* (Ann Arbor MI: UMI Research Press, 1988); and the most recent and programmatic N. H. Reeve, ed., *Henry James: The Shorter Fiction: Reassessments* (London: Macmillan; New York: St. Martin's Press, 1997). An invaluable guide to James's short stories, including complete bibliographies, critical histories, and short interpretative essays on each, is Christina E. Albers, *A Reader's Guide to the Short Stories of Henry James* (New York: G. K. Hall, 1997). While in my chapters I will keep bibliographic references to those titles that appear more relevant to my argument, I refer the reader to Albers's book for complete bibliographies on each tale.

40 For a detailed reading in this key see my own essay "'Daisy Miller' e il discorso dell'ideologia," *RSA Journal* 1 (1990): 45–68. I will briefly come back to the function of the "international theme" when I examine "A London Life" further on.

41 Roland Barthes, "Sade II," in *Sade, Fourier, Loyola*, trans. Richard Miller (New York: Hill and Wang, 1976), 131; originally published as *Sade Fourier Loyola*, (Paris: Seuil, 1971).

42 Angela Carter, *The Sadeian Woman: An Exercise in Cultural History* (London: Virago, 1979), 19–20. I will further discuss the "pornographic" representation in James in the chapter on "Glasses."

43 See Bertolt Brecht, *Brecht on Theatre: The Development of an Aesthetic*, ed. and trans. John Willett (New York: Hill and Wang, 1964); originally published as *Schriften zum Theater: Über eine nicht-aristotelische Dramatik* (Frankfurt: Suhrkamp, 1957). Brecht's résumé of the basic differences between the dramatic and the epic theatre is particularly suggestive of their possible connections, respectively, with the classic realistic novel and the Jamesian novel. As will be clear, despite a few points of contact, my argument here does not coincide with Peter Brooks's view of James's "theatre." In Brooks's view, hyperbole, theatrical hypersignification, and expressionistic excess in James's writings are connected to the world of melodrama and its conflict between good and evil; they represent James's "nostalgia" for a world of stable ethical values. To my mind, they are, rather, features of a textual strategy whose overall aim is to undermine that very stability once and for all. See Peter Brooks, *The Melodramatic Imagination: Balzac, Henry James, Melodrama, and the Mode of Excess* (New Haven: Yale University Press, 1976).

44 I have read *The Portrait of a Lady* along these lines in an attempt to give relevance to Isabel's unconsciousness about the signs of patriarchal ideology that are inscribed in her own imagination; see "Setting a Free Woman Free: *The Portrait(s) of a Lady*," QWERTY 8 (October 1998): 169–79.

45 Carren Kaston makes this point explicitly (*Imagination and Desire*, 15); elsewhere in her book she argues that in order to be perceived as innovative, representations must necessarily move from "earlier demarcations and definitions whose boundaries they challenge, push off from, extend, remake. The difficulty is deciding when old forms or fictions have undergone sufficient activity to become new, when revision is indeed not merely rewriting" (166).

46 Let me incidentally note that, at least in principle, the same applies to biographical sources. Critical attention has recently been given to James's relationships with women in his life, with the welcome effect of limning the closeness and significance of such relations and the strong impact of women in James's life, as witness, for instance, Lyndall Gordon's *A Private Life of Henry James: Two Women and His Art* (New York: Norton, 1998), focusing on James's relations with Minnie Temple and Constance Fenimore Woolson, and the volume edited by Susan E. Gunter *Dear Munificent Friends: Henry James's Letters to Four Women* (Ann Arbor: University of Michigan Press, 1999), collecting James's letters to four women whose significance had been largely underrated by previous criticism, i.e., Alice Howe Gibbens, Mary Cadwalader, Margaret Frances Prothero, and Louisa Wolseley. These recent works certainly encourage the opinion that, living among women and corresponding with them all his life, James could hardly fail to be aware of and sympathize with their predicament, their limited options, and their efforts to live with these limits or to overcome them. All the same, let me repeat, these sources have the same *textual* quality and are potentially involved in the same dynamics of ideology, consciousness, and the unconscious as the other writings I have examined here, and consequently do not lend themselves to grounding the interpretation with any degree of "objective" certainty.

47 For interesting commentaries on psycho-Marxist theory, see *Psycho-Marxism: Marxism and Psychoanalysis Late in the Twentieth Century*, ed. Robert Miklitsch, special issue of *The South Atlantic Quarterly* 97:2 (spring 1998).

48 Kaja Silverman, "Too Early/Too Late: Male Subjectivity and the Primal Scene," in *Male Subjectivity at the Margins*, 157.

49 Eve Kosofsky Sedgwick, "Shame and Performativity: Henry James's New York Edition Prefaces," in *Henry James's New York Edition: The Construction of Authorship*, ed. David McWhirter (Stanford CA: Stanford University Press, 1995), 229. See also by Sedgwick the essay on the "The Beast in the Jungle" already quoted and "Is the Rectum Straight? Identification and Identity in *The Wings of the Dove*," in *Tendencies* (Durham NC: Duke University Press, 1993).

50 Stevens, *Henry James and Sexuality*, 167.

51 Among the most recent and intelligent contributions are David McWhirter, "Restaging the Hurt: Henry James and the Artist as Masochist," *Texas Studies in Literature and Language* 33:4 (winter 1991): 464–91; Person, "Henry James, George Sand, and the Suspense of Masculinity," 515–28; Kelly Cannon, *Henry James and Masculinity: The Man at the Margins* (Basingstoke UK: Macmillan, 1994); Lynda Zwinger, "Bodies That Don't Matter: The Queering of 'Henry James,'" *Modern Fiction Studies* 41:3–4 (1995): 657–80; Susan M. Griffin, "Scar Texts: Tracing the Marks of Jamesian Masculinity," *Arizona Quarterly* 53:4 (winter 1997): 61–82; Moon, *Small Boy and Others*.

52 Jean Laplanche and Jean-Bertrand Pontalis, *The Language of Psychoanalysis* (London: Hogarth Press and The Institute of Psychoanalysis, 1973); Michel Foucault, *The History of Sexuality*, vol. 1, *An Introduction*, trans. Robert Hurley (New York: Vintage, 1980), 95; originally published as *Histoire de la sexualité: I: La volonté de savoir* (Paris: Gallimard, 1976).

53 Ross Posnock, "The Politics of Nonidentity: A Genealogy," in *National Identities and*

Post-Americanist Narratives, ed. Donald E. Pease (Durham NC: Duke University Press, 1994).

54 Carren Kaston reminds us, very aptly (*Imagination and Desire*, 14), that notwithstanding the image of the Master as absolute proprietor of his artistic forms, inherited by the critics, James believed in textual collaboration to the point that he took part in a project that foreshadows some of the experiments circulating today on the Net: the collective novel *The Whole Family: A Novel by Twelve Authors*, designed by Howells and published in installments in *Harper's Bazaar* in 1908. That this novel is by and large ignored by most scholars is the best demonstration of their implicit notion of authorship. One of the few critical discussions of this novel is to be found in chapter 4 of Sergio Perosa, *Henry James and the Experimental Novel* (Charlottesville: University Press of Virginia, 1978).

55 Joseph Litvak, *Caught in the Act: Theatricality in the Nineteenth-Century English Novel* (Berkeley: University of California Press, 1992), 216, 214.

Part 1. In the Museum of Women

1 Classic studies of James and visual arts are Viola Hopkins Winner, *Henry James and the Visual Arts* (Charlottesville: University Press of Virginia, 1970); Marianna Torgovnick, *The Visual Arts, Pictorialism, and the Novel: James, Lawrence, Woolf* (Princeton NJ: Princeton University Press, 1985); Tintner, *Museum World of Henry James*. On James's use of portraiture as both thematic motif and representational technique, see Moshe Ron, "The Art of the Portrait according to James," *Yale French Studies* 69 (1985): 222–37; Graziella Pagliano, "Il gioco pericoloso: Henry James e il ritratto," *Letterature d'America* 7 (1986): 71–91; J. A. Ward, "The Portraits of Henry James," *The Henry James Review* 10:1 (winter 1989): 1–14; and chapter 4 in Sergio Perosa, *L'isola la donna il ritratto: Quattro variazioni* (Turin: Bollati Boringhieri, 1996). For an investigation of a special aspect of the woman-portrait relation, involving the woman's death, in James as well as in a wide range of literary and nonliterary sources, see Elisabeth Bronfen, *Over Her Dead Body: Death, Femininity and the Aesthetic* (Manchester: Manchester University Press, 1992).

2 I will take this opportunity to confront a possible objection to the argument I develop in part 1 of this book, where I take the representation of *woman*, rather than representation *tout court*, as the central issue addressed in each text. The conflict between the aesthetic and the existential sphere is, to be sure, a recurring motif in James's work, where the confrontation between person and portrait often takes place with a man as protagonist, as is the case with "The Special Type," "The Tone of Time," "The Liar," and *The Tragic Muse*, to name a few. It might be argued, then, that the problem of representation is not gender-specific. The wide range and heterogeneous quality of the objects entering a relation of antagonism, comparison, or exchange with women protagonists, however, go beyond James's usual interest in the portrait and in artistic representation: to my mind, they point to a specific engagement with the axis of gender, which—as I will try to show—displays its own consistency in these tales beside and beyond the art/life opposition. The reification and aestheticization of women in these stories are made to

appear as phenomena of representation in the widest—cultural and ideological—sense: of these, artistic representation is but *one* possible version.

3   Francette Pacteau, *The Symptom of Beauty* (London: Reaktion Books, 1994), 12.

4   The best study of this visual dimension in James's work is still Porter, *Seeing and Being*.

5   Laura Mulvey, "Visual Pleasure and Narrative Cinema", in *Visual and Other Pleasures* (London: Macmillan, 1989), first published in *Screen* 16:3 (1975); Jacqueline Rose, *Sexuality in the Field of Vision* (London: Verso, 1986); Griselda Pollock, *Vision and Difference: Femininity, Feminism and the Histories of Art* (London: Routledge, 1988). This coincidence between James and late-twentieth-century feminist theory in defining the gaze as male is all the more remarkable since such a gender arrangement in the scopic field, however endemic as a regulation of visual relations between men and women, seems to have been perceived in opposite terms at the time. With reference to W. D. Howells, William James, and several other sources, Emily Fourmy Coutrer reconstructs the widespread interest in the debate on the physiological and epistemological implications of vision in turn-of-the-century America and argues that the prevailing notion was the traditional one, associating man with the rational and verbal sphere and gendering the unreliable, fickle, and superficial sense of sight as feminine: see Emily Fourmy Coutrer, "A Pragmatic Mode of Seeing: James, Howells, and the Politics of Vision," in *American Iconology: New Approaches to Nineteenth-Century Art and Literature*, ed. David C. Miller (New Haven: Yale University Press, 1993).

6   Jonathan Freedman, *Professions of Taste: Henry James, British Aestheticism, and Commodity Culture* (Stanford CA: Stanford University Press, 1990).

7   On the "spectacularization" of society at the beginning of the age of consumption, see Alan Trachtenberg, *The Incorporation of America: Culture and Society in the Gilded Age* (New York: Hill and Wang, 1982); on the accompanying phenomenon of the creation of the "literary field" and, more generally, on the aesthetic sphere as a way of endowing art with value both *against* and *within* the marketplace, see Pierre Bourdieu, *The Rules of Art: Genesis and Structure of the Literary Field*, trans. Susan Emanuel (Stanford: Stanford University Press, 1996); originally published as *Les règles de l'art: Genèse et structure du champ littéraire* (Paris: Seuil, 1992).

8   This, I would like to add, is my only reason for dissatisfaction with Freedman's admirable book. While I share the overall thrust of his argument, and while his analysis of *The Portrait of a Lady* and *The Wings of the Dove* seems to me perfectly consistent with the results of my own reading of the short stories, Freedman's otherwise subtle and suggestive reading of *The Golden Bowl* as "James's turn toward the aesthetic" (243), in making James's position coincide with Maggie's fails to do justice to the complexity of James's narrative strategy.

Chapter 1. Women, Portraits, and Painters

1   The story was first published in *Atlantic Monthly*, March 1873, and reprinted in *A Passionate Pilgrim and Other Tales* (Boston: James R. Osgood, 1875) and *The Madonna of the Future and Other Tales* (London: Macmillan, 1879). Quotations are from Henry James, *Complete Stories 1864–1874*, edited by Jean Strouse (New York: Library of

America, 1999), reproducing the text of the 1879 volume publication. Page numbers will henceforth be included parenthetically in the text.

2   For an analysis of the relation between James's story and its sources see: Cornelia P. Kelley, *The Early Development of Henry James* (Urbana: Illinois University Press, 1965); Giorgio Melchiori, "La lezione al maestro: Robert Browning," in Barbara and Giorgio Melchiori, *Il gusto di Henry James* (Turin: Einaudi, 1974); Michael L. Ross, "Henry James's 'Half-man': The Legacy of Browning in 'The Madonna of the Future,'" *Browning Institute Studies* 2 (1974): 25–42; Tintner, *Museum World of Henry James.*

3   Alfred de Musset, *Lorenzaccio*, in *Five Plays*, ed. Claude Schumacher, trans. Donald Watson (London: Methuen, 1995), 114.

4   As many critics have noted, the appropriation of woman's otherness by a male voice is recurrent in Browning's monologues, and it is frequently represented in an ironic key. Taking Browning as an intertext, therefore, amounted in itself to evoking a theme revolving around the possession of woman and her aesthetic congealment. See U. K. Knoepflmacher, "Projection and the Female Other: Romanticism, Browning, and the Victorian Dramatic Monologue," in *Out of Bounds*, eds. Claridge and Langland.

5   Pearce, *Woman/Image/Text*, 35.

6   James had already made use of the woman-Madonna-portrait triangle in "Travelling Companions," 1870; for a detailed analysis of his treatment of this thematic cluster in the story, see Anna De Biasio, "Bright With Reflected Color: The Woman as Portrait in 'Travelling Companions,'" *Igitur*, n.s., 1:1(2000): 29–47.

7   On the Virgin Mary and the cultural implications of her myth as related to patterns of femininity, see Marina Warner, *Alone of All Her Sex: The Myth of the Virgin Mary* (New York: Knopf, 1976).

8   Elisabetta Rasy, *Le donne e la letteratura: Scrittrici eroine e ispiratrici nel mondo delle lettere* (Rome: Editori Riuniti, 1984), 83 (my translation).

9   M. L. Ross, "Henry James's 'Half-man,'" 35. Cristina Giorcelli also blames Theobald's failure on Serafina's "inert, sordid, and vulgar personality" and on her "massive passive resistance" (my translation): Cristina Giorcelli, *Henry James e l'Italia* (Rome: Edizioni di Storia e letteratura, 1968), 140. Guido Fink explicitly dissociates himself from what he deems the "moralistic judgments, out of context with the character" on Serafina, and he traces Theobald's failure back to the "disproportion between a delirious aesthetic dream and objective reality, a conflict far from unusual in James": Guido Fink, "Il colore sul vuoto: James e Malamud a Firenze," in *America-Europa: la circolazione delle idee*, ed. Tiziano Bonazzi (Bologna: Il Mulino, 1976), 22 (my translation).

10 Theobald prides himself on this patience: "'I have chosen never to manifest myself by imperfection. . . . I may say, with some satisfaction, that I have not added a mite to the rubbish of the world. . . . Art is long. If we work for ourselves, of course we must hurry. If we work for her, we must often pause. She can wait!'" (734–35). A little later, while contemplating a painting by Mantegna, he lovingly comments: "'*He* was not in a hurry'" (736).

11 "'As a proof of my conscientiousness . . . I have never sold a picture! "At least no merchant traffics in my heart!" Do you remember that divine line in Browning? My little studio has never been profaned by superficial, feverish, mercenary work. It's a temple of labour, but of leisure!'" (735).

12   James did not entirely share the enthusiastic, frequently acritical tribute his age paid to Raphael. In some letters of 1869, for instance, he expressed his reservations about the "general formal indifferent beauty," lacking in intellectual content, of his painting, and he had declared himself "actually surprised at its thinness": Henry James, *Letters*, vol. I, *1843–1875* (Cambridge: Belknap Press, 1974), 150, 165–66. In the "Florentine Notes," published in *Transatlantic Sketches* (1875), James would be critical of the compunctious, fetishistic attitude of the public when facing the *Madonna of the Chair*, gazed at like "a kind of semi-sacred, an almost miraculous, manifestation." For James's views on Raphael and their relevance to this story, see Lynne P. Shackelford, "The Significance of the Raphael References in Henry James's 'The Madonna of the Future,'" *Studies in Short Fiction* 27:1 (winter 1990): 101–4.

13   Past/present and America/Europe are of course the most prominent, but several other oppositions are connected to these within a coherent system: reality vs. dream (Theobald's sudden apparition in his Raphaelesque costume makes him look "picturesque, fantastic, slightly unreal" like a ghost, while in the moonlight "'the past hovers about us like a dream made visible,'" [731]); light vs. shadow (both physically and metaphorically: the masterpieces in the Uffizi, for instance, are glowing "in a luminous atmosphere of their own," [737], whereas nowadays "'the days of illumination are gone,'" [739]); the barrenness of America as a "thirsty land" vs. the expected gush of a "slender stream of beauty" (734); exile vs. the promised land, with the artist as a possible Moses (733); the critical vs. the idealistic approach to art. The list could continue.

14   Another, well-known instance where a meditation on the intersections of capitalist technology, modernity, art, religion, sex, and femininity, in the framework of a contrast between American and European civilization, is epitomized by the image of a Madonna is, of course, Henry Adams's chapter on "The Dynamo and the Virgin" in *The Education of Henry Adams*—a chapter, however, that James preceded by several years, since it is dated 1900. In fact, more than a faint echo of James's story can be heard in Adams's portrayal of Saint-Gaudens as "in mind and person . . . a survival of the 1500" who "bore the stamp of the Renaissance, and should have carried an image of the Virgin round his neck," since "[i]n mere time he was a lost soul that had strayed by chance into the twentieth century, and forgotten where it came from," "a child of Benvenuto Cellini, smothered in an American cradle": Henry Adams, *The Education of Henry Adams* (New York: Modern Library, 1931), 387.

15   The story was published in *Galaxy*, June 1873, and never appeared in book form in James's lifetime. Quotations are from Henry James, *Complete Stories 1864–1874*; page numbers will henceforth be included parenthetically in the text.

16   The protagonist's refusal of a statue-man is especially significant when read in connection with the reifying implications of the statue in "The Last of the Valerii," which are examined in the next chapter.

17   Even while altering names and titles, James's story makes clear reference to debates in French painting in the 1830s and particularly to the controversy between Ingres's academism and Delacroix's romantic colorism—the latter, as is well known, very much admired by James. For an analysis of the debate as background for the story, see Tintner, *Museum World of Henry James*, 9–10, 49–51. Further reference to Romanticism and a further occasion for disagreement between the unnamed protagonist and her fiancé

are provided by her mention of Shelley's "Stanzas Written in Dejection near Naples," which Staines dismisses as childish (781).

18 " 'You make me nervous,' he suddenly declared. . . . I began to pity him. . . . 'If it wearies you,' I said, 'give it up.' He . . . was hesitating to ask me seriously whether in giving up his picture he gave up something more" (786).

19 On James's use of Mona Lisa in this story, see Adeline R. Tintner, "Henry James's Mona Lisa," *Essays in Literature* 8:1 (spring 1981): 105–8.

20 For a classical study of the myth of the artist, see Ernst Kris and Otto Kurz, *Legend, Myth, and Magic in the Image of the Artist: A Historical Experiment* (New Haven: Yale University Press, 1979), originally published as *Die Legende vom Künstler: Ein historischer Versuch* (Vienna: Krystall Verlag, 1934); on the portrait motif and its literary and cultural implications (with particular but not exclusive reference to classical culture) see Maurizio Bettini, *The Portrait of the Lover* (Berkeley: University of California Press, 1999), originally published as *Il ritratto dell'amante* (Turin: Einaudi, 1992). On James's fascination with the portrait motif, see Giorgio Melchiori, 32 and note to 43, as well as the works quoted in note 1 to the previous chapter.

21 Henry James, "The Story of a Masterpiece", in *Complete Stories 1864–1874*, 238. The story was first published in *Galaxy*, January–February 1868. For a critical reading examining the relation of this story with Browning's poetry, see Frederick Wegener, " 'Looking as if She Were Alive': The 'Duchess Effect,' The Representation of Women, and Henry James's Use of Portraits," *The Centennial Review* 38:3 (fall 1994): 539–77.

22 A precedent for this incident is in "The Story of a Masterpiece," where Lennox furiously stabs Marian's portrait: " 'Come! . . . Marian may be what God has made her; but *this* detestable creature I can neither love nor respect!' " (241).

23 On the debate accompanying the institution of museums, see Francis Haskell, *Past and Present in Art and Taste: Selected Essays* (New Haven: Yale University Press, 1987) and Tony Bennett, *The Birth of the Museum: History, Theory, Politics* (London: Routledge, 1995).

24 Interestingly enough, another example of the same basic narrative situation—a generous woman sacrificing herself to grant a painter life and success—can be found in the popular fiction of those very years, in Ouida's novel *Folle-Farine* (1871). On the ideology of selflessness and on the domestic sphere, see, among others, Judith Lowder Newton, *Women, Power, and Subversion: Social Strategies in British Fiction, 1778–1860* (Athens: University of Georgia Press, 1981); Nancy Armstrong, *Desire and Domestic Fiction: A Political History of the Novel* (New York: Oxford University Press, 1987); Lynda Nead, *Myths of Sexuality: Representations of Women in Victorian Britain* (Oxford: Blackwell, 1988); Kimberley Reynolds and Nicola Humble, *Victorian Heroines: Representations of Femininity in Nineteenth-Century Literature and Art* (Hemel Hempstead UK: Harvester Wheatsheaf, 1993).

Chapter 2. Women, Statues, and Lovers

1 "The Last of the Valerii" was published in *Atlantic Monthly* in January 1874, included in James's first collection of stories, *A Passionate Pilgrim and Other Tales* (Boston: James R. Osgood, 1875), and revised for publication in *The Madonna of the Future and Other*

Tales (London: Macmillan, 1879). All quotations are from Henry James, *Complete Stories 1864–1874*, which reproduces the text of the 1879 volume. Page numbers will henceforth be included parenthetically in the text.

2 About the literary and sculptural "sources" of the tale see P. R. Grover, "Mérimée's Influence on Henry James," *Modern Language Review* 63 (1968): 810–17; Melchiori and Melchiori, *Il gusto di Henry James*; Theodore Ziolkowski, *Disenchanted Images: A Literary Iconology* (Princeton: Princeton University Press, 1977); Tintner, *Museum World of Henry James* and *Book World of Henry James*. Jean Perrot, *Henry James: Une écriture énigmatique* (Paris: Aubier, 1982) provides an interesting reading of the tale based on the identification—albeit an undemonstrated and possibly undemonstrable one—of Sacher-Masoch's *Venus in Furs* as one of its sources. To these might be added, just as hypothetically, Joseph von Eichendorff's *Das Marmorbild* (1819), also featuring the *unheimlich* phenomenon of a statue coming to life in the moonlight. The question is also open about James's direct knowledge of the rich tradition going back to the classical motif of love for a statue and to the medieval one of Venus and the ring, about which see Ziolkowski, as well as Bettini, *Portrait of the Lover*; and Kenneth Gross, *The Dream of the Moving Statue* (Ithaca: Cornell University Press, 1992).

3 Leon Edel, *The Life of Henry James*, vol. 1 (London: Rupert Hart-Davis, 1953; reprint, Harmondsworth UK: Penguin, 1977), 354. The interpretation is basically the same in Edel's introductions to the two collections, edited by himself, which include "The Last of the Valerii": *The Ghostly Tales of Henry James* (New Brunswick NJ: Rutgers University Press, 1948) and *Stories of the Supernatural* (New York: Taplinger, 1970).

4 Andrea Mariani, *Il sorriso del Fauno: La scultura classica in Hawthorne, Melville e James* (Chieti: Solfanelli, 1992), 125 (my translation).

5 Sigmund Freud, "Delusions and Dreams in Jensen's 'Gradiva'" (1906), in *The Standard Edition of the Complete Psychological Works of Sigmund Freud*, vol. 9, trans. and ed. James Strachey (London: Hogarth Press and The Institute of Psycho-analysis, 1959); originally published as *Der Wahn und die Träume in Wilhelm Jensens "Gradiva"* (Leipzig: Hugo Heller, 1907). Quotations will henceforth be included parenthetically in the text. For a feminist reading of Freud's essay, rich in suggestions that are potentially relevant to this tale, see Rachel Bowlby, "One Foot in the Grave: Freud on Jensen's *Gradiva*," in *Still Crazy After All These Years: Women, Writing and Psychoanalysis* (London: Routledge, 1992).

6 In his recent *The Other Henry James* (Durham NC: Duke University Press, 1998), which appeared some years after the first version of this chapter had been published, John Carlos Rowe also reads the tale in terms of gender. Both his focus and his interpretation, however, are different from my own: he reads the tale as a "heterosexual containment narrative" (54–55) where James expresses his anxieties about the threat of a powerful female figure through the image of Juno, who to Rowe is associated with Margaret Fuller. The statue's phallic connotations feminize the count and destabilize gender boundaries; Martha, on the contrary, is the embodiment of a reassuring, weak American femininity, associated through the final scene with Penelope's patience and submissiveness.

7 J. Hillis Miller, *Versions of Pygmalion* (Cambridge MA: Harvard University Press, 1990), 211–43.

8 Barbara Johnson, "Apostrophe, Animation, and Abortion," *Diacritics* 16 (spring 1986): 29–47.

9 It is far from accidental, therefore, that before the statue is unearthed the count is recurrently connoted as childish, full of animal spirits, lacking in moral conscience, in a way clearly reminiscent of Hawthorne's faun: "he seemed to me . . . to be fundamentally unfurnished with 'ideas.' He had no beliefs nor hopes nor fears,—nothing but senses, appetites, and serenely luxurious tastes. . . . I often wondered whether he had anything that could properly be termed a soul, and whether good health and good-nature were not the sum of his advantages" (803). The situation is changed by the advent of the statue, when Valerio loses his animal tranquillity in his inner turmoil and even displays humor and irony in his defense of the statue ("The Count had suddenly become witty!" 811): in other words, the count achieves the status of an aware subject, thus acquiring the "soul" he supposedly lacked.

10 Paul de Man, "Autobiography as De-Facement," in *The Rhetoric of Romanticism* (New York: Columbia University Press, 1984), 78. Paul de Man's analysis of prosopopoeia develops into a discussion of language, which always designates the absence of the thing: "it is indeed not the thing itself but the representation, the picture of the thing and, as such, it is silent, mute as pictures are mute. Language, as trope, is always privative." Consequently, "[a]s soon as we understand the rhetorical function of prosopopeia as positing voice or face by means of language, we also understand that what we are deprived of is not life but the shape and the sense of a world accessible only in the privative way of understanding. Death is a displaced name for a linguistic predicament" (80–81). For a discussion of this point, see Gross, *Dream of the Moving Statue*, 149 ff.

11 " 'It's the Villa she's in love with, quite as much as the Count,' said her mother. 'She dreams of converting the Count; that's all very well. But she dreams of refurnishing the Villa!' " (799); "next after that slow-coming, slow-going smile of her lover, it was the rusty complexion of his patrimonial marbles that she most prized" (800).

12 Mariani suggests that the count's attitude may be modeled on the Barberini Faun (116).

13 On the strength of this scene, Edwin Sill Fussell includes "The Last of the Valerii" in his chapter on "The Narratives of Catholic Conversion," contrasting Martha's wish to become Catholic with the "happy pluralism" voiced by the count, in this instance "more American than the Americans"; see Edwin Sill Fussell, *The Catholic Side of Henry James* (Cambridge: Cambridge University Press, 1993), 70.

14 " 'He has crossed the Acheron, but he has left you behind, as a pledge to the present. We'll bring him back to redeem it. The old ancestral ghosts ought to be propitiated when a pretty creature like you has sacrificed the fragrance of her life' " (822–23).

15 "The silliest American woman is too good for the best foreigner, and the poorest of us have moral needs that the cleverest Frenchman is quite unable to appreciate": Henry James, "Madame de Mauves," in *Complete Stories 1864–1874* (reproducing the text of the 1879 volume publication of the tale, in *The Madonna of the Future*), 832. Page numbers will henceforth be included parenthetically in the text.

16 The image of the bucolic shepherd and shepherdess and their "childlike caresses," incidentally, also explicitly reinforces the desexualized quality of their relationship,

where sublimation seems to have taken over and moved from the religious to the aesthetic sphere.

17   Nathaniel Hawthorne, *The Marble Faun* (New York: New American Library, 1961), 330. It is worth recalling that his love for angel-like Hilda makes sculptor Kenyon, unlike Valerio, quite impervious to the appeal of the Venus whose recovery he watches on the via Appia: "He could hardly, we fear, be reckoned a consummate artist, because there was something dearer to him than his art; and, by the greater strength of a human affection, the divine statue seemed to fall asunder again, and become only a heap of worthless fragments" (305).

18   Regarding the statue, Dorothy Berkson writes that "there is no mistaking the parallel to the nineteenth-century woman who was treated like an empedestaled goddess of virtue and benevolence, a dehumanized marble fulfillment of male fantasy, whose home was considered her temple, though it was often a prison in which her talents and charms were locked away for the exclusive benefit of her husband and family": Dorothy Berkson, "Tender-Minded Idealism and Erotic Repression in James's 'Madame de Mauves' and 'The Last of the Valerii,'" *The Henry James Review* 2:2 (winter 1981): 78–86, here 84.

19   Miller, *Versions of Pygmalion*, 220.

20   W. J. T. Mitchell, *Iconology: Image, Text, Ideology* (Chicago: University of Chicago Press, 1986), 113.

21   Even though it may be no more than a curiosity, I think it worth mentioning the connection the narrator establishes, when confronted with the blood sacrifice, between Latins and cannibals, trying to get reassurance about the nature of the sacrifice from the remark that "there is blood and blood, and the Latins were posterior to the cannibals" (823). The remark is an obvious historical blunder, although it is uncertain whether it should be blamed on the narrator or the author: "cannibal" is a term coined and circulated by the voyage of Columbus; it designated the Caribbean Indians as man-eaters, thus paving the way to their extermination from the ideological point of view. The Latins, therefore, were not at all "posterior" to cannibals (unless the narrator is thinking in generic evolutionary terms); but the hint undoubtedly creates a common connotative context for both, stressing both the narrator's racist ideology and the sinister connections implied in Western people's violent extinction of different populations and cultures. James's attitude to the racial question has only recently become the subject of specific criticism (mostly limited to the Jewish question): see Jonathan Freedman, who, in an interesting essay on "The Poetics of Cultural Decline: Degeneracy, Assimilation, and the Jew in James's *The Golden Bowl*," *American Literary History* 7:3 (fall 1995): 476–99, reads the figure and function of the Jewish antiquarian in the novel as the touchstone, in his unassimilability ("the Jew's persistence as a Jew," [496]), of the way traveled by Amerigo, "a figure represented as an emblem of racial and cultural degeneracy, whose task is understood to be nothing less than a successful assimilation of the norms and even the identity of the dominant Anglo-American order" (477): words exactly describing, as can be seen, Count Valerio's position in this tale. Freedman argues that James has an ultimately ambiguous attitude to the race question, vacillating between an acceptance of his age's canonical notions (race as nationality or as genetic identity) and an attempt to go beyond the ideology of race *tout court*. Remarks on this subject can also be found in Posnock, *Trial of Curiosity*, 276 ff. To Posnock, the Jew, in his rootlessness is an

identification figure for James, who makes him "a repository of all that unsettles the discipline of the hotel-spirit" (276); "[i]n pursuing new forms of human agency and cultural inquiry that seek power and value by deliberately eluding direct identification and affiliation, [the James brothers] practiced a politics of nonidentity" (285). The expression "politics of nonidentity", as Posnock explicitly acknowledges in a footnote, derives from feminist theorist Leslie Rabine: a significant fact in the framework of my argument for what it suggests about the convergence of the race question with the woman question. J. C. Rowe also touches on the question of race in *The Other Henry James*. The widest and most thorough study of this issue, which deals exhaustively with James's complex and problematic cultural negotiation of the categories of race and nationality in his work (although it only gives cursory treatment to the stereotypes of Italianness), is Blair, *Henry James and the Writing of Race and Nation*.

22 On the origins and ideological import of the museum as an institution in the nineteenth century and on the accompanying debate, see Bennett, *Birth of the Museum*.

23 Quotations are from Henry James, *Complete Stories 1864–1874*. Page numbers will henceforth be included parenthetically in the text. Two recent critical interpretations on this story (formerly nearly ignored by critics) are John Carlos Rowe, "Hawthorne's Ghost in Henry James's Italy: Sculptural Form, Romantic Narrative, and the Function of Sexuality," *The Henry James Review* 20:2 (spring 1999): 107–34 (which explores James's response to the feminist movement and the homoerotic implications of the tale through an exploration of its sculptural citations and parallels) and Pierre A. Walker, "'Adina': Henry James's Roman Allegory of Power and the Representation of the Foreign," *The Henry James Review* 21:1 (winter 2000): 14–26, a careful teasing out of the political implications of the Scrope-Angelo conflict and of the allusions to Wagner, through which (and through the more obvious allusions to the Roman Empire) James stages an "intercultural class struggle." I wish to thank Pierre Walker for allowing me to benefit from a reading of his article prior to its publication.

24 The comparison with Endymion is a revealing one, since Endymion causes Selene to love him by his mere presence, as well as for the associations, both classical and romantic, which the character conveys.

Chapter 3. Woman as Object

1 The original title, "Théodolinde," was changed to "Rose-Agathe" when the story was collected in *Stories Revived* (London: Macmillan, 1885). Quotations are from Henry James, *Complete Stories 1874–1884*, edited by William L. Vance (New York: Library of America, 1999), which reproduces the text of the volume edition; page numbers will henceforth be included parenthetically in the text.

2 The motif of the protagonist's love for a puppet would seem to be borrowed from E. T. A. Hoffmann's *Der Sandmann*. In Hoffmann's tale, however (and the difference is no minor one), the protagonist is under powerful psychic and fantastic influences and is deceived into loving the mechanical puppet, whereas James's Sanguinetti is perfectly aware of the true nature of his love object. I will return to James's use of Hoffmann's puppet motif in the next chapter on "Glasses." One of the few extensive readings ever devoted to "Rose-Agathe" is Perrot, *Henry James: Une écriture énigmatique*, 183 ff. Perrot

points to *Mademoiselle de Maupin* by Théophile Gautier as the main source for James's tale on the strength of the original title (later discarded by James as too explicit) recalling both Théodore, Gautier's protagonist, and Rosalinde, from a version of *As You Like It* staged within the story. Gautier's theme of androgyny, *en abyme* in the play within the story, is thus taken up again in James's tale "by displacing Gautier's questioning of the heroine's sex on her nature as human or fetish" (188, my translation). Perrot goes on to argue that, in echoing *Mademoiselle de Maupin*'s critique of the social boundaries confining women, James was "denouncing women's modern alienation and the social sadism (Sanguinetti's name is not without reason) which made it possible" (188, my translation). The same literary source is also suggested by Tintner in *Book World of Henry James*); Tintner also briefly touches on "Rose-Agathe" in her chapter "The Cabinet of Curiosities" in *Museum World of Henry James*.

3   Freud, "Three Essays on the Theory of Sexuality" (1905), in *Standard Edition*, vol. 7 (1953), 153.

4   Freud, "Fragment of an Analysis of a Case of Hysteria" (1901), in *Standard Edition*, vol. 7 (1953), 76–77, and "The Psychopathology of Everyday Life," in *Standard Edition*, vol. 6 (1960), 202.

5   Freud, "Fetishism" (1927), in *Standard Edition*, vol. 21 (1961). Freud deals with fetishism again in two later works, "Splitting of the Ego in the Process of Defence" (1938) and "Some Elementary Lessons in Psycho-analysis" (1938), both in volume 22 (1964) of *Standard Edition*.

6   Among James's writings, *The Spoils of Poynton* has, of course, been the most frequently studied in terms of fetishism: see Luisa Villa, "L'incendio di Poynton: Su Henry James, la merce, il feticcio e l'amore per i morti," *Nuova Corrente* 35 (1988): 239–82, and Fotios Sarris, "Fetishism in *The Spoils of Poynton*," *Nineteenth-Century Literature* 51:1 (June 1996): 53–83.

7   Emily Apter, *Feminizing the Fetish: Psychoanalysis and Narrative Obsession in Turn-of-the Century France* (Ithaca NY: Cornell University Press, 1991), 43.

8   Pollock, *Vision and Difference*, 123.

9   Significantly enough, the narrator contrasts the china women his friend has adored so far with the real woman he believes him to have now fallen in love with, defining the latter "a charmer who would, as the phrase is, have something to say for herself" (226). As for Rose-Agathe as repository of Sanguinetti's projections, here is one of his rapturous statements: "'You may laugh at the idea, but, upon my word, to me she is different every day; she has never the same expression. Sometimes she's a little melancholy—sometimes she's in high spirits'" (233).

10   The association between women and the drawing room was a veritable topos in the French nineteenth-century novel. In her analysis of Balzac, Flaubert, and Proust, Juliette Frølich (who borrows the expression from Benjamin) terms the topos "femme meublée" (furnished woman), pointing out that the constant narrative association between woman and her rich *intérieur*, full of glass cases and precious objects, results in making her appear as another precious (and marketable) object—a connotation that "Rose-Agathe" effectively literalizes. See Juliette Frølich, *Des hommes, des femmes et des choses: Langages de l'objet dans le roman de Balzac à Proust* (Saint-Denis: Presses Universitaires de Vincennes, 1997), 32. As for Rose-Agathe's connection to a Madonna,

it is made explicit in the dialogue: " 'Shall I tell you what she looks like? . . . like a Madonna who should have had her hair dressed—over there. . . . It is a real Madonna type' " (224).

11 " 'She's weary of her position there, it's so public.—Yesterday she was very pale,' he would say at another time; 'I'm sure she wants rest' " (233).

12 See his frequent use of patronizing expressions such as "the poor fellow" (221); "I was inclined to humour his enthusiasm" (226); "I was not too much shocked to be still a good deal amused" (228); "I looked at him, and—I couldn't help it—I began to laugh" (231).

13 See Mitchell, *Iconology*.

14 "When I first saw him, on coming to Paris, I asked him if he meant never to go back to New York, and I very well remember his answer. 'My dear fellow' (in a very mournful tone), 'What *can* you get there? The things are all second-rate, and during the Louis Quinze period, you know, our poor dear country was really—really——' And he shook his head very slowly and expressively. I answered that there were (as I had been told) very good spinning-wheels and kitchen-settles, but he rejoined that he cared only for things that were truly elegant" (226).

15 On the bachelor as a recurring presence in Victorian fiction, which "both narrowed the venue, and startlingly desexualized the question, of male sexual choice," see Sedgwick, "Beast in the Closet," 188.

16 Freud devotes some paragraphs of "Three Essays on the Theory of Sexuality" to scopophilia, connecting the *Schaulust*, or pleasure in looking, to the "instinct for knowledge or research" (*Wisstrieb*), "a sublimated manner of obtaining mastery" originally related to the child's wish for sexual knowledge (194). In a 1915 note to the essay, he relates fetishism to scopophilia as originally addressed to the female genitals (155). For a feminist antiessentialist reading of this issue, see Toril Moi, "Patriarchal Thought and the Drive for Knowledge," in *Between Feminism and Psychoanalysis*, ed. Teresa Brennan (London: Routledge, 1989): 189–205.

17 Pollock, *Vision and Difference*, 87, 79. Over the last two decades feminist film criticism has produced some classic studies of gender and the gaze: see Mulvey, "Visual Pleasure and Narrative Cinema"; E. Ann Kaplan, *Women and Film: Both Sides of the Camera* (London: Methuen, 1983); Teresa de Lauretis, *Alice Doesn't: Feminism, Semiotics, Cinema* (Bloomington: Indiana University Press, 1984); Rose, *Sexuality in the Field of Vision*. Jean-Paul Sartre had already commented on the objectifying gaze and on the asymmetrical power relation it produces in *Being and Nothingness* (New York: Philosophical Library, 1956); originally published as *L'être et le néant* (Paris: Gallimard, 1943). For a bibliography on the critique of the gaze in contemporary culture, see Martin Jay, "The Rise of Hermeneutics and the Crisis of Ocularcentrism," *Poetics Today* 9:2 (1988): 307–26.

18 Peter Brooks, *Body Work: Objects of Desire in Modern Narrative* (Cambridge MA: Harvard University Press, 1993), 5, 88. Page numbers will henceforth be quoted parenthetically in the text.

19 "The castration complex, which dictates that post-infantile desire emerges subject to interdictions and repressions, founds a narrative 'law' whereby direct access to the object of desire never can be unproblematic or linear." Brooks, *Body Work*, 19.

20 In his analysis of *The American* (1877) in *Bodies and Machines* (New York: Routledge,

1992), Seltzer makes some strikingly similar points about the novel: "an association of a way of seeing and a desire of acquisition . . . of girl-watching and window-shopping is scarcely surprising in a novel that conceives of sexual relations in terms of market relations: the marriage market or prostitution" (50). I will return to Seltzer's stimulating book and to the questions it raises later in this chapter.

21 Pierre Macherey, *A Theory of Literary Production*, trans. Geoffrey Wall (London: Routledge, 1978); originally published as *Pour une théorie de la production littéraire* (Paris: François Maspero, 1980).

22 Karl Marx, *Capital: A Critique of Political Economy*, trans. Ben Fowkes, with an introduction by J. M. Cohen (Harmondsworth UK: Penguin, 1992). Luce Irigaray, "Women on the Market," in *This Sex Which Is Not One* (Ithaca NY: Cornell University Press, 1985); originally published as "Le marché des femmes," in *Ce sexe qui n'en est pas un*, (Paris: Minuit, 1977). For a discussion of Marx's analysis of fetishism, see Giorgio Agamben, *Stanzas: Word and Phantasm in Western Culture*, trans. Ronald L. Martinez (Minneapolis: University of Minnesota Press, 1993); originally published as *Stanze: La parola e il fantasma nella cultura occidentale*, (Turin: Einaudi, 1977) and Mitchell, *Iconology*, 160–208. For an updated survey of the theory of commodity fetishism and a reformulation of the issue based on a reading of Marx's *Grundrisse* filtered through the work of Baudrillard, Spivak, and Appadurai, among others, see Robert Miklitsch, "The Commodity-Body-Sign: Toward a General Economy of 'Commodity Fetishism,'" *Cultural Critique* 33 (spring 1996): 5–40.

23 "Something else has taken its place, has been appointed its substitute, as it were, and now inherits the interest which was formerly directed to its predecessor. But this interest suffers an extraordinary increase as well, because the horror of castration has set up a memorial to itself in the creation of this substitute," Freud, "Fetishism," 154.

24 For a semiotic definition of "encyclopaedia," see Umberto Eco, *The Role of the Reader* (Bloomington: Indiana University Press, 1979); for its relation to the interpretation of metaphor, Eco, *Semiotics and the Philosophy of Language* (Bloomington: Indiana University Press, 1986); originally published as *Semiotica e filosofia del linguaggio*, (Turin: Einaudi, 1984). On metaphoric representations of woman in nineteenth-century culture, see Bram Dijkstra, *Idols of Perversity: Fantasies of Feminine Evil in Fin-de-siècle Culture* (Oxford: Oxford University Press, 1986). As for the "sociological" ground of women's association with flowers, it is worth recalling that in nineteenth-century France the cult of flowers in interior decoration had become a veritable bourgeois ritual, minutely codified and prescribing, for instance, that at least two jardinieres of fresh flowers be present in every drawing room. This connection between flowers and women—the usual inhabitants of the bourgeois *intérieur*—was later to be circulated and made into a cliché by innumerable journals and novels of the age.

25 Quoting a study by Laure Adler, *La vie quotidienne dans les maisons closes, 1830–1930* (Paris: Hachette, 1990), Apter mentions the institutionalization of voyeurism as a codified practice within turn-of-the-century brothels: prostitutes would stand in various poses, motionless, composing *tableaux vivants* on revolving floors lit by candelabra or else within *cabinets* provided with curtains and optical devices, forerunners of today's peep shows. As can be seen, the situation Adler describes has several traits in common with the one found in "Rose-Agathe," even to the point of prostitutes being compared

to "wax dolls fixed for eternity in voluptuous poses": see Apter, *Feminizing the Fetish*, 42. As for the Madonna image, it is applied both by the narrator to the coiffeur's wife and by Sanguinetti to the wax head—a fact that underscores the hidden affinity between the two couples: "the character of her beauty being suggestive of purity and gentleness, she looked . . . like a Madonna who should have been *coiffée* by M. Anatole" (220); "the pretty woman with the face of a Madonna and the coiffure of a Parisienne" (222); " 'Shall I tell you what she looks like? . . . like a Madonna who should have had her hair dressed—over there. . . . It is a real Madonna type' " (224).

26 Apter cites "[t]he image of woman as commodity and rare specimen, who, as a bonus, wards off castration anxiety with her prosthetic coiffure" as appearing in E. de Goncourt's "La Fille Elisa" and Huysmans's "Marthe," both published in the same year as "Rose-Agathe" (54–55). The critic also provides an ample bibliography to illustrate the appeal of artificial tresses and other elaborate hairdressing styles to the fin-de-siècle imagination (100 n.3).

27 Seltzer, *Bodies and Machines*, 6. Page numbers will henceforth be included parenthetically in the text.

28 Seltzer's historically specific "body-machine complex" might be usefully compared with Irigaray's synthesis of the issue of women in modern patriarchy: "The circulation of women among men is what establishes the operations of society, at least of patriarchal society. Whose presuppositions include the following: the appropriation of nature by man; the transformation of nature according to 'human' criteria, defined by men alone; the submission of nature to labor and technology; the reduction of its material, corporeal, perceptible qualities to man's practical concrete activity [the original here has "valeur abstraite d'échange," which would be more suitably rendered as "an abstract exchange value" rather than "practical concrete activity"]; the equality of women among themselves, but in terms of laws of equivalence that remain external to them; the constitution of women as 'objects' that emblematize the materialization of relations among men, and so on" (184–85).

29 Andreas Huyssen, "The Vamp and the Machine: Fritz Lang's *Metropolis*," reprinted in *After the Great Divide: Modernism, Mass Culture, Postmodernism* (London: Macmillan, 1988), 70. First published in *New German Critique* 24–25 (fall–winter 1981–82): 221–37. Page numbers will henceforth be included parenthetically in the text.

30 Pacteau, *Symptom of Beauty*, 36.

31 Walter Benjamin, "Paris, Capital of the Nineteenth Century," in *Reflections: Essays, Aphorisms, Autobiographical Writings*, ed. and with an introduction by Peter Demetz, trans. Edmund Jephcott (New York: Harcourt Brace Jovanovich, 1978; New York: Schocken Books, 1986), originally published as "Paris, die Hauptstadt des XIX. Jahrhunderts," in *Illuminationen* (Frankfurt: Suhrkamp Verlag, 1955). For an analysis of the relation between the collector and the experience of modernity in Benjamin as well as in other crucial figures of the twentieth century, see Ackbar Abbas, "Walter Benjamin's Collector: The Fate of Modern Experience," in *Modernity and the Text: Revisions of German Modernism*, eds. Andreas Huyssen and David Bathrick (New York: Columbia University Press, 1989). An interesting special issue on Benjamin that deals with various aspects of his thought (but devotes little attention to the question of collecting) has recently been published by *Critical Inquiry* 25:2 (winter 1999).

32 Collecting was, of course, a very modern phenomenon and a very topical subject in James's times, as Freedman repeatedly notes in *Professions of Taste*. In an essay opening up interesting perspectives on the relations between collecting and gender, Judith Weissman connects the frequent presence of collectors in James's works (as well as in contemporary texts such as *The Picture of Dorian Gray*) to the collapse of old families and the dispersal of their estates, on one hand, and to the secret and taboo of homosexuality (another symptom of alienation from the traditional family), on the other, in "Antique Secrets in Henry James," *The Sewanee Review* 93 (1985): 196–215.

33 Angelika Rauch, "The *Trauerspiel* of the Prostituted Body, or Woman as Allegory of Modernity," *Cultural Critique* 10 (fall 1988): 77–88, here 85.

Chapter 4. Woman as Image

1 First published in *Atlantic Monthly* in February 1896, the tale was reprinted in the same year in the collection *Embarrassments* (London: Heinemann; New York: Macmillan). James excluded it from the New York Edition, but revised it for the British Uniform Edition of 1915–19. Quotations are from Henry James, *Complete Stories 1892–1898*, eds. David Bromwich and John Hollander (New York: Library of America, 1996), reproducing the text of the Heinemann edition; page numbers will henceforth be included in the text parenthetically.

2 *The Complete Notebooks of Henry James*, eds. Leon Edel and Lyall H. Powers (New York: Oxford University Press, 1987), 125; page numbers will henceforth be included parenthetically in the text.

3 Freud, "On Narcissism: An Introduction" (1914), in *Standard Edition*, vol. 14, (1957), 88, 89.

4 "I wanted him to give her up and luminously informed him why; on which he never protested nor contradicted, never was even so alembicated as to declare just for the sake of the drama that he wouldn't. He simply and undramatically didn't, and when at the end of three months I asked him what was the use of talking with such a fellow his nearest approach to a justification was to say that what made him want to help her was just the deficiencies I dwelt on" (542).

5 "Mr. Dawling, smitten . . . by the doom-dealing gods" (540). "She might have been an ancient woman responding with humility at the church door to the patronage of the parson" (559). The Christ-figure image, foreshadowing Flora's sacrifice, is taken up again in the end with reference to her transfiguration and resurrection: "she was altered only, as it were, by resurrection . . . she was simply transfigured" (565).

6 Titles such as *The Cult of Chiffon*, by Mrs. Eric Pritchard (London: Grant Richards, 1902), or *Le Bréviaire de la femme* and *L'Evangile profane: Rite féminin* by Comtesse de Tramar (Paris: Victor Havard, 1903, 1905), became increasingly common: see Valerie Steele, *Fashion and Eroticism: Ideals of Feminine Beauty from the Victorian Era to the Jazz Age* (New York: Oxford University Press, 1985), 214.

7 Irigaray, "Women on the Market," 180.

8 On beauty as representation, investigated in a wide range of texts, genres, and media in the past and present, see Pacteau, *Symptom of Beauty*.

9 Simone de Beauvoir, *The Second Sex*, trans. and ed. H. M. Parshley (New York: Vintage,

1989), 632; originally published as *Le deuxième sexe* (Paris: Gallimard, 1949). Page numbers will henceforth be included parenthetically in the text.

10 Freud had already suggested as much in "On Narcissism," when stating that women's narcissistic self-contentment "compensates them for the social restrictions that are imposed upon them in their choice of object" (89).

11 Sandra Lee Bartky, *Femininity and Domination: Studies in the Phenomenology of Oppression* (New York: Routledge, 1990), 42.

12 See Bartky, *Femininity and Domination,* 42, who is here elaborating on a notion first introduced by Herbert Marcuse.

13 Rose, *Sexuality in the Field of Vision,* 177; Rose's quotations are from Freud's essay on narcissism, quoted above.

14 Rose, *Sexuality in the Field of Vision,* 177. Jacques Lacan, *The Four Fundamental Concepts of Psychoanalysis,* trans. Alan Sheridan (London: Hogarth Press, 1977), 106; here I'm using Jacqueline Rose's quotation of the passage in her *Sexuality in the Field of Vision,* 190, where Sheridan's translation is modified to highlight relevant elements. The French original of Lacan's passage reads as follows: "[D]ans le champ scopique, le regard est au-dehors, je suis regardé, c'est-à-dire je suis tableau. C'est là la fonction qui se trouve au plus intime de l'institution du sujet dans le visible. Ce qui me détermine foncièrement dans le visible, c'est le regard qui est au-dehors." Jacques Lacan, *Le séminaire—Livre XI: Les quatre concepts fondamentaux de la psychanalyse* (1964), ed. and comp. J-A. Miller (Paris: Seuil, 1973), 121.

15 Bartky, *Femininity and Domination,* 72.

16 Flora's self-awareness with regard to her weaknesses seems to reflect contemporary paradigms of beauty codified by guidebooks and magazines: "Woman's beauty depends on the perfection of face and figure," read a sententious advertisement in a fashion magazine published a year after James's story (quoted in Steele, *Fashion and Eroticism,* 108).

17 For an interesting analysis of the human face as subjectively revealed to others, see J. Hillis Miller, *Hawthorne and History: Defacing It* (Oxford UK: Basil Blackwell, 1991), 73 ff. For a cultural history of the face, see Jean-Jacques Courtine and Claudine Haroche, *Histoire du visage: Exprimer et taire ses émotions. XVIeme–début XIX siècle* (Paris: Rivages, 1988). For Freud's reading of the face, see "Medusa's Head" (1922), in *Standard Edition,* vol. 18 (1955). A rather explicit link between Medusa's mask and Flora's face is the mention of the onlookers' "petrification" (538) at the sight of her beauty. Bataille's reading of the face can be found in Georges Bataille, *Erotism: Death and Sensuality,* trans. Mary Dalwood (San Francisco: City Light Books, 1986); originally published as *L'Erotisme,* (Paris: Editions de Minuit, 1957). On the face as fetishistic fragment, with particular reference to fashion photography, see Diana Fuss, "Fashion and the Homospectatorial Look," *Critical Inquiry* 18:4 (summer 1992): 713–37.

18 See Dijkstra, *Idols of Perversity.* Dijkstra devotes most of his fifth chapter to this motif. In chapter 6, he interprets the figurative topos of representing women with dim, vacant eyes as an immediate reflection of contemporary scientific theories on the inferiority of women's intellect: to my mind, a rather shallow and mechanical interpretation, begging the question of the common epistemic foundation of *both* practices. On the literature of the looking glass and its varying cultural significance and implications, see the classic

study by Jenijoy La Belle, *Herself Beheld: The Literature of the Looking Glass* (Ithaca: Cornell University Press, 1988).

19   Mulvey, "Visual Pleasure and Narrative Cinema," 19.

20   Sharon Dean, "The Myopic Narrator in Henry James's 'Glasses,'" *The Henry James Review* 4:3 (spring 1983): 191–95; George Bishop, "Shattered Notions of Mastery: 'Glasses,'" in *When the Master Relents*. These have been the only extended readings of "Glasses" until the recent publication (when this chapter had long been completed) of an essay that briefly touches on some of the points I analyze here: see Adrian Poole, "Through 'Glasses', Darkly," in *Henry James: The Shorter Fiction*, ed. Reeve, 1–16.

21   In identifying the symbolic value of glasses as connected to gender roles, James seems to be critically forerunning some topoi of Hollywood movies—the sexually available woman who takes off her glasses in comedies, on one hand; the self-sacrificial woman who conceals her blindness out of love and devotion in melodrama, like Bette Davis in *Dark Victory* (1939), on the other. See Mary Ann Doane, *The Desire to Desire: The Woman's Film of the 1940s* (Bloomington: Indiana University Press, 1987).

22   In typical late Jamesian fashion, the adjective "queer" is here applied to a character who is *both* subversive of gender identities as represented in the diegetic world *and* a destabilizing factor with regard to the ideology voiced by other characters. This need not imply that Mrs. Meldrum is a lesbian—indeed, her masculine traits would in that case be offensively stereotypical—although, of course, such a reading would open interesting perspectives on the narrator's misinterpretation of her relation to Flora and of her supposed love for Dawling. Interestingly, Flora too, we are told, would become "queer" if she agreed to wear glasses (547).

23   The wing image recurs in the final scene: "She presently moved her eyes over the house, and I felt them brush me again like the wings of a dove" (566).

24   "What were most of his friends—what were all of them—but repudiated idiots? I was perfectly aware that in her conversations and confidences I myself for instance had a niche in the gallery" (550).

25   The scene in which the narrator tries to dissuade Dawling is another rather ambiguous instance of active interference, even verging on homosexual innuendo, as witness the following passage: "He doubtless told me his simple story, but the matter comes back to me in a kind of sense of *my* being rather the mouthpiece, of my having had to thresh it out for him. He took it from me without a groan, and I gave it to him, as we used to say, pretty hot; he took it again and again, spending his odd half-hours with me as if for the very purpose of learning how idiotically he was in love" (542).

26   Brooks, *Body Work*, 35. On the connection between scopophilia and epistemophilia as male modes of knowledge, see Toril Moi, "Patriarchal Thought and the Drive for Knowledge," in *Between Feminism and Psychoanalysis*, ed. Brennan.

27   "The irony of old judgments" (570) is retrospectively underscored in the last scene. According to Tintner, the citation of Gibbon in the tale is used as an allusion to the historian's celebrated irony, drawing the reader's attention to the narrator's ironic stance: cf. Tintner, *Book World of Henry James*, 173.

28   "'Woman' as generality . . . is only seen in pieces (in part-objects, in the 'trash-can' of overvalued zones of her body—breast, eyebrow, ankle, smile)." Juliet Flower MacCan-

nell, *Figuring Lacan: Criticism and the Cultural Unconscious* (Lincoln: University of Nebraska Press, 1986), 108.

29 Mitchell, *Iconology*, 113.

30 Mulvey, "Visual Pleasure and Narrative Cinema," 21–22.

31 The narrator mentions no love story of his own; he only refers at one point to the "nymphs and naiads . . . in the American depths" who "may have had something to do with the duration of my dive" (563). Incidentally, nymphs and naiads were another iconographic topos of femininity at the time.

32 Ovid, *Metamorphoses*, III, 348, trans. A. D. Malville (Oxford: Oxford University Press, 1986), 61. Bettini, *Portrait of the Lover*, provides an ample bibliography on Narcissus as literary and iconographic motif in his chapter on this subject. A somewhat arduous but stimulating reading of the role of woman in the myth of Narcissus is offered by Gayatri Chakravorty Spivak, "Echo," *New Literary History* 24:1 (winter 1993): 17–43.

33 Such is, for instance, Lord Iffield's comparison to a "jockeyed customer," highly connotative with regard to both the character to whom it refers and the narrator who employs it. Other animal metaphors are used in direct speech, and consequently can be immediately attributed to the characters making use of them.

34 Both Sharon Dean and George Bishop note this in their essays, with different emphases.

35 Bishop, *When the Master Relents*, 33. As Roland Barthes remarks, the tableau is itself linked to fetishism: "the *tableau vivant*, despite the apparently total character of the figuration, is a fetish object (to immobilize, to light, to frame, means to *cut up*)." Barthes, "Sade II," 154.

36 W. J. T. Mitchell, "Ekphrasis and the Other," SAQ 91:3 (summer 1992): 695–719, here 705–6.

37 Lynda Nead, "The Female Nude: Pornography, Art, and Sexuality," *Signs* 15:2 (1990): 323–35, here 333. A more complete and articulate treatment of the same issues by the same author is *The Female Nude: Art, Obscenity and Sexuality* (London: Routledge, 1992).

38 Susanne Kappeler, *The Pornography of Representation* (Minneapolis: University of Minnesota Press, 1986), 103. Pornography has been the object of much controversial attention in feminist criticism over the last two decades, starting with Angela Carter's classic essay *The Sadeian Woman*. For a few representative samples of the critical debate, see Eva Feder Kittay, "Pornography and the Erotics of Domination," in *Beyond Domination: New Perspectives on Women and Philosophy*, ed. Carol C. Gould (Totowa NJ: Barnes and Noble, 1984); Gary Day and Clive Bloom, eds., *Perspectives on Pornography: Sexuality in Film and Literature* (London: Macmillan, 1988); Robin Sheets, "Pornography and Art: The Case of 'Jenny,'" *Critical Inquiry* 14:2 (winter 1988): 315–34; Lynn Hunt, ed., *The Invention of Pornography: Obscenity and the Origins of Modernity, 1500–1800* (New York: Zone Books, 1993); Frances Ferguson, "Pornography: The Theory," *Critical Inquiry* 21:3 (spring 1995): 670–95.

39 Brooks, *Body Work*, 32 ff.

40 Clive Bloom, "Grinding with the Bachelors: Pornography in a Machine Age," in Day and Bloom, eds., *Perspectives on Pornography*, 22.

41 Mrs. Meldrum's stubborn silence in the last few paragraphs of the tale, however, should possibly be taken as protest rather than complicity in view of her explicit refusal to

consort with the Dawlings after their marriage; unless, of course, one wishes to read it as an expression of her jealousy and her frustrated passion (be it for Dawling or for Flora herself). The textual effect of Mrs. Meldrum's unexplained silence, in any case, is to undermine the stability and completion of the narrator's final version of the story.

42 "Fate," "destiny," "doom," and so on frequently recur in the tale: for a few instances, see 535, 541, 559, 562.

43 Roland Barthes, *Mythologies*, selected and translated by Annette Lavers (London: Paladin Grafton, 1973); originally published as *Mythologies* (Paris: Editions du Seuil, 1957), 143.

44 For an analysis of this picture and of its spatial and visual dynamics, see Pollock, *Vision and Difference*, 75 ff.

45 Tintner, *Book World of Henry James*, 187–89, singles out "The Spectacles" as the source of James's story on the strength of the fact that James had recently reread Poe's work when he wrote "Glasses." Another influence might be Poe's "The Sphinx": Flora's metamorphosis into a giant insect behind her glasses recalls the optical phenomenon whereby in Poe's tale a small insect on a nearby windowpane is perceived as a distant giant monster.

46 "Der Sandmann" in particular was collected several times, in such popular volumes as *Tales from the German* (New York: Harper, 1844), *Hoffmann's Strange Stories* (Boston: Burnham, 1855), and *Weird Tales* (New York: Scribner, 1885)—a two-volume edition, featuring a new translation of "Der Sandmann" by J. T. Bealby.

47 Freud, "The 'Uncanny'" (1919), in *Standard Edition*, vol. 17 (1955).

48 In an interesting reading based on a sort of 'critical embedding,' Naomi Schor takes up Hélène Cixous's reading of Freud's repression, in his essay on the uncanny, of Ernst Jentsch's essay on the same issue, which had been his actual starting point. Freud's strategies of misunderstanding with regard to Jentsch revolve precisely around the repression of the puppet: Freud tries to ignore both her gender, as argued by Cixous, and her tridimensionality. The latter feature, Schor notes, had been explicitly singled out by Jentsch as a decisive *unheimlich* element in wax statues, dolls, and automata, because of the uncertainty it created between animate and inanimate beings. See Hélène Cixous, "La fiction et ses fantômes," *Poétique* 10 (1972): 199–216, and Naomi Schor, *Reading in Detail: Aesthetics and the Feminine* (New York: Methuen, 1987), 134 ff.

49 E. T. A. Hoffmann, "Der Sandmann," in *Poetische Werke*, vol. 2 (Berlin: Aufbau-Verlag, 1958), 408–9 (my translation).

50 Significantly enough, at one point Nathanael angrily rejects Klara's impassive and untroubled attitude in the face of mystery, calling her "'You damned lifeless automaton!'" (393, my translation).

51 Bloom, "Grinding with the Bachelors," 19.

Epilogue 1. Woman as Museum

1 "Maud-Evelyn" was published in *Atlantic Monthly*, April 1900, and reprinted in the volume *The Soft Side* (London: Methuen; New York: Macmillan, 1900). Quotations are from Henry James, *Complete Stories 1898–1910*, ed. Denis Donoghue (New York:

Library of America, 1996), reproducing the text of the Methuen edition; page numbers will henceforth be included parenthetically in the text.

2 Such is the reading provided by Jean Perrot, who sees "Maud-Evelyn" as I do, albeit on different grounds, as a development of Count Valerio's and Sanguinetti's fetishistic perversion: "a ghost—a shadow—has replaced the concrete being and this cult, which abolishes object relations in an intense narcissism, plunges into necrophiliac fetishism enhanced by fashionable mysticism and primitivism. Death was at that time, as is well known, an object of conspicuous consumption, involving the sacralization and social ritualization of perversion; the ritual of death in James's work is simultaneously a defence against sinking into neurosis and a sign of its actual imminence." Perrot, *Henry James: Une écriture énigmatique*, 189 (my translation).

3 Tzvetan Todorov, *The Poetics of Prose*, trans. Richard Howard (Oxford UK: Blackwell, 1977); originally published as *Poétique de la prose* (Paris: Seuil, 1971). Richard Gage also takes Todorov as his starting point, applying his theory of the fantastic to the story: Richard Gage, "Henry James's 'Maud-Evelyn': Ménage à trois fantastique," in *The Shape of the Fantastic: Selected Essays from the Seventh International Conference on the Fantastic in the Arts*, ed. Olena H. Saciuk (New York: Greenwood, 1990): 67–73. Other critical studies of the tale are N. B. Houston, "Henry James's 'Maud-Evelyn': Classic *Folie à deux*," *Research Studies* 41 (1973): 28–41 (who reads the tale's characters as displaying symptoms of a psychosis that A. Gralnick would later theorize as "folie à deux"); Gennaro A. Santangelo, "Henry James's 'Maud-Evelyn' and the Web of Consciousness," *Amerikastudien* 20:1 (1975): 45–54 (who reads the tale with reference to William James's philosophy of consciousness). On the literary sources of "Maud-Evelyn," see Mario L. D'Avanzo, "James's 'Maud-Evelyn': Source, Allusion, and Meaning," *Iowa English Yearbook* 13 (fall 1968): 24–33 (who identifies one source of the tale in Browning's "Evelyn Hope"); and Adeline R. Tintner, "A Source for James's 'Maud-Evelyn' in Henry Harland's 'The House of Eulalie,'" *Notes on Modern American Literature* 7:2 (fall 1983) (in Harland's story, a couple builds a house for their dead daughter). Tintner also briefly refers to "Maud-Evelyn" in *The Museum World of Henry James*, 169–70, where she connects it to "Rose-Agathe" as both being representations of a collector's mania and defines the Dedricks as "certainly the most bizarre collectors in a body of work that teems with the type."

4 An example of banal misunderstanding worthy of a couple of comedians: "I thought a moment. 'Are they ladies?' Her own imagination meanwhile had also strayed a little. 'I think about forty.' 'Forty ladies?' She quickly came back. 'Oh no; I mean Mrs. Dedrick is.' . . . 'And how old is *he*?' Lavinia followed my example. 'Well, about forty, too.' 'About forty-two?'" (182–83).

5 Santangelo, "Henry James's 'Maud-Evelyn,'" 48.

6 "There were mixed in her then, in a puzzling way, two qualities that mostly exclude each other—an extreme timidity and . . . a self-complacency hard in tiny, unexpected spots . . . which, I subsequently saw, would have done something for the flatness of her life had they not evaporated with everything else. She was at any rate one of those persons as to whom you don't know whether they might have been attractive if they had been happy, or might have been happy if they had been attractive" (179).

7 Edel and Powers, eds., *Complete Notebooks of Henry James*, 169. Page numbers will henceforth be included parenthetically in the text.

8 The basic narrative situation of the imaginary portrait of an imaginary child was later developed in James's posthumous and unfinished tale "Hugh Merrow."

9 Among the numerous studies existing on the subject, see Beth Ann Bassein, *Women and Death: Linkages in Western Thought and Literature* (Westport CT: Greenwood Press, 1984) and Bronfen, *Over Her Dead Body*.

10 Santangelo, "Henry James's 'Maud-Evelyn,'" 53.

Epilogue 2. Objectified Woman

1 "Julia Bride" was published in *Harper's Monthly Magazine*, March–April 1908, and collected in volume 17 of the New York Edition, published by Scribner in 1909. Quotations are from Henry James, *Complete Stories 1898–1910*, reproducing the text of the New York edition; page numbers will henceforth be included parenthetically in the text.

2 Numerous animal images reinforce this dehumanization: Julia figures as a "minx" (663), a "parrakeet" (666), a wild animal that "scented some lion in her path" (672), a "swan" (682), and, together with her mother, as "antelope and zebra" (669). She is surrounded by a bestiary made up of elephants (Mrs. Drack), kittens (Mrs. Maule's daughters, her competitors for French), and a pig (Brush).

3 Bartky, *Femininity and Domination*, 38–39. Francette Pacteau also deals with this issue in terms that read as a paraphrase of James's story: "a sense of beauty in oneself can only ever be alien to oneself, can only be in an image: a 'beautiful work' formed in the gaze of another, and in the guise of another. . . . the pleasure of self-display . . . the pleasure of identifying with the gaze of another . . . is therefore fundamentally scopophilic: the subject exhibiting herself . . . derives her pleasure from seeing herself through the eyes of the other who watches," Pacteau, *Symptom of Beauty*, 186–87.

4 Lacan, *Four Fundamental Concepts*, 106; as I did when dealing with "Glasses," I use Rose's quotation of the passage in her *Sexuality in the Field of Vision*, 190, where Sheridan's translation is modified to highlight relevant elements. Again, I provide the French original of Lacan's passage, which reads as follows: "Ce qui me détermine foncièrement dans le visible, c'est le regard qui est au-dehors. C'est par le regard que j'entre dans la lumière, et c'est du regard que j'en reçois l'effet. D'où il ressort que le regard est l'instrument par où la lumière s'incarne, et par où . . . je suis *photo-graphié*." Jacques Lacan, "Qu'est-ce qu'un tableau?", in *Le Séminaire—Livre XI*, 121.

5 Lacan, *Four Fundamental Concepts*, 106.

6 Tintner, *Museum World of Henry James*, 183.

7 Henry James, *The American Scene*, in *Collected Travel Writings: Great Britain and America*, ed. Richard Howard (New York: Library of America, 1993), 514. Page numbers will henceforth be included parenthetically in the text.

8 Although divorce had been legally possible for women since the mid–nineteenth century, it was ill regarded by high society, as *The Age of Innocence* would also illustrate. In contemporary middle-class culture and in the typology created by the sensation novel, both Julia and her mother would qualify as varieties of the "unchaste woman":

the latter because of her divorces, which were regarded as evidence of immorality; the former as an "adventuress," that is, a woman bent on using her beauty to attain a high social position through marriage. On "fallen women" in the nineteenth-century novel, see Sally Mitchell, *The Fallen Angel: Chastity, Class, and Women's Reading, 1835–1880* (Bowling Green KY: Bowling Green University Popular Press, 1981). An interesting analysis of divorce and gender is provided by Mary Poovey, *Uneven Developments: The Ideological Work of Gender in Mid-Victorian England* (Chicago: University of Chicago Press, 1988). I take up these issues again when discussing the tales in part 2.

9 Foucault, *History of Sexuality*, vol. 1, 61. I go back to this passage several times in the chapters that follow. Here as elsewhere, I have slightly modified the current English translation, which by its use of the past tense seems to limit the scope of Foucault's analysis to a specific historical moment rather than present it as a generalized and lasting mode of operation as implied by the present tense in the French original: "Ce qu'on cache, dit-on. Et si c'était au contraire ce que, d'une façon toute particulière, on avoue? Si l'obligation de le cacher n'était qu'un autre aspect du devoir de l'avouer?" (82).

10 For a reading of "Daisy Miller" as staging and laying bare the operation of patriarchal ideology through confrontation between Winterbourne, its representative, and the transgressive, self-directed, and self-aware heroine, see Izzo, " 'Daisy Miller' e il discorso dell'ideologia," 45–68.

11 Sartre, *Being and Nothingness*, 222.

12 For a stimulating discussion of shame as related to gender and to James, see Sedgwick, "Shame and Performativity."

13 Richard Godden discusses Olmsted's projects as related to contemporary literature in *Fictions of Capital: The American Novel from James to Mailer* (Cambridge: Cambridge University Press, 1990), 2 ff.

14 Bennett, *Birth of the Museum* and "The Multiplication of Culture's Utility," *Critical Inquiry* 21:4 (summer 1995): 861–89.

15 See Peter Buitenhuis, *The Grasping Imagination: The American Writings of Henry James* (Toronto: University of Toronto Press, 1970), 226 ff.; Michel Zéraffa, "Présentation de 'Julia Bride,' " in *Henry James, L'Art de la fiction*, ed. Michel Zéraffa (Paris: Klincksieck, 1978), 279–80; Lauren T. Cowdery, " 'Julia Bride': 'The Mantle of Iridescence,' " in *The Nouvelle of Henry James in Theory and Practice* (Ann Arbor MI: UMI Research Press, 1986), 35–51. Incidentally, Cowdery's reading of the tale is as "comedy," "slender farce," and "mixture of existential crisis and slapstick farce"; it takes the "official" value system of the diegetic world absolutely for granted, and sees Julia Bride as a "scatterbrained character," a "clown," "always bouncing back full of chatter and energy," while the narrator's voice has a "high-spirited, playful tone" and "drolling," which are particularly manifest in the imagery. To my mind, this reading is so arbitrary that it is hard to believe that Cowdery and I have read the same story. Another "ex-centric" reading of "Julia Bride" is provided by Perrot, *Henry James*, 285 ff., who reads the tale in a metalinguistic and psychoanalytical framework, as translating the problems of "the bachelor writer, Henry James, hesitating between 'settling down' to a way of writing directly inspired by the 'psychological' French writers (the Frenches) and a purely descriptive kind of narration—such as J. Murray might have proposed in his tourist guidebooks" (286, my translation).

16   Although the tale is collected in volume 17 of the New York Edition, James significantly chose to discuss it primarily in the preface to volume 18, that is, in connection with other tales centering on women protagonists such as "Daisy Miller," "Pandora," and "The Patagonia." Henry James, *Prefaces to the New York Edition*, in *Literary Criticism: French Writers, Other European Writers, The Prefaces to the New York Edition*, ed. Leon Edel and Mark Wilson (New York: Library of America, 1984), 1265. Page numbers will henceforth be included parenthetically in the text.

17   For an analysis of this issue in *The American Scene*, see Peter Conn, *The Divided Mind: Ideology and Imagination in America, 1898–1917* (Cambridge: Cambridge University Press, 1983).

18   A classic discussion of the origins and social significance of chastity and propriety is Mary Poovey, *The Proper Lady and the Woman Writer: Ideology as Style in the Works of Mary Wollstonecraft, Mary Shelley, and Jane Austen* (Chicago: University of Chicago Press, 1984).

19   These hypercodified motions are contrasted with the playful spontaneity conveyed by the metaphors through which Julia envisages her past conduct: "the forecourt, as she now imagined it, had been dishonoured by her younger romps. She had tumbled over the walls with this, that and the other raw playmate, and had played 'tag' and leap-frog, as she might say, from corner to corner" (669)—an image that, incidentally, reinforces the innocent connotations of Julia's past behavior.

Part 2. Discourses of Silence

1   For some approaches in these directions, see Bernard P. Dauenhauer, *Silence: The Phenomenon and Its Ontological Significance* (Bloomington: Indiana University Press, 1980); Paolo Valesio, *Novantiqua: Rhetoric as a Contemporary Theory* (Bloomington: Indiana University Press, 1980); and the innumerable discussions of silence in the works of Blanchot, Derrida, and Foucault.

2   Besides the classical studies by Chatman, Rimmon, and Todorov, see for example Mimi Kairshner, "The Traces of Capitalist Patriarchy in the Silences of *The Golden Bowl*," *The Henry James Review* 5:3 (spring 1984): 187–92; John Auchard, *Silence in Henry James: The Heritage of Symbolism and Decadence* (University Park: Pennsylvania State University Press, 1986); Boren, *Eurydice Reclaimed*.

3   Pierre Bourdieu, *Language and Symbolic Power*, ed. and with an introduction by John B. Thompson, trans. Gino Raymond and Matthew Adamson (Cambridge: Harvard University Press, 1991); originally published as *Ce que parler veut dire: L'économie des échanges linguistiques* (Paris: Fayard, 1982).

4   The obvious reference here is to Eve Kosofsky Sedgwick, *Between Men: English Literature and Male Homosocial Desire* (New York: Columbia University Press, 1985) and *Epistemology of the Closet*.

5   A minimalist sampling of feminist critiques of silence would have to include Robin Lakoff, *Language and Woman's Place* (New York: Harper, 1975); Tillie Olsen, *Silences* (New York: Delta, 1979); Adrienne Rich, *On Lies, Secrets, and Silence: Selected Prose 1966–1978* (New York: Norton, 1976); Sandra M. Gilbert and Susan Gubar, *The Madwoman in the Attic: The Woman Writer and the Nineteenth-Century Literary Imagination* (New

Haven: Yale University Press, 1979); Susan Gubar, " 'The Blank Page' and the Issue of Female Creativity," *Critical Inquiry* 8:2 (winter 1981): 243–64; Deborah Cameron, *Feminism and Linguistic Theory* (London: Macmillan, 1985) and "Introduction: Why Is Language a Feminist Issue?" in *The Feminist Critique of Language: A Reader*, ed. Deborah Cameron (London: Routledge, 1990); Janis P. Stout, *Strategies of Reticence: Silence and Meaning in the Works of Jane Austen, Willa Cather, Katherine Anne Porter, and Joan Didion* (Charlottesville: University Press of Virginia, 1990); Lena B. Ross, ed., *To Speak or Be Silent: The Paradox of Disobedience in the Lives of Women* (Wilmette IL: Chiron, 1993); Elaine Hedges and Shelley Fisher Fishkin, eds., *Listening to Silences: New Essays in Feminist Criticism* (New York: Oxford University Press, 1994).

6 The only exception is the book by Boren quoted above: the Lacanian concepts she utilizes differ from those I use here and turn the feminine into a linguistic-psychoanalytical notion rather than into a sociological-cultural one.

7 Foucault, *History of Sexuality*, vol. 1. Page numbers will henceforth be included parenthetically in the text.

8 I have slightly revised the translation of this passage—which is crucial to the analyses that follow—to make it more literal and to emphasize the value of Foucault's statement as a description of a general mode of operation rather than of a historically contingent phenomenon. The French original reads as follows: "Ce qu'on cache, dit-on. Et si c'était au contraire ce que, d'une façon toute particulière, on avoue? Si l'obligation de le cacher n'était qu'un autre aspect du devoir de l'avouer? . . . Pour nous, c'est dans l'aveu que se lient la vérité et le sexe, par l'expression obligatoire et exhaustive d'un secret individuel" (82). Foucault's present tense leaves no doubt as to the *general* and *lasting* implications of the system he is describing, a system that the past tense of the English translation somewhat tends to limit.

9 French edition, 96. In the English translation that follows, I have again reinstated the present tense as more faithful to the implications of the original expression.

10 Foucault's position on sexuality, though widely influential, has been criticized by feminists for its apparent disinterest in gender issues. For a relevant sample of feminist discussions of Foucault, see the essays in the following sources: Irene Diamond and Lee Quinby, eds., *Feminism and Foucault: Reflections on Resistance* (Boston: Northeastern University Press, 1988); Lois McNay, *Foucault and Feminism: Power, Gender and the Self* (Cambridge: Polity Press, 1992); Caroline Ramazanoglu, ed., *Up Against Foucault: Explorations of Some Tensions between Foucault and Feminism* (London: Routledge, 1993).

11 Roger Bozzetto examines "aveu" and "secret" in James from the point of view of the enigmatic quality and anamorphic posture of the short stories—a point of view totally divergent from mine: see "L'aveu et le secret," in *Henry James ou le fluide sacré de la fiction*, ed. and comp. Sophie Geoffroy-Menoux (Paris-Montréal: L'Harmattan, 1998).

Chapter 5. Of Shame and Horror

1 Edel and Powers, eds. *Complete Notebooks of Henry James*, 36 ff.

2 Henry James, "A London Life," *Scribner's Magazine* (June, July–September 1888). The story was republished in the volume titled *A London Life, The Patagonia, The Liar,*

Mrs. Temperley (London: Macmillan, 1889) and again in volume 10 of the New York Edition, together with *The Spoils of Poynton* and "The Chaperon." Quotations are from Henry James, *Complete Stories 1884–1891*, ed. Edward Said (New York: Library of America, 1999), which reproduces the first book edition of the story; page numbers will henceforth be included parenthetically in the text.

3   " 'A London Life' breaks down altogether, I have had to recognise, as a contribution to my comprehensive picture of bewildered Americanism. I fail to make out to-day why I need have conceived my three principal persons as sharers in that particular bewilderment," from the preface to *The Spoils of Poynton, A London Life, The Chaperon,* in James, *Prefaces,* in *Literary Criticism: French Writers,* eds. Edel and Wilson, 1150.

4   Heath Moon, "James's 'A London Life' and the Campbell Divorce Scandal," *American Literary Realism 1870–1910* 13:2 (autumn 1980): 246–58.

5   On the Matrimonial Causes Act and the ensuing debate, see Poovey, *Uneven Developments,* 51 ff., and Nead, *Myths of Sexuality,* 48 ff.

6   Nead, *Myths of Sexuality,* 56.

7   William Acton, *The Functions and Disorders of the Reproductive Organs, in Childhood, Youth, Adult Age, and Advanced Life, considered in their Physiological, Social and Moral Relations,* 3rd enlarged edition (London: Churchill, 1862), 101–2. For an examination of the scientific theories on sexual difference and on Victorian femininity, see Cynthia Eagle Russett, *Sexual Science: The Victorian Construction of Womanhood* (Cambridge MA: Harvard University Press, 1989).

8   On the cultural and ideological implications of the role of governess—who enjoyed a standing halfway between the bourgeoisie and the servants, was frequently of bourgeois origins, and as such, was a living memento of the potential threat to the social status of young women whose fathers suffered financial set-backs—see Poovey, *Uneven Developments,* 126 ff., and Deirdre David, *Rule Britannia: Women, Empire, and Victorian Writing* (Ithaca NY: Cornell University Press, 1995), 77 ff.

9   Armstrong, *Desire and Domestic Fiction.* James makes Laura (and the reader, with her) fully aware of the class implication, as is shown by her parenthetical remark "and both what we are, otherwise."

10   The judicial connotation reappears and is developed on the occasion of Laura's dialogue with her brother-in-law, which forecasts the possibility of being heard in court: " 'Why, of course you'll be cross-examined' " (466).

11   Here as elsewhere I have slightly revised the terms used in the English translation, which reads "duty to admit to it" (61), thus sacrificing Foucault's insistence on the recurrent verb "avouer" and noun "aveu."

12   On the Victorian iconography of the adulteress, see Nead, *Myths of Sexuality.*

13   " 'He oughtn't to have left that to you' " (524), " 'I'm sure that whatever you said it was very charming' " (525).

14   Edel, *Life of Henry James,* vol. 1, 821, 815.

15   S. Gorley Putt, *The Fiction of Henry James: A Reader's Guide* (Harmondsworth UK: Penguin, 1968), 241–43.

16   According to John Kimmey, "James's London Tales of the 1880s," *The Henry James Review* 8:1 (fall 1986): 37–46, James intends to make Laura into a complex and nonunilateral character, even though the quote from *The Huguenots* underscores her

puritan mindset. Heath Moon criticizes explicitly Edel's reading and sees Laura as the faithful representative of James's social conservatism; James would appear to criticize the degradation of the upper class in the name of the best British traditions and not in that of abstract moralism. According to Adeline R. Tintner, *Henry James and the Lust of the Eyes: Thirteen Artists in His Work* (Baton Rouge: Louisiana State University Press, 1993), 36–55, the story's model is Hogarth's cycle of *Marriage à la mode*; James would appear to share its moralizing intent, voiced by Laura.

17 Unsigned review, in *Henry James: The Critical Heritage*, ed. Roger Gard (London: Routledge and Kegan Paul, 1968), 192. First published in *Spectator* (August 1889): 211–13.

18 "The quiet old lady in the firelight, encompassed with the symbolic security of chintz and water-color, . . . safely, sensibly, with a cap and gloves and consideration and memories" epitomizes in Laura's eyes the blessings of old age as opposed to "all the middle dangers of life" (444).

19 Putt, *Fiction of Henry James*, 242.

20 Acton, *Functions and Disorders*, 79.

21 For an analysis of this mythology see: Nead, *Myths of Sexuality*, 62 ff.; Reynolds and Humble, *Victorian Heroines*, 98 ff.; Nina Auerbach, *Woman and the Demon: The Life of a Victorian Myth* (Cambridge MA: Harvard University Press, 1982), 150 ff.; Mitchell, *Fallen Angel.*

22 Laura had already deplored the fact that the Berrington children could not be reduced to the sentimental stereotype of childhood: "Their mother had certainly gone too far; but there was nevertheless a limit to the tenderness one could feel for the neglected, compromised bairns. It was difficult to take a sentimental view of them—they would never take such a view of themselves" (451).

23 See Nead, *Myths of Sexuality*, 196 ff.

24 In this regard, it is interesting to note that through her submissive internalization of all the Victorian stereotypes of womanhood Laura renounces completely her native heritage of free American girl, which at the beginning of the story had induced her to protest the idea of marriage as a way of acquiring male protection ("'But to be only protected—always protected: is that a life?'" [443]) and to react within herself, in the middle of the story, against being treated as "a marriageable article"(507) in Lady Davenant's matrimonial tactics. As several scholars of women's history and culture have noted, by the middle of the nineteenth century an alternative ideal, different from the suffocating and submissive ideal of "True Womanhood," had taken hold in the United States. Frances B. Cogan calls it the ideal of "Real Womanhood," which, though still centered around the exaltation of the domestic sphere, juxtaposed to idealizations a certain corrective realism that allowed women more physical, economic, and intellectual self-reliance, thus making the young American girl a partial prototype of the "New Woman." See Frances B. Cogan, *All-American Girl: The Ideal of Real Womanhood in Mid-Nineteenth-Century America* (Athens: University of Georgia Press, 1989); Claudia Nelson and Lynne Vallone, eds., *The Girl's Own: Cultural Histories of the Anglo-American Girl, 1830–1915* (Athens: University of Georgia Press, 1994); Kate Flint, "The American Girl and the New Woman," *Women's Writing* 3:3 (1996): 217–29. I wish to thank Daniela Daniele for drawing my attention to the issue of the specific

and differential conceptualizations of womanhood in the American context. I take this opportunity to mention a wonderful critical inventory of images of American womanhood that has in many ways inspired my reading of James: Martha Banta, *Imaging American Women: Idea and Ideals in Cultural History* (New York: Columbia University Press, 1987).

25 "[N]o doubt she had been to the vicarage—she was capable even of that. She could pay 'duty-visits,' like that (she called at the vicarage about three times a year), and she could go and be nice to her mother-in-law with her fresh lips still fresher for the lie she had just told" (474).

26 Judith Butler, *Gender Trouble: Feminism and the Subversion of Identity* (New York: Routledge, 1990), 25.

27 Judith Butler, *Bodies That Matter: On the Discursive Limits of "Sex"* (New York: Routledge, 1993), 94.

28 Butler, *Bodies That Matter*, 95.

29 To be precise: "shame" seventeen times; "horror" thirteen; "dreadful" twelve; "awful" eight; "horrible" six; "hideous" five; "abominable" and "terrible" once each.

30 See Michel Foucault, "The Order of Discourse," trans. Ian McLeod, in *Untying the Text: A Post-Structuralist Reader*, ed. Robert Young (Boston: Routledge, 1981); originally published as *L'ordre du discours* (Paris: Gallimard, 1970). Like other key words in this discourse, "monster" and "monstrous" are the epithets that Laura and Selina attribute to each other repeatedly, always in reference to "unnatural" transgressions of the behavioral and symbolic codes of femininity.

Chapter 6. Dying to Speak

1 The story was published in *Black and White*, on May 28, 1892, with the title "The Visit"; the following year it appeared under the title "The Visits" in the volume *The Private Life, The Wheel of Time, Lord Beaupré, The Visits, Collaboration, Owen Wingrave* (London: James R. Osgood, McIlvaine & Co.) and in *The Private Life, Lord Beaupré, The Visits* (New York: Harper and Brothers); it was not included in the New York Edition. Quotations are from Henry James, *Complete Stories 1892–1898*, which reproduces the Osgood book edition of the story; page numbers will henceforth be included parenthetically in the text.

2 The symmetric structure of this tale, organized around the narrator's two visits to two different country houses, which in turn embed Louisa's own fateful visit and the record of its consequences, possibly accounts for James's decision to change the original title, "The Visit," into the more allusive plural, which embraces the experience of both characters at once.

3 On the production of feminine sexuality in the Victorian age, the cultural and sociological categories it created, and their complex interactions, see especially Nead, *Myths of Sexuality*; Mary Poovey, *Uneven Developments*; and Reynolds and Humble, *Victorian Heroines*.

4 On the image of the young girl as cultural construct, see especially Judith Rowbotham, *Good Girls Make Good Wives: Guidance for Girls in Victorian Fiction* (Oxford: Blackwell, 1989); Ruth Bernard Yeazell, *Fictions of Modesty: Women and Courtship in the English*

Novel (Chicago: University of Chicago Press, 1991); Reynolds and Humble, *Victorian Heroines*.

5 William Cobbett, *Advice to Young Men, and (Incidentally) to Young Women, in the Middle and Higher Ranks of Life* (London, 1829); quoted in Yeazell, *Fictions of Modesty*, 56.

6 Sarah Stickney Ellis, *The Daughters of England, Their Position in Society, Character & Responsibilities* (London: 1842); quoted in Yeazell, *Fictions of Modesty*, 58.

7 Yeazell, *Fictions of Modesty*, 57.

8 Reynolds and Humble, *Victorian Heroines*, 16. Further investigation is warranted into the reasons why control over young women's sexuality was so crucial in those years. In her recent essay on the notion of sacrifice in the emerging social sciences at the turn of the century, Susan Mizruchi relates modern systems of social control to the conservative continuation of traditional gender roles, which were used to soothe anxieties about the unknown by anchoring crucial societal functions to the reproductive and protective role of women. Hence the central importance of the maternal role, thus transposed from the body of women to the social body, and of its control: "women's reproduction was cultural capital too precious to be controlled by women themselves" (236). Mizruchi also argues that the ensuing centrality of adolescent "rites of passage" for young girls, which James focalizes in *The Awkward Age*, within the framework of a general interest in primitive rituals on the part of the social sciences is "a more general effort to locate the transhistorical and transcultural foundations of male control over female sexuality and reproduction" (239); see Susan L. Mizruchi, *The Science of Sacrifice: American Literature and Modern Social Theory* (Princeton: Princeton University Press, 1998). Laura Wing's and especially Louisa Chantry's destiny seems to fit perfectly this logic of scapegoating, which revives the notion of the sacrifice of the individual (in this case, of the *female* individual) on the altar of social engineering, to guarantee the survival and health of the social body as a whole.

9 Yeazell, *Fictions of Modesty*, 51.

10 The debate over the young girl had raged for twenty years, since the anonymous publication of Eliza Lynn Linton's article "The Girl of the Period" in the *Saturday Review* of March 14, 1868: the article had named and branded the tendency on the part of well-bred young girls to seek the thrill of transgression by imitating the clothes and habits of the women of the demimonde. James, who was a friend and correspondent of Eliza Lynn Linton, was well aware of this debate; in 1868, in *The Nation* (October 22), he had reviewed the American edition of *Modern Women, and What Is Said of Them*, an anonymous collection of articles published by the *Saturday Review*, which included Linton's article mentioned above. In 1876 James revisits the theme of the English "fast young girl" as reader of sensation fiction in his negative review of Rhoda Broughton's novel *Joan* (*Nation*, December 21, 1876). Both essays are reprinted in Henry James, *Literary Criticism: Essays on Literature, American Writers, English Writers*, eds. Leon Edel and Mark Wilson (New York: Library of America, 1984), 19–25 and 511–15. On Linton's essay and the debate it provoked, see Christina Boufis, " 'Of Home Birth and Breeding': Eliza Lynn Linton and the Girl of the Period," in *The Girl's Own*, eds. Nelson and Vallone.

11 Even though it may be just a casual coincidence, it is worth noting that the name of James's protagonist is identical to the name of the addressee of Reverend John Bennett's

Letters to a Young Lady, a famous and popular conduct book published in 1789, which, through the teachings offered in the letters, construed its protagonist as a paragon of a young girl and model of feminine modesty.

Chapter 7. Gender Trouble

1 On sensation fiction, its implications, themes and reading protocols, and the debate surrounding it, see Mitchell, *The Fallen Angel*; Patrick Brantlinger, "What Is 'Sensational' about the Sensation Novel?" *Nineteenth-Century Fiction* 37 (1982): 1–28; David A. Miller, *The Novel and the Police* (Berkeley: University of California Press, 1988); Kate Flint, *The Woman Reader: 1837–1914* (Oxford UK: Clarendon Press, 1993).

2 [Alfred Austin], "Our Novels: The Sensational School," *Temple Bar* 29 (1870): 424; cited in Flint, *Woman Reader*, 276.

3 Henry James, "Mary Elizabeth Braddon," in *Literary Criticism: Essays on Literature*, eds. Edel and Wilson, 742, 743–44; originally published in *Nation* (November 9, 1865).

4 "These works are censured and ridiculed, but they are extensively read. The author has a hold upon the public. It is, assuredly, worth our while to enquire more particularly how she has obtained it.... Miss Braddon... goes to work like an artist. Let not the curious public take for granted that, from a literary point of view, her works are contemptible.... She writes what we may call very knowing English.... with a telling subject and a knowing style she proceeds to get up her photograph. These require shrewd observation and wide experience; Miss Braddon has both" (744–45).

5 The critical essays on the relationship between James and popular culture are numerous by now. Among the most significant see Veeder, *Lessons of the Master*; Jacobson, *Henry James and the Mass Market*; Margolis, *Problem of Audience*; Anesko, *"Friction with the Market"*; Tintner, *Pop World of Henry James*.

6 Syndication—a publishing arrangement involving simultaneous publication of stories and installments of novels in several newspapers, constituting a "syndicate"—was promoted in the United States by Charles A. Dana, the editor and owner of the *Sun*, as a way of maximizing profits and reducing costs for publishing fiction by well-known authors; James was among the first writers to agree to sell him stories ("Georgina's Reasons" and "Pandora"). For a detailed analysis of James's attitude to this publishing venture and of the events accompanying it, and for a documented critique of Edel's assumptions on the subject, see Charles Johanningsmeier, "Henry James's Dalliance with the Newspaper World," *The Henry James Review* 19:1 (1998): 36–52. In 1885 "Georgina's Reasons" was reprinted in *The Author of Beltraffio* (Boston: James R. Osgood) and in *Stories Revived* (London: Macmillan). Quotations are from James, *Complete Stories 1884–1891*, which reproduces the text of the English book edition; page numbers will henceforth be included parenthetically in the text.

7 The information is from the article by Johanningsmeier just quoted; both Leon Edel and Dan Laurence in *A Bibliography of Henry James* (Oxford UK: Clarendon, 1982) and Roger Gard as editor of *Henry James: The Critical Heritage* mistakenly attribute this headline to the *Cincinnati Enquirer*.

8 On the analogies between James's story and M. E. Braddon's novels see Tintner, "Henry James and Miss Braddon: 'Georgina's Reasons' and the Victorian Sensation Novel," in

Pop World of Henry James; originally published in *Essays in Literature* 10:1 (spring 1983): 119–24.

9 On the motif of the adventuress in James's short stories, see P. R. Grover, "Henry James and the Theme of the Adventuress," *Revue de Littérature Comparée* 47 (1973): 586–96; on the influence and functions of French melodrama, see Walker, *Reading Henry James*.

10 Reynolds and Humble, *Victorian Heroines*, 113.

11 Mrs. Oliphant, "Novels," *Blackwood's Magazine* 102 (September 11, 1867), 263.

12 The adjective "imperial" recurs several other times in the story. It is perhaps worth noting that the analogy with Josephine in relation to the plot of James's story provides us with yet another example of reversal of gender expectations: it was Napoleon who repudiated her and proceeded to remarry.

13 Auerbach, *Woman and the Demon*, 36.

14 The first three and last six of the fifteen sections of the text are filtered through Benyon's point of view; sections four to seven are filtered through Mrs. Portico's; sections eight and nine are focalized on the Theory sisters.

15 *Henry James and Robert Louis Stevenson*, ed. Janet Adam Smith (London: Rupert Hart-Davis, 1948), 108; cit. in A. Tintner, *Pop World of Henry James*. Unsigned review, *Critic* (May 1885): 206–7; in *Henry James: The Critical Heritage*, ed. Gard.

16 "He had nothing in the world but his pay, and he felt that this was a rather 'mean' income to offer Miss Gressie. Therefore he didn't put it forward; what he offered, instead, was the expression—crude often, and almost boyishly extravagant—of a delighted admiration of her beauty, the tenderest tones of his voice, the softest assurances of his eye, and the most insinuating pressure of her hand . . . it was as plain that he expected, in general, she would marry him, as it was indefinite that he counted upon her for living on a few hundred a year" (7). "She never told him how she arranged the matter at home, how she found it possible always to keep the appointments (to meet him out of the house) that she so boldly made, in what degree she dissimulated to her parents" (6).

17 "She had, in her daughterless condition, a certain ideal of a girl who should be beautiful and romantic, with wistful eyes, and a little persecuted, so that she, Mrs. Portico, might get her out of her troubles. She looked to Georgina, to a considerable degree, to give actuality to this vision" (13–14).

18 The fundamentally sexual reason for their marriage is stated again retrospectively by Benyon himself: "She did him the honour of wishing to enjoy his society, and she did herself the honour of thinking that their intimacy, however brief, must have a certain consecration" (52).

19 At one point Georgina, urged by Mrs. Portico to "normalize" her marriage, argues that she does not want Benyon to sacrifice his brilliant career by asking that he leave his post to live with her: " 'I wouldn't for the world interfere with his prospects—with his promotion. . . . He is devoted to his profession; it would ruin him to leave it' " (19)—a position, it must be noted, inspired more by middle-class individualism than by the ideology of domesticity.

20 The only allusion to madness, tentatively uttered and promptly discarded, is in Benyon's words when Georgina in their final dialogue mentions her son and her devotion to him: " 'I wonder if you are insane,' he murmured" (56). For this reason, I completely disagree, on this point, with Tintner, who argues that Georgina's reasons are so contradictory

and irrational that she is "a casebook representation of the psychopathic personality" (122) and that with this story James refurbishes Mrs. Braddon's sensation plot with the reference to the "contemporary scientific interest in abnormal behavior" (123). To the contrary, I would argue that, as David Miller writes about Lady Audley's evident "insanity," Georgina's actions, if anything, are all "crimes" in the legal sense of the term, that is, they are motivated "by impeccably rational considerations of self-interest" (*Novel and the Police*, 169). The point of the story is not the scientific study of "abnormal behavior" but quite the reverse, the laying bare of the foundations of "normalcy."

21 Foucault, *History of Sexuality*, vol. 1, 55.

22 The passage about Benyon's "mat[ing] himself with . . . a monster" might be read as another reversal of roles: the expression used here would seem to point to the nonhuman mating, typical of mythology, except that in myth it is *women* who mate with the monster or with the god who appears in the shape of an animal.

23 Miller, *Novel and the Police*, 169.

24 As most critics of the genre have noted, the conclusion of the sensation novel coincides with order returning in the form of the bourgeois domestic sphere: "Herein, one might argue, lies the 'morality' of sensation fiction, in its ultimately fulfilled wish to abolish itself: to abandon its grotesque aberrations of character and situation that have typified its representation, which now coincides with the norm of the Victorian household" (Miller, *Novel and the Police*, 165–66).

25 Among the few critics who have written on this story, Granville H. Jones (who reads it along with *Washington Square*) is the only one to bring to light the subversive character of the ending and to compare "Georgina's Reasons" to *Hedda Gabler* (which James could not have known at that time): "But perhaps Georgina herself has the ultimate disdainful, contented reward: she knows that the whole false fabric is supported by bigamy and lie." Granville H. Jones, "Henry James's 'Georgina's Reasons': The Underside of *Washington Square*," *Studies in Short Fiction* 11 (1974): 189–94, 193.

26 Reynolds and Humble, *Victorian Heroines*, 113.

27 It is significant that at least one critic accuses Benyon of having used his promise as an excuse to evade his human engagement toward Kate and marriage thanks to "as thorough a protection as any of the Jamesian non-marriers enjoys." Putt, *Fiction of Henry James*, 237.

28 Miller, *Novel and the Police*, 166; the italics are the author's.

29 Already in the first dialogue, in section 3, Georgina had touched on this: " 'You are your own master, but you don't know what I go through' " (8).

30 "[Her] polished windows seemed to shine defiance at him" (54); "they met now as adversaries" (55); "satisfied, apparently, that she was not to receive a broadside, she advanced" (55).

31 *Complete Notebooks of Henry James*, eds. Edel and Powers, 26, 27. Page numbers will henceforth be included parenthetically in the text.

32 On the relevance of the readers' process of identification in sensation fiction see in particular the works by D. A. Miller and K. Flint, already quoted.

33 This is Leon Edel's reading: "a strange unmotivated sensational story, written in the belief that this was what newspaper-readers wanted" (*Life of Henry James*, vol. 1, 723).

296 NOTES TO PAGES 213–216

Gorley Putt is of the contrary opinion: he finds the story unsatisfactory but credits James with intentional artistic decisions: "If, on occasion, he seems perverse in aim and direction, we must always pay him the credit, or discredit, of having known precisely what he *was* doing" (*Fiction of Henry James*, 237). Finally, F. O. Matthiessen and Kenneth B. Murdock's commentary on James's entry in their edition of *The Notebooks of Henry James* (Chicago: University of Chicago Press, 1947) is typical of the most classic trend of critical canonization of Henry James: it redeems James from the accusation of sensational writing and underlines his ability at psychological characterization, which makes Georgina's character credible and human (61).

Chapter 8. The Word Not to Say It

1 Edel and Powers, eds., *Complete Notebooks of Henry James*, 170. Page numbers will henceforth be included parenthetically in the text. The story was published in *The Anglo-American Magazine* (January 1902), was reprinted in 1903 in the collection *The Better Sort* (London: Methuen; New York: Charles Scribner's Sons), and finally collected in volume 18 of the New York Edition. Quotations are from James, *Complete Stories 1898–1910*, which reproduces the text of the Methuen book edition; page numbers will henceforth be included parenthetically in the text.

2 On the debate about the French novel, a label used by the press of the times as an "instant signifier of immorality," see Flint, *Woman Reader*.

3 James, *Prefaces*, in *Literary Criticism: French Writers*, eds. Edel and Wilson, 1285.

4 Critics of this tale have dealt especially with its aesthetic discussion: see, for example, Ellen Tremper, "Henry James's 'The Story in It': A Successful Aesthetic Adventure," *The Henry James Review*, 3:1 (fall 1981): 11–16; Adeline R. Tintner, "Henry James's 'The Story in It' and Gabriele D'Annunzio," in *The Cosmopolitan World of Henry James: An Intertextual Study* (Baton Rouge: Louisiana State University Press, 1991); originally published in *Modern Fiction Studies* 28:2 (summer 1982): 201–14; Catherine Vieilledent, "Literary Pornographics: Henry James's Politics of Suppression," *The Henry James Review* 10:3 (fall 1989): 185–96; Sara S. Chapman, *Henry James's Portrait of the Writer as Hero* (London: Macmillan, 1990); Donata Meneghelli, "'A Certain High Lucidity': le 'storie' di Henry James," in *Studi sulla modernità-II*, ed. Fausto Curi (Bologna: Printer, 1993): 243–86.

5 Beside the "orientalist" connotations that reinforce his attractiveness and suggest his sensuality, Voyt is also introduced as having part Irish, part Jewish features. This eminently racial description probably has sexual suggestions (according to the current stereotypes, Irish and Jewish men were very prolific) and is possibly used to "justify," on the basis of racial stereotyping, his unscrupulous behavior (a behavior, however, that in other texts James does not scruple to attribute to pureblood Britons). These connotations are not univocal in that, immediately afterward, Voyt is defined as a "pleasant Briton"; the reader also learns that he is a Conservative M.P. in the House of Commons and, therefore, part and parcel of the British establishment. The one unequivocal element in this unstable presentation, underneath the uncertain racial overtone, is Voyt's very "essentialist" gender connotation.

6 "'Well, my dear, I think he understands you're here.' 'So that as he evidently isn't

coming,' Maud laughed, 'it's particularly flattering! Or rather . . . it would be, I think, quite extraordinarily flattering if he did. Except that, of course,' she subjoined, 'he might come partly for you.' ' "Partly" is charming. Thank you for 'partly' " (405).

7   On gender relations in language and communication, see the classic studies by Lakoff, *Language and Woman's Place*; Marina Mizzau, *Eco e Narciso: Parole e silenzi nel conflitto uomo-donna* (Turin: Bollati Boringhieri, 1979); Cameron, *Feminism and Linguistic Theory*; Patrizia Violi, *L'infinito singolare: Considerazioni sulla differenza sessuale nel linguaggio* (Verona: Essedue, 1986).

8   On the moralistic debate on the "French novels" and on the prohibition of their being read by women, see Flint, *Woman Reader*, 287 ff. In this sense, by separating into two different characters transgression as lived and transgression as read and thus criticizing the position of the moralizers who argued that reading immoral novels would induce immorality in women, James defends a position already voiced by contemporary women novelists.

9   This is Susanne Kappeler's reading of the story in *Writing and Reading in Henry James* (London: Macmillan, 1980), 101–5.

10 See Roland Barthes, *S/Z*, trans. Richard Miller (New York: Hill and Wang, 1974); originally published as *S/Z*, (Paris: Seuil, 1970).

11 Nancy K. Miller, "Emphasis Added: Plots and Plausibilities in Women's Fiction," in *The New Feminist Criticism: Essays on Women, Literature and Theory*, ed. Elaine Showalter (New York: Pantheon Books, 1985), 339–60, here 341; originally published in PMLA 96 (1981). Page numbers will henceforth be included parenthetically in the text.

12 Meneghelli, " 'Certain High Lucidity,' " also discusses the metafictional aspect of James's intervention on literary models.

13 Villa, *Esperienza e memoria*, 116, my translation.

14 Villa, "L'incendio di Poynton," 260, my translation.

15 Freud, "Creative Writers and Day-Dreaming", in *Standard Edition*, vol. 9, 150. Freud's essay, originally titled "Der Dichter und das Phantasieren," was written in 1907 and first published on *Neue Revue* in March 1908.

16 Kaston focuses on the dialectics of mastery/submission, author/character in *Imagination and Desire*.

17 On this aspect see the interesting observations by Elizabeth Cowie, "Fantasia," *m/f* 9 (1984) and Catherine Belsey, *Desire: Love Stories in Western Culture* (Oxford UK: Blackwell, 1994).

18 Freud, *The Interpretation of Dreams*, in *Standard Edition*, vol. 5, 148; Jacques Lacan, "Direction of Treatment and Principles of its Power," in *Ecrits: A Selection* (New York: Norton, 1977), 261. For an analysis of literary representations of desire and fantasy in this key, see Pacteau, *Symptom of Beauty*, 172 ff.

19 Villa, in "L'incendio di Poynton," notes that in psychoanalytic terms the secret is connected to an anal strategy of mastery over one's own space (255).

20 Miller, *Novel and the Police*, 195.

21 Kappeler, in *Writing and Reading* (105), notes that, as far as we know, the object of Maud's love may not be Colonel Voyt.

Epilogue 3. Silence of the Sphinx

1   "The Beast in the Jungle" was first published in the volume *The Better Sort* (London: Methuen; New York: Charles Scribner's Sons, 1903), and later included in volume 17 of the New York Edition (1909). Quotations are from James, *Complete Stories 1898–1910*, which reproduces the text of the Methuen edition; page numbers will henceforth be included parenthetically in the text. Criticism of this tale is so extensive that I will have to confine myself to a few samples. For examinations of language and style, see Jane P. Tompkins, " 'The Beast in the Jungle': An Analysis of James's Late Style," *Modern Fiction Studies* 16:2 (summer 1970): 185–91; Michael P. Peinovich and Richard F. Patteson, "The Cognitive Beast in the Syntactic Jungle: A Study of James' Language," *Language and Style* 11:2 (spring 1978): 82–93; Elizabeth Shapland, "Duration and Frequency: Prominent Aspects of Time in Henry James' 'The Beast in the Jungle,' " *Papers on Language and Literature* 17:1 (winter 1981): 33–47; David Smit, "The Leap of the Beast: The Dramatic Style of Henry James's 'The Beast in the Jungle,' " *The Henry James Review* 4:3 (spring 1983): 219–30. On author, narrator, irony, and point of view, see William R. Goetz, *Henry James and the Darkest Abyss of Romance* (Baton Rouge: Louisiana State University Press, 1986), 174 ff.; James Phelan, "Character in Fictional Narrative: The Case of John Marcher," *The Henry James Review* 9:2 (spring 1988): 105–13. Several critics have read the tale in a symbolic, mythic, or religious key: among these, Courtney Johnson, "John Marcher and the Paradox of the 'Unfortunate' Fall," *Studies in Short Fiction* 6:2 (winter 1969): 121–35; Joseph Kau, "Henry James and the Garden: A Symbolic Setting for 'The Beast in the Jungle,' " *Studies in Short Fiction* 10 (1973): 187–98; William Nance, " 'The Beast in the Jungle': Two Versions of Oedipus," *Studies in Short Fiction* 13 (1976): 433–40; Rachel Salmon, "Naming and Knowing in Henry James's 'The Beast in the Jungle': The Hermeneutics of a Sacred Text," *Orbis Litterarum* 36 (1981): 302–22. Thematic studies include O. P. Jones, "The Cold World of London in 'The Beast in the Jungle,' " *Studies in American Fiction* 6:2 (autumn 1978): 227–35; Janice H. Harris, "Bushes, Bears, and 'The Beast in the Jungle,' " *Studies in Short Fiction* 18:2 (spring 1981): 147–54; Cannon, *Henry James and Masculinity*. Several readings combine a psychological and/or psychoanalytic framework with a metafictional one: Todorov, *The Poetics of Prose*; Giovanna Mochi Gioli, " 'The Beast in the Jungle' e l'assenza del referente," *Paragone* 314 (1976): 51–76; Ruth Bernard Yeazell, *Language and Knowledge in the Late Novels of Henry James* (Chicago: University of Chicago Press, 1976); Patricia Bleu, "Fantastique et révélation dans *The Beast in the Jungle*," *Delta* 15 (November 1982): 91–102; Kaston, *Imagination and Desire*; Donna Przybylowicz, *Desire and Repression: The Dialectics of Self and Other in the Late Works of Henry James* (Tuscaloosa: University of Alabama Press, 1986); Herbert Perluck, "The Dramatics of the Unspoken and Unspeakable in James's 'The Beast in the Jungle,' " *The Henry James Review* 12:3 (fall 1991): 231–54; Paola Castellucci, " 'The Beast in the Jungle' e l'avventura negativa di Henry James," in *Letteratura dell'assenza* (Rome: Bulzoni, 1992); Bernard Terramorsi, "La 'bête' et la 'vieille terreur sacrée': la morsure du Fantastique," in *Henry James ou le fluide sacré de la fiction*, ed. and comp. Sophie Geoffroy-Menoux (Paris: L'Harmattan, 1998).

2   As far as I know, Kelly Cannon is the only critic to note this explicitly (59), besides touching briefly on May's function of keeping rather than revealing the secret, as I will in this chapter. Cannon's reading, however, differs from mine, as it centers on Marcher's

self-defense as "marginal male" against that knowledge of his own sexuality that would socially destroy him.

3 Tintner, *Pop World of Henry James* points to Kipling as the main source for the image of the beast. Other sources include romances of exotic adventure ("The Lady, or the Tiger?" by Frank R. Stockton and *Mr. Isaacs: A Tale of Modern India* by F. M. Crawford), as suggested by George Monteiro, "Henry James, Great White Hunter," *Modern Language Studies* 13:4 (fall 1983): 96–108; Hawthorne's notebooks, as suggested by Michael Coulson Berthold, "The Idea of 'Too Late' in James's 'The Beast in the Jungle,'" *The Henry James Review* 4:2 (winter 1983): 128–39; the fourth book of the *Aeneid*, as suggested by Paul J. Lindholdt, "Pragmatism and 'The Beast in the Jungle,'" *Studies in Short Fiction* 25:3 (summer 1988): 275–84; William James's *The Varieties of Religious Experience*, as suggested by Bruce Fogelman, "John Marcher's Journey for Knowledge: The Heroic Background of 'The Beast in the Jungle,'" *The Henry James Review* 10:1 (winter 1989): 68–73; and William James's lecture titled "The Tigers in India," as suggested by H. Lewis Ulman, "A Possible Lair: 'The Tigers in India' and 'The Beast in the Jungle,'" *The Henry James Review* 12:1 (winter 1991): 1–8.

4 "Matilde Serao," in *Literary Criticism: French Writers*, eds. Edel and Wilson, 957; originally published in *North American Review* (March 1901). As James Ellis suggests, the different settings that Marcher and Bartram respectively provide for their first meeting are significant in this sense: Marcher places their meeting in Rome at the Palace of the Caesars, a setting evoking imperial grandiosity and egocentrism; May corrects this recollection shifting the setting to Pompeii, a place connected to the rediscovery of past life and death. See James Ellis, "The Archaeology of Ancient Rome: Sexual Metaphor in 'The Beast in the Jungle,'" *The Henry James Review* 6:1 (fall 1984): 27–31.

5 The phrase is Henry James's own, in his preface to the tale, James, *Prefaces*, in *Literary Criticism: French Writers*, eds. Edel and Wilson, 1251.

6 May Bartram reads as the perfect embodiment of the Angel in the House and the everlasting principle of femininity as polemically described by Gilbert and Gubar in their classic *Madwoman in the Attic*, 20 ff.

7 Among the few who touch on this question, however tangentially, are Kau, "Henry James and the Garden," and Carla L. Peterson, "Constant's *Adolphe*, James's 'The Beast in the Jungle,' and the Quest for the Mother," *Essays in Literature* 9:2 (fall 1982): 224–39. On the other hand, even some subtle and original recent readings, that—running counter to a well-established critical tradition—underscore the role of May's secret as an instrument of power and mastery within the relationship, take her silence on herself absolutely for granted, as an obvious and natural fact: see Michiel Heyns, "The Double Narrative of 'The Beast in the Jungle': Ethical Plot, Ironical Plot and the Play of Power," in *Enacting History in Henry James: Narrative, Power and Ethics*, ed. Gert Buelens (Cambridge: Cambridge University Press, 1997): 109–25, and Gert Buelens, "In Possession of a Secret: Rhythms of Mastery and Surrender in 'The Beast in the Jungle,'" *The Henry James Review* 19:1 (winter 1998): 17–35.

8 Sedgwick, "Beast in the Closet." Page numbers will henceforth be included parenthetically in the text.

9 Sedgwick's essay has been very controversial both on the critical and on the theoretical plane: its "farfetched" interpretations, questionable or contradictory premises, and naive

political categories have been variously attacked and discussed. See David Van Leer, "The Beast of the Closet: Homosociality and the Pathology of Manhood," *Critical Inquiry* 15:3 (spring 1989): 587–605, and Philip Horne, "The Master and the 'Queer Affair' of 'The Pupil,'" in *Henry James: The Shorter Fiction*, ed. Reeve. Apart from its "classic" status in gender studies, Sedgwick's critical reading of James is, to my mind, a bold and stimulating one, and I entirely share its overall thrust. Sedgwick's reading of Marcher's secret as centering on homosexuality (not as fact, but as potential and panic) is compatible with my reading revolving around gender roles rather than around sexuality. Indeed, the extraordinary intensity and significance of this tale lies in the tension it creates between the homosexual panic as closeted secret, the stereotypes of manhood as the only possible conceivable figurations of it, and the utterly naturalized way in which *gender roles* are distributed in spite of a problematic *sexual identity*.

10 The confession motif is explicitly resumed in section 4, immediately before the climactic moment of May's standing up to offer Marcher his last chance: "her whole manner was a virtual confession, though still with a small, fine, inner stiffness, an imperfect surrender" (524). Again, the confession is not verbalized, and it reveals the existence of a secret without spelling out its content.

11 "She spoke as with the softness almost of a sick child, yet now at last, at the end of all, with the perfect straightness of a sibyl. She visibly knew that she knew, and the effect on him was of something co-ordinate, in its high character, with the law that had ruled him. It was the true voice of the law; so on her lips would the law itself have sounded" (529). On the sibyl as figure of the knowledge and wisdom the Jamesian hero strives for, see Larry A. Gray, "Sibyls, Seekers, and Sacred Founts in the Tales of Henry James," *The Henry James Review* 11:3 (fall 1990): 189–201.

12 On Wilde's and Swinburne's poems as related to James's decadent heroine, Maggie Verver, see Freedman, *Professions of Taste*, 234–35. Interestingly, in chapter 9 of *Idols of Perversity*, Dijkstra associates sphinxes with Circe and with animalized women as representations of men's fear of female beastlike sensuality.

13 On the Oedipus myth as connotative background for the tale and on its sexual implications, see Courtney Johnson and William Nance. In an exploration of the relevance of the sphinx's riddle in the tale, Johnson is the first who, in 1969, evokes an issue of sexual identity for this tale, although curiously the critic no sooner evokes than negates it, emphatically denying the possibility that James had codified this particular meaning: "the Sphinx legend . . . depicts a struggle with the unrecognized or unrecognizable feminine side of man's nature. . . . this would certainly have been no secret to Henry James; not that he consciously intended the specific sexual meaning expressed. But, conscious or no, the sense of the parallel is unmistakable," Johnson, "John Marcher and the Paradox," 133.

14 Henry James, *The Portrait of a Lady*, ed. Robert D. Bamberg (New York: Norton, 1975), 64.

15 A similar position is held by William Goetz, to whom Marcher's consciousness "is framed not only by that of the impersonal, Jamesian narrator who looks down at Marcher from an ironic height, but also by that of May, the second consciousness within the tale, who contains his consciousness and keeps it from becoming fluid but who is also the index to Marcher's failure to attain an autonomous sense of identity"

(178); as a result, "[i]f there is a character in the tale who participates in James's vision, it is not Marcher but May. James's authorial view comes close to coinciding not with the supposed center of consciousness but with the tale's second consciousness" (178).

16 Significantly, in view of my contention of the undecidability of this part of the tale, Goetz, whose book is totally devoted to an analysis of the relation between author and "central consciousness" in James's fiction, on this point completely diverges from Sedgwick. To him, "'The Beast in the Jungle' shows [James] as author drawing progressively away from his character until, at the moment when Marcher loses consciousness, author and character are totally detached from each other" (178).

17 Such is Eco's definition of catachresis in *Semiotics and the Philosophy of Language*, 101. The definition of catachresis as a "pseudoname," however, does not exist in the English version, which modifies the relevant paragraph (121), and can only be found in the Italian original, *Semiotica e filosofia del linguaggio*, 188.

18 James W. Gargano in "Imagery as Action in 'The Beast in the Jungle,'" (in *The Arizona Quarterly* 42:4 [1986]: 351-67) argues that "[b]y filling the void resulting from Marcher's inaction, imagery itself becomes a kind of dominant action" (351). Many other "mobile" metaphoric fields might be added to Gargano's exemplification. A short but interesting analysis of the role of metaphor as "foreshortening" detail, capable of simultaneously conveying Marcher's whole destiny and confirming (like the elusive trope it is) its undecipherability, is provided by Giovanni Bottiroli, *Teoria dello stile* (Florence: La Nuova Italia, 1997), 264 ff.

19 Gayatri Chakravorty Spivak, "Can the Subaltern Speak?" in *Marxism and the Interpretation of Culture*, eds. Cary Nelson and Lawrence Grossberg (London: Macmillan, 1988).

20 For the notion of "compassionate authority" and its connection with women's non-hierarchical definition of authority, see Kathleen B. Jones, "On Authority: Or, Why Women Are Not Entitled to Speak," in *Feminism and Foucault*, eds. Diamond and Quinby.

21 Miller, *Novel and the Police*, 195. Page numbers will henceforth be included parenthetically in the text.

22 A similar point, albeit in a very different theoretical framework, is made by Shoshana Felman in her reading of *The Turn of the Screw*: "Turning the Screw of Interpretation," *Yale French Studies* 55/56 (1977): 94-207.

23 Frank Moore Colby, "The Queerness of Henry James," in *Henry James. The Critical Heritage*, ed. Gard, 335-38; originally published in *Bookman* (June 1902): 396-97.

The End of the Story

1 Even if three other short stories—"Crapy Cornelia," "The Bench of Desolation" and "A Round of Visits"—present a later publication date, "Mora Montravers" was the last story the writer completed in April 1909, according to James's unpublished letters to his agent J. B. Pinker (in the Bienecke Library at Yale); see N. H. Reeve, "Living Up to the Name: 'Mora Montravers,'" in *Henry James: The Shorter Fiction*, 155, note 1.

"Mora Montravers" was published on *The English Review*, August–September 1909, and then in the collection *The Finer Grain* (New York: Charles Scribner's Sons; London: Methuen, 1910) together with "The Velvet Glove" and the three short stories cited above. Quotations are from Henry James, *Complete Stories 1898–1910*, which reproduces the text of the Scribner edition; page numbers will henceforth be included parenthetically in the text.

2 Through Winterbourne's point of view (the perfect incarnation of phallogocentrism), ironically framed and undermined by the narrating voice, James stages the normative character of the patriarchal ideology, thus revealing its partiality and pretense to universality and denouncing its deadening character for women (and its constricting character for men themselves). See Izzo, "'Daisy Miller,'" 45–68.

3 "Extraordinary" is the fourth word of the story, used in relation to the strange destiny that has befallen the Traffles; it recurs throughout the story and in relation to Mora on pages 761, 763, 772, 783, 792, 796.

4 Even her family status is unstable, according to different points of view: "Miss Montravers, their unspeakable niece, though not, absolutely not and never, as every one would have it, their adopted daughter" (761); "'my sister's child'" (770).

5 On this aspect of the story and how it reveals James's camp tendency to use terms that are borderline indecent or have a double meaning, see Stevens, *Henry James and Sexuality*, 119 ff.

6 For a few hypotheses on the name of the protagonist, see the essay by Reeve, as well as W. R. Martin, "'Superior to Oak': The Part of Mora Montravers in James's *The Finer Grain*," *American Literary Realism 1870–1910* 16:1 (spring 1983): 121–28. A possible literary source that, as far as I know, has never been noted is Bulwer-Lytton's novel *Ernest Maltravers* (1837), the story of the protagonist's seduction and abandonment of Alice, an angelic young girl who flees from her father (who wanted to turn her into a prostitute) and finds social redemption—an interesting case of ironic reversal of the intertext, if James indeed had read the novel.

7 See the following reflection in which Traffle thinks about their neighbors' attitude during the period in which they have no news of Mora. He displays here a clear grasp of the relation between pseudo-morality and scandalmongering, which is typical of mass media: "'Never was a scandal, therefore, less scandalous—more naturally a disappointment, that is, to our good friends, whose resentment of this holy calm, this absence of any echo of any convulsion, of any sensation of any kind to be picked up, strikes me as ushering in the only form of ostracism our dissimulated taint, our connection with lurid facts that *might* have gone on making us rather eminently worth while, will have earned for us'" (789).

8 The phrase "new fact," in quotes as if to signal a self-conscious citational quality, is also employed during the meeting with Mora at the National Gallery, 794.

9 James had followed the case with passion, defending Dreyfus's innocence without any hesitation, taking Zola's side during the trial following the famous "J'accuse!" and publicly criticizing the reactionary and anti-Semitic stance of many French intellectuals. See Leon Edel, *The Life of Henry James*, vol. 2 (Harmondsworth UK: Penguin, 1963), 303 ff. For an insightful summary of the Dreyfus case and its repercussions in the artistic and literary world, see the essays in Norman L. Kleeblatt, ed., *The Dreyfus Affair: Art,*

Truth, and Justice (Berkeley: University of California Press, 1987). For James's use of the Dreyfus case in this story, see Tintner, *Pop World of Henry James,* 271 ff.

10 It is worth noting the specific legal term employed to describe Mora's "contumacy" (789).

11 I would like to thank Manuela Vastolo, who, as a second year student at the Istituto Universitario Orientale, brought to my attention this detail of "Daisy Miller," a story I thought I knew almost by heart.

12 The arrival of the orphaned Mora is "her coming to them bereft and homeless, addressed, packed and registered after the fashion of a postal packet" (768); and this is how her aunt describes the civil marriage to Puddick: "'They looked in somewhere, at some dingy office, jabbered a word or two to a man without h's and with a pen behind his ear, and then came out as good as you and me; very much as you and I the other day sent off that little postal-packet to Paris from our grocer's back-shop'" (804).

13 As Martin notes (125), Mora's "serene and dispassionate offhandedness" toward marriage is unparalleled: not even D. H. Lawrence's characters are as radical in their attitudes towards this institution.

14 See 761, 768, 780, 784 twice, 799, 803. On the implications of the term in contemporary culture, see Stevens, *Henry James and Sexuality,* 12.

15 On the mirror image and more generally on the spell-breaking strategies of postmodern heroines, see Cristina Bacchilega, *Postmodern Fairy Tales: Gender and Narrative Strategies* (Philadelphia: University of Pennsylvania Press, 1997).

16 On the siren as disturbing and powerful image of femininity, "creature of transformations and mysterious interrelations, able to kill and to regenerate but not to die" (7), which recurs in Victorian literature, arts, and iconography, see Auerbach, *Woman and the Demon.*

17 Reeve too notices in this scene "the presence of an anarchic, vengeful, utopian joy . . . at the spectacle of so absolute a repudiation and so final a judgement of the kind of world which Mora leaves beneath her"(154).

18 With a significant lexical reference, the gesture with which Mora frees herself from the prejudices of others is described twice by the verb "to brush" (772 and 796). It would seem almost unnecessary to point out the phallic connotation of the paintbrush, according to a long-standing correlation between creative powers and virility.

19 This is perhaps why some of the critics focus exclusively on him and ignore, by and large, the character of Mora Montravers; see, for example, Richard S. Lyons, "Ironies of Loss in *The Finer Grain,*" *The Henry James Review* 11:3 (fall 1990): 202–12. Also J. Peter Dyson, in "Bartolozzi and Henry James's 'Mora Montravers,'" *The Henry James Review* 1:3 (spring 1980): 264–66 (a short essay in which the reference to Bartolozzi, the engraver, is seen as connoting the sort of derivative, limited, and commercialized art that defines the Traffles world) states without any hesitation that the protagonist of the story is Sidney Traffle.

20 Significantly, the term recurs in an unequivocally emasculating context, at the end of the second dialogue between Traffle and Puddick: "Traffle accompanied him to the gate, but wondering, as they went, if it was quite inevitable one should come back to feeling, as the result of every sort of brush with people who were really living, like so very small a boy" (788).

21 Shoshana Felman, *What Does a Woman Want? Reading and Sexual Difference* (Baltimore: Johns Hopkins University Press, 1993), 73.

22 The prevailing and eminently social notion is that of "taking a liberty" at the level of conversational rules: see 775, 778, 794; add to it the "freedom of thought" that Traffle claims for himself in relation to his wife's mental framework, 786.

Index